A Custom Edition for Westchester Community College

Frank L. Friedman ▪ Elliot B. Koffman

PROBLEM SOLVING, ABSTRACTION, AND DESIGN USING

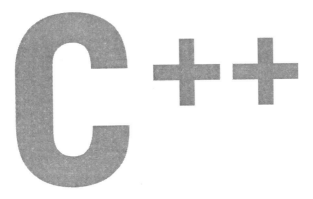

C++

Taken from:
Problem Solving, Abstraction, and Design Using C++, Sixth Edition
by Frank L. Friedman and Elliot B. Koffman

Learning Solutions

New York   Boston   San Francisco
London   Toronto   Sydney   Tokyo   Singapore   Madrid
Mexico City   Munich   Paris   Cape Town   Hong Kong   Montreal

Cover Art: Pattern 7.

Taken from:

Problem Solving, Abstraction, and Design Using C++, Sixth Edition
by Frank L. Friedman and Elliot B. Koffman
Copyright © 2011, 2007, 2004, 2000, 1997 by Pearson Education, Inc.
Published by Addison Wesley
Boston, Massachusetts 02116

This special edition published in cooperation with Pearson Learning Solutions.

Pearson Learning Solutions, 501 Boylston Street, Suite 900, Boston, MA 02116
A Pearson Education Company
www.pearsoned.com

Printed in the United States of America

3 4 5 6 7 8 9 10 V202 15 14 13 12 11

000200010270583428

KB

ISBN 10: 0-558-76102-X
ISBN 13: 978-0-558-76102-8

To Martha, Dara, Shelley,
and my parents George and Sylvia
whose limitless support made everything possible.
And to Sammy, the little miracle who brightened my life.

FLF

To my wife, Caryn
my children, Richard, Deborah, and Robin
my daughter- and son-in-law Jacquie and Jeff
and my grandchildren Dustin, Jonathan, and Eliana
with much thanks for your love and support.

EBK

Preface

This is a textbook for a one- or two-semester course in problem solving and program design. It is suitable for use by students with no programming background as well as those with a one-semester course, or the equivalent, in another programming language. Students' backgrounds will determine the time required to cover the earlier chapters of the text and the extent of coverage possible for later chapters.

The earlier editions of this book represented the culmination of an eight-year effort, partially sponsored by the National Science Foundation, to define an introductory-level course that presented the rudimentary principles of software engineering and object-oriented programming along with an introduction to the C++ programming language. Our primary goal is to motivate and introduce sound principles of program design and abstraction in a first programming course. Early in the book we introduce topics such as program style, documentation, algorithm and data structuring, procedure- and data-oriented modularization, component reuse, and program verification. The focus throughout is on the problem solving/software design process, from problem analysis to program design and coding.

The textbook fits the objectives of the first course in programming, following an imperative first approach as described in the ACM/IEEE Computing Curricula 2001 (courses CS101 or CS111). Because it also introduces object-oriented programming and the C++ Standard Template Library (STL) as well as recursion and dynamic data structures, it may also be used as the textbook for the second course in the three-semester sequence, CS102. The textbook can also be used in an objects early approach to the first programming course as classes are introduced in Chapter 1 and used in Chapter 3. In that case, we recommend that you move Chapter 10, Class Definition and Use, forward. It could be studied anytime after Chapter 6.

New to the Sixth Edition

Students will benefit from a variety of new content, including:

- Graphics coverage implemented throughout the book. Many Computer Science faculty have recommended the use of graphics to help motivate the study of introductory programming and as a vehicle to help students understand how to use libraries and to call functions. We agree with this viewpoint and have included several optional sections with graphics examples in this edition. The new graphics sections include:

  Section 3.8: Introduction to Computer Graphics

  Section 5.10: Loops in Graphics Programs

  Section 7.6: Using Type char Data to Control a Graphics Program

  Section 9.12: Graphics Programs with Arrays

  To reduce the overhead required to introduce graphics, we decided to use WinBGIm (Windows BGI with mouse), which is a package based on the Turbo Pascal BGI (Borland Graphics Interface) library. WinBGIm was created to run on top of the Win32 library by Michael Main and his students at the University of Colorado. Several development platforms appropriate for CS 1 courses have incorporated WinBGIm. Quincy (developed by Al Stevens) is an open-source student-oriented C++ IDE that includes WinBGIm as well as more advanced libraries (http://www.codecutter.net/tools/quincy). A command-line platform based on the open-source GNU g++ compiler and the emacs program editor is distributed by the University of Colorado (http://www.codecutter.net/tools/winbgim). WinBGIm is also available for Bloodshed Software's Dev-C++ and Microsoft's Visual Studio C++.

- New Chapter 0 is designed to elucidate the opportunities and structures of the field of computing to introductory students. We hope this chapter encourages students to consider a major or minor in computing by illustrating a world in which they can envision themselves.

- Reorganization of coverage of multidimensional arrays and arrays of structs. These topics were moved from Chapter 11 (Data Abstraction and Object-Oriented Design) to Chapter 9 (Arrays and Structs) to keep all coverage of arrays and structs in one chapter and to enable students to complete their study of procedural programming topics before learning how to write classes.

- New Section 7.6 on iterative approximations including a case study on finding roots of an equation.

- New case study in Chapter 11 (An Address Book for an email Provider) that uses the C++ vector class as its underlying data structure.

- New end-of-section exercises and updated case studies.

- New end-of-chapter quick-check and review exercises and new programming project assignments including graphics programming assignments.

Balancing Object–Oriented and Procedural Approaches

Object-oriented concepts and classes are introduced early in the book, starting in Section 1.3. Sections 2.4 and 3.7 discuss the use of two system-defined classes, iostream and string, and we refer to the use of classes and objects throughout most of the text.

An issue of concern to faculty is the relative order of arrays, structs, and classes. As in the last edition, we introduce arrays and structs first (Chapter 9) and then introduce the definition and coding of classes (Chapter 10). Some faculty may prefer to reverse the order, and this is entirely possible. The chapter on classes uses arrays only in the implementation of class simpleString, which can be omitted or deferred until after arrays are covered.

We continue to emphasize the design of classes and data modeling in Chapter 11, which introduces template classes, an indexed-list class, the STL vector class, friend functions, and operator overloading. We also use template classes in Chapter 13, where we discuss dynamic data structures: lists, stacks, queues, and trees. We discuss the use of the STL container classes and iterators and also show students how to implement their own classes. An illustration of the C++ inheritance and virtual function mechanisms is provided in Appendix E in the publisher's Web site. We've done our best to follow a balanced path between the strictly objects-first and totally procedure-focused programming metaphors. We agree with the objects-first concept, but not at the expense of the fundamentals of algorithm organization and design. Students in a first course can and should be taught the basic elements of procedural design. Our task is to do so within the context of an early focus on the importance of data modeling, reuse, and other fundamental principles of good software development.

Software Engineering and Object–Oriented Concepts

Many fundamental software engineering and object-oriented concepts are illustrated in the text: user-defined types, modeling problem-domain entities and their relationships, minimal interfaces, high-level cohesion, information hiding, separation of concerns, parameterized components, and inheritance. Abstraction is stressed from the start. Numerous complete case examples are provided throughout the text; these follow a standard software development method, from the specification and analysis of a problem to the first stage of design to the final coding.

Issues of program style are presented throughout in special displays. The concept of a program as a sequence of control structures is introduced in Chapter 3 and discussed in more detail in Chapters 4 (on selection structures) and 5 (on repetition structures). Our decision to introduce software engineering concepts in a first-year course is apparent in these early chapters. We've introduced functions and classes as early as possible at the introductory level—functions in Chapters 3 and 6 and the use and definition of classes in Chapters 3 and 10, respectively. We also provide several sections that discuss testing, debugging, and program verification.

Outline of Contents

Conceptually, the text may be partitioned into three sections. Chapters 1 through 6 provide introductory material on functions and top-down design, presenting detailed coverage of selection and repetition structures and program design strategies for using these structures. The connection between good problem-solving skills and effective software development is established early in the first three chapters. Included in the first two chapters are sections on problem solving and an introduction to a software development methodology based on a systematic approach to problem solving. The problem-solving approach outlined in these chapters is applied consistently to all other case studies in the text. Chapter 2 also contains an introduction to the basic elements of C++, including two sections in which we discuss abstraction, data modeling, and object-oriented programming. In Chapter 3, we continue the emphasis on basic problem-solving skills with a discussion of top-down design and divide and conquer. The reuse of program components is discussed, and additional detail is provided on the string class and its member functions.

Top-down procedural decomposition is further illustrated in Chapters 4 through 6. Decision structures are introduced in Chapter 4, and repetition structures are presented in Chapter 5. In Chapter 6, we revisit the C++ function, introducing functions with output arguments and providing a complete case study illustrating much of what has been learned to this point. An optional section on recursion is also included at the end of Chapter 6.

Chapters 7 through 9 cover simple data types, input and output, structured data types (arrays and structs), and classes. Chapter 7 contains a more detailed discussion of simple data types, including additional commentary on data abstraction as well as a description of the internal and external distinctions among the simple types. In Chapter 9, the structured types (arrays and structs) are first introduced. Simple searching and sorting algorithms are discussed, and the use of structured types as function arguments is illustrated. Chapter 9 also covers multidimensional arrays and arrays of structs.

Chapter 8 provides an introduction to external file input/output. Although studying external files may seem premature at this point, we believe it is appropriate. Programs don't exist in a vacuum; they manipulate data that often come from external sources, and they produce results that may subsequently be manipulated by other programs. It's therefore important for students to gain a relatively early exposure to some fundamental concepts related to file input and output, as long as this exposure does not disrupt the presentation of other essential ideas. Of course, by the time students reach Chapter 8, they will already have been introduced to the basics of stream input and output, including a minimal use of formatting functions and input/output manipulators (Chapter 5).

For students with the equivalent of a one-semester programming course in another language, Chapters 1 through 9 can be covered fairly quickly, perhaps in as little as five or six weeks. For students with little or no background, this may take ten to twelve weeks.

Chapters 10 and 11 cover intermediate-level concepts that would normally be introduced at the end of CS1 or the beginning of CS2. Chapter 10 covers the definition and use of classes and objects. Chapter 11 focuses on data modeling. We begin with a discussion of template classes and develop our own indexed-list template class. Next, we introduce the Standard Template Library and provide a new case study which uses the C++ vector class to process an address book.

Chapters 12, 13, and 14 cover more advanced topics in some depth: recursion (Chapter 12), linked lists, stacks, queues, and trees (Chapter 13), and multiprocessing and threads (Chapter 14). Chapters 12 and 13 are normally covered in the second semester of the first-year sequence. Chapter 14 could also be included in this course or a later one on Operating Systems.

Coverage of Pointers

Pointers are introduced only where they really belong—in the discussion of dynamic data structures (Chapter 13). The pointer is one of the more dangerous, relatively unprotected aspects of the C++ language and need not be an essential part of an introductory text. Use of the new and delete operators and the allocation and deallocation of memory cells in the heap are discussed at the beginning of Chapter 13. We illustrate the manipulation of dynamic data structures such as simple linked lists, stacks and queues, and binary trees.

Pedagogical Features

Several pedagogical features also enhance the usefulness of the text as an instructional tool. These include the following:

- Consistent use of analysis and design aids such as data requirements tables and program structure charts
- End-of-section self-check and programming exercises (answers to the odd-numbered self-check exercises are available in the publisher's Web site.)
- End-of-chapter quick-check exercises (answers are provided) and programming projects
- Numerous examples and case studies carried through from analysis and design to implementation
- Syntax displays containing the syntax and semantics of each new C++ feature introduced
- Program style and design guideline displays
- Detailed syntax and run-time error discussions at the end of each chapter
- Chapter reviews and review questions

Appendices

Separate appendices are available in the publisher's Web site summarizing information about character sets, C++ reserved words, C++ operators, and function libraries (with descriptions and section numbers). There is also an appendix illustrating inheritance and virtual functions.

Supplemental Materials

The following supplements are available to all readers of this book at www.aw.com/cssupport:

Source Code

Answers to Odd-Numbered Questions

Appendices

The following instructor supplements are only available to qualified instructors at Addison-Wesley's Instructor Resource Center. Visit www.pearsonhighered.com/irc or send an e-mail to computing@aw.com for information about how to access them.

PowerPoint Slides

Instructor's Manual with Solutions

Test Bank

Source Code

Acknowledgments

Many people participated in the development of this textbook. For this edition, we want to thank Michael Main for his assistance with WinBGIm and help with some of the graphics examples. We would also like to acknowledge the contributions of his students at the University of Colorado who adapted WinBGI to create WinBGIm (Grant Macklem, Gregory Schmelter, Alan Schmidt, and Ivan Stashak).

We also want to thank Charlotte Young of South Plains College for her help in creating Chapter 0, and Jeff Warsaw of Temple University and WaveRules, LLC, who contributed substantially to the chapter on multiprocessing in the fifth edition. Paul LaFollette and Paul Wolfgang of Temple University were primary contributors to the first edition. Temple graduate students Donna Chrupcala, Bruce Weiner, and Judith Wilson also contributed significantly to the development of the original textbook. Steve Vinoski provided detailed comments concerning the C++ material in many of the later chapters.

The principal reviewers and class testers have been enormously helpful in suggesting improvements and finding errors. For the first edition, these included Allen Alexander (Delaware Technical and Community College), Ruth Barton and Richard Reid (Michigan State University), Larry Cottrell (University of Central Florida), H. E. Dunsmore and Russell Quong (Purdue University), Donna Krabbe (College of Mount St. Joseph), Sally Kyvernitis (Neumann College), Xiaoping Jia (DePaul University), Xiannong Meng and Rick Zaccone (Bucknell), Jeff Buckwalter and Kim Summerhays (University of San Francisco), and Jo Ellen Perry (University of North Carolina). Valuable proofreading and editing assistance were provided by Sally Kyvernitis, Donna Skalski, and Frank Friedman's daughters Dara and Shelley.

We are also very grateful to the principal reviewers of other editions of this book for their hard work and timely responses. They include William E. Bulley (Merit Network, Inc.), Greg Comeau (Comeau Computing), Bruce Gilland (University of Colorado at Boulder), William I. Grosky (Wayne State University), Bina Ramamurthy (SUNY at Buffalo), and W. Brent Seales (University of Kentucky).

Frank Friedman is particularly indebted to several members of the staff at the Software Engineering Institute (Pittsburgh), particularly Mary Shaw, Norm Gibbs (Guilford College), and Gary Ford, for their support during the year in which the seeds that lead to this book were sown.

As always, it has been a pleasure working with the people of Addison-Wesley throughout this endeavor. Editor-in-Chief Michael Hirsch, along with Editorial Assistant Stephanie Sellinger, provided guidance and encouragement throughout all phases of manuscript revision. Heather McNally and Wanda Rockwell supervised the production of the book, while Margaret Waples and Kathryn Ferranti developed the marketing campaign.

F. L. F.
E. B. K.

Brief Contents

The following are available online:

Contents

chapter three   Top-Down Design with Functions and Classes   117

chapter nine

The following are available online:

chapter one

Introduction to Computers, Problem Solving, and Programming

Chapter Objectives

- To learn the different categories of computers
- To understand the role of each component in a computer
- To understand the purpose of an operating system
- To learn the differences between machine language, assembly language, and higher level languages
- To understand what processes are required to run a C++ program
- To learn how to solve a programming problem in a careful, disciplined way
- To understand and appreciate ethical issues related to the use of computers and programming

SINCE THE 1940s—a period of little more than 70 years—the development of the computer has spurred the growth of technology into realms only dreamed of at the turn of the twentieth century. Computers have changed the way we live and how we do business. Many of us use computers to register for courses, to send and receive electronic mail (e-mail), to shop and bank from home, to retrieve information from the World Wide Web, to research and write term papers, and to do other homework assignments. Computers are a key component of automatic teller machines (ATMs), and computers are built into our cars and most household appliances. Computers can receive, store, process, and output information of all kinds: numbers, text, images, graphics, video, and sound, to name a few.

Although we're often led to believe otherwise, computers cannot "think." Basically, computers are devices for performing computations at incredible speeds (more than a billion instructions per second) and with great accuracy. But, to accomplish anything useful, a computer must be provided with a list of instructions, or a program. Programs are usually written in special computer programming languages—such as C++, the subject of this book and one of the most versatile programming languages available today.

This chapter introduces the computer and its components and then presents an overview of programming languages. We describe a systematic approach to solving problems called the software development method, and we use it to write a basic C++ program. The chapter ends with a discussion of ethics for programmers.

1.1 Overview of Computers

Most of us deal with computers every day, and we probably use computers for word processing or for surfing the World Wide Web. And some of us may even have studied programming in high school. But it wasn't always this way. Not long ago, most people considered computers to be mysterious devices whose secrets were known only by a few computer wizards.

Early Computers

If we take the literal definition for a computer as "a device for counting or computing," then we could consider the abacus to have been the first computer. The first electronic digital computer was designed in the late 1930s by Dr. John Atanasoff and graduate student Clifford Berry at Iowa State University. They designed their computer to help them perform mathematical computations in nuclear physics.

The first large-scale, general-purpose electronic digital computer, called the ENIAC, was completed in 1946 at the University of Pennsylvania with funding from the U.S. Army. The ENIAC weighed 30 tons and occupied a 30-by-50-foot space. It was used to compute ballistics tables, predict the weather, and make atomic energy calculations. Its designers were J. Presper Eckert and John Mauchley.

stored-program computer (von Neumann architecture)
A computer design based on the concept of storing a computer program along with its data in computer memory.

To program the ENIAC, engineers had to connect hundreds of wires and arrange thousands of switches in a certain way. In 1946, Dr. John von Neumann of Princeton University proposed the concept of a **stored-program** computer—a computer whose program was stored in computer memory. Von Neumann knew that the data stored in computer memory could easily be changed by a program. He reasoned that programs, too, could be stored in computer memory and changed far more easily than by connecting wires and setting switches. Von Neumann designed a computer based on this idea. His design was a success and greatly simplified computer programming. The **von Neumann architecture** is the basis of the digital computer as we know it today.

Categories of Computers

Early computers used vacuum tubes as their basic electronic component. Technological advances in the design and manufacture of these components led to new generations of computers that were considerably smaller, faster, and less expensive than their predecessors.

In the 1970s, the Altair and Apple computer companies manufactured the first **microcomputers**. The computer processor in a microcomputer is an electronic component called a **microprocessor**, which is about the size of a postage stamp. Because they are so small and relatively inexpensive, microprocessors are found in watches, pocket calculators, cameras, home appliances, and automobiles, as well as in computers.

Most offices have one or more personal computers. Typical models cost less than $2000 and sit on a desk, yet have as much computational power as the giants of 20 years ago that cost more than $100,000 and filled a 9-by-12-foot room. Today's computers come in even smaller models that can fit inside a backpack or a person's hand (see Figure 1.1).

Personal computers are used by one person at a time. Businesses and research labs use larger and faster computers called **minicomputers** and **mainframes**, which can be used by many people simultaneously.

microcomputer
A computer that uses a very small processor.

microprocessor
The processor found in a microcomputer.

minicomputer
A computer for businesses or research laboratories that can be used by many people simultaneously.

mainframe
A computer with more computational power than a minicomputer that is often used by major corporations.

Figure 1.1   Netbook computer and hand-held computer

supercomputer
The most powerful kind of mainframe computer, performing in seconds computations that might take hours or days on other computers.

Supercomputers, the most powerful mainframe computers, can perform in seconds computations that might take hours or even days on other computers.

Sharing Computer Resources

time sharing
A process that allows simultaneous access to a single computer by a number of users.

Time sharing is used on mainframes and minicomputers to allow simultaneous access to the computing resources. The problem with time sharing is that users have to wait for their turn to access the resources. In the early days, these waits could take minutes. And if the computer stops working, all users are affected, as they must wait for the computer to be restarted.

Although microcomputers don't have the huge resources of minicomputers and mainframes, they provide their users with dedicated resources. Also if one microcomputer stops working, others are not affected. The major disadvantage of early personal or workstation computers was that they were isolated from the vast resources of the larger machines. In Section 1.2, we see how computer networks solve this problem.

EXERCISES FOR SECTION 1.1

Self-Check

1. List the different kinds of computers from smallest to largest.

2. Why do you think each computer user in a time-shared environment is unaware that others are also using the computer?

3. Describe the contributions of Atanasoff and Berry, Eckert and Mauchley, and von Neumann.

1.2   Computer Hardware

hardware
The actual computer equipment.
software
The set of programs associated with a computer.
program
A list of instructions that a computer uses to manipulate data to perform a task.

A computer system consists of two major components: **hardware**—the actual equipment used to perform the computations—and **software**—that is, the programs. **Programs** let us communicate with a computer by giving it the instructions it needs to operate. We discuss hardware in this section and software in the next.

Despite their differences in cost, size, and capabilities, modern computers resemble each other in many basic ways. Essentially, most consist of the following hardware components:

- Main memory
- Secondary memory, including storage media such as hard disks, flash drives, and CD-ROMs

- Central processing unit (CPU)
- Input devices, such as a keyboard and mouse
- Output devices, such as a monitor and printer
- Network connection, such as a modem or Ethernet interface

Figure 1.2 shows how these components interact in a computer when a program is executed; the arrows show the direction of information flow.

The program must be transferred from *secondary memory* (or *secondary storage*) to *main memory* before it can be executed. Data must be supplied from some source. The person using a program (the *program user*) may supply data through an *input device* such as a mouse or a keyboard, from a *data file* located in secondary storage, or from a remote machine via the network connection. The data are stored in the computer's *main memory* where they can be accessed and manipulated by the *central processing unit.* The results of this manipulation are stored back in *main memory.* Finally, the information (results) in main memory may be displayed through an *output device* such as a monitor or printer, stored in secondary storage, or sent to another computer via the network. In the remainder of this section, we describe these components in more detail.

Figure 1.2   Computer components

Memory

Memory is an essential component in any computer. Before discussing the types of memory—main and secondary—let's look at what it consists of and how the computer works with it.

Anatomy of Memory

memory cell
An individual storage location in memory.

address of a memory cell
The relative position of a memory cell in the computer's main memory.

contents of a memory cell
The information stored in a memory cell, either a program instruction or data.

Imagine the memory of a computer as a sequence of storage locations called **memory cells**. To store and access information, the computer must have some way of identifying the individual memory cells, so each memory cell has a unique **address** that indicates its position in memory. Figure 1.3 shows a computer memory consisting of 1000 memory cells with addresses 0 through 999. Most computers have millions of individual memory cells, each with its own address.

The data stored in a memory cell are called the **contents** of the cell. In Figure 1.3, the contents of memory cell 3 is the number −26 and the contents of memory cell 4 is the letter H.

Memory cells can also contain program instructions. Cells 6 through 8 in Figure 1.3 store instructions to add two numbers (from cells 1 and 3) and store the result in memory cell 5. You'll recall that in a von Neumann computer, a program's instructions must be stored in main memory before they

Address	Contents
0	−27.2
1	354
2	0.005
3	−26
4	H
5	400
6	RTV 001
7	ADD 003
8	STO 005
⋮	⋮
998	X
999	75.62

Figure 1.3   A thousand memory cells in main memory

can be executed. Whenever we open a new program, we change the computer's operation by storing the new instructions in memory.

Bytes and Bits

A memory cell is actually a grouping of smaller units called bytes. A **byte** is the amount of storage required to store a single character, such as the letter H in cell 4 of Figure 1.3. The number of bytes a memory cell can contain varies from computer to computer.

byte
The amount of storage required to store a single character.

A byte is composed of even smaller units of storage called bits (see Figure 1.4). There are eight bits to a byte. "**Bit**" derives from the words *binary* digi*t* and is the smallest element a computer can deal with. Binary refers to a number system based on two numbers, 0 and 1; therefore, a bit is either a 0 or a 1.

bit (binary digit)
A binary unit representing a 0 or a 1.

Storing and Retrieving Information in Memory

A particular pattern of zeros and ones (that is, bits) represents each value in memory, whether it's a number, a letter, or an instruction such as ADD 003. A computer can either store or retrieve a value. When **storing** a value, the computer sends electronic signals to set each bit of a selected memory cell to either 0 or 1; storing a value destroys the previous contents of the cell. When **retrieving** a value from a memory cell, the computer copies the pattern of 0s and 1s stored in that cell to another storage area for processing; copying does *not* destroy the contents of the cell whose value is retrieved. This process is the same regardless of the kind of information—character, number, or program instruction—to be stored or retrieved.

storing a value in memory
Setting the individual bits of a memory cell to 0 or 1, destroying its previous contents.
retrieving a value from memory
Copying the contents of a particular memory cell to another storage area for processing.

Main Memory

Main memory, made of electronic circuitry on small computer chips, stores programs, data, and results. Most computers have two types of main memory: **random access memory (RAM)** for temporary storage of programs, data, and results, and **read-only memory (ROM)**, which stores programs or data permanently.

random access memory (RAM)
The part of main memory that temporarily stores programs, data, and results.

RAM temporarily stores programs while they are being executed by the computer. It also temporarily stores information—for example, numbers,

read-only memory (ROM)
The part of main memory that permanently stores programs or data.

Figure 1.4   Relationship between a byte and a bit

volatile memory
Memory whose contents disappear when you switch off the computer.

names, or pictures—that is being processed by the computer. RAM is usually **volatile memory**, which means that when you switch off the computer, you will lose everything stored in RAM. To prevent this, you should store the contents of RAM in semipermanent secondary memory (discussed below) before switching off your computer.

In contrast, ROM stores information permanently. The computer can retrieve (or read) information but it can't store (or write) information in ROM— hence its name, read-only memory. Because they're not volatile, the instructions and data stored in ROM don't disappear when you switch off the computer. Most modern computers contain an internal ROM that stores the instructions needed to get the computer running when you first switch it on.

Usually a computer contains much more RAM than internal ROM. The amount of RAM can often be increased (up to a specified maximum), but the amount of internal ROM is usually fixed. When we refer to main memory in this text, we mean RAM because that is the part of main memory that is normally accessible to the programmer.

RAM is relatively fast memory, but is limited in size and is not permanent memory. These features are in contrast to secondary memory, which, although slower than RAM, is larger and more permanent.

Secondary Memory

Computer systems provide storage in addition to main memory for two reasons. First, computers need storage that is permanent or semipermanent so that information can be retained during a power loss or when the computer is turned off. Second, systems typically store more information than will fit in memory.

secondary storage
Units such as disks or flash drives that retain data even when the power to the drive is off.
disk
Thin platter of metal or plastic on which data are represented by magnetized spots arranged in tracks.

Figure 1.5 shows some of the most frequently used **secondary storage** devices and storage media. Most personal computers use two types of disk drives as their secondary storage devices—hard drives and optical drives. Hard **disks** are attached to their disk drives and are coated with a magnetic material. Each data bit is a magnetized spot on the disk, and the spots are arranged in concentric circles called tracks. The disk drive read/write head accesses data by moving across the spinning disk to the correct track and

CD   Flash   Hard
            drive   disk

Figure 1.5   Secondary storage media

then sensing the spots as they move by. The hard disks in personal computers usually hold from one to several hundred gigabytes (GB) of data, but clusters of hard drives that store data for an entire network may provide many terabytes (TB) of storage (see Table 1.1).

Most of today's personal computers are equipped with **optical drives** for storing and retrieving data on compact disks (CDs) or digital versatile disks (DVDs) that can be removed from the drive. A CD is a silvery plastic platter on which a laser records data as a sequence of tiny pits in a spiral track on one side of the disk. One CD can hold 680 MB of data. A DVD uses smaller pits packed in a tighter spiral, allowing storage of 4.7 GB of data on one layer. Some DVDs can hold four layers of data—two on each side—for a total capacity of 17 GB, sufficient storage for as much as nine hours of studio-quality video and multichannel audio.

optical drive
Device that uses a laser to access or store data on a CD or DVD.

Flash drives such as the one pictured in Figure 1.5 use flash memory packaged in small plastic cases about three inches long that can be plugged into any of a computer's USB (Universal Serial Bus) ports. Unlike hard drives and optical drives that must spin their disks for access to data, flash drives have no moving parts and all data transfer is by electronic signal only. In flash memory, bits are represented as electrons trapped in microscopic chambers of silicon dioxide. Typical USB flash drives store 1 to a few GB of data, but 64-GB drives are also available.

flash drive
Device that plugs into USB port and stores data bits as trapped electrons.

Information stored on a disk is organized into separate collections called **files**. One file may contain a C++ program. Another file may contain the data to be processed by that program (a *data file*). A third file could contain the results generated by a program (an *output file*). The names of all files stored on a disk are listed in the disk's **directory**. This directory may be broken into one or more levels of subdirectories or folders, where each **subdirectory** stores the names of files that relate to the same general topic. For example, you might have separate subdirectories of files that contain homework assignments and programs for each course you are taking this

file
Named collection of data stored on a disk.

directory
A list of the names of files stored on a disk.

subdirectory
A list of the names of files that relate to a particular topic.

Table 1.1 Terms Used to Quantify Storage Capacities

Term	Abbreviation	Equivalent to	Comparison to Power of 10
Byte	B	8 bits	
Kilobyte	KB	1,024 (2^{10}) bytes	$> 10^3$
Megabyte	MB	1,048,576 (2^{20}) bytes	$> 10^6$
Gigabyte	GB	1,073,741,824 (2^{30}) bytes	$> 10^9$
Terabyte	TB	1,099,511,627,776 (2^{40}) bytes	$> 10^{12}$

semester. The details of how files are named and grouped in directories vary with each computer system. Follow the naming conventions that apply to your system.

Central Processing Unit

central processing unit (CPU)
Coordinates all computer operations and performs arithmetic and logical operations on data.

The **central processing unit (CPU)** has two roles: coordinating all computer operations and performing arithmetic and logical operations on data. The CPU follows instructions in computer programs to determine which operations to carry out and in what order. It then transmits control signals to the other computer components. For example, when instructed to read a data item, the CPU sends the necessary control signals to the input device.

fetching an instruction
Retrieving an instruction from main memory.

To process a program stored in main memory, the CPU retrieves each instruction in sequence (called **fetching an instruction**), decodes the instruction, and then retrieves any data needed to carry out that instruction. Next, the CPU processes the data it retrieved and stores the results in main memory.

The CPU can perform arithmetic operations such as addition, subtraction, multiplication, and division. It can also compare the contents of two memory cells—for example, deciding which contains the larger value or if the values are equal—and make decisions based on the results of that comparison.

integrated circuit (IC)
An electronic device containing a large number of circuits/components housed inside a silicon case.
microprocessor
A central processing unit packaged in an integrated circuit.
register
A high-speed memory location inside the CPU.
keyboard
A computer input device for typing sequences of letter or digit characters.
cursor
A moving place marker that indicates the position on the screen where the next character will be displayed.
function keys
A special keyboard key used to select a particular operation; the operation selected depends on the program being used.

The circuitry of a modern CPU is housed in a single **integrated circuit** (IC) or chip—millions of miniature circuits manufactured on a sliver of silicon. An integrated circuit that is a full central processing unit is called a **microprocessor**. A CPU's current instruction and data values are stored temporarily inside the CPU in special high-speed memory locations called **registers**.

Input/Output Devices

We use input/output (I/O) devices to communicate with the computer—to enter data for a computation and to observe the results of that computation. The most common input device is a keyboard and the most common output device is a monitor.

A computer **keyboard** resembles a typewriter keyboard (see Figure 1.6). When you press a letter or digit key, that character is sent to main memory and is displayed on the monitor at the position of the **cursor**, a moving place marker. A computer keyboard has extra keys for special purposes. For example, on the keyboard shown in Figure 1.6, the 12 keys in the top row labeled F1 through F12 are **function keys**. The functions of these keys depend on the program currently being executed; that is, pressing F4 in one program will usually not produce the same results as pressing F4 in another program.

Figure 1.6 Computer keyboard

Other special keys let you delete characters, move the cursor, and "enter" a line of data you typed at the keyboard.

Another common input device is a **mouse**, a handheld pointing device. Moving the mouse on your desk causes the mouse cursor, a small arrow or symbol on the screen, to move in the same direction as the mouse. You can use the mouse to select an operation by pointing and clicking: moving the mouse cursor to a word or picture (called an **icon**) that represents the computer operation and then pressing a mouse button to start the operation selected.

A **scanner** is used to process a page of text or a picture and to generate a sequence of bits as its digital image. This digital image is sent to memory so it can be processed and stored on disk. Some printers include a scanner.

A Webcam (abbreviation for Web camera) is a device that sends a video to a computer. Webcams are often used to send a video of the person using the computer over the Internet.

A **monitor** displays the output of currect computer operations. Once the image disappears from the monitor screen, it is lost. If you want a hard copy (a printed version) of some information, you must send that information to a different output device, a printer.

mouse
A handheld input device that moves a cursor on the computer screen to select an operation.

icon
A picture representing a computer operation that is activated by clicking a mouse.

scanner
A device for generating a digital image of a document or picture.

monitor
A computer output device for providing a temporary display of information.

Computer Networks

Network technology was invented to connect computers together and let them share resources. Unlike a mainframe, which is a single computer shared by many users, a **network** is made of many computers that share resources. Within an organization, a **local area network (LAN)** lets many personal computers access sharable resources from a larger computer called

network
An interconnected collection of computers that share resources.

local area network (LAN)
A network of computers in a single organization.

server
A computer that provides resources to other computers in a network.

wide area network (WAN)
A network such as the Internet that connects computers and LANs over a large geographic area.

Internet
An interconnected grouping of computer networks from all over the world; provides access to the World Wide Web.

Figure 1.7   Local area network

a **server** (see Figure 1.7). A network that links individual computers and local area networks over a large geographic area is called a **wide area network (WAN)** (see Figure 1.8). The best-known WAN is the **Internet**, which is composed of university, corporate, government, and public-access networks. The World Wide Web is accessed via the Internet.

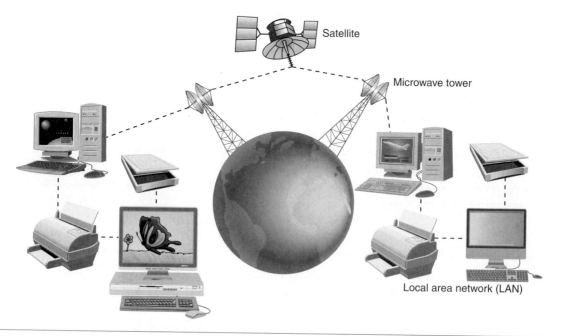

Figure 1.8   A wide area network with satellite relays of microwave signals

If your computer is connected to a modem, you can connect to the Internet through a telephone line or television or fiber-optic cable. A **modem** (**mo**dulator **dem**odulator) converts binary computer data into a form that can be transmitted to another computer. At the computer on the receiving end, another modem converts the signal received back to binary data. Early modems for telephone lines transmitted at only 300 baud (300 bits per second). Today's telephone modems transmit over 50,000 bits per second, or if you have a digital subscriber line (**DSL connection**), the associated modem can transmit 1.5 million bits per second while allowing you to use the same line simultaneously for voice calls. Another high-speed option is **cable Internet access**, which brings Internet data to your computer along a channel just like a television channel, using the same coaxial cable that carries cable TV.

modem
A device that converts binary data into a form that can be transmitted between computers over telephone lines or coaxial cable.

DSL connection (digital subscriber line)
A high-speed Internet connection that uses a telephone line and does not interfere with simultaneous voice communication on the same line.

cable Internet access
Two-way high-speed transmission of Internet data over the coaxial cable that carries cable television signals.

The World Wide Web

The **World Wide Web (the Web)** was introduced in 1989; it is the newest and the most popular feature on the Internet. The Web was developed at CERN (the European Laboratory for Particle Physics) as an effective and uniform way of accessing all the information on the Internet. Today you can use the Web to send, view, retrieve, and search for information or to create a Web page. (There are no controls or checks for accuracy on the Web; you should keep this in mind when reading or using such information.)

To access and navigate the Web, you need a **Web browser**. A Web browser is a program with a **graphical user interface (GUI)** that displays the text and graphics in a Web document and activates the **hyperlinks** to other documents. Clicking on a link to a Web document causes that document to be transferred from the computer where it is stored to your own computer.

World Wide Web
A collection of interconnected documents that may be accessed from virtually any computer in the world.

Web browser
A program that lets users display and view a Web document and activate links to other documents.

graphical user interface (GUI)
Displayed pictures and menus that allow users to select commands and data.

hyperlink
A connection in a Web document to other related documents that users can activate by pressing a mouse button.

EXERCISES FOR SECTION 1.2

Self-Check

1. What are the contents of memory cells 1 and 998 in Figure 1.3? What memory cells contain the letter H and the number 75.62?

2. Explain the purpose of main memory, secondary memory, CPU, and the disk. What input and output devices will be used with your computer? What is a computer network?

3. List the following in order of smallest to largest: byte, bit, main memory, WAN, memory cell, secondary memory, LAN.

4. What do you think each of the instructions in memory cells 6 though 8 in Figure 1.3 means?

5. Which came first, the Internet or the World Wide Web?

6. Indicate whether each of these devices usually provides temporary, semi-permanent, or permanent storage: ROM, RAM, flash drive, CD, hard disk.

7. Which device from the list in Exercise 6 does a word processor use to store a letter while it is being typed? To store the letter after you are finished? To store a software package you purchase? To store some very large files you no longer need?

8. Explain the use of a Web browser and hyperlinks in a Web document.

9. If a computer were instructed to sum the contents of memory cells 1 and 3 of Figure 1.3 and store the result in memory cell 5, what would be stored in memory cell 5?

10. One bit can have two values, 0 or 1. A combination of 2 bits can have values 00, 01, 10, 11. List the values you can have with 3 bits. Do the same for 4 bits. Write a formula that tells you how many values you can have with n bits.

1.3   Computer Software

In the previous section, we surveyed the components of a computer system, collectively called hardware. We also covered the basic operations by which a computer accomplishes tasks: repeated fetching and execution of instructions. In this section, we focus on these all-important lists of instructions, called computer programs or computer software. We will first consider the software that makes the hardware accessible to the user, then look at the various levels of computer languages in which software is written and at the process of creating and running a new program.

Operating System

operating system (OS)
Software that controls a user's interaction with the computer hardware and software and that manages the computer resources.

The computer programs that control the interaction of the user with the computer hardware compose the **operating system (OS)**. The operating system may be compared to the conductor of an orchestra, for it is responsible for directing all computer operations and managing all computer resources. Usually, part of the operating system is stored permanently in a read-only memory (ROM) chip so it will be available as soon as the computer is turned on. (A computer can look at the values in ROM but can't write new values to the chip.) This portion of the OS contains the instructions that will load into RAM the rest of the operating system code, which typically resides on disk. Loading the operating system into RAM is called **booting the computer**.

Among the operating system's many responsibilities are the following:

1. Communicating with the computer user: receiving commands and carrying them out or rejecting them with an error message.

2. Managing allocation of memory, processor time, and other resources for various tasks.

3. Collecting input from the keyboard, mouse, and other input devices, and providing this data to the currently running program.

4. Conveying program output to the screen, printer, or other output device.

5. Accessing data from secondary storage.

6. Writing data to secondary storage.

In addition, the OS of a computer with multiple users must verify each user's right to use the computer and ensure that each user can access only data for which he or she has authorization.

Table 1.2 lists some widely used operating systems. An OS with a command-line interface displays a brief message called a **prompt** that indicates readiness to receive input; the user can then type a command at the keyboard. Listing 1.1 shows the entry of a UNIX command (ls temp/misc) requesting a list of the names of all the files (`Gridvar.cpp`, `Gridvar.exe`, `Gridok.dat`) in subdirectory `misc` of directory `temp`. Here, the prompt is

booting the computer
Starting the computer by loading part of the operating system from disk into memory (RAM) and executing it.

prompt
A message displayed by the computer indicating its readiness to receive data or a command from the user.

Table 1.2 Some Widely Used Operating Systems Characterized by Interface Type

Command-Line Interface	Graphical User Interface
UNIX	Macintosh OS
MS-DOS	Windows 7
VMS	Windows Vista
	OS/2 Warp
	UNIX + X Window System
	Linux

Listing 1.1 Entering a UNIX command to display a directory

```
mycomputer:~> ls temp/misc
Gridvar.cpp      Gridvar.exe      Gridok.dat

mycomputer:~>
```

`mycomputer:~>`. (In this and all subsequent listings showing program runs, input typed by the user is shown in color to distinguish it from computer-generated text.)

In contrast, operating systems with a graphical user interface provide the user with a system of icons and menus. To issue commands, the user moves the mouse or touch-pad cursor to point to the appropriate icon or menu selection and pushes a button once or twice. Figure 1.9 shows the window that pops up when you double-click on the My Computer icon on the desktop of a Windows GUI. You can view the directories of the hard drive (C:), backup drive (D:), optical drive (E:), or flash drive (F:) by double-clicking the appropriate icon.

Application Software

application programs
Software used for a specific task such as word processing, accounting, or database management.

Application programs are designed to accomplish specific tasks. For example, a word-processing application such as Microsoft Word or WordPerfect creates a document, a spreadsheet application such as Excel automates tedious numerical calculations and generates charts that depict data, and

Figure 1.9 Accessing secondary storage devices through Windows

a database management application such as Access or dBASE enables data storage and quick keyword-based access to large collections of records.

Computer users typically buy application software on CDs or they download software files from a Web site. The software is saved on the hard disk and then *installed* which makes it ready to use. When buying software, verify that the program you are purchasing is compatible with both your operating system and your computer hardware. Programmers use programming languages, the subject of the next section, to write most commercial software.

installing software
Making an application available on a computer by copying it from a CD or downloading it from a Web site.

Programming Languages

Developing new software requires writing lists of instructions for a computer to execute. Software developers rarely write instructions in **machine language**, a language of binary numbers directly understood by a computer. A drawback of machine language is that it is not standardized: every type of CPU has a different machine language. This same drawback also applies to the somewhat more readable **assembly language**, a language in which computer operations are represented by mnemonic codes rather than binary numbers, and variables can be given names rather than binary memory addresses.

machine language
A list of binary instructions for a particular CPU.

assembly language
A language whose instructions are in the form of mnemonic codes and variable names.

Table 1.3 shows a small machine language program fragment that adds two numbers and an equivalent fragment in assembly language. Notice that each assembly language instruction corresponds to exactly one machine language instruction. (The assembly language memory cells labeled A and B are space for data; they are not instructions.) The symbol ? indicates that we don't know the contents of the memory cells with addresses 00000100 and 00000101.

To write programs that are independent of the CPU on which they will be executed, software designers use **high-level languages**, which combine algebraic expressions and English words. For example, the machine/assembly

high-level language
A machine programming language that combines algebraic expressions and English words.

Table 1.3 A Program in Machine and Assembly Language

Memory Addresses	Machine Language Instructions	Assembly Language Instructions
00000000	00010101	RTV A
00000001	00010110	ADD B
00000010	00110101	STO A
00000011	01110111	HLT
00000100	?	A ?
00000101	?	B ?

language program fragment shown in Table 1.3 would be a single statement in a high-level language:

```
a = a + b;
```

This statement means "Add the data in memory cells a and b, and store the result in memory cell a (replacing its previous value)."

Many high-level languages are available. Table 1.4 lists some of the most widely used ones along with the application areas that first popularized them.

Object-Oriented Programming

We will focus on C++, an object-oriented programming language derived from C. C++ was developed by Bjarne Stroustrup of AT&T's Bell Laboratories in the mid-1980s and was formally standardized in 1998. Object-oriented programming languages are popular because they make it easier to reuse and adapt previously written software. Another object-oriented language listed in Table 1.4 is Java, which is widely used on the Web.

An object is an entity that has particular properties. Some of these properties can be encoded into a computer program as data and some can be encoded as **methods** for operating on the data.

method
An operation that can be performed on an object's data.

As an example of an object, consider a hypothetical automobile. You may visualize wheels, a steering wheel, a body shape, and a color. These are the attributes, or data, of the automobile. You can also imagine the actions associated with operating an automobile, such as starting the engine, driving forward or in reverse, and applying the brakes. These activities are analogous to methods. The attributes and methods we use to characterize an automobile are an **abstraction**, or model, of an automobile.

abstraction
A representation or model of a physical object.

Table 1.4   Common High-Level Languages

High-Level Language	Original Purpose
BASIC	Teaching college students how to use the computer in their courses
C	Writing system software
C++	Extension of C supporting object-oriented programming
COBOL	Performing business data processing
FORTRAN (**For**mula **tran**slation)	Performing engineering and scientific applications
Java	A highly portable object-oriented language used for programming on the Web
Lisp	Performing artificial intelligence applications that require manipulating abstract symbols

The description of an automobile thus provides a definition of a hypo-thetical automobile. As such, it describes a **class**—the class *automobile*. The class definition can be used as a template to construct actual **objects**, or instances of the class, such as your car and your parents' car. Both cars have all the attributes of an automobile, but they differ in detail—for example, one may be red and the other white.

The distinction between the terms *class* and *object* sometimes gets a bit blurry. A class definition, or class, describes the properties (attributes) of an abstract or hypothetical object. Actual objects are instances of the class. An object's data fields provide storage for information, and an object's methods process or manipulate this information. Some of the data stored in an object may be computed using a method. For example, fuel efficiency can be com-puted from the power of the engine and the weight of the car (along with some other factors). Table 1.5 shows some attributes of the class *automobile* and two objects of that class.

Classes can have other classes as components. For example, a car has an engine and wheels; both components can be defined as separate classes. Finally, classes can be organized into a hierarchy of **subclasses** and **superclasses**, where a subclass has all the properties of a superclass and some additional properties that are not part of the superclass. Figure 1.10 shows that the class *automobile* is a subclass of the class *vehicle* (an automo-bile is a vehicle that has passenger seats), and the class *vehicle* is a superclass of the class *automobile*. The class *truck* is also a subclass of the class *vehicle* (a truck is a vehicle that has a truck bed), and the class *vehicle* is also a super-class of the class *truck*. The class *sports car* is a subclass of the class *automobile* (a sports car is an automobile with a powerful engine), so it is also a subclass of the class *vehicle* but not of the class *truck*. The classes *vehicle* and *automobile* are both superclasses of the class *sports car*.

Objects in a subclass inherit properties (both data and methods) from a superclass. For example, all three subclasses shown in Figure 1.10 have a driver's seat and can be driven (properties inherited from class *vehicle*).

These basic principles help programmers organize their solutions to problems. In particular, rather than starting each program from scratch, programmers use object-oriented programming because it encourages reuse

class
An entity that defines the properties of a hypo-thetical object.
object
A member, or instance, of a class that has all the properties described by the class definition.

subclass
A class that is derived from a superclass but with additional attributes.
superclass
A class that serves as a base class for other classes with additional attributes.

Table 1.5 The Relationship Between a Class and Objects of the Class

Class **automobile**	Object **yourCar**	Object parentsCar
Color	Red	White
Make	Toyota	Buick
Model	Coupe	Sedan
Year	1999	2003

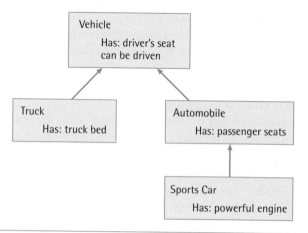

Figure 1.10   A class hierarchy

of code (programs) that are already written. They can use existing classes as components of new classes, or they can create new classes that are subclasses of existing classes. Either way, methods that were programmed for the existing classes can be used with objects of the new classes. In this book, we will focus on using existing classes as components of new classes rather than creating subclasses of existing classes.

EXERCISES FOR SECTION 1.3

Self-Check

1. What do you think the six high-level language statements below mean?
   a. `profit = gross - net;`
   b. `fahren = 1.8 * celsius + 32;`
   c. `fraction = percent / 100.0;`
   d. `sum = sum + x;`
   e. `newPrincipal = oldPrincipal * (1.0 + interest);`
   f. `celsius = 5 * (fahren - 32.0) / 9;`

2. List two reasons why it would be preferable to write a program in C++ rather than machine language.

3. Explain the relationship between the data and methods of a class.

4. What are two ways that object-oriented programming facilitates code reuse by programmers?

5. What is an abstraction in programming?

6. Is an object an instance of a class or vice versa?

1.4 Processing a High-Level Language Program

Although programmers find it much easier to express problem solutions in high-level languages, computers do NOT understand these languages. Before a high-level language program can be executed, it must be translated into the target computer's machine language. The program that does this translation is called a **compiler**. Figure 1.11 illustrates the role of the compiler in the process of developing and testing a high-level language program. Both the input to and (when successful) the output from the compiler are programs.

The input to the compiler is a **source file** containing the text of a high-level language program. The software developer creates this file with a word processor or **editor**. The source file is in text format, which means that it is a collection of character codes. For example, you might type a program into a file called `myprog.cpp`. The compiler will scan this source file, checking to see if it follows the high-level language's rules of **syntax** (grammar). If the program is syntactically correct, the compiler saves, in an **object file**, the machine language instructions that carry out the program's purpose. For program `myprog.cpp`, the object file created might be named `myprog.obj`. This file's format is binary, which means that you should not send it to a printer, display it on your monitor, or try to work with it in a word processor because it will appear to be meaningless garbage. If the source program contains syntax errors, the compiler lists these errors but does not create an object file. The developer must return to the editor, correct the errors, and recompile the program.

Although an object file contains machine language instructions, not all of the instructions are complete. High-level languages provide the software developer with many named chunks of code for operations that he or she will likely need. Almost all high-level language programs use at least one of these code chunks, which reside in other object files available to the system. The **linker program** combines code from other object files with the new object file, creating a complete machine language program that is ready to run. For your sample program, the linker might name the executable file it creates `myprog.exe`.

As long as `myprog.exe` is just stored on your disk, it does nothing. To run it, the **loader** must copy all its instructions into memory and direct the CPU to begin execution with the first instruction. As the program runs, it takes input data from one or more sources and sends results to output and/or secondary storage devices.

Some computer systems require the user to ask the OS to separately carry out each step illustrated in Figure 1.11. However, many high-level language compilers are now sold as part of an **integrated development environment (IDE)**, a package that combines a simple editor with a compiler, linker, and loader. IDEs give the developer menus from which to select steps, and if the developer tries a step that is out of sequence, the environment simply fills in the missing steps automatically.

compiler
Software that translates a high-level language program into machine language.

source file
File containing a program written in a high-level language; the input for a compiler.

editor
Software used to create, edit (change), and store a source file on disk.

syntax
Grammar rules of a programming language.

object file
File of machine language instructions that is the output of a compiler.

linker
Software that combines object files to create an executable machine language program.

loader
Software that copies an executable machine language program into memory and starts its execution.

integrated development environment (IDE)
Software package combining an editor, a compiler, a linker, a loader, and tools for finding errors.

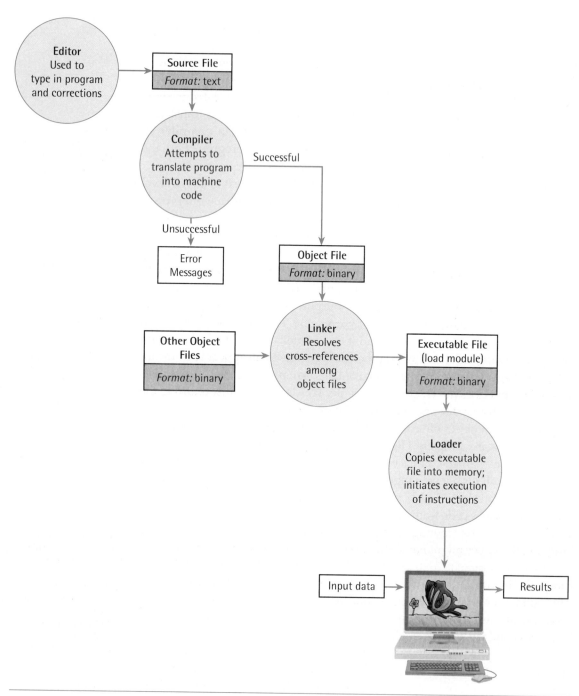

Figure 1.11   Preparing a high-level language program for execution

One caution: the IDE might not automatically save to disk the source, object, and executable files created by the programmer; it may simply leave these programs in memory. This approach saves the time and disk space needed to make copies, and keeps the code available in memory for application of the next step in the translation/execution process. But the developer can risk losing the only copy of the source file if a serious program error causes termination of the IDE program. To prevent such a loss, users must explicitly save the source file to disk after every modification before attempting to run the program.

Executing a Program

To execute a program, the CPU must examine each program instruction in memory and send out the command signals required to carry out the instruction. Although normally the instructions are executed in sequence, as we will discuss later, it is possible to have the CPU skip over some instructions or execute some instructions more than once.

While a program runs, data can be entered into memory and manipulated in some specified way. Special program instructions are used for entering a program's data (called **input data**) into memory. After the input data have been processed, instructions for displaying or printing values in memory can be executed to display the program results. The lines displayed by a program are called the **program output**.

input data
The data values that are entered by a program.

program output
The lines displayed by a program.

Let's look at the example shown in Figure 1.12—executing a water bill program stored in memory. Step 1 of the program enters into memory data that describe the amount of water used. In Step 2, the program manipulates the data and stores the results of the computations in memory. In the final step, the computed results are displayed as a water bill.

EXERCISES FOR SECTION 1.4

Self-Check

1. Would a syntax error be found in a source program or an object program? What system program would find a syntax error if one existed? What system program would you use to correct it?

2. Explain the differences between a source program, an object program, and an executable program. Which do you create, and which does the compiler create? Which does the linker or loader create?

3. What is an IDE? What does the program developer need to be concerned about when using an IDE?

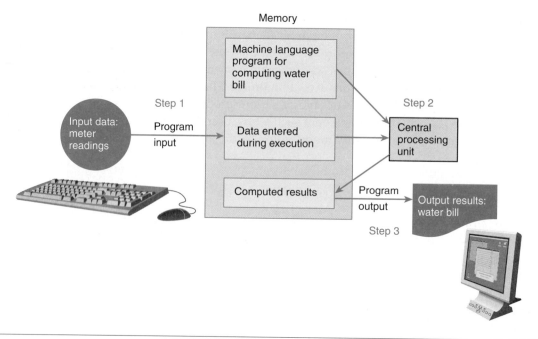

Figure 1.12   Flow of information during program execution

4. Explain how you could lose your source program if an error occurs while running a program using an IDE.

5. Explain the role of the compiler, linker, loader, and editor.

1.5   The Software Development Method

Programming is a problem-solving activity. If you are a good problem solver, you have the potential to become a good programmer, so one goal of this book is to help you improve your problem-solving ability. Problem-solving methods vary with subject area. Business students learn to solve problems with a *systems approach*, while engineering and science students use the *engineering and scientific method*. Programmers use the *software development method*.

We will focus on the first five steps listed below. The last step applies to commercial software, not student programs.

1. Specify the problem requirements.
2. Analyze the problem.
3. Design the algorithm to solve the problem.
4. Implement the algorithm.

5. Test and verify the completed program.

6. Maintain and update the program.

PROBLEM

Specifying the problem requirements forces you to state the problem clearly and unambiguously to gain a precise understanding of what is required for its solution. Your objective is to eliminate unimportant aspects and zero in on the root problem. This goal may not be as easy to achieve as it sounds. You may, for instance, need more information from the person who posed the problem.

ANALYSIS

Analyzing the problem involves identifying the problem *inputs* (the data you have to work with), *outputs* (the desired results), and any additional requirements for or constraints on the solution. At this stage, you should also determine the format in which the results should be displayed (for example, as a table with specific column headings) and develop a list of problem variables and their relationships. These relationships may be expressed as formulas.

If Steps 1 and 2 are not done properly, you will solve the wrong problem. Read the problem statement carefully (1) to obtain a clear idea of the problem and (2) to determine the inputs and outputs. It may be helpful to underline phrases in the problem statement that identify the inputs and outputs, as in the following example:

> Compute and display the *total cost of apples* given the number of *pounds of apples* purchased and the *cost per pound of apples*.

Next, summarize the information contained in the underlined phrases:

Problem Inputs
quantity of apples purchased (in pounds)
cost per pound of apples (in dollars per pound)

Problem Output
total cost of apples (in dollars)

Once you know the problem inputs and outputs, develop a list of formulas that specify relationships between them. The general formula

Total cost = Unit cost × Number of units

computes the total cost of any item purchased. Using the variables for our particular problem, we get the formula

Total cost of apples = Cost per pound × Pounds of apples

abstraction
The process of modeling a problem to extract the essential variables and their relationships.

This process of modeling a problem to extract the essential variables and their relationships is called **abstraction**.

DESIGN

Designing the algorithm to solve the problem requires you to develop a list of steps (an **algorithm**) to solve the problem and then verify that the algorithm solves the problem as intended. Writing the algorithm is often the hardest part of the problem-solving process. Don't try to solve every detail of the problem at the beginning; instead, use top-down design. In **top-down design** (also called *divide and conquer*), you first list the major steps, or subproblems, that need to be solved, then solve the original problem by solving each of its subproblems. Most computer algorithms consist of at least the following subproblems.

algorithm
A list of steps for solving a problem.

top-down design
Breaking a problem into its major subproblems and then solving the subproblems.

ALGORITHM FOR A PROGRAMMING PROBLEM
1. Get the data.
2. Perform the computations.
3. Display the results.

algorithm refinement
Developing a detailed list of steps to solve a particular step in an algorithm.

Once you know the subproblems, you can attack each one individually. The perform-the-computations step, for example, may need to be broken down into a more detailed list of steps through a process called **algorithm refinement**.

You are using top-down design when creating an outline for a term paper. You first create an outline of the major topics, then refine it by filling in subtopics for each major topic. Once the outline is complete, you begin writing the text for each subtopic.

desk-checking
The step-by-step simulation of the computer execution of an algorithm.

Desk-checking is an important, and often overlooked, part of algorithm design. To desk check an algorithm, you must carefully perform each algorithm step (or its refinements) just as a computer would and verify that the algorithm works as intended. You'll save time and effort if you locate algorithm errors early in the problem-solving process.

IMPLEMENTATION

Implementing the algorithm (Step 4 in the software development method) involves writing it as a program—converting each algorithm step into one or more statements in a programming language.

TESTING

Testing and verifying the program requires testing the completed program to verify that it works as desired. Don't rely on just one test case; run the program several times using different sets of data, making sure that it works correctly for every situation provided for in the algorithm.

MAINTENANCE

Maintaining and updating the program involves modifying a program to remove previously undetected errors and to keep it up-to-date as government regulations or company policies change. Many organizations maintain a program for five years or more, often after the programmers who originally coded it have left.

A disciplined approach is essential if you want to create programs that are easy to read, understand, and maintain. You must follow accepted program style guidelines (which will be stressed in this book) and avoid tricks and programming shortcuts.

Caution: Failure Is Part of the Process

Although a step-by-step approach to problem solving is helpful, it does not guarantee that following these steps will result in a correct solution the first time, every time. The importance of verification highlights an essential truth of problem solving: The first (and also the second, third, or twentieth) attempt at a solution *may be wrong*. Probably the most important distinction between outstanding problem solvers and less proficient ones is that the former are not discouraged by initial failures. Instead, they see the faulty and near-correct early solutions as pointing toward a better understanding of the problem. One of the most inventive problem solvers of all time, Thomas Edison, is noted for his positive interpretation of the thousands of failed experiments that contributed to his incredible record of invention; he always saw those failures in terms of the helpful data they yielded about what did *not* work.

EXERCISES FOR SECTION 1.5

Self-Check

1. List the steps of the software development method.

2. Do you desk-check an algorithm before you refine it or after you refine it? Explain your answer.

1.6 Applying the Software Development Method

Throughout this book, we use the first five steps of the software development method to solve programming problems. These example problems, presented as *Case Studies*, begin with a statement of the *problem*. This is followed by an *analysis,* where we identify the data requirements for the problem: the problem inputs and the desired outputs. Next, we formulate the *design* of the initial algorithm and then we refine it. Finally, we *implement* the algorithm as a C++ program. We also provide a sample run of the program and discuss how to *test* the program.

Now let's walk through a sample case study. This example includes a running commentary on the process, which you can use as a model in solving other problems.

case study   **Converting Miles to Kilometers**

PROBLEM

Your summer internship has you working with a surveyor. Part of your job is to study some maps that give distances in kilometers and some that use miles. The surveyor prefers to deal in metric measurements. Write a program that performs the necessary conversion.

ANALYSIS

The first step in solving this problem is to determine what you are asked to do. You must convert from one system of measurement to another, but are you supposed to convert from kilometers to miles, or vice versa? The problem states that you prefer to deal in metric measurements, so you must convert distance measurements in miles to kilometers. Therefore, the problem input is *distance in miles* and the problem output is *distance in kilometers*. To write the program, you need to know the relationship between miles and kilometers. Consulting a metric table shows that one mile equals 1.609 kilometers.

The data requirements and relevant formulas are listed below. The memory cell that will contain the problem input is identified by `miles`, and `kms` identifies the memory cell that will contain the program result, or the problem output.

DATA REQUIREMENTS

Problem Input

`miles`   *the distance in miles*

Problem Output

`kms`   *the distance in kilometers*

Relevant Formula

1 mile = 1.609 kilometers

DESIGN

The next step is to formulate the algorithm that solves the problem. Begin by listing the three major steps, or subproblems, of the algorithm.

ALGORITHM

1. Get the distance in miles.

2. Convert the distance to kilometers.

3. Display the distance in kilometers.

Now decide whether any steps of the algorithm need further refinement or whether they are perfectly clear as stated. Step 1 (getting the data) and Step 3 (displaying a value) are basic steps and require no further refinement. Step 2 is fairly straightforward, but some detail might help:

Step 2 Refinement

2.1 The distance in kilometers is 1.609 times the distance in miles.

We list the complete algorithm with refinements below to show you how it all fits together. The refinement of Step 2 is numbered as Step 2.1 and is indented under Step 2.

ALGORITHM WITH REFINEMENTS

1. Get the distance in miles.

2. Convert the distance to kilometers.

    2.1 The distance in kilometers is 1.609 times the distance in miles.

3. Display the distance in kilometers.

Let's desk check the algorithm before going further. If Step 1 gets a distance of 10.0 miles, Step 2.1 would convert it to 1.609×10.00 or 16.09 kilometers. This correct result would be displayed by Step 3.

IMPLEMENTATION

To implement the solution, you must write the algorithm as a C++ program. You would first tell the C++ compiler about the problem data requirements— that is, what memory cell names you are using and what kind of data will be stored in each memory cell. Next, convert each algorithm step into one or more C++ statements. If an algorithm step has been refined, convert the refinements, not the original step, into C++ statements.

Listing 1.2 shows the C++ program along with a sample execution. The algorithm steps are in lines that begin with //; the program statements follow the algorithm steps. The sample execution is highlighted in the color screen. The input data typed in by the program user are in color. Don't worry about understanding the details of this program yet; we explain the program in the next chapter.

TESTING

How do you know the sample run is correct? You should always examine program results carefully to make sure that they make sense. In this run, a distance of 10.0 miles is converted to 16.09 kilometers, as it should be. To verify that the program works properly, enter a few more test values of miles. You don't need to try more than a few test cases to verify that a simple program like this is correct.

Listing 1.2   Converting miles to kilometers

```cpp
// miles.cpp
// Converts distance in miles to kilometers.

#include <iostream>
using namespace std;

int main()                                // start of main function
{
     const float KM_PER_MILE = 1.609;     // 1.609 km in a mile
     float miles,                         // input: distance in miles
           kms;                           // output: distance in kilometers

     // Get the distance in miles.
     cout << "Enter the distance in miles: ";
     cin >> miles;

     // Convert the distance to kilometers.
     kms = km_per_mile * miles;

     // Display the distance in kilometers.
     cout << "The distance in kilometers is " << kms << endl;

     return 0;                            //Exit the main function
}
```

(handwritten note: should be all capital *pointing to* `km_per_mile`)*

```
Enter the distance in miles: 10.0
The distance in kilometers is 16.09
```

EXERCISES FOR SECTION 1.6

Self-Check

1. Change the algorithm for the metric conversion program to convert distance in kilometers to miles.

2. List the data requirements, formulas, and algorithm for a program that converts a volume from quarts to liters.

1.7 Professional Ethics for Computer Programmers

We end this introductory chapter with a discussion of professional ethics for computer programmers. Like other professionals, computer programmers and software system designers (called software engineers) need to follow certain standards of professional conduct.

Privacy and Misuse of Data

As part of their jobs, programmers may have access to large data banks or databases containing sensitive information on financial transactions or personnel, or information that is classified as "secret" or "top secret." Programmers should always behave in a socially responsible manner and not retrieve information that they are not entitled to see. They should not use information to which they are given access for their own personal gain, or do anything that would be considered illegal, unethical, or harmful to others. Just as doctors and lawyers must keep patient information confidential, programmers must respect an individual's rights to privacy.

A programmer who changes information in a database containing financial records for his or her own personal gain—for example, changes the amount of money in a bank account—is guilty of **computer theft** or **computer fraud**. This is a felony that can lead to fines and imprisonment.

> **computer theft (computer fraud)** Illegally obtaining money by falsifying information in a computer database.

Computer Hacking

You may have heard about "computer hackers" who break into secure data banks by using their own computer to call the computer that controls access to the data bank. Classified or confidential information retrieved in this way has been sold to intelligence agencies of other countries. Other hackers have tried to break into computers to retrieve information for their own amusement or as a prank, or just to demonstrate that they can do it. Regardless of the intent, this activity is illegal, and the government will prosecute anyone who does it. Your university probably addresses this kind of activity in your student handbook. The punishment is likely similar to that for other criminal activity, because that is exactly what it is.

Another illegal activity sometimes practiced by hackers is attaching harmful code, called a **virus**, to another program so that the virus code copies itself throughout a computer's disk memory. A virus can cause sporadic activities to disrupt the operation of the host computer—for example, unusual messages may appear on the screen at certain times—or cause the host computer to erase portions of its own disk memory, destroying valuable information and programs. Viruses are spread from one computer

> **virus** Code attached to another program that spreads through a computer's disk memory, disrupting the computer or erasing information.

to another in various ways—for example, if you copy a file that originated on another computer that has a virus, or if you open an e-mail message that is sent from an infected computer. A computer **worm** is a virus that can replicate itself on other network computers, causing these computers to send multiple messages over the network to disrupt its operation or shut it down. Certainly, data theft and virus propagation should not be considered harmless pranks; they are illegal and carry serious penalties.

worm
A virus that can disrupt a network by replicating itself on other network computers.

Plagiarism and Software Piracy

Using someone else's programs without permission is also unprofessional behavior. Although it is certainly permissible to use modules from libraries that have been developed for reuse by their own company's programmers, you cannot use another programmer's personal programs or programs from another company without getting permission beforehand. Doing so could lead to a lawsuit, with you or your company having to pay damages.

Modifying another student's code and submitting it as your own is a fraudulent practice—specifically, plagiarism—and is no different than copying paragraphs of information from a book or journal article and calling it your own. Most universities have severe penalties for plagiarism that may include failing the course and/or being dismissed from the university. Be aware that even if you modify the code slightly or substitute your own comments or different variable names, you are still guilty of plagiarism if you are using another person's ideas and code. To avoid any question of plagiarism, find out beforehand your instructor's rules about working with others on a project. If group efforts are not allowed, make sure that you work independently and submit only your own code.

software piracy
Violating copyright agreements by illegally copying software for use in another computer.

Many commercial software packages are protected by copyright laws against **software piracy**—the practice of illegally copying software for use on another computer. If you violate this law, your company or university can be fined heavily for allowing this activity to occur. Besides the fact that software piracy is against the law, using software copied from another computer increases the possibility that your computer will receive a virus. For all these reasons, you should read the copyright restrictions on each software package and adhere to them.

Misuse of a Computer Resource

Computer system access privileges or user account codes are private property. These privileges are usually granted for a specific purpose—for example, for work to be done in a particular course or for work to be done during the time you are a student at your university. The privilege should be protected; it should not be loaned to or shared with anyone else and should not be used for any purpose for which it was not intended. When you leave the institution, this privilege is normally terminated and any accounts associated with the privilege will be closed.

Computers, computer programs, data, and access (account) codes are like any other property. If they belong to someone else and you are not explicitly given permission to use them, then do not use them. If you are granted a use privilege for a specific purpose, do not abuse the privilege or it will be taken away.

Legal issues aside, it is important that we apply the same principles of right and wrong to computerized property and access rights as to all other property rights and privileges. If you are not sure about the propriety of something you want to do, ask first. As students and professionals in computing, we set an example for others. If we set a bad example, others are sure to follow.

EXERCISES FOR SECTION 1.7

Self-Check

1. Some computer users will not open an e-mail message unless they know the person who sent it. Why might someone adopt this policy?

2. Find out the penalty for plagiarism at your school.

3. Why is it a good policy to be selective about opening e-mail attachments?

4. Define the terms *virus* and *worm*.

Chapter Review

1. The basic components of a computer are main and secondary memory, the CPU, and input and output devices.

2. Main memory is organized into individual storage locations called memory cells.

   - Each memory cell has a unique address.
   - A memory cell is a collection of bytes; a byte is a collection of eight bits.
   - A memory cell is never empty, but its initial contents may be meaningless to your program.
   - The current contents of a memory cell are destroyed whenever new information is stored in that cell.
   - Programs must be copied into the memory of the computer before they can be executed.
   - Data cannot be manipulated by the computer until they are first stored in memory.

3. Information in secondary memory is of two types: program files and data files. Secondary memory stores information in semipermanent form and is less expensive than main memory.

4. A computer cannot think for itself; a programming language is used to instruct it in a precise and unambiguous manner to perform a task.

5. The three categories of programming languages are machine language (meaningful to the computer), high-level language (meaningful to the programmer), and assembly language, which is similar to machine language except that it uses special mnemonic codes for operations and names for memory cells instead of numeric addresses.

6. Several system programs are used to prepare a high-level language program for execution. An *editor* enters a high-level language program into memory. A *compiler* translates a high-level language program (the source program) into machine language (the object program). The *linker* links this object program to other object files, creating an executable program, and the *loader* loads the executable program into memory. Sometimes these steps are combined into an Integrated Development Environment (IDE).

7. Programming a computer can be fun, if you're patient, organized, and careful. The software development method for solving problems using a computer can be of considerable help in your programming work. We emphasize five major steps in this problem-solving process:

   ■ Problem specification
   ■ Problem analysis
   ■ Program design
   ■ Program implementation
   ■ Program testing

8. Through the operating system, you can issue commands to the computer and manage files.

9. Follow ethical standards of conduct in everything you do pertaining to computers. This means don't copy software that is copyright protected, don't hack into someone else's computer, don't send files that may be infected to others, and don't submit someone else's work as your own or lend your work to another student.

Quick-Check Exercises

1. A _____ may translate statements in _____ language into several statements in _____ language while a statement in _____ language usually is translated into one statement in _____ language.

2. After a program has been executed, all program results are automatically displayed. True or false?

3. Specify the correct order for these operations: execution, translation, loading, linking.

4. A high-level language program is saved on disk as a(n) _____ file.

5. The _____ finds syntax errors in the _____ file.

6. Before linking, a machine-language program is saved on disk as a(n) _____ file.

7. After linking, a machine-language program is saved on disk as a(n) _____ file.

8. The _____ program is used to create and save the source file.

9. Computers are becoming (more/less) expensive and (bigger/smaller) in size.

10. List the five steps of the software development method that you should use to write your programs.

11. Determine whether each characteristic below applies to main memory or secondary memory.
    a. Faster to access
    b. Volatile
    c. May be extended almost without limit
    d. Less expensive
    e. Used to store files
    f. Central processor accesses it to obtain the next machine-language instruction for execution
    g. Provides semipermanent data storage

12. In object-oriented programming, explain the difference between the terms *class* and *object*.

13. The _____ of an object operate on the _____ of the object.

14. In a class hierarchy, a _____ class inherits data and methods from its _____ class.

Review Questions

1. List at least three kinds of information stored in a computer.

2. List two functions of the CPU.

3. List two input devices, two output devices, and two secondary storage devices.

4. A computer can think. True or false?

5. What programs are combined in an IDE?

6. Describe two advantages of programming in a high-level language such as C++.

7. What processes are needed to transform a C++ program to a machine language program that is ready for execution?

8. Explain the relationship between memory cells, bytes, and bits.

9. What is the difference between a command-line interface and a GUI? Which are you using? Which kind is used on a PC?

10. Name three high-level languages and describe their main usage.

11. What are the differences between RAM and ROM? Which contains the instructions that execute when you first boot your computer? Which can be extended? Which contains information that does not disappear when you turn your computer off?

12. What is the major reason for programming in an object-oriented language?

13. In the following problem statement, identify the problem inputs, problem outputs, and some relevant formulas.

You are writing a program to help balance your checkbook. This program displays the new balance in your account after you enter the starting balance and a transaction. Each transaction has two data items: an indication of whether the transaction is a deposit or a withdrawal and the dollar amount of the transaction.

Answers to Quick–Check Exercises

1. Compiler, high-level, machine, assembler, machine

2. false

3. translation, linking, loading, execution

4. source

5. compiler, source

6. object

7. executable

8. editor

9. less, smaller

10. problem specification, problem analysis, program design, program implementation, program testing

11. main (a, b, f), secondary (c, d, e, g)

12. A class describes the properties of a category of objects whereas an object is a specific instance of a class.

13. methods, data or attributes

14. sub, super

Bjarne Stroustrup

Bjarne Stroustrup is the designer of the C++ programming language. He is currently the College of Engineering Chair in Computer Science professor at Texas A&M University and an AT&T Labs' Fellow. He is a member of the National Academy of Engineering, an ACM Fellow, and an IEEE Fellow. In 1993 Stroustrup won the ACM Grace Murray Hopper award for his early work on C++, and in 1990 he was named one of America's twelve top young scientists by Fortune *magazine. Stroustrup has also authored several books, including* The C++ Programming Language *and* The Design and Evolution of C++, *which are the definitive C++ reference books.*

What is your educational background? Why did you decide to study computer science?

I have a master's degree in mathematics with computer science from the University of Århus in Denmark and a Ph.D. in computer science from Cambridge University in England. I liked math, but wanted something that had a practical application. Thinking about that led me to computers.

What was your first job in the computer industry? What did it entail?

I first had a series of programming jobs while I was studying in Århus, which helped me avoid serious study debts. I programmed ledger [billing] systems for small firms such as lumberyards, accounting systems, payroll systems, etc. Interestingly enough, this involved my collaborating with both computer salesmen and people running businesses. (They knew their businesses, but nothing about computers.)

In such collaboration, I designed a system and modified it for better usability. In addition, I did the complete detailed design, implementation, and documentation. That taught me a lot—especially that a program is only a part of a larger system and that people directly depend on it.

My first full-time job was as a researcher at AT&T Bell Labs. I experimented with distributed systems and eventually with programming and programming languages as tools for building systems.

What drove the development of C++? Which specific issues were you trying to address when you developed the language?

I was working with some problems in distributed systems and networking. I needed a tool that would help me to structure my programs well and also allow me to write efficient code. I designed C++ to give me the design techniques of Simula and the low-level flexibility and efficiency of C. The further evolution of C++ has been dominated by the same aim of enabling code that is simultaneously elegant and efficient.

What is a typical day like for you?

Usually the first thing I do when I get up (at about 7 A.M.) and the last thing I do before I go to bed (after 11 P.M.) is look at my e-mail. In between, things vary. I read a bit, go to a few talks, and write a lot—both code and text. I avoid meetings whenever I can. As a professor, I naturally lecture a couple of times a week during term-time and see a lot of students.

I try to do something that has nothing to do with work every day. I spend time with my family, read a lot of literature and history, and run a few miles when time and the weather allows it.

Which person in the computer science field has inspired you?

I have always had a deep respect for Kristen Nygaard. He is one of the designers of Simula [the first programming language to support object-oriented programming, designed in the mid-1960s], a gentleman, and a thoroughly enjoyable person to be with. Together with his friend and colleague, Ole-Johan Dahl, he received the 2002 Turing award.

Do you have any advice for students learning C++?

Study systems and programming, not just programming languages. A language is a tool, so it should be studied in the context of problems that deserve to be solved. Studying a language in isolation is sterile.

Start C++ with an up-to-date ISO-standard-conforming implementation and use standard library facilities, such as strings, vectors, maps, and iostreams, right from the beginning. Do not fiddle with pointers, C-style strings, and other low-level facilities until you understand the basics of scope, functions, looks, variables, etc. and until you have a real need. Focus on concepts and techniques. Learn programming language features as needed to express ideas. Don't think that a single programming language is all you'll ever need to know.

What advice do you have for students entering the computer science field?

Don't just study computers. Learn something that will give you an idea of what to use computers for. Consider making computer science a minor or the major with some other interesting field as a minor.

Study something just because it is hard and interesting at least once in your life; not everything has to be obviously useful or directly applicable to something specific.

How do you see C++ evolving over the next few years?

In 2003, the standards committee issued a set of minor corrections and clarifications. That shows the dedication to stability and detail that is necessary for a mature language. However, no living language can remain unchanged for more than a few years, and a more significant revision of the standard, called C++0x, is in progress. The emphasis will be on providing a larger and better standard library. The changes to the core language will be close to 100% compatible and focus on providing better support for systems programming and library building. You can get an idea of some of the libraries considered for the next standard by looking at boost.org. These include smart pointers, regular expressions, threads, and file system access. The language extensions currently under consideration focus on better support for generic programming and on making the language (and standard library) rules more regular and easier to understand. The emphasis on performance and suitability for systems programming will be maintained. See my home pages for more information about C++0x.

chapter two

Overview of C++

Chapter Objectives

- To become familiar with the general form of a C++ program and the basic elements in a program
- To learn how to include standard library files in a program
- To appreciate the importance of writing comments in a program
- To understand the use of data types and the differences between the numeric types for real numbers and integers
- To be able to declare variables with and without initial values
- To understand how to write assignment statements to change the values of variables
- To learn how C++ evaluates arithmetic expressions and how to write them
- To learn how to read data values into a program and to display results
- To learn how to use files for input/output
- To understand the differences between syntax errors, run-time errors, and logic errors, and how to avoid them and to correct them.

THIS CHAPTER INTRODUCES C++—a high-level programming language developed in the mid-1980s by Bjarne Stroustrup at AT&T's Bell Laboratories. C++ is widely used in industry because it supports object-oriented programming and incorporates all of the features of the popular C programming language. Throughout this book, we will follow the standard for the C++ language approved in 1998. Our focus in this chapter will be on the C++ statements for entering data, performing simple computations, and displaying results.

2.1   C++ Language Elements

One advantage of C++ is that it allows programmers to write programs that resemble everyday English. Even though you don't yet know how to write your own programs, you can probably read and understand parts of the program in Listing 1.2, which is repeated in Listing 2.1. In this section, we will describe the different language elements in this program and explain their syntax.

Comments

The first two lines in the program shown in Listing 2.1

```
// miles.cpp
// Converts distances from miles to kilometers.
```

comment
Text in a program that makes the code more understandable to the human reader but is ignored—that is, not translated—by the compiler.

start with the symbol pair // that indicates that these lines are **comments**—text used to clarify the program to the person who is reading it but ignored by the C++ compiler, which does not attempt to translate comments into machine language. We show all comments in italics; your C++ system may not. The first comment line gives the name of the file containing this program (`miles.cpp`), and the second describes in English what the program does. (You can download all program files from the Web site for this book—see the Preface.) We discuss the use of comments in Section 2.5.

The C++ syntax for comments is described in the syntax display that follows. We use this stylistic form throughout the text to describe C++ language features.

Listing 2.1   Converting miles to kilometers

```
// miles.cpp
// Converts distance in miles to kilometers.

#include <iostream>
using namespace std;

int main()              // start of main function
{

    const float KM_PER_MILE = 1.609;   // 1.609 km in a mile
    float miles,                       // input: distance in miles
          kms;                         // output: distance in kilometers
```

(continued)

Listing 2.1 Converting miles to kilometers (continued)

```
    // Get the distance in miles.
    cout << "Enter the distance in miles: ";
    cin >> miles;

    // Convert the distance to kilometers.

    kms = KM_PER_MILE * miles;

    // Display the distance in kilometers.

    cout << "The distance in kilometers is " << kms << endl;

    return 0;                        // Exit main function

}
```

Comment

Form: // comment
             /* comment */

Example: // This is a comment
             /* and so is this */

Interpretation: A double slash indicates the start of a comment. Alternatively, the symbol pair /* may be used to mark the beginning of a comment that is terminated by the symbol pair */. Comments are listed with the program but are otherwise ignored by the C++ compiler.

Compiler Directive #include

The first line of Listing 2.1 after the comments—

```
#include <iostream>
```

is a **compiler directive**, a statement that is processed before the program is translated. This directive causes the statements from the header file for class iostream to be inserted at this spot in our program. A **header file** describes the data and operations in a class so that the compiler can check that the class is used correctly.

The left and right angle brackets < > indicate that class iostream is part of the C++ **standard library**, a component that contains a number of

compiler directive
A C++ program line beginning with # that is processed by the compiler before translation begins.

header file
A file that describes the data and operations in a class.

standard library
A collection of C++ predefined classes provided with a C++ system.

predefined classes such as `iostream` that provide important functionality for the C++ language. For example, class `iostream` has operators that enable a program to read input data typed at the keyboard and to display information on the screen. Libraries enable us to *reuse* C++ code modules that have already been written and tested, saving us from the burden of creating this code ourselves. There may be many `#include` statements, and possibly other compiler directives, in each program that you write.

Compiler Directive `#include`

Form: `#include <filename>`

Example: `#include <iostream>`

Interpretation: Prior to translation, this line is replaced by the C++ standard library file header named inside the angle brackets. Usually compiler directives, such as `#include`, appear at the beginning of a program, but they will work as long as they appear before they are used.

Note: A compiler directive should not end with a semicolon.

Namespace `std`

The line

```
using namespace std;
```

indicates that we will be using objects that are named in a special region of the C++ compiler called `namespace std` (short for standard). Because the C++ standard library is defined in the standard namespace, this line will appear in all our programs. The using statement ends with a semicolon.

`using namespace`

Form: `using namespace region;`

Example: `using namespace std;`

Interpretation: This line indicates that our program uses objects defined in the namespace specified by *region*. This line should follow the `#include` lines.

Function `main`

The line

```
int main()          // start of function main
```

indicates the start of function `main`. A **function** is a collection of related statements that perform a specific operation. For example, the `main` function in Listing 2.1 is the program for converting from kilometers to miles. The word `int` indicates that the `main` function should return an integer value to the operating system. The empty parentheses after `main` indicate that no special information is passed to this function by the operating system. We added a comment (beginning with `//`) to the end of this line to clarify its meaning to you, the program reader. The body of function `main`, or any other function, is enclosed in curly braces `{ }` and it consists of the rest of the lines in Listing 2.1. Execution of a C++ program always begins with the first line in the body of function `main`.

> **function**
> A collection of related statements that perform a specific operation. These statements are executed as a unit.

`main` function definition

Form:
```
int main()
{
      function body
}
```

Example:
```
int main()
{
      cout << "Enjoy C++" << endl;
      return 0;
}
```

Interpretation: A program begins its execution with function `main`. The body of the function is enclosed in curly braces. The function body should end with the line

```
return 0;
```

which causes function `main` to return a value of 0 to the operating system when it finishes execution.

Declaration Statements

A function body consists of two kinds of statements: *declaration statements* and *executable statements*. The declarations tell the compiler what data are needed in the function. For example, the declaration statements

```
const float KM_PER_MILE = 1.609;   // 1.609 km in a mile
float miles,          // input: distance in miles
         kms;         // output: distance in kilometers
```

tell the compiler that the function main needs three data items named `KM_PER_MILE`, `miles`, and `kms`. `KM_PER_MILE` is the conversion constant

1.609. To create this part of the function, the programmer uses the problem data requirements identified during problem analysis. We describe the syntax of declaration statements in Section 2.3.

Executable Statements

The executable statements cause some action to take place when a program is executed. Executable statements that begin with cout (pronounced c-out) display output on the screen. The first such line

```
cout << "Enter the distance in miles: ";
```

displays the prompt (in black type) in the first line of the sample execution repeated below:

```
Enter the distance in miles: 10.0
```

cout (pronounced c-out) refers to the standard output device, the screen. The symbol pair << is the insertion operator, so named because it inserts characters into the text displayed on the screen. In this case, it inserts the characters shown in quotes, which ask the user to type in a distance in miles. The program user types in the number 10.0. The next statement in function main

```
cin >> miles;
```

reads the data value (10.0) into the variable miles. cin (pronounced c-in) refers to the standard input device, the keyboard. The symbol pair >> is the extraction operator, so named because it "extracts" characters typed at the keyboard and stores them in memory. The statement

```
kms = KM_PER_MILE * miles;
```

computes the equivalent distance in kilometers by multiplying miles by the number (1.609) stored in KM_PER_MILE; the result (16.09) is stored in memory cell kms.

Then, the statement

```
cout << "The distance in kilometers is " << kms << endl;
```

displays a *string* (the characters enclosed in double quotes) followed by the value contained in kms. The word endl stands for "endline" and ends the output line shown next:

```
The distance in kilometers is 16.09
```

Finally, the line

```
return 0;                    // Exit main function
```

causes the function exit. The function returns a value of 0 to the operating system which indicates that it exited normally. We describe these executable statements in Section 2.4.

EXERCISES FOR SECTION 2.1

Self-Check

1. Explain what is wrong with the following declaration statement and correct it.

```
float miles,     /* input: distance in miles
       kms;         output: distance in kilometers */
```

2. Explain what is wrong with the comments below and correct them.

   a. `/* This is a comment? /*`

   b. `/* How about this one /* it seems like a comment`
      `*/ doesn't it? */`

3. Indicate which of the following are translated into machine language: compiler directives, comments, using namespace statement, variable declarations, executable statements.

4. What is the purpose of the #include? Of the using namespace statement? Which does not end with a semicolon?

5. What are the symbols >> and << ?

6. Why do you think C++ uses cin >> x instead of cin << x ?

7. Correct the errors in the statement sequence below:

```
cout >> "weight";
cin << "Enter weight in pounds: ";
```

Programming

1. Write the declarations for a program that converts a weight in pounds to a weight in kilograms.

2. Write the C++ statements to ask for and read the weight in pounds.

2.2   Reserved Words and Identifiers

Reserved Words

reserved word
(keyword)
A word that has a specific meaning in C++.

Each line of the program in Listing 2.1 contains a number of different syntactic elements, such as reserved words, identifiers, and special character symbols (for example, //). The **reserved words** (or **keywords**) have a specific meaning in C++, and they cannot be used for other purposes. Table 2.1 lists the reserved words used in Listing 2.1.

Table 2.1   Reserved Words in Listing 2.1

Reserved Words	Meaning
const	Constant; indicates a data element whose value cannot change
float	Floating point; indicates that a data item is a real number
include	Preprocessor directive; used to insert a library file
int	Integer; indicates that the main function returns an integer value
namespace	Region where program elements are defined
return	Causes a return from a function to the unit that activates it
using	Indicates that a program is using elements from a particular namespace

Identifiers

Table 2.2 lists the identifiers from Listing 2.1. We use identifiers to name the data elements and objects manipulated by a program. The identifiers cin, cout, and std are predefined in C++, but the others were chosen by us. You have quite a bit of freedom in selecting the identifiers that you use as long as you follow these syntactic rules:

1. An identifier must always begin with a letter or underscore symbol (the latter is not recommended).

Table 2.2   Identifiers in Listing 2.1

Identifier	Use
cin	C++ name for standard input stream
cout	C++ name for standard output stream
km	Data element used for storing the distance in kilometers
KM_PER_MILE	Data element used for storing the conversion constant
miles	Data element used for storing the distance in miles
std	C++ name for the standard namespace

2. An identifier can consist only of letters, digits, and underscores.

3. You cannot use a C++ reserved word as an identifier.

The following are some valid identifiers.

```
letter1, Letter1, letter2, inches, cent, centPerInch,
cent_per_inch, hello
```

Table 2.3 shows some invalid identifiers.

Uppercase and Lowercase Letters

The C++ programmer must use uppercase and lowercase letters with care, because the compiler considers such usage significant. The names Rate, rate, and RATE are viewed by the compiler as *different* identifiers. Adopting a consistent pattern in the way you use uppercase and lowercase letters will be helpful to the readers of your programs. All reserved words in C++ use only lowercase letters.

PROGRAM STYLE   Choosing Identifier Names

We discuss program style throughout the text in displays like this one. A program that "looks good" is easier to read and understand than one that is sloppy. Most programs will be examined or studied by someone other than the original programmers. In industry, programmers spend considerably more time on program maintenance (that is, updating and modifying the program) than they do on its original design or coding. A program that is neatly stated and whose meaning is clear makes everyone's job simpler.

Pick a meaningful name for a user-defined identifier, so its use is immediately clear. For example, the identifier salary would be a good name for a memory cell used to store a person's salary, whereas the identifier s or bagel would be a bad choice.

If an identifier consists of two or more words, C programmers place the underscore character (_) between words to improve the readability of the

Table 2.3   Invalid Identifiers

Invalid Identifier	Reason Invalid
1Letter	Begins with a number
float	Reserved word
const	Reserved word
Two*Four	Character * not allowed
Joe's	Character ' not allowed
two-dimensional	Underscore allowed but not hyphen

name (`dollars_per_hour` rather than `dollarsperhour`). C programmers write constants in all uppercase letters (for example, `KM_PER_MILE`).

In this book, we will follow the C style for constants, but we will use a different naming convention for multiple-word variables called "Hungarian notation." Instead of using underscore characters, we will capitalize the first letter of each word—except for the first word. Therefore, we prefer the identifier `dollarsPerHour` to `dollars_per_hour`. Your instructor may recommend a different convention. Whichever convention you choose, make sure you use it consistently.

Choose identifiers long enough to convey your meaning, but avoid excessively long names because you are more likely to make a typing error in a longer name. For example, use the shorter identifier `lbsPerSqIn` instead of the longer identifier `poundsPerSquareInch`.

If you mistype an identifier, the compiler may detect this as a syntax error and display an *undefined identifier* error message during program translation. But if you mistype a name so that the identifier looks like another, the compiler may not detect your error. For this reason and to avoid confusion, do not choose names that are similar to each other. Especially avoid selecting two names that are different only in their use of uppercase and lowercase letters (such as `LARGE` and `large`), or in the presence or absence of an underscore (`xcoord` and `x_coord`).

EXERCISES FOR SECTION 2.2

Self-Check

1. Can reserved words be used as identifiers?

2. Why is it important to use consistent programming style?

3. Indicate which of the symbols below are C++ reserved words, or valid or invalid identifiers.

```
float        cout        Bill         "hello"   rate      start
var          xyz123      123xyz       'a'       include
return
x=y*z        Prog#2      thisIsLong
so_is_this   hyphen-ate  under_score
```

4. Explain the difference between Hungarian notation and C-style notation.

5. Why should e (2.7182818) be defined as a constant instead of a variable?

Programming

1. Write a multiline comment with your name, your instructor's name, and the course name. Use both methods for multiline comments.

2. (Continuation of programming Exercises 1 and 2 from Section 2.1) Write the C++ statement to multiply the weight in pounds by the conversion constant and store the resulting weight in kilograms. Write the C++ statement(s) to display the weight in kilograms.

2.3 Data Types and Declarations

Data Types

A **data type** is a set of values and operations that can be performed on those values. (A value that appears in a C++ program line is called a **literal**. In C++, some data types are predefined in the language and some are defined in class libraries. In this section, we describe four predefined data types and one that is defined in the standard library.

> **data type**
> A set of values and operations that can be performed on those values.
> **literal**
> A value that appears in a C++ program line.

Data Type `int`

In mathematics, integers are positive or negative whole numbers. Examples are 5, –52, and 343,222 (written in C++ as 343222). A number without a sign is assumed to be positive. C++ has three data types to represent integers—short, int, and long. Each data type is considered to be an abstraction (or model) for the integers because it represents a subset of all the integers. Each integer is represented as a binary number. The number of bytes allocated for storing an integer value limits the range of integers that can be represented. The difference between these three types is that some compilers use more bytes to represent int values than short values and more bytes to represent long values than int values. In these compilers, you can represent larger integers with type int than you can with type short, and larger integers with type long that you can with type int.

We will use the data type int throughout this text. The predefined constants INT_MIN and INT_MAX represent the smallest and largest values of type int, respectively. Use the line

```
cout << INT_MIN << "through" << INT_MAX << endl;
```

in a program to show the range of integer values for your computer.

In C++, you write integers (and all other numbers) without commas. Some valid integers are

    −10500   435   15   −25

We can read and display integer values and can perform the common arithmetic operations (add, subtract, multiply, and divide) on type int values.

Data Type float

A real number has an integral part and a fractional part that are separated by a decimal point. Examples are 2.5, 3.66666666, −.000034, and 5.0. C++ has three data types to represent real numbers—float, double, and long double. Just as it is for integers, the number of bytes used to represent each of these types is different, so the range and precision of real numbers that can be represented varies. We will use type float in this text.

We can use scientific notation to represent very large and very small values. In normal scientific notation, the real number 1.23×10^5 is equivalent to 123000.0, where the exponent 5 means "move the decimal point 5 places to the right." In C++ scientific notation, we write this number as 1.23e5 or 1.23e+5. If the exponent has a minus sign, the decimal point is moved to the left (for example, 0.34e−4 is equivalent to 0.000034). Table 2.4 shows examples of both valid and invalid real numbers in C++.

C++ uses different formats (see Figure 2.1) to represent real numbers (floating-point format) and integers (fixed-point format). In **fixed-point format**, the binary number corresponding to an integer value is stored directly in memory. In **floating point-format**, a positive real number is represented as a **mantissa** (a binary fraction between 0.5 and 1.0) and an integer exponent (power of 2) analogous to scientific notation. Therefore, the

fixed-point format
The internal storage form for an integer.

floating-point format
The internal storage form for a real number.

mantissa
A binary fraction between 0.5 and 1.0 used in floating-point format.

Table 2.4   Valid and Invalid Real Numbers

Valid	Invalid
3.14159	−15e−0.3 (0.3 invalid exponent)
0.005	12.5e.3 (.3 invalid exponent)
.12345	.123E3 (needs lowercase *e*)
12345.0	e32 (doesn't start with a digit)
16	a34e03 (doesn't start with a digit)
15.0e−04 (value is 0.0015)	
2.345e2 (value is 234.5)	
1.15e−3 (value is 0.00115)	
12e+5 (value is 1200000.0)	

Figure 2.1 Internal formats for integers and real numbers

integer 10 and the real number 10.0 are stored differently in memory, so they can't be used interchangeably. As with integers, we can read and display real numbers and perform the common arithmetic operations (add, subtract, multiply, and divide).

Data Type `bool`

The `bool` data type (named after mathematician George Boole who invented a two-valued algebra) has just two possible values: false and true. We can use this data type to represent conditional values so that a program can make decisions. For example, "if the first number is bigger than the second number, then switch their values." We discuss this data type in more detail in Chapter 4.

Data Type `char`

Data type `char` represents an individual character value—a letter, digit, or special symbol that can be typed at the keyboard. Each character is unique. For example, the character for the digit one (`'1'`) is distinct from the character for the letter "el" (`'l'`), even though they might look identical on a computer screen. Each type `char` literal is enclosed in apostrophes (single quotes) as shown below.

    'A' 'z' '2' '9' '*' ':' '"' ' '

The next-to-last literal above represents the character "(a quotation mark); the last literal represents the blank character, which is typed by pressing the apostrophe key, the space bar, and the apostrophe key.

Each type `char` value is stored in a byte of memory. The digit character `'1'` has a different storage representation than the integer 1.

Although a type `char` literal in a program requires apostrophes, you don't need them for a type `char` data value. When entering the letter z as a character data item to be read by a program, press just the z key.

Characters are used primarily in strings, a topic we will introduce shortly. A special set of symbols, called an **escape sequence**, allows you to do simple textual control. Each escape sequence is written as a type `char` literal consisting of a backslash \ followed by another character. Table 2.5 shows some

escape sequence
A two-character sequence beginning with a backslash \ that represents a special character.

Table 2.5   Escape Sequences

Escape Sequence	Meaning
`'\n'`	linefeed
`'\b'`	backspace
`'\r'`	carriage return
`'\t'`	tab
`'\"'`	double quote
`'\'`	single quote
`'\f'`	formfeed
`'\\'`	backslash

common escape sequences. The first four escape sequences represent characters that control the appearance of text that is displayed. The last row shows that C++ uses two backslash characters to represent the backslash character.

`string` Class

Besides these built-in data types, C++ provides definitions for a number of other data types in its standard library. The ability to extend C++ by using data types defined in libraries is one of the primary advantages of C++ and object-oriented languages in general. We will use two of these classes, `string` and `iostream`, in much of our programming. We discuss the `string` class next and some features of class `iostream` in Section 2.4.

string literal
A sequence of characters enclosed in quotation marks displayed as prompts or as labels for a program's results.

A **string literal** (or string) is a sequence of characters enclosed in quotation marks. String literals are often displayed as prompts or as labels for a program's results ("the value of x is"). The next line contains five string literals.

```
"A"    "1234"    "true"    "the value of x is "
"Enter speed in mph: "
```

Note that the string `"A"` is stored differently from the character `'A'`. Similarly, the string `"1234"` is not stored the same way as the integer `1234` and cannot be used in a numerical computation. The string `"true"` is also stored differently from the `bool` value `true`. A string can contain any number of characters, but all must be on the same line. Programmers often use string literals in lines that begin with `cout`. C++ displays the characters in the string literal exactly as they appear without the enclosing quotes.

In C++, strings can be read, stored, compared, joined together, and taken apart. A program that performs any of these operations on string data must contain the compiler directive

```
#include <string>
```

before the main function definition. This directive is not needed if you only use strings as literals in lines that begin with cout.

Purpose of Data Types

Why have different data types? The reason is that they allow the compiler to know what operations are valid and how to represent a particular value in memory. For example, a whole number is stored differently in a type float variable than in a type int variable. Also, a type float value usually requires more memory space than an int value. A string will also take up more memory space than a float or char under most circumstances.

If you try to manipulate a value in memory in an incorrect way (for example, adding two bool values), the C++ compiler displays an error message telling you that this is an incorrect operation. Or if you try to store the wrong kind of value (such as a string in a data field that is type int), you get an error message. Detecting these errors keeps the computer from performing operations that don't make sense.

Declarations

The memory cells used for storing a program's input data and its computational results are called **variables** because the values stored in variables can change (and usually do) as the program executes. The **variable declarations** in a C++ program communicate to the compiler the names of all variables used in a program. They also tell the compiler what kind of information will be stored in each variable and how that information will be represented in memory. You must declare each variable before its first use in a function.

A variable declaration begins with an identifier (for example, float) that tells the C++ compiler the type of data (for example, a real number) stored in a particular variable. The declaration statement

variable
A name associated with a memory cell whose contents can change during program execution.

variable declarations
Statements that communicate to the compiler the names of variables and the kind of information stored in each variable.

```
float miles,      // input: distance in miles
      kms;        // output: distance in kilometers
```

gives the names of two variables (miles, kms) used to store real numbers. Note that C++ ignores the comments on the right of each line describing the use of each variable. The two lines above make up a single C++ declaration statement.

The statement

```
string lastName;
```

declares an identifier, `lastName`, for storing a string. Since `string` is a class, it is more accurate to refer to `lastName` as an object (or class instance) instead of a variable.

Variable and Object Declarations

Form: `type identifier-list;`

Examples: `float x, y;`
             `int me, you;`
             `float week = 40.0;`
             `string flower = "rose";`

Interpretation: Storage is allocated for each identifier in the *identifier-list*. The *type* of data (`float, int`, etc.) to be stored in each variable or object is specified. Commas are used to separate the identifiers in the *identifier-list*. The last two lines show how to store an initial value (`40.0`, `"rose"`) in a variable or object. This value can be changed during program execution. A semicolon appears at the end of each declaration.

Constant Declarations

constant
A memory cell whose contents cannot change.

constant declaration
A statement that communicates to the compiler the name of a constant and the value associated with it.

We often want to associate names with special program **constants**—memory cells whose values cannot change. This association may be done using a **constant declaration**. The constant declaration

```
const float KM_PER_MILE = 1.609; // 1.609 km in a mile
```

specifies that the identifier `KM_PER_MILE` will be associated with the program constant 1.609. Because the identifier `KM_PER_MILE` is a constant, C++ will not allow you to change its value. You should consistently use `KM_PER_MILE` instead of the value 1.609 in the program. This makes it easier to read and understand the program. Make sure you only associate constant identifiers with data values that should never change (for example, the

---

Constant Declaration

Form: `const type constant-identifier = value;`

Example: `const float PI = 3.14159;`

Interpretation: The specified *value* is associated with the *constant-identifier*. This *value* cannot be changed at any time by the program. A semicolon appears at the end of each declaration.

Note: By convention, we place constant declarations before any variable or object declarations in a C++ function.

number of kilometers in a mile is always 1.609). You should never declare an input data item or output result as a constant.

EXAMPLE 2.1

Listing 2.2 contains a C++ program that reads character and string data and displays a personalized message to the program user.

The line starting with **char** declares two variables (**letter1, letter2**) used to store the first two initials of the name of the program user. The line beginning with **string** declares an object **lastName** used to store the last name of the user. The instruction

```
cin >> letter1 >> letter2 >> lastName;
```

reads the two letters, **E** and **B**, and the last name, **Koffman**, all typed by the program user, and stores them in the three variables listed (**E** in **letter1**, **B** in **letter2**, and **Koffman** in **lastName**). The next line

```
cout << "Hello " << letter1 << ". " << letter2 << ". "
     << lastName << "!";
```

displays **Hello E. B. Koffman!**. The two string literals **". "** cause a period and one blank space to be displayed after each initial. Finally, the last **cout** line displays the rest of the second line shown in the program output.

Listing 2.2   Printing a welcoming message

```cpp
// File: hello.cpp
// Displays a user's name

#include <iostream>
#include <string>
using namespace std;

int main()
{
    char letter1, letter2;  // input and output: first two initials
    string lastName;        // input and output: last name

    // Enter letters and print message.
    cout << "Enter 2 initials and a last name:";
    cin >> letter1 >> letter2 >> lastName;
    cout << "Hello " << letter1 << "." << letter2 << "."
         << lastName << "!";
    cout << "We hope you enjoy studying C++." << endl;
    return 0;
}
```

(continued)

Listing 2.2   Printing a welcoming message (continued)

```
Enter 2 initials and a last name: EB Koffman
Hello E. B. Koffman! We hope you enjoy studying C++.
```

EXERCISES FOR SECTION 2.3

Self-Check

1. What is the difference between a predefined type and a class type? Which has data stores that are variables and which has data stores that are objects? Is string a predefined type or a class type?

2. List the four types of predefined data.

3. **a.** Write the following C++ scientific notation numbers in normal decimal notation:

   345E-4   3.456E+6   345.678E+3

   b. Write the following numbers in C++ scientific notation with one digit before the decimal point:

   5678   567.89   0.00567

4. Indicate which of the following literal values are legal in C++ and which are not. Identify the data type of each valid literal value.

   15   'XYZ'   '*' $ 25.123   15.   -999   .123   'x'
   "X"   '9'   '-5'   True   'True'

5. What would be the best variable type for the area of a circle in square inches? How about the number of cars passing through an intersection in an hour? Your name? The first letter of your last name?

6. Distinguish between character and integer types.

7. What is the difference between:

   ```
   char color = 'r';
   string colorS = "r";
   ```

8. What is the difference between these three declarations?

   ```
   string aPresident;
   string pres = "Obama";
   const string LAST_PRES = "Bush";
   ```

9. What is the difference between these three declarations?

```
string name;
string pres = "Obama";
const string FIRST_PRES = "Washington";
```

Programming

1. Write the variable declarations and a constant declaration for a program that calculates the area and circumference of a circle given its radius.

2. Write declarations for variables to store the number of seconds it takes to run the 50-yard dash, the number of siblings a person has, a person's street address, a person's grade point average (G.P.A.), and a person's gender (M or F).

3. Write the declarations for a program with variables for `firstName`, `lastName`, and `middleInitial`.

2.4 Executable Statements

The **executable statements** follow the declarations in a function. They are the C++ statements used to write or code the algorithm and its refinements. The C++ compiler translates the executable statements into machine language; the computer executes the machine language version of these statements when we run the program.

executable statement
A C++ statement that is translated into machine language instructions that are executed.

Programs in Memory

Before examining the executable statements in the miles-to-kilometers conversion program (Listing 2.1), let's see what computer memory looks like before and after that program executes. Figure 2.2(a) shows the program loaded into memory and the program memory area before the program executes. The question marks in memory cells `miles` and `kms` indicate that the values of these cells are undefined before program execution begins. During program execution, the data value 10.0 is copied from the input device into the variable `miles`. After the program executes, the variables are defined as shown in Figure 2.2(b). We will see why next.

Assignment Statements

An **assignment statement** stores a value or a computed result in a variable, and is used to perform most arithmetic operations in a program. The assignment statement

assignment statement
A statement used to store a value or a computed result in a variable.

```
kms = KM_PER_MILE * miles;
```

Figure 2.2   Memory (a) before and (b) after execution of a program

assigns a value to the variable `kms`. The value assigned is the result of the multiplication (* means multiply) of the constant `KM_PER_MILE` (`1.609`) by the variable `miles`. The memory cell for `miles` must contain valid information (in this case, a real number) before the assignment statement is executed. Figure 2.3 shows the contents of memory before and after the assignment statement executes; only the value of `kms` is changed.

In C++ the symbol = is the assignment operator. Read it as "becomes," "gets," or "takes the value of" rather than "equals" because it is *not* equivalent to the "equal sign" of mathematics. In mathematics, this symbol states a relationship between two values, but in C++ it represents an action to be carried out by the computer.

Section 2.6 continues the discussion of type `int` and `float` expressions and operators.

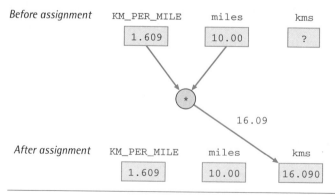

Figure 2.3   Effect of kms = KM_PER_MILE * miles;

EXAMPLE 2.2

In C++ you can write assignment statements of the form

```
sum = sum + item;
```

where the variable sum appears on both sides of the assignment operator. This is obviously not an algebraic equation, but it illustrates a common programming practice. This statement instructs the computer to add the current value of **sum** to the value of **item**; the result is then stored back into **sum**. The previous value of **sum** is destroyed in the process, as illustrated in Figure 2.4. The value of **item**, however, is unchanged.

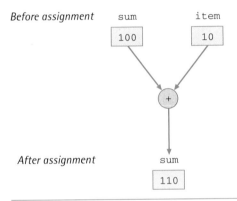

Figure 2.4   Effect of **sum = sum + item;**

EXAMPLE 2.3

You can also write assignment statements that assign the value of a single variable or constant to a variable. If **x** and **newX** are type **float** variables, the statement

```
newX = x;
```

copies the value of variable **x** into variable **newX**. The statement

```
newX = -x;
```

instructs the computer to get the value of **x**, negate that value, and store the result in **newX**. For example, if **x** is **3.5**, **newX** is **-3.5**. Neither of the assignment statements above changes the value of **x**.

Input/Output Operations

input operation
An instruction that reads data from an input device into memory.

Data can be stored in memory in two different ways: through assignment to a variable or by reading the data from an input device through an **input operation**. Use an input operation if you want the program to manipulate different data each time it executes.

As it executes, a program performs computations and assigns new values to variables and objects. These program results can be displayed on the screen through an **output operation**.

output operation
An instruction that displays information stored in memory.

stream
A sequence of characters associated with an input device, an output device, or a disk file.

Several C++ class libraries provide instructions for performing input and output. In this section, we will discuss how to use the input/output operations defined in the C++ class iostream.

In C++, a **stream** is a sequence of characters associated with an input device, an output device, or a disk file. Class iostream defines object cin as the stream associated with the standard input device (the keyboard). Class iostream defines object cout as the stream associated with the standard output device (the screen). Class iostream also defines the input operator >> and output operator <<. If you insert the compiler directive

```
#include <iostream>
```

before the main function, you can use cin and cout and the operators >> and << in your program. You also need to insert the statement

```
using namespace std;
```

Input Statements

The statement

```
cin >> miles;
```

indicates that the input operator >> (also called the *extraction operator*) should read data into the variable miles. Where does the extraction operator get the data it stores in variable miles? It gets the data from cin, the standard input device. In most cases the standard input device is the keyboard; consequently, the computer will attempt to store in miles whatever data the program user types at the keyboard.

If miles is declared as type float, the input operation will proceed correctly only if the program user types in a number. Figure 2.5 shows the effect of this input statement.

When finished entering data, the program user should press the RETURN or ENTER key. Any space characters preceding the data item will be ignored during the input operation. This is true for the input of type int, float, char, bool, and string data.

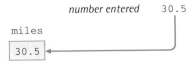

Figure 2.5 Effect of `cin >> miles;`

> **The Input (Extraction) Operator >>**
>
> **Form:** `cin >> data-store;`
>
> **Example:** `cin >> age >> firstInitial;`
>
> **Interpretation:** The extraction operator >> causes data typed at the keyboard to be read into the indicated *data-store* (variable or object) during program execution. The program extracts one data item for each data-store. The symbol pair >> precedes each data-store.
>
> The order of the data you type in must correspond to the order of the data-stores in the input statement. You must insert one or more blank characters between numeric and string data items, and you may insert blanks between consecutive character data items and strings. The input operator >> skips any blanks that precede the data value to be read. This operator stops reading when a character (normally a space) that cannot legally be a part of the value being read in is encountered. Press the ENTER or RETURN key after entering all data items.

The program in Listing 2.2 reads a person's first two initials and last name. The input statement

```
cin >> letter1 >> letter2 >> lastName;
```

causes data to be extracted from the input stream object `cin` and stored in the variables `letter1` and `letter2` and object `lastName`. One character will be stored in `letter1` and one in `letter2` (type `char`). Figure 2.6 shows the effect of this statement when the characters `EBKoffman` are typed. Note that the result would be the same if one or more blanks appear before `E`, `B`, or `Koffman`.

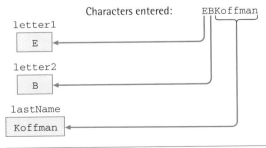

Figure 2.6 Effect of `cin >> letter1 >> letter2 >> lastName;`

The number of characters extracted from cin depends on the type of the variable or object in which the data will be stored. The next nonblank character is stored for a type char variable. For a type float, int, or string variable, the program continues to extract characters until it reaches a character that cannot be part of the data item (usually the result of pressing the space bar or the RETURN or ENTER key).

How do we know when to enter the input data and what data to enter? Your program should display a prompt as a signal that informs the program user what data to enter and when. (Prompts are discussed in the next section.)

Program Output

In order to see the results of a program execution, we must have some way of displaying data stored in variables. In Listing 2.1, the output statement

```
cout << "The distance in kilometers is "
     << kms << endl;
```

displays a line of program output containing two data elements: the string literal "The distance . . . is " and the value of kms (type float). The characters inside the quotes are displayed, but the quotes are not. The output operator << (also called the *insertion operator*) causes the data on the right of each occurrence of the operator to be inserted into the output stream object cout. Thus the previous output statement displays the line

```
The distance in kilometers is 16.09
```

In Listing 2.2, the line

```
cout << "Hello" << letter1 << ". " << letter2 << ". "
     << lastName << "! ";
```

displays

```
Hello E. B. Koffman!
```

In this case, the values of letter1, letter2, and lastName are displayed after the string "Hello". The punctuation and space characters come from the other strings in the output statement.

Finally, the lines

```
cout << "Enter the distance in miles: ";
cout << "Enter 2 initials and a last name: ";
```

The Output (Insertion) Operator <<

Form: cout << *data-element*;

Example: cout << "My height in inches is" << height
             << endl;

Interpretation: The *data-element* can be a variable, object, constant, or literal (such as a **string** or **float** literal). Each data-element must be preceded by the output operator. The output operator causes the value of the data-element that follows it to be displayed. Each value is displayed in the order in which it appears. An **endl** at the end of the output statement advances the screen cursor to the next line. A string is displayed without the quotes.
   If no **endl** appears, the screen cursor will not advance to the next line. The next output statement will display characters on the same line as the previous one.

---

in Listings 2.1 and 2.2, respectively, display **prompts** or **prompting messages**. You should always display a prompt just before an input statement executes to inform the program user to enter data. The prompt should provide a description of the data to be entered—for example, distance in miles. If you don't display a prompt, the user will not know that the program is waiting for data or what data to enter.

The **screen cursor** is a moving place marker that indicates the position on the screen where the next character will be displayed. After executing an output statement, the cursor does not automatically advance to the next line of the screen. For this reason, the data you type in after a prompt will normally appear on the same line as the prompt. This is also the reason the two output statements in Listing 2.2

prompt (prompting message)
A message displayed by the computer indicating its readiness to receive data or a command from the user.

screen cursor
A moving place marker that indicates the position on the screen where the next character will be displayed.

```
cout << "Hello" << letter1 << ". " << letter2 << ". "
     << lastName << "! ";
cout << "We hope you enjoy studying C++." << endl;
```

display the single output line

```
Hello E. B. Koffman! We hope you enjoy studying C++.
```

But there are also many times when we would like to end one line and start a new one. We can do this by displaying the predefined constant endl (pronounced as *end-line*) when we wish to end a line.

To help you remember which operator follows cin and which follows cout, visualize the operator as an arrow indicating the direction of information flow. Data flows from cin to a variable (cin >>) and from a variable to cout (cout <<).

EXAMPLE 2.4

INSERTING BLANK LINES

The statements

```
cout << "The distance in kilometers is "
     << kms << endl << endl;
cout << "Conversion completed." << endl;
```

display the lines

```
The distance in kilometers is 16.09

Conversion completed.
```

A blank line occurs because we inserted `endl` twice in succession (`<< endl << endl`). Inserting `endl` always causes the display to be advanced to the next line. If there is nothing between the two `endl`s, a blank line appears in the program output. Most of the time, you will want to place `<< endl` at the end of an output statement.

The **return** Statement

The last line in the `main` function (Listing 2.1)

```
return 0;
```

transfers control from your program to the operating system. The value `0` is considered the result of function `main`'s execution. By convention, returning `0` from function `main` indicates to the operating system that your program executed without error.

Return Statement

Form: return *expression*;

Example: return 0;

Interpretation: The **return** statement transfers control from a function back to the activator of the function. For function **main**, control is transferred back to the operating system. The value of *expression* is returned as the result of function execution.

EXERCISES FOR SECTION 2.4

Self–Check

1. Show the output displayed by the program lines below when the data entered are 3.0 and 5.0.

```
cout << "Enter two numbers: ";
cin >> a >> b;
a = a - 5.0;
b = a * b;
cout << "a = " << a << endl;
cout << "b = " << b << endl;
```

2. Show the contents of memory before and after the execution of the program lines shown in Self-Check Exercise 1.

3. Show the output displayed by the lines below.

```
cout << "My name is: ";
cout << "Doe, Jane" << endl;
cout << "I live in ";
cout << "Ann Arbor, MI ";
cout << "and my zip code is " << 48109 << endl;
```

4. How would you modify the code in Exercise 3 so that a blank line would be displayed between the two sentences?

5. Which library contains the definition of endl?

6. Explain the purpose of the statement

```
using namespace std;
```

Programming

1. Write the C++ instructions that first ask a user to type three integers and then read the three user responses into the variables first, second, and third. Do this in two different ways.

2. a. Write a C++ statement that displays the value of x as indicated in the line below.

```
The value of x is _____
```

b. Assuming radius and area are type `float` variables, write a statement that displays this information in the following form:

```
The area of a circle with radius _____ is _____
```

3. Write a program that asks the user to enter the list price of an item and the discount as a percentage, and then computes and displays the sale price and the savings to the buyer. For example, if the list price is $40 and the discount percentage is 25%, the sale price would be $30 and the savings to the buyer would be $10. Use the formulas

percentAsFraction = percent / 100.0

discount = listPrice* percentAsFraction

salePrice = listPrice discount

2.5   General Form of a C++ Program

Now that we have discussed the individual statements that can appear in C++ programs, we'll review the rules for combining them into programs. We'll also discuss the use of punctuation, spacing, and comments in a program.

As shown in Listing 2.3, each program begins with compiler directives that provide information about classes to be included from libraries. Examples of such directives are `#include <iostream>` and `#include <string>`. Unlike the `using` statement and the statements of the `main` function body, the compiler directives do not end in semicolons.

A C++ program defines the `main` function after the `using` statement. An open curly brace `{` signals the beginning of the `main` function body. Within this body, we first see the declarations of all the variables and objects to be used by the `main` function. Next come the executable statements that are translated into machine language and eventually executed. The executable statements we have looked at so far perform computations or input/output operations. The end of the `main` function body is marked by a closing curly brace `}`.

Listing 2.3   General form of a C++ program

```
compiler directives
using namespace std;

int main()
{
    declaration statements
    executable statements
}
```

C++ treats most line breaks like spaces, so a C++ statement can extend over more than one line. (For example, the variable declaration in Listing 2.1 extends over two lines.) You should not split a statement that extends over more than one line in the middle of an identifier, a reserved word, or a numeric or string literal.

You can write more than one statement on a line. For example, the line

```
cout << "Enter the distance in miles: "; cin >> miles;
```

contains an output statement that displays a prompt and an input statement that gets the data requested. We recommend that you place only one statement on a line; that will improve readability and make it easier to maintain a program.

PROGRAM STYLE   Spaces in Programs

The consistent and careful use of blank spaces can improve the style of a program. A blank space is required between consecutive words in a program line.

The compiler ignores extra blanks between words and symbols, but you may insert space to improve the readability and style of a program. You should always leave a blank space after a comma and before and after operators such as *, -, and =. You should indent the body of the main function and insert blank lines between sections of the main function.

Although stylistic issues have no effect whatever on the meaning of the program as far as the computer is concerned, they can make it easier for people to read and understand the program. But take care not to insert blank spaces where they do not belong. You can't place a space between special character pairs (for example, //, /*, */, >>, or <<), or write the identifier MAX_ITEMS as MAX ITEMS.

Comments in Programs

Programmers can make a program easier to understand by using comments to describe the purpose of the program, the use of identifiers, and the purpose of each program step. Comments are part of the **program documentation** because they help others read and understand the program. The compiler, however, ignores comments and they are not translated into machine language.

A comment can appear by itself on a program line, at the end of a line following a statement, or embedded in a statement. In the following variable

program documentation Information (comments) that make it easier to read and understand a program.

declaration statement, the first comment is embedded in the declaration, while the second one follows the semicolon that terminates the declaration.

```
float miles,     // input - distance in miles
        kms;     // output - distance in kilometers
```

We document most variables in this way.

PROGRAM STYLE   Using Comments

Each program should begin with a header section that consists of a series of comments specifying

- The programmer's name
- The date of the current version
- A brief description of what the program does

If you write the program for a class assignment, you should also list the class identification and your instructor's name:

```
/*
 * Programmer: William Bell Date completed: May 9, 2003
 * Instructor: Janet Smith Class: CIS61
 *
 * Calculates and displays the area and circumference of
 * a circle
 */
```

As shown above, programmers often use the symbol pairs /*, */ to surround multiline comments instead of placing the symbol pair // before each line.

Before you implement each step in the initial algorithm, you should write a comment that summarizes the purpose of the algorithm step. This comment should describe what the step does rather than simply restate the step in English. For example, the comment

```
// Convert the distance to kilometers.
kms = KM_PER_MILE * miles;
```

is more descriptive than (so preferable to)

```
// Multiply KM_PER_MILE by miles and store result in kms.
kms = KM_PER_MILE * miles;
```

EXERCISES FOR SECTION 2.5

Self-Check

1. Change the following comments so they are syntactically correct.

```
/* This is a comment? *\
/* This one /* is a comment */ isn't it? */
```

2. Correct the syntax errors in the following program, and rewrite the program so that it follows our style conventions. What does each statement of your corrected program do? What output does it display?

```
/*
 * Calculate and display the product of two input values
//
#include [iostream]
void main(float)
{int Y,    /* first input value */
       y,      /* second input value */
     sum; /* product of inputs */
cin << Y << sum;
Y * y = sum;
cout >> sum >> " = " >> Y " * " y;
return 0;}
```

Programming

1. Write a program that performs the implementation step for the case study presented in Section 1.5.

   Problem: Determine the total cost of apples given the number of pounds of apples purchased and the cost per pound of apples.

   Run this using several sets of input data. Try special values such as 0 and 1 for pounds of apples.

2.6 Arithmetic Expressions

To solve most programming problems, you will need to write arithmetic expressions that manipulate numeric data. This section describes the operators used in arithmetic expressions and rules for writing and evaluating the expressions.

Table 2.6   Arithmetic Operators

Arithmetic Operator	Meaning	Examples
+	addition	5 + 2 is 7
		5.0 + 2.0 is 7.0
−	subtraction	5 - 2 is 3
		5.0 - 2.0 is 3.0
*	multiplication	5 * 2 is 10
		5.0 * 2.0 is 10.0
/	division	5.0 / 2.0 is 2.5
		5 / 2 is 2
%	remainder	5 % 2 is 1

Table 2.6 shows all the arithmetic operators. Each operator manipulates two *operands,* which may be constants, variables, or other arithmetic expressions. The operators +, -, *, and / may be used with type int or float operands. As shown in the last column, the data type of the result is the same as the data type of its operands. An additional operator, the remainder operator (%), can be used with integer operands to find the remainder of longhand division. We will discuss the division and remainder operators next.

Operators / and %

When applied to two positive integers, the division operator (/) computes the integral part of the result of dividing its first operand by its second. For example, the value of 7.0 / 2.0 is 3.5, but the value of 7 / 2 is the integral part of this result, or 3. Similarly, the value of 299.0 / 100.0 is 2.99, but the value of 299 / 100 is the integral part of this result, or 2. If the / operator is used with a negative and a positive integer, the result may vary from one C++ implementation to another. For this reason, you should avoid using division with negative integers. The / operation is undefined when the divisor (the second operand) is 0. Table 2.7 shows some examples of integer division.

Table 2.7   Results of Integer Division

3 / 15 = 0	18 / 3 = 6
15 / 3 = 5	16 / −3 system dependent
16 / 3 = 5	0 / 4 = 0
17 / 3 = 5	4 / 0 is undefined

The remainder operator (%) returns the *integer remainder* of the result of dividing its first operand by its second. For example, the value of 7 % 2 is 1 because the integer remainder is 1.

You can use longhand division to determine the result of a / or % operation with integers. The calculation on the left shows the effect of dividing 7 by 2 using longhand division: we get a quotient of 3 (7 / 2) and a remainder of 1 (7 % 2). The calculation on the right shows that 299 % 100 is 99 because we get a remainder of 99 when we divide 299 by 100.

The magnitude of m % n must always be less than the divisor n, so if m is positive, the value of m % 100 must be between 0 and 99. The % operation is undefined when n is zero and varies from one implementation to another if n is negative. Table 2.8 shows some examples of the % operator.

The formula

m equals $(m / n) * n + (m \% n)$

defines the relationship between the operators / and % for an integer dividend of m and an integer divisor of n. We can see that this formula holds for the two problems discussed earlier by plugging in values for $m, n, m / n,$ and m % n. In the first example that follows, m is 7 and n is 2; in the second, m is 299 and n is 100.

```
  7   equals  (7 / 2)      * 2 + (7 % 2)
      equals      3        * 2 + 1
290   equals  (299 / 100)  * 100 + (299 % 100)
      equals      2        * 100 + 99
```

Table 2.8   Results of % Operation

3 % 5 = 3	5 % 3 = 2
4 % 5 = 4	5 % 4 = 1
5 % 5 = 0	15 % 5 = 0
6 % 5 = 1	15 % 6 = 3
7 % 5 = 2	15 % -7 system dependent
8 % 5 = 3	15 % 0 is undefined

EXAMPLE 2.5

If you have **p** people and **b** identical boats, the expression

    p / b

tells you how many people to put in each boat. For example, if **p** is **18** and **b** is **4**, then four people would go in each boat. The formula

    p % b

tells you how many people would be left over (18 % 4 is 2).

Data Type of a Mixed–Type Expression

The data type of each variable must be specified in its declaration, but how does C++ determine the type of an expression? The data type of an expression depends on the type of its operands. For example, the expression

    m + n

is type int if both m and n are type int; otherwise, it is type float. A C++ expression is type int only if all its operands are type int, and a C++ expression is type float if any of its operands are type float. For example, 5 / 2 is type int, but 5 / 2.5 is type float. The latter expression, containing an integer and a floating-point operand, is called a **mixed-type expression**. The type of a mixed-type expression involving integer and floating-point data must be float.

mixed-type expression
An expression involving operands of type int and type float

In evaluating a mixed-type expression such as 5 / 2.5, C++ cannot perform the division directly because the internal representations of the numbers 5 and 2.5 are in different formats (fixed-point for 5, floating-point for 2.5). Consequently, C++ must first compute and store the floating-point equivalent of 5 in a new memory cell and then divide the contents of that cell (5.0) by the contents of the cell containing 2.5. C++ "converts" the type int value to type float instead of the other way around because there is no type int value that is equivalent to the real number 2.5.

Mixed–Type Assignment Statement

When an assignment statement is executed, the expression is first evaluated and then the result is assigned to the variable listed to the left of the assignment operator (=). Either a type float or type int expression may be assigned to a type `float` variable. If the expression is type `int`, a real number with a fractional part of zero will be stored in a type `float` variable. For example, if a is type `float`, the statement

```
a = 10;
```

stores the floating-point value `10.0` in a. In a mixed-type assignment such as

```
a = 10 / 3;
```

the expression is type `int` and the variable a is type `float`. A common error is to assume that since a is type `float`, the expression should be evaluated as if its operands were type `float` as well. If you make this error, you will calculate the expression value incorrectly as `3.3333....` Remember, the expression is evaluated before the assignment is made, and the type of the variable being assigned has no effect on the expression value. The expression `10 / 3` evaluates to `3`, so `3.0` is stored in a.

In a similar vein, consider the assignment statement below when n is type `int`.

```
n = 10.5 + 3.7;
```

The expression is type `float`, and it is evaluated before the assignment. Its value is `14.2`, so the integral part of `14.2`, or `14`, is stored in n. Again, be careful not to evaluate the expression as if its operands were the same type as the variable being assigned. If you make this error, you might calculate the expression result incorrectly as `13` (`10 + 3`).

Expressions with Multiple Operators

In our programs so far, most expressions have involved a single arithmetic operator; however, expressions with multiple operators are common in C++. Expressions can include both unary and binary operators. **Unary operators** take only one operand. In these expressions, we see the unary negation (-) and plus (+) operators.

unary operator
An operator that has one operand.

```
x = -y;
p = +x * y;
```

Binary operators require two operands. When + and – are used to represent addition and subtraction, they are binary operators.

binary operator
An operator that has two operands.

```
x = y + z;
z = y - x;
```

To understand and write expressions with multiple operators, we must know the C++ rules for evaluating expressions. For example, in the expression x + y / z, is + performed before / or is + performed after /? Is the expression x / y * z evaluated as (x / y) * z or as x / (y * z)? Verify for yourself that the order of evaluation does make a difference by substituting some simple values for x, y, and z. In both expressions, the / operator is evaluated first; the reasons are explained in the C++ rules for evaluation of arithmetic expressions that follow. These rules are based on familiar algebraic rules.

Rules for Evaluating Expressions

1. *Parentheses rule:* All expressions in parentheses must be evaluated separately. Nested parenthesized expressions must be evaluated from the inside out, with the innermost expression evaluated first.

2. *Operator precedence rule:* Operators in the same expression are evaluated in the following order:

```
unary +, -    first
*, /, %       next
binary +, -   last
```

3. *Associativity rule:* Binary operators in the same subexpression and at the same precedence level (such as + and -) are evaluated left to right (*left associativity*). Unary operators in the same subexpression and at the same precedence level (such as + and -) are evaluated right to left (*right associativity*).

These rules will help you understand how C++ evaluates expressions. Use parentheses as needed to specify the order of evaluation. Often it is a good idea in complicated expressions to use extra parentheses to document clearly the order of operator evaluation. For example, the expression

```
x * y * z + a / b - c * d
```

can be written in a more readable form using parentheses:

```
(x * y * z ) + (a / b) - (c * d)
```

In Figure 2.8, we see a step-by-step evaluation of the same expression for a radius value of 2.0. You may want to use a similar notation when computing by hand the value of an expression with multiple operators.

EXAMPLE 2.6

The formula for the area of a circle

    a = πr2

can be written in C++ as

    area = PI * radius * radius;

where the value of the constant `PI` is `3.14159`. Figure 2.7 shows the *evaluation tree* for this formula. In this tree, which you read from top to bottom, arrows connect each operand with its operator. The order of operator evaluation is shown by the number to the left of each operator; the letter to the right of the operator indicates which evaluation rule applies.

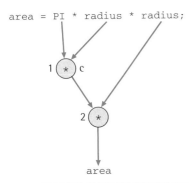

Figure 2.7   Evaluation tree for `area = PI * radius * radius;`

```
area    =   PI    *    radius    *    radius
            3.14159 *       2.0            2.0
                    6.28318          *     2.0
                           12.56636
```

Figure 2.8   Step-by-step evaluation

EXAMPLE 2.7

The formula for the average velocity, v, of a particle traveling on a line between points p_1 and p_2 in time t_1 to t_2 is

$$v = \frac{p_2 - p_1}{t_2 - t_1}$$

This formula can be written and evaluated in C++ as shown in Figure 2.9.

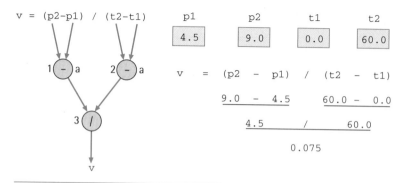

Figure 2.9   Evaluation for v = (p2 - p1) / (t2 - t1);

EXAMPLE 2.8

Consider the expression

    z - (a + b / 2) + w * -y

containing type int variables only. The parenthesized expression

    (a + b / 2)

is evaluated first (rule 1) beginning with b / 2 (rule 2). Once the value of b / 2 is determined, it can be added to a to obtain the value of (a + b / 2). Next, y is negated (rule 2). The multiplication operation can now be performed (rule 2) and the value for w * -y is determined. Then, the value of (a + b / 2) is subtracted from z (rule 3). Finally, this result is added to w * -y. The evaluation tree and step-by-step evaluation for this expression are shown in Figure 2.10.

EXAMPLE 2.9

The evaluation of multiple operator expressions containing both type int and float values can be quite tricky to follow. Don't make the mistake of just converting all operands to type float, but evaluate each operator and its operands separately. Consider the statement

    m = x + k / 2;

shown in Figure 2.11, with x = 5.5 (type float), k = 5 (type int), and m (type int). First, k / 2 is evaluated (rule 2). Because both k and 2 are type int, the result is type int (k / 2 = 2). Next, x + 2 is evaluated. Because x is type float, 2 is first converted to 2.0 so the expression 5.5 + 2.0 is evaluated. The result 7.5 is then truncated to 7 before it is assigned to the type int variable m.

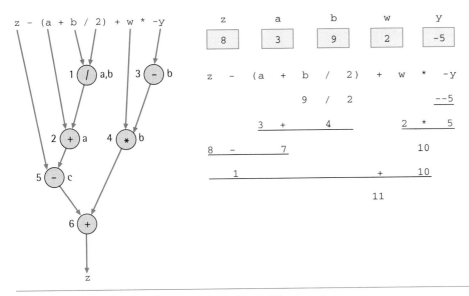

Figure 2.10   Evaluation for z - (a + b / 2) + w * -y;

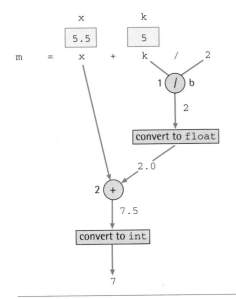

Figure 2.11   Evaluation tree for m = x + k / 2;

Writing Mathematical Formulas in C++

You may encounter two problems when writing mathematical formulas in C++: The first concerns multiplication, which is often implied in a mathematical formula by writing the two multiplicands next to each other—for example, $a = bc$. In C++, however, you must always use the $*$ operator to indicate multiplication, as in

```
a = b * c;
```

The other difficulty arises in formulas using division in which we normally write the numerator and denominator on separate lines:

$$m = \frac{y - b}{x - a}$$

In C++, however, all assignment statements must be written in a linear form. Consequently, parentheses are often needed to separate the numerator from the denominator and to clearly indicate the order of evaluation of the operators in the expression. The formula above would thus be written in C++ as

```
m = (y - b) / (x - a);
```

EXAMPLE 2.10

This example illustrates how several mathematical formulas can be written in C++.

Mathematical Formula	C++ Expression
1. $b^2 - 4ac$	b * b - 4 * a * c
2. $a + b - c$	a + b - c
3. $\dfrac{a + b}{c + d}$	(a + b) / (c + d)
4. $\dfrac{1}{1 + y^2}$	1 / (1 + y * y)
5. $a \times - (b + c)$	a * -(b + c)

The points illustrated are summarized as follows:

- Always specify multiplication explicitly by using the operator $*$ where needed (formulas 1 and 4).
- Use parentheses when required to control the order of operator evaluation (formulas 3 and 4).
- Two arithmetic operators can be written in succession if the second is a unary operator (formula 5).

case study   Supermarket Coin Processor

This case study provides an example of manipulating type `int` data (using `/` and `%`).

PROBLEM

You are writing software for the machines placed at the front of supermarkets to convert change to personalized credit slips. In this version, the user will manually enter the number of each kind of coin in the collection, but in the final version, these counts will be provided by code that interfaces with the counting devices in the machine.

ANALYSIS

To solve this problem, you need to get the customer's name to personalize the credit slip. You also need the count of each type of coin (dollars, quarters, dimes, nickels, pennies). From those counts, you determine the total value of coins in cents. Next, you can do an integer division using 100 as the divisor to get the dollar value; the remainder of this division will be the loose change that she should receive. In the data requirements table below, you list the total value in cents (`totalCents`) as a **program variable** because it is needed as part of the computation process but is not a required problem output.

program variable
A variable needed to store a computation in a program.

DATA REQUIREMENTS

Problem Input

`string name`	// user's first name
`int dollars`	// count of dollars
`int quarters`	// count of quarters
`int dimes`	// count of dimes
`int nickels`	// count of nickels
`int pennies`	// count of pennies

Problem Output

`int totalDollars`	// the number of dollars
`int change`	// the change

Additional Program Variable

`int totalCents`	// the total number of cents

FORMULAS

one dollar equals 100 pennies
one nickel equals 5 pennies

DESIGN

The algorithm is straightforward and is presented next.

INITIAL ALGORITHM
1. Read in the user's first name.

2. Read in the count of each kind of coin.

3. Compute the total value in cents.

4. Find the value in dollars and change.

5. Display the value in dollars and change.

Steps 3 and 4 require further refinement.

Step 3 Refinement
3.1. Find the value of each kind of coin in pennies and add these values.

Step 4 Refinement
4.1. totalDollars is the integer quotient of totalCents and 100.

4.2. change is the integer remainder of totalCents and 100.

IMPLEMENTATION

Listing 2.4 shows the program. The statement

```
totalCents = 100 * dollars + 25 * quarters + 10 * dimes +
             5 * nickels + pennies;
```

implements algorithm Step 3.1. The statements

```
totalDollars = totalCents / 100;
change = totalCents % 100;
```

use the / and % operators to implement algorithm Steps 4.1 and 4.2, respectively.

TESTING

To test this program, try running it with a combination of coins that yields an exact dollar amount with no change left over. For example, 1 dollar, 8 quarters, 0 dimes, 35 nickels, and 25 pennies should yield a value of 5 dollars and 0 cents. Then increase and decrease the amount of pennies by 1 (26 and 24 pennies) to make sure that these cases are also handled properly.

Listing 2.4 Value of a coin collection

```cpp
// File: Coins.cpp
// Determines the value of a coin collection

#include <iostream>
using namespace std;

int main ()
{
    string name;            // input: user's first name
    int pennies;            // input: count of pennies
    int nickels;            // input: count of nickels
    int dimes;              // input: count of dimes
    int quarters;           // input: count of quarters
    int dollars;            // input: count of coins in dollars
    int totalDollars;       // output: value of coins in dollars
    int change;             // output: value of coins in cents
    int totalCents;         // total cents represented

    // Read user's first name.
    cout << "Enter your first name: ";
    cin >> name;

    // Read in the count of nickels and pennies.
    cout << "Enter the number of dollars: ";
    cin >> dollars;
    cout << "Enter the number of quarters: ";
    cin >> quarters;
    cout << "Enter the number of dimes: ";
    cin >> dimes;
    cout << "Enter the number of nickels: ";
    cin >> nickels;
    cout << "Enter the number of pennies: ";
    cin >> pennies;

    // Compute the total value in cents.
    totalCents = 100 * dollars + 25 * quarters + 10 * dimes +
                 5 * nickels + pennies;

    // Find the value in dollars and change.
    totalDollars = totalCents / 100;
    change = totalCents % 100;
    // Display the value in dollars and change.
    cout << "Coin credit: " << name << endl;
    cout << "Dollars: " << totalDollars << endl;
```

(continued)

Listing 2.4   Value of a coin collection (continued)

```
    cout << "Cents: " << change << endl;

    return 0;
}
```

```
Enter your first name: Richard
Enter the number of dollars: 2
Enter the number of quarters: 3
Enter the number of dimes: 11
Enter the number of nickels: 1
Enter the number of pennies: 5
Coin credit: Richard
Dollars: 3
Cents: 95
```

PROGRAM STYLE   Use of Color to Highlight New Constructs

In Listing 2.1, program lines that illustrate key constructs are in color, so that you can find them easily. We will continue to use color for this purpose in listings.

EXERCISES FOR SECTION 2.6

Self-Check

1. For the program fragment below, what values are printed?

```
int x, y, z;
float w;
x = 15;
w = x / 2;
y = 2 * x % 4;
z = 2 + x % 4;
cout << w << " " << x << " " << y << " " << z;
```

2. Evaluate the following expressions with 7 and 22 as operands:

    a. 22 /7   **b.** 7/ 22   **c.** 22 % 7   **d.** 7 % 22

    Repeat this exercise for the following pairs of integers:

    e. 15, 16   **f.** 3, 23   **g.** −3, 16

3. Show that the formula $m = (m \ / \ n) * n + (m \ \% \ n)$ holds when $m = 45$ and $n = 5$ (both of type int).

4. Show the step-by-step evaluation of the expressions below.

```
(y % z * (5 + w)) + x / y
(w + x / z) - x / (w - 5)
```

5. Given the declarations

```
const float PI = 3.14159;
const int MAX_I = 1000;
float x, y;
int a, b, i;
```

indicate which C++ statements below are valid and find the value of each valid statement. Also, indicate which are invalid and why. Assume that a is 3, b is 4, and y is –1.0.

a. `i = a % b;`
b. `i = (MAX_I - 990) / a;`
c. `i = a % y;`
d. `i = (990 - MAX_I) / a;`
e. `i = PI * a;`
f. `x = PI * y;`
g. `x = PI / y;`
h. `i = (MAX_I - 990) % a;`
i. `x = a % (a / b);`
j. `i = a % 0;`
k. `i = b / 0;`
l. `i = a % (MAX_I - 990);`
m. `x = a / y;`
n. `i = a % (990 - MAX_I);`
o. `x = a / b;`

6. What values are assigned by the legal statements in Exercise 5 above, assuming a is 2, b is 5, and y is 2.0?

7. Assume that you have the following variable declarations:

```
int color, lime, straw, yellow, red, orange;
float black, white, green, blue, purple, crayon;
```

Evaluate each of the statements below given the following values: color is 2, black is 2.5, crayon is –1.3, straw is 1, red is 3, and purple is 0.3e+1.

a. `white = color * 2.5 / purple;`
b. `green = color / purple;`
c. `orange = color / red;`
d. `blue = (color + straw) / (crayon + 0.3);`
e. `lime = red / color + red % color;`
f. `purple = straw / red * color;`

8. Let a, b, c, and x be the names of four type float variables, and let i, j, and k be the names of three type int variables. Each of the statements below contains a violation of the rules for forming arithmetic expressions. Rewrite each statement so that it is consistent with these rules.

a. `x = 4.0 a * c;`
b. `a = ac;`
c. `i = 5j3;`
d. `k = 3(i + j);`
e. `x = 5a / bc;`

Programming

1. Write an assignment statement that might be used to implement the equation below in C++.

$$q = \frac{ka(t_1 - t_2)}{b}$$

2. Write a program that reads two int values into m, n and displays their sum, their differences ($m - n$ and $n - m$), their product, their quotients (m / n and n / m) and both $m \% n$ and $n \% m$. If the numbers are 4 and 5, the line that shows their sum should be displayed as:

    5 + 4 = 9

Use this format for each output line.

3. Extend the program in Listing 2.4 to handle two-dollar coins and half-dollars.

2.7   Interactive Mode, Batch Mode, and Data Files

interactive mode
A mode of program execution in which the user interacts with a running program, entering data as requested.

batch mode
A noninteractive mode of program execution that requires all program data to be supplied before execution begins.

There are two basic modes of computer operation: interactive and batch. The programs we have written so far are intended to be run in **interactive mode**, a mode of program execution in which the user can interact with the program and enter data while the program is executing. In **batch mode**, all data must be supplied beforehand and the program user cannot interact with the program while it is executing. Batch mode is an option on most computers.

If you use batch mode, you must prepare a batch data file before executing your program. On a time-shared or personal computer, a batch data file is created and saved in the same way as a program or source file.

Input Redirection

input/output redirection
Using operating system commands to associate the standard input device with an input file instead of the keyboard and/or the standard output device with an output file instead of the screen.

Listing 2.5 shows the miles to kilometers conversion program rewritten as a batch program. We assume that the input is associated with a data file instead of the keyboard. In most systems this can be done relatively easily through **input/output redirection** using operating system commands. For example, in the UNIX operating system, you can instruct your program to take its input from file `mydata` instead of the keyboard, by placing the symbols

    < mydata

at the end of the command line that causes your compiled and linked program to execute. If you normally used the UNIX command line

```
metric
```

to execute this program, your new command line would be

```
metric < mydata
```

PROGRAM STYLE   Echo Prints versus Prompts

In Listing 2.5, the statement

```
cin >> miles;
```

Listing 2.5   Batch version of miles-to-kilometers conversion program

```cpp
// File: milesBatch.cpp
// Converts distance in miles to kilometers.

#include <iostream>
using namespace std;

int main()
{
      const float KM_PER_MILE = 1.609; // 1.609 km in a mile
      float miles,                     // input: distance in miles
            kms;                       // output: distance in kilometers

      // Get the distance in miles.
      cin >> miles;
      cout << "The distance in miles is " << miles << endl;

      // Convert the distance to kilometers.
      kms = KM_PER_MILE * miles;

      // Display the distance in kilometers.
      cout << "The distance in kilometers is " << kms << endl;

      return 0;
}
```

```
The distance in miles is 10
The distance in kilometers is 16.09
```

reads the value of miles from the first (and only) line of the data file. Because the program input comes from a data file, there is no need to precede this statement with a prompt. Instead, we follow the input statement with the output statement

```
cout << "The distance in miles is " << miles << endl;
```

which displays, or *echo prints*, the value just read into miles. This statement provides a record of the data to be manipulated by the program; without it, we would have no easy way of knowing what value was read. Whenever you convert an interactive program to a batch program, make sure you replace each prompt with an echo print that follows each input statement.

Output Redirection

You can also redirect program output to a disk file instead of the screen. Then you could print the output file to obtain a hard-copy version of the program output. In UNIX, you would type

```
> myoutput
```

to redirect output from the screen to file myoutput. The command

```
metric > myoutput
```

executes the compiled and linked code for the metric conversion program, reading program input from the keyboard and writing program output to the file myoutput. However, it would be difficult to interact with the running program because all program output, including any prompts, are sent to the output file. It would be better to use the command

```
metric < mydata > myoutput
```

which reads program input from the data file mydata and sends program output to the output file myoutput.

EXERCISES FOR SECTION 2.7

Self-Check

1. Explain the difference in placement of cout statements used to display prompts and cout statements used to echo data. Which are used in

interactive programs and which are used in batch programs? How are input data provided to an interactive program? How are input data provided to a batch program?

Programming

1. Rewrite the program in Listing 2.4 as a batch program. Assume data are read from the file `mydata`.

2. Change the main function below to an interactive version.

```
int main() {
    int m, n;          // input - 2 numbers
    int sum;           // output - their sum

    cin >> m >> n;
    cout << "m is " << m << ", n is " << n << endl;

    sum = m + n;
    cout << "Their sum is " << sum << endl;

    return 0;
}
```

3. Write a batch version of the solution to Programming Exercise 2 in Section 2.6 (repeated below). Your output should be sent to an output file. Show the UNIX command that reads data from file `inData` and writes results to output file `outData`.

   Write a program that reads two int values into m, n and displays their sum, their differences ($m - n$ and $n - m$), their product, their quotients (m / n and n / m) and both $m \% n$ and $n \% m$. If the numbers are 4 and 5, the line that shows their sum should be displayed as:

   $$5 + 4 = 9$$

   Use this format for each output line.

2.8 Common Programming Errors

As you begin to program, you will soon discover that a program rarely runs correctly on the first try. Murphy's law—"If something can go wrong, it will"—seems to have been written with the computer program in mind. In fact, errors are so common that they have their own special name—*bugs*—and

debugging
The process of removing errors from a program.

the process of correcting them is called **debugging**. (According to computer folklore, computer pioneer Dr. Grace Murray Hopper diagnosed the first hardware error caused by a large insect found inside a computer component.) To alert you to potential problems, we will provide a section on common errors at the end of each chapter.

When the compiler detects an error, it displays an error message that indicates you made a mistake and what the likely cause of the error might be. Unfortunately, error messages are often difficult to interpret and are sometimes misleading. As you gain some experience, you will become more proficient at locating and correcting errors.

Three kinds of errors—syntax errors, run-time errors, and logic errors—can occur, as discussed in the following sections.

Syntax Errors

syntax error
A violation of a C++ grammar rule that prevents a program from being translated.

A **syntax error** occurs when your code violates one or more of the grammar rules of C++ and is detected by the compiler as it attempts to translate your program. If a statement has a syntax error, it cannot be completely translated, and your program will not execute.

Listing 2.6 shows a version of the miles-to-kilometers conversion program with errors introduced.

One C++ system gives the following error messages:

```
[C++ Error] miles.cpp(12): E2141 Declaration syntax error.
[C++ Error] miles.cpp(15): E2380 Unterminated string or
    character constant.
[C++ Error] miles.cpp(16): E2379 Statement missing ;.
[C++ Error] miles.cpp(19): E2451 Undefined symbol 'kms'.
[C++ Warning] miles.cpp(25): W8080 'miles' is declared but
    never used.
[C++ Warning] miles.cpp(25): W8004 'KM_PER_MILE' is
    assigned a value that is never used.
```

On some systems, if you click on an error message, the statement containing the error will be highlighted. The missing comma after miles in the variable declaration statement causes error message E2141 above (Declaration syntax error). The missing quote at the end of the prompt string in the first executable statement causes error message E2380. Because of the missing quote, C++ considers the rest of the line to be part of the string including the ; at the end of the line. This causes error message E2379. If you click on this message, you will find that the line beginning with cin is highlighted; however, the missing ; is actually in the line just above. This kind of displacement of error messages is fairly common—you sometimes

Listing 2.6   Miles-to-kilometers conversion program with syntax errors

```cpp
// milesError.cpp
// Converts distances from miles to kilometers.

#include <iostream>
using namespace std;

int main()          // start of function main
{
        const float KM_PER_MILE = 1.609; // 1.609 km in a mile
        float miles                       // input: distance in miles
            kms;                          // output: distance in kilometers
        // Get the distance in miles.
        cout << "Enter the distance in miles: ";
        cin >> miles;

        // Convert the distance to kilometers.
        kms = KM_PER_MILE * miles;

        // Display the distance in kilometers.
        cout << "The distance in kilometers is " << kms << endl;
        return 0;
}
```

need to check one or more lines that precede the highlighted line to find an error. The incorrect variable declaration statement also causes error message E2451, which is associated with the assignment statement. If you fix the variable declaration, this error message will also go away. Finally, the last two error messages (W8080 and W8004) are considered warning messages. They will not stop the program from being executed, but they do indicate suspicious behavior in the program.

Your strategy for correcting syntax errors should take into account the fact that one error can lead to many error messages. It is often a good idea to concentrate on correcting the errors in the declaration statements first. Then recompile the program before you attempt to fix other errors. Many of the other error messages will disappear once the declarations are correct.

Run–Time Errors

Run-time errors are detected and displayed by the computer during the execution of a program. A run-time error occurs when the program directs the computer to perform an illegal operation, such as dividing a number by

run-time error
An error detected by the computer during program execution.

Listing 2.7   Program with a potential run-time error

```cpp
// File: runtimeError.cpp
// Provides a possible "division by zero" run-time error.

#include <iostream>
using namespace std;

int main()
{

    int first, second;
    float temp, ans;

    cout << "Enter 2 integers: ";
    cin >> first >> second;

    temp = second / first;
    ans = first / temp;

    cout << "The result is " << ans << endl;

    return 0;
}
```

zero. When a run-time error occurs, the computer will stop executing your program and will display a diagnostic message that indicates the line where the error was detected.

The program in Listing 2.7 compiles successfully but cannot run to completion if the first integer entered is greater than the second. In this case, integer division causes the first assignment statement to store zero in `temp`. Using `temp` as a divisor in the next line causes a run-time error such as "`Floating point division by zero`".

Undetected Errors

Some execution errors will not prevent a C++ program from running to completion, but they may lead to incorrect results. It is essential that you predict the results your program should produce and verify that the actual output is correct.

A very common source of incorrect results is the input of character and numeric data. Listing 2.8 shows the data entry statements for the coin program from Listing 2.4 If your niece happens to type in her entire name instead of just her first name, a curious result will occur. You indicate the

Listing 2.8   Data entry statements for coins program

```
// Read in the user's first name.
cout << "Enter your first name: ";
cin >> name;

// Read in the count of each kind of coin.
cout << "Enter the number of dollars: ";
cin >> dollars;
cout << "Enter the number of quarters: ";
cin >> quarters;
```

end of a string data item by pressing the space bar or the return key, so her first name will be extracted correctly. But the characters that remain in the input stream (the space and last name) will mess up the data entry for variables `nickels` and `pennies`. Because the input stream is not empty, C++ attempts to extract these data from the current input stream instead of waiting for the user to type in these numbers. Since the next data character to be processed is a letter, C++ will simply leave the values of `dollars` and `quarters` unchanged, which will lead to unpredictable results.

The output from one incorrect run of the program is shown below. Notice that the prompts for `dollars` and `quarters` appear are on the second and third lines and the user is unable to type in any numbers. The program runs to completion using whatever "garbage" values were originally in all input variables.

```
Enter your first name: Sally Smith
Enter the number of dollars: Enter the number of
quarters: . . .
Coin Credit: Sally
Dollars: 210060
Change: 0 cents
```

Logic Errors

Logic errors occur when a program follows a faulty algorithm. Because such errors usually do not cause run-time errors and do not display error messages, they are very difficult to detect. You can detect logic errors by testing the program thoroughly, comparing its output to calculated results. You can prevent logic errors by carefully desk checking the algorithm and the program before you type it in.

Because debugging a program can be very time-consuming, plan your program solutions carefully and desk-check them to eliminate bugs early. If you are unsure of the syntax for a particular statement, look it up in the text.

Chapter Review

1. You learned how to use C++ statements to perform some basic operations: to read information into memory, to perform computations, and to display the results of the computation. You can do all of this using symbols (variable names and operators, such as +, -, *, and /) that are familiar and easy to remember.

2. Use the compiler directive #include to reuse files containing classes and functions in previously defined libraries. Use the statement using namespace std; to indicate that you are referencing C++ elements defined in the standard namespace.

3. Comments make programs easier to read and understand. Use comments to document the use of variables and to introduce the major steps of the algorithm. A comment in a program line is preceded by the symbol pair // and it extends to the end of a line. You can also use the symbol pairs /*, */ to bracket multiline comments.

4. C++ statements contain reserved words (predefined in C++) and identifiers chosen by the programmer. Identifiers should begin with a letter and can consist of letters, digits, and the underscore character only. Use a standard naming convention for identifiers. We suggest using all uppercase for constants and using all lowercase for one-word names of variables and objects. For variables with multiword names, start each word after the first with an uppercase letter (no underscores). Use underscore characters between words of a constant identifier.

5. A data type specifies a set of values and the operations that can be performed on those values. We will use the C++ predefined data types float, int, char, and bool. Types float and int are abstractions for the integers and real numbers. C++ uses floating-point representation for real numbers and fixed-point representation for integers. C++ uses the data type char to represent single characters that are enclosed in apostrophes in a program. The apostrophes are not considered part of the data element and are not stored in memory. Data type bool represents the two values false and true.

6. C++ uses the data type string (defined in the standard library) to represent sequences of characters that are enclosed in quotes in a program. The quotes are not considered part of the data element and are not stored in memory.

7. We can write arithmetic expressions using type float and int data. The rules of evaluation are similar to the rules of algebra, but we must be aware of the data type of an expression. If an operator has only type int data for its operands, the result will be type int; otherwise, it will be type float. Be careful when evaluating expressions with type int and type float

data. If an operator has both kinds of data for its operands, C++ converts the type `int` value to a type `float` value before performing the operation.

8. C++ uses assignment statements to assign a computational result to a variable. Remember, the expression is evaluated first, following the rules summarized in point 7 above. Afterward, the result is assigned to the indicated variable. For a mixed-type assignment, C++ must perform a type conversion just before storing the expression result.

9. C++ uses the standard library class `iostream` for modeling input and output streams—sequences of characters associated with a file or device. C++ uses `cin` and `cout` to represent the keyboard and screen, respectively. C++ uses `<<` as the stream insertion operator, also called the output operator because it writes data to an output stream. C++ uses `>>` as the stream extraction operator, also called the input operator because it reads data into a variable.

10. The syntax rules of C++ are precise and allow no exceptions. The compiler will be unable to translate C++ instructions that violate these rules. Remember to declare every identifier used as a constant or variable and to terminate program statements with semicolons.

The table below summarizes the new C++ constructs.

Summary of New C++ Constructs

Construct	Effect
Compiler Directive `#include <iostream>`	A compiler directive that causes the class `iostream` to be placed in the program where the directive appears.
Using Statement `using namespace std;`	Indicates that the program is using names defined in the region `namespace std` (standard).

Constant Declaration
`const float TAX = 25.00;`
`const char STAR = '*';`
	Associates the constant identifier `TAX` with the floating-point constant `25.00` and the constant identifier `STAR` with the character constant `'*'`.

Variable Declaration
`float x, y, z;`
`int me, it;`
	Allocates memory cells named `x`, `y`, and `z` for storage of floating-point numbers and cells named `me` and `it` for storage of integers.

Assignment Statement `distance = speed * time;`	Assigns the product of `speed` and `time` as the value of `distance`.
Input Statement `cin >> hours >> rate;`	Enters data into the variables `hours` and `rate`.
Output Statement `cout << "Net = " << net << endl;`	Displays the string `"Net = "` followed by the value of `net`. `endl` advances the screen cursor to the next line after this information is displayed.

Quick-Check Exercises

1. What value is assigned to x (type `float`) by the following statement?

   ```
   x = 25 % 3 / 3.0;
   ```

2. What value is assigned to x by the statement below, assuming x is 10.0?

   ```
   x = x / 20;
   ```

3. Show the form of the output line displayed by the following `cout` lines when `total` is 152.55.

   ```
   cout << "The value of total is: " << endl;
   cout << "$" << total << endl;
   ```

4. Show the form of the output line displayed by the following `cout` line when `total` is 352.74.

   ```
   cout << "The final total is $" << total << endl;
   ```

5. Indicate which type of data you use to represent the following items: number of cats in your house; each initial of your name; your full name; the average temperature during the last month.

6. In which step of the software development method are the problem input and output data identified? In which step do you develop and refine the algorithm?

7. In reading two integers using the statement

   ```
   cin >> m >> n;
   ```

   what character should be entered following the first value? What should be entered after the second number?

8. When reading two characters using the input operator >>, does it matter how many blanks (if any) appear

   a. before the first character?

   b. between the first and second characters?

   c. after the second character?

9. How does the compiler determine how many and what type of data values are to be entered when an input statement is executed?

10. What is the syntactic purpose of the semicolon in a C++ program?

11. Does the compiler listing show syntax or run-time errors?

Review Questions

1. What type of information should be specified in the program header section comments?

2. Circle those identifiers below that are valid names for variables.

```
salary        two fold      amount*pct      myprogram
1stTime       R2D2          firstTime       program
CONST         income#1      main            MAIN
Jane's        int           variable        PI
```

3. What is illegal about the following declarations and assignment statement?

```
const float PI = 3.14159;
float c, r;
PI = c % (2 * r * r);
```

4. What do the following statements do? Which identifier cannot have its value changed?

```
a. float x = 3.5;
b. string flower = "rose";
c. const int FEETINMILE = 5280;
```

5. List and define the rules of order of evaluation for arithmetic expressions.

6. Write the data requirements, necessary formulas, and algorithm for Programming Project 6 in the next section.

7. If the average size of a family is 2.8 and this value is stored in the variable `familySize`, provide the C++ statement to display this fact in a readable way (leave the display on the same line).

8. List three language-defined data types of C++.

9. Convert the program statements below to read and echo data in batch mode.

```
cout << "Enter three numbers separated by spaces:"
     << endl;
cin >> x >> y >> z;
cout << "Enter two characters: ";
cin >> ch1 >> ch2;
```

10. Write an algorithm that allows for the input of an integer value, triples it, adds your age to it (also an input), and displays the result.

11. Assuming a (10) and b (6) are type int variables, what are the values of the following expressions:

   a. a / b
   b. a % b
   c. a * b
   d. a + b

12. Assuming a and b are type int variables, which of the following expressions evaluate to the same value?

   a. a + b * c
   b. (a + b) * c
   c. a + (b * c)

13. Differentiate among syntax errors, run-time errors, and logic errors.

Programming Projects

1. Write a program to convert a temperature in degrees Fahrenheit to degrees Celsius.

   DATA REQUIREMENTS
   Problem Input
   `int fahrenheit`   // *temperature in degrees Fahrenheit*

   Problem Output
   `float celsius`   // *temperature in degrees Celsius*

   Formula
   celsius = (5/9) * (fahrenheit – 32)

2. Write a program to read two data items and print their sum, difference, product, and quotient.

   DATA REQUIREMENTS
   Problem Input
   `int x, y`   // *two items*

   Problem Output
   `int sum`   // *sum of x and y*
   `int difference`   // *difference of x and y*
   `int product`   // *product of x and y*
   `float quotient`   // *quotient of x divided by y*

3. You have been watching the World's Strongest Man competition on television. The competitors perform amazing feats of strength such as pulling trucks along a course, flipping huge tires, lifting large objects

onto raised platforms, etc. You can tell the items are quite heavy but the British announcer keeps referring to the weights in stones. Write a program that converts the weight in stones to the equivalent weight in pounds where 1 stone is 14 pounds.

4. Write a program that prints your first initial as a block letter. (Hint: Use a 6 × 6 grid for the letter and print six strings. Each string should consist of asterisks (*) interspersed with blanks.)

5. Write a program that reads in the length and width of a rectangular yard (in meters) and the length and width of a rectangular house (in meters) placed in the yard. Your program should compute the time (in minutes) required to cut the lawn around the house. Assume the mowing rate in square meters per minutes is entered as a data item.

6. Write a program that reads and stores the numerators and denominators of two fractions as integer values. For example, if the numbers 1 and 4 are entered for the first fraction, the fraction is $1/4$. The program should print the product of the two fractions as a fraction and as a decimal value. For example, $1/4 * 1/2 = 1/8$ or 0.125.

7. Write a program that reads the number of years ago that a dinosaur lived and then computes the equivalent number of months, days, and seconds ago. Use 365.25 days per year. Test your program with a triceratops that lived 145 million years ago and a brontosaurus that lived 182 million years ago. (Hint: Use type double for all variables.)

8. Arnie likes to jog in the morning. As he jogs, he counts the number of strides he makes during the first minute and then again during the last minute of his jogging. Arnie then averages these two and calls this average the number of strides he makes in a minute when he jogs. Write a program that accepts this average and the total time Arnie spends jogging in hours and minutes and then displays the distance Arnie has jogged in miles. Assume Arnie's stride is 2.5 feet (also a data item). There are 5280 feet in a mile (a constant).

9. Write a program that reads a number of seconds between 0 and 18,000 (5 hours) and displays the hours, minutes, and seconds equivalent.

10. Redo Programming Project 6—but this time compute the sum of the two fractions.

11. The Pythagorean theorem states that the sum of the squares of the sides of a right triangle is equal to the square of the hypotenuse. For example, if two sides of a right triangle have lengths 3 and 4, then the hypotenuse must have a length of 5. The integers 3, 4, and 5 together form a Pythagorean triple. There is an infinite number of such triples. Given

two positive integers, m and n, where $m > n$, a Pythagorean triple can be generated by the following formulas:

$$side1 = m^2 - n^2$$
$$side2 = 2mn$$
$$hypotenuse = \sqrt{side1^2 + side2^2}$$

Write a program that reads in values for m and n and prints the values of the Pythagorean triple generated by the formulas above.

12. Write a program to compute the rate of growth, expressed as a percentage, of an insect population. Take as input the initial size of the population and its size one week later. Then compute the rate of growth and predict the size of the population in yet another week, assuming that growth continues at the same rate.

13. Write a program that reads in an integer that is greater than 1,000 and less than 1,000,000. Recall that the number must be entered without a comma. Display the number with a comma inserted where it belongs. (Hint: use the % operator.)

14. Write a program that asks a user to enter the distance of a trip in miles, the miles per gallon estimate for the user's car, and the average cost of a gallon of gas. Your program should calculate and display the number of gallons of gas needed and the estimated cost of the trip.

15. Write a program that dispenses change. The program should read the amount of the purchase and the amount paid and then display the number of dollars, quarters, dimes, nickels, and pennies given in change. (Hint: Convert the purchase amount and the amount paid to pennies.) Calculate the difference (changeDue). Use the % operator to determine how many dollars to pay. Subtract that number of pennies from changeDue and continue this process for quarters, dimes, etc. Your answer may be off by a penny. Do you have any idea why this might be the case? How could you correct this?

16. Write a program that calculates mileage reimbursement for a salesperson at a rate of $.35 per mile. Your program should interact with the user in this manner:

```
MILEAGE REIMBURSEMENT CALCULATOR
Enter beginning odometer reading=> 13505.2
Enter ending odometer reading=> 13810.6
You traveled 305.4 miles. At $0.35 per mile,
your reimbursement is $106.89.
```

17. Write a program to assist in the design of a hydroelectric dam. Prompt the user for the height of the dam and for the number of cubic meters of water that are projected to flow from the top to the

bottom of the dam each second. Predict how many megawatts ($1MW = 10^6W$) of power will be produced if 90% of the work done on the water by gravity is converted to electrical energy. Note that the mass of one cubic meter of water is 1000 kg. Use 9.80 meters/ second^2 as the gravitational constant g. Be sure to use meaningful names for both the gravitational constant and the 90% efficiency constant. For one run, use a height of 170 m and flow of $1.30 \times\_ 10^3 \, m^3/s$. The relevant formula ($w$ = work, m = mass, g = gravity, h = height) is $w = mgh$.

18. Hospitals use programmable pumps to deliver medications and fluids to intravenous lines at a set number of milliliters per hour. Write a program to output information for the labels the hospital pharmacy places on bags of I.V. medications indicating the volume of medication to be infused and the rate at which the pump should be set. The program should prompt the user to enter the quantity of fluid in the bag and the number of minutes over which it should be infused. Output the VTBI (volume to be infused) in ml and the infusion rate in ml/hr.

```
Sample run:
Volume to be infused (ml) => 100
Minutes over which to infuse => 20

VTBI: 100 ml
Rate: 300 ml/hr
```

19. Metro City Planners proposes that a community conserve its water supply by replacing all the community's toilets with low-flush models that use only 2 liters per flush. Assume that there is about 1 toilet for every 3 persons, that existing toilets use an average of 15 liters per flush, that a toilet is flushed on average 14 times per day, and that the cost to install each new toilet is $150. Write a program that would estimate the magnitude (liters/day) and cost of the water saved based on the community's population.

Answers to Quick-Check Exercises

1. `0.333333`

2. `0.5`

3. The value of total is:

   `$152.55`

4. The final total is `$352.74`

5. `int, char, string, float`

6. problem analysis, design

7. a blank, RETURN key

8. For (a) and (b), the number of blanks is irrelevant; any number is allowed or there may be no blanks; the input operator will simply skip all leading blanks and stop reading after the first nonblank is read. For (c), there is no need for any blanks; press the return key after entering the second character.

9. The number of values to be entered depends on the number of variables in the input list. The type of data is determined by the type of each variable.

10. It terminates a C++ statement.

11. syntax errors

Josée Lajoie

Josée Lajoie served as chair of the core language working group for the ANSI/ISO C++ Standard Committee and worked as a staff development analyst in the IBM Canada Laboratory C/C++ Compiler group. In addition, she coauthored The C++ Primer *and was a regular columnist on the evolution of the C++ language standard for the* C++ Report.

What is your educational background?
I have a bachelor's degree in electrical engineering, from L'École Polytechnique at the University of Montreal and I am currently pursuing a master's degree in computer graphics at the University of Waterloo. This master's degree includes both computer science and fine arts courses.

What was your first job in the computer industry? What did it entail?
I worked at IBM as a member of a team building a C compiler for IBM's mainframes. My work was to help develop the compiler front end—that is, the portion of the compiler that analyzes C programs for their syntactic and semantic validity. Over the course of a year and half, I developed with two other coworkers a C compiler front end to support the syntax and semantic requirements of the ANSI C standard.

Which person in the computer science field has inspired you?
Grace Hopper, for her pioneering spirit and her determination. Before computers were widely used, Grace Hopper believed that a much wider audience could use computers if tools existed that were both programmer-friendly and application-friendly. She worked on the development of early compilers to facilitate the use of computers in business and other nonscientific applications.

Do you have any advice for students learning C++?
I think people should learn by first using existing C++ libraries and code. They should start by writing small programs that use the features of an existing library. Then, when they become familiar with how to use the library, they should examine the library interface more closely, look at how the library features were designed and implemented, and if they can, read up on the design decisions behind the library implementation. The C++ Standard Library is a good example of a library that can be used in this way.

Do you have any advice for students entering the computer science field?
I would like to encourage students who are interested in studying computer science, but who do not see themselves as fitting the stereotypical description of a computer scientist as portrayed in the

media, to pursue their interests. The field needs people who are innovative, artistic, and good communicators just as much as it needs people who are good in math.

What do you think the future of the C++ language is?

I think the language itself will remain the way it is for very many years to come. The C++ language tool set is quite extensive and, I think, sufficient to implement a great variety of good libraries.

What I hope will happen is that the support offered by the C++ Standard Library will grow importantly over the next few iterations of the C++ standard. Five years after a standard has been published, individuals and companies can request changes to bring the standard closer to widely accepted industry practices. I hope that as more C++ libraries become available, they will be added to the list of C++ Standard Libraries and that users developing new products will be able to choose from a wide variety of domain-specific libraries available with every standard C++ implementation.

You were a key member of the ANSI/ISO C++ Standard committee. Why was it important to standardize C++?

Standardization is important for users, especially for users writing applications that must be ported to a great variety of architectures. A standard gives these users the guarantee that the code they are writing on one platform will compile and run on another platform where standard C++ is supported, provided that their implementation follows the rules prescribed in the standard. Similarly with the library, the standard guarantees that the standard libraries used by their implementation will be available on other platforms where the C++ standard library is supported and that they won't have to rewrite their code to use another, sometimes quite different, system-specific library. Having a standard means that implementers can port their applications faster to other platforms.

What were the main changes to the C++ definition?

The most important change to the original definition of C++ is the addition of the Standard Template Library, which is a good library not only because it provides important basic tools such as containers and algorithms that programmers use very often, but also because it is a very well-designed piece of software that shows better than anything else the power of C++ and how it can be used to write very good libraries.

Top-Down Design with Functions and Classes

Chapter Objectives

- To learn about functions and how to use them to modularize programs
- To understand the capabilities of functions in the C++ math library
- To introduce structure charts as a system documentation tool
- To understand how control flows between functions
- To learn how to pass information to functions using arguments
- To learn how to return a value from a function
- To understand how to use class `string` and `string` objects and functions

PROGRAMMERS WHO SOLVE PROBLEMS using the software development method can use information collected during the analysis and design phases to help plan and complete the finished program. Also, programmers can use segments of earlier program solutions as components in their new programs. Therefore, they don't have to construct each new program from square one.

In the first section of this chapter, we demonstrate how you can tap existing information and code in the form of predefined functions to write programs. In addition to using existing information, you can use top-down design techniques to simplify the development of algorithms and the structure of the resulting programs. To apply top-down design, you start with the broadest statement of the problem solution and work down to more detailed subproblems.

We also introduce the structure chart, which documents the relationships among subproblems. We illustrate the use of procedural abstraction to develop modular programs that use separate functions to implement each subproblem's solution. Finally, we continue our discussion of data abstraction and provide further detail on class `string` and its member functions.

3.1 Building Programs from Existing Information

Programmers seldom start off with a blank slate (or empty screen) when they develop a program. Often some—or all—of the solution can be developed from information that already exists or from the solution to another problem, as we demonstrate next.

Carefully following the software development method generates important system documentation before you even begin coding. This documentation—a description of a problem's data requirements (developed during the analysis phase) and its solution algorithm (developed during the design phase)—summarizes your intentions and thought processes.

You can use this documentation as a starting point in coding your program. For example, you can begin by editing the problem data requirements to conform to the C++ syntax for constant and variable declarations, as shown in Listing 3.1 for the miles-to-kilometers conversion program. This approach is especially helpful if the documentation was created with a word processor and is in a file that you can edit.

Listing 3.1   Edited data requirements and algorithm for a conversion program

```cpp
// File: miles.cpp
// Converts distance in miles to kilometers.

#include <iostream>
using namespace std;

int main()                  // start of main function
{
    const float KM_PER_MILE = 1.609; // 1.609 km in a mile
    float miles,                       // input: distance in miles
          kms;                         // output: distance in kilometers

    // Get the distance in miles.

    // Convert the distance to kilometers.
        // Distance in kilometers is 1.609 * distance in miles.

    // Display the distance in kilometers.

    return 0;
}
```

To develop the executable statements in the `main` function, first use the initial algorithm and its refinements as program comments. The comments describe each algorithm step and provide program documentation that guides your C++ code. Listing 3.1 shows how the program will look at this point. After the comments are in place in the `main` function, you can begin to write the C++ statements. Place the C++ code for an unrefined step directly under that step. For a step that is refined, either edit the refinement to change it from English to C++ or replace it with C++ code. We illustrate this entire process in the next case study.

case study   Finding the Area and Circumference of a Circle

PROBLEM

Get the radius of a circle. Compute and display the circle's area and circumference.

ANALYSIS

Clearly, the problem input is the circle radius. Two output values are requested: the circle's area and circumference. These variables should be type `float` because the inputs and outputs may contain fractional parts. The geometric relationship of a circle's radius to its area and circumference are listed below, along with the data requirements.

DATA REQUIREMENTS

Problem Constant

```
PI = 3.14159
```

Problem Input

```
float radius        // radius of a circle
```

Problem Output

```
float area          // area of a circle
float circum        // circumference of a circle
```

FORMULAS

area of a circle = $\pi \times radius^2$
circumference of a circle = $2 \times \pi \times radius$

DESIGN

After identifying the problem inputs and outputs, list the steps necessary to solve the problem. Pay close attention to the order of the steps.

INITIAL ALGORITHM

1. Get the circle radius.
2. Compute the area of circle.

3. Compute the circumference of circle.

ALGORITHM REFINEMENTS
Next, refine any steps that don't have an obvious solution (Steps 2 and 3).

Step 2 Refinement
2.1. Assign `PI * radius * radius` to area.

Step 3 Refinement
3.1. Assign `2 * PI * radius` to circum.

IMPLEMENTATION

Listing 3.2 shows the C++ program so far. Function `main` consists of the initial algorithm with its refinements as comments. To write the final program, convert the refinements (Steps 2.1 and 3.1) to C++ and write C++ code for the unrefined steps (Steps 1 and 4). Listing 3.3 shows the final program.

TESTING

The sample output in Listing 3.3 provides a good test of the solution because it is relatively easy to compute by hand the area and circumference for a radius value of 5.0. The radius squared is 25.0, so the value of the area is correct. The circumference should be ten times π, which is also an easy number to compute by hand.

Listing 3.2   Outline of area and circumference program

```
// Computes and displays the area and circumference of a circle

int main()
{
    const float PI = 3.14159;
    float radius;        // input: radius of circle
    float area;          // output: area of circle
    float circum;        // output: circumference of circle

    // Get the circle radius.

    // Compute area of circle.
        // Assign PI * radius * radius to area.

    // Compute circumference of circle.
        // Assign 2 * PI * radius to circum.

    // Display area and circumference.

    return 0;
```

Listing 3.3   Finding the area and circumference of a circle

```cpp
// File: circle.cpp
// Computes and displays the area and circumference of a circle

#include <iostream>
using namespace std;

int main()
{
    const float PI = 3.14159;
    float radius;       // input: radius of circle
    float area;         // output: area of circle
    float circum;       // output: circumference of circle

    // Get the circle radius.
    cout << "Enter the circle radius: ";
    cin >> radius;

    // Compute area of circle.
    area = PI * radius * radius;

    // Compute circumference of circle.
    circum = 2 * PI * radius;

    // Display area and circumference.
    cout << "The area of the circle is " << area << endl;
    cout << "The circumference of the circle is " << circum << endl;

    return 0;
}
```

```
Enter the circle radius: 5.0
The area of the circle is 78.539749
The circumference of the circle is 31.415901
```

case study   Computing the Weight of a Batch of Flat Washers

Another way in which programmers use existing information is by *extending the solution for one problem to solve another*. For example, you can easily solve this new problem by building on the solution to the previous one.

PROBLEM

You work for a hardware company that manufactures flat washers. To estimate shipping costs, your company needs a program that computes the weight of a specified quantity of flat washers.

ANALYSIS

A flat washer resembles a small donut. To compute the weight of a single flat washer, you need to know its rim area, its thickness, and the density of the material used in its construction. The last two quantities are problem inputs. However, the rim area (see Figure 3.1) must be computed from two measurements that are provided as inputs: the washer's outer diameter and its inner diameter (diameter of the hole).

In the following data requirements, we list the washer's inner and outer radius (half the diameter) as program variables. We also list the rim area and weight of one washer (`unitWeight`) as program variables.

DATA REQUIREMENTS
Problem Constant

```
PI = 3.14159
```

Problem Inputs

```
float holeDiameter     // diameter of hole
float edgeDiameter     // diameter of outer edge
float thickness        // thickness of washer
float density          // density of material used
float quantity         // number of washers made
```

Problem Outputs

```
float weight           // weight of batch of washers
```

Program Variables

```
float holeRadius       // radius of hole
float edgeRadius       // radius of outer edge
float rimArea          // area of rim
float unitWeight       // weight of 1 washer
```

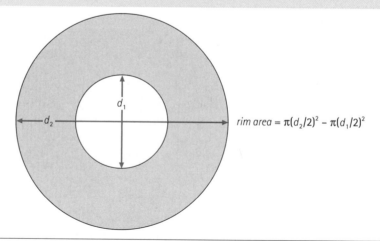

$$\text{rim area} = \pi(d_2/2)^2 - \pi(d_1/2)^2$$

Figure 3.1   The rim area of a washer

Relevant Formulas

area of circle = $\pi \times radius^2$
radius of circle = *diameter* / 2
rim area = *area of outer circle* − *area of hole*
unit weight = *rim area* × *thickness* × *density*

DESIGN

We list the algorithm next, followed by the refinement of Steps 3 and 4.

INITIAL ALGORITHM

1. Get the washer's inner diameter, outer diameter, and thickness.

2. Get the material density and quantity of washers manufactured.

3. Compute the rim area.

4. Compute the weight of one flat washer.

5. Compute the weight of the batch of washers.

6. Display the weight of the batch of washers.

ALGORITHM REFINEMENTS

Step 3 Refinement
3.1 Compute `holeRadius` and `edgeRadius`.
3.2 `rimArea` is `PI * edgeRadius * edgeRadius -`
`            PI * holeRadius * holeRadius`

Step 4 Refinement
4.1 `unitWeight` is `rimArea * thickness * density`

IMPLEMENTATION

To write this program, edit the data requirements to write the variable declarations and use the initial algorithm with refinements as a starting point for the executable statements. Listing 3.4 shows the C++ program.

TESTING

To test this program, run it with inner and outer diameters such as 2 centimeters and 4 centimeters that lead to easy calculations for rim area (`3 * PI` square centimeters). You can verify that the program is computing the correct unit weight by entering 1 for quantity, and then verify that the batch weight is correct by running it for larger quantities.

Listing 3.4   Washer program

```cpp
// File: washers.cpp
// Computes the weight of a batch of flat washers.

#include <iostream>
using namespace std;

int main()
{
      const float PI = 3.14159;
      float holeDiameter;   // input - diameter of hole
      float edgeDiameter;   // input - diameter of outer edge
      float thickness;      // input - thickness of washer
      float density;        // input - density of material used
      float quantity;       // input - number of washers made
      float weight;         // output - weight of washer batch
      float holeRadius;     // radius of hole
      float edgeRadius;     // radius of outer edge
      float rimArea;        // area of rim
      float unitWeight;     // weight of 1 washer

      // Get the inner diameter, outer diameter, and thickness.
      cout << "Inner diameter in centimeters: ";
      cin >> holeDiameter;
      cout << "Outer diameter in centimeters: ";
      cin >> edgeDiameter;
      cout << "Thickness in centimeters: ";
      cin >> thickness;

      // Get the material density and quantity manufactured.
      cout << "Material density in grams per cubic centimeter: ";
      cin >> density;
      cout << "Quantity in batch: ";
      cin >> quantity;

      // Compute the rim area.
      holeRadius = holeDiameter / 2.0;
      edgeRadius = edgeDiameter / 2.0;
      rimArea = PI * edgeRadius * edgeRadius -
                PI * holeRadius * holeRadius;

      // Compute the weight of a flat washer.
      unitWeight = rimArea * thickness * density;

      // Compute the weight of the batch of washers.
      weight = unitWeight * quantity;
```

(continued)

Listing 3.4   Washer program (continued)

```
            // Display the weight of the batch of washers.
            cout << "The expected weight of the batch is "
                 << weight << " grams." << endl;
            return 0;
    }
    Inner diameter in centimeters: 1.2
    Outer diameter in centimeters: 2.4
    Thickness in centimeters: 0.1
    Material density in grams per cubic centimeter: 7.87
    Quantity in batch: 1000
    The expected weight of the batch is 2670.23 grams.
```

EXERCISES FOR SECTION 3.1

Self-Check

1. Describe the data requirements and algorithm for a program that computes the number of miles you can drive a car given the estimated number of miles per gallon and the number of gallons of gas you purchased as input data. Also compute and display the cost of the gasoline based on the cost per gallon (a data item).

2. Write a program outline from the algorithm you developed in Exercise 1. Show the declaration part of the program and the program comments corresponding to the algorithm and its refinements.

3. Change the solution to Exercise 1 to calculate the estimated cost of a trip given the distance of the trip, the estimated number of miles per gallon, and the average cost of a gallon of gasoline.

4. Describe the problem inputs and outputs and write the algorithm for a program that computes an employee's gross salary given the hours worked and the hourly rate.

5. Write a preliminary version of the program for Self-Check Exercise 4 showing the declaration part of the program and the program comments corresponding to the algorithm and its refinements.

6. In computing gross salary, what changes should you make in order to include overtime hours to be paid at 1.5 times an employee's normal hourly rate? Assume that overtime hours are entered separately.

Programming

1. Add refinements to the program outline below and write the final C++ program.

```
// Computes the sum and average of two numbers
#include <iostream>
using namespace std;

int main()
{
    // Declare any constants and variables you need.
    // Read two numbers.
    // Compute the sum of the two numbers.
    // Compute the average of the two numbers.
    // Display sum and average.
    return 0;
}
```

2. Write a complete C++ program for Self-Check Exercise 2.

3. Write a complete C++ program for Self-Check Exercise 3.

4. Assume that flat washers are manufactured by stamping them out from a rectangular piece of material of uniform thickness. Extend the washer program to compute (a) the number of square centimeters of material needed to manufacture a specified quantity of flat washers and (b) the weight of the leftover material.

5. Write a complete C++ program for Self-Check Exercise 5.

6. Write a complete C++ program for Self-Check Exercise 6.

3.2 Library Functions

A main goal of software engineering is to write error-free code. Code reuse—reusing program fragments that have already been written and tested whenever possible—is one efficient way to accomplish this goal. Stated more simply, why reinvent the wheel?

C++ promotes reuse by providing many predefined classes and functions in its standard library. The standard library cmath contains many functions that perform mathematical computations. For example, it defines a function named sqrt that performs the square root computation. The function call in the assignment statement

Figure 3.2   Function `sqrt` as a "black box"

activates the code for function `sqrt`, passing the *argument* x to the function. You activate a function by writing a *function call*. After the function executes, the function result is substituted for the function call. If x is 16.0, the assignment statement above is evaluated as follows:

1. x is 16.0, so function `sqrt` computes $\sqrt{16.0}$, or 4.0.

2. The function result 4.0 is assigned to y.

A function can be thought of as a "black box" that is passed one or more input values and automatically returns a single output value. Figure 3.2 illustrates this for the call to function `sqrt`. The value of x (16.0) is the function input, and the function result, or output, is $\sqrt{16.0}$ (result is 4.0).

If w is 9.0, C++ evaluates the assignment statement

```
z = 5.7 + sqrt(w);
```

as follows:

1. w is 9.0, so function `sqrt` computes $\sqrt{9.0}$, or 3.0.

2. The values 5.7 and 3.0 are added together.

3. The sum, 8.7, is stored in z.

EXAMPLE 3.1

The program in Listing 3.5 displays the square root of two numbers provided as input data (`first` and `second`) and the square root of their sum. To do so, we must call the function `sqrt` three times:

```
answer = sqrt(first);
answer = sqrt(second);
answer = sqrt(first + second);
```

For the first two calls, the function arguments are variables (`first` and `second`). The third call shows that a function argument can also be an expression (`first + sec-ond`). For all three calls, the result returned by function `sqrt` is assigned to variable `answer`. Because the definition of function `sqrt` is found in the standard library `cmath`, the program begins with

```
#include <cmath>          // sqrt function
```

Listing 3.5   Illustration of the use of the C++ `sqrt` function

```cpp
// File: squareRoot.cpp
// Performs three square root computations

#include <cmath>              // sqrt function
#include <iostream>           // i/o functions
using namespace std;

int main()
{
    float first;             // input: one of two data values
    float second;            // input: second of two data values
    float answer;            // output: a square root value

    // Get first number and display its square root.
    cout << "Enter the first number: ";
    cin >> first;
    answer = sqrt(first);
    cout << "The square root of the first number is "
         << answer << endl;

    // Get second number and display its square root.
    cout << "Enter the second number: ";
    cin >> second;
    answer = sqrt(second);
    cout << "The square root of the second number is "
         << answer << endl;

    // Display the square root of the sum of first and second.
    answer = sqrt(first + second);
    cout << "The square root of the sum of both numbers is "
         << answer << endl;
    return 0;
}
```

```
Enter the first number: 9
The square root of the first number is 3
Enter the second number: 25
The square root of the second number is 5
The square root of the sum of both numbers is 5.83095
```

C++ Library Functions

Table 3.1 lists the names and descriptions of some of the most commonly used functions along with the name of the standard file to #include in order to have access to each function.

If one of the functions in Table 3.1 is called with a numeric argument that is not of the argument type listed, the argument value is converted to the required

Table 3.1 Some Mathematical Library Functions

Function	Standard Library	Purpose: Example	Argument(s)	Result
abs(x)	<cstdlib>	Returns the absolute value of its integer argument: if x is −5, abs(x) is 5	int	int
ceil(x)	<cmath>	Returns the smallest integral value that is not less than x: if x is 45.23, ceil(x) is 46.0	double	double
cos(x)	<cmath>	Returns the cosine of angle x: if x is 0.0, cos(x) is 1.0	double (radians)	double
exp(x)	<cmath>	Returns e^x where $e = 2.71828 . . . .$: if x is 1.0, exp(x) is 2.71828	double	double
fabs(x)	<cmath>	Returns the absolute value of its type double argument: if x is −8.432, fabs(x) is 8.432	double	double
floor(x)	<cmath>	Returns the largest integral value that is not greater than x: if x is 45.23, floor(x) is 45.0	double	double
log(x)	<cmath>	Returns the natural logarithm of x for x > 0.0: if x is 2.71828, log(x) is 1.0	double	double
log10(x)	<cmath>	Returns the base-10 logarithm of x for x > 0.0: if x is 100.0, log10(x) is 2.0	double	double
pow(x, y)	<cmath>	Returns x^y. If x is negative, y must be integral: if x is 0.16 and y is 0.5, pow(x, y) is 0.4	double, double	double
sin(x)	<cmath>	Returns the sine of angle x: if x is 1.5708, sin(x) is 1.0	double (radians)	double
sqrt(x)	<cmath>	Returns the non-negative square root of x $\sqrt{x}$ for x ≥ 0.0: if x is 2.25, sqrt(x) is 1.5	double	double
tan(x)	<cmath>	Returns the tangent of angle x: if x is 0.0, tan(x) is 0.0	double (radians)	double

type before it is used. Conversions of type int or type float to type double cause no problems, but a conversion of type float or type double to type int leads to the loss of any fractional part, just as in a mixed-type assignment. For example, if we call the abs function (in library cstdlib) with an argument value of −3.47, the argument is converted to −3 and the result returned is the type int value 3. For this reason, there is another absolute value function (fabs in library cmath) for floating-point arguments.

Most of the functions in Table 3.1 perform common mathematical computations. The arguments for `log` and `log10` must be positive; the argument for `sqrt` cannot be negative. The arguments for `sin`, `cos`, and `tan` must be expressed in radians, not in degrees.

EXAMPLE 3.2

We can use the C++ functions `sqrt` and `pow` to compute the roots of a quadratic equation in x of the form

$$ax^2 + bx + c = 0.$$

These two roots are defined as

$$root_1 = \frac{-b + \sqrt{b^2 - 4ac}}{2a} \qquad root_2 = \frac{-b - \sqrt{b^2 - 4ac}}{2a}$$

when the discriminant $(b^2 - 4ac)$ is greater than zero. If we assume that this is the case, we can use these assignment statements to assign values to `root1` and `root2`.

```
// Compute 2 roots, root1 & root2, for discriminant values > 0.
disc = pow(b, 2) - 4.0 * a * c;
root1 = (-b + sqrt(disc)) / (2.0 * a);
root2 = (-b - sqrt(disc)) / (2.0 * a);
```

EXAMPLE 3.3

If we know the lengths of two sides (b and c) of a triangle and the angle between them in degrees (α) (see Figure 3.3), we can compute the length of the third side, a, by using the formula

$$a^2 = b^2 + c^2 - 2bc(\cos(\alpha))$$

To use the `cmath` library cosine function (`cos`), we must express its argument angle in radians instead of degrees. To convert an angle from degrees to radians, we multiply the angle by $\pi/180$. If we assume `PI` represents the constant π, the assignment statement that follows computes the length of the unknown side.

```
a = sqrt(pow(b,2) + pow(c,2)
    - 2 * b * c * cos(alpha * PI / 180.0));
```

A Look Ahead

C++ allows us to write our own functions such as `findArea` and `findCircum`:

- Function `findArea(r)` returns the area of a circle with radius r.
- Function `findCircum(r)` returns the circumference of a circle with radius r.

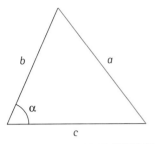

Figure 3.3 Triangle with unknown side *a*

We can reuse these functions in two programs shown earlier in this chapter (see Listings 3.3 and 3.4). The program in Listing 3.3 computes the area and the circumference of a circle. The statements

```
area = findArea(radius);
circum = findCircum(radius);
```

can be used to find these values. The expression part for each of the assignment statements is a function call with argument `radius` (the circle radius). The result returned by each function execution is assigned to the variable listed to the left of the = (assignment) operator.

For the flat washer program (Listing 3.4), we can use the statement

```
rimArea = findArea(edgeRadius) - findArea(holeRadius);
```

to compute the rim area for a washer. This statement is clearer than the one shown in the original program. We show how to write these functions in Section 3.5.

EXERCISES FOR SECTION 3.2

Self-Check

1. Rewrite the following mathematical expressions using C++ functions:

   a. $\sqrt{u + v} \times w^2$ **c.** $\sqrt{(x - y)^3}$

   b. $\log_e (x^y)$ **d.** $|a/c - wz|$

2. Evaluate the following:

   a. `floor(16.2)`

   b. `floor(16.7 + 0.5)`

   c. `ceil(-9.2) * pow(4.0, 3)`

   d. `sqrt(fabs(floor(-24.8)))`

   e. `log10(10000.0)`

3. What happens if you call `abs` with a type `float` argument?

4. What happens if you call `ceil` with a type `int` argument?

Programming

1. Write statements that compute and display the absolute difference of two type double variables, x and y ($|x - y|$).

2. Write a complete program that prompts the user for the Cartesian coordinates of two points (x_1, y_1) and (x_2, y_2) and displays the distance between them computed using the following formula:

$$distance = \sqrt{(x_1 - x_2)^2 + (y_1 - y_2)^2}$$

3. Write a program that prompts the user for the lengths of two sides of a triangle and the angle between them (in degrees) and calculates the length of the third side.

3.3 Top–Down Design and Structure Charts

top-down design
A problem-solving method in which the programmer breaks a problem up into its major subproblems and then solves the subproblems to derive the solution to the original problem.

structure chart
A documentation tool that shows the relationships among the subproblems of a problem.

Often the algorithm needed to solve a problem is more complex than those we have seen so far and the programmer has to break up the problem into subproblems to develop the program solution. In attempting to solve a subproblem at one level, we introduce new subproblems at lower levels. This process, called **top-down design,** proceeds from the original problem at the top level to the subproblems at each lower level. The splitting of a problem into its related subproblems is analogous to the process of refining an algorithm. The following case study introduces a documentation tool—the **structure chart**—that will help you to keep track of the relationships among subproblems.

case study   Drawing Simple Figures

PROBLEM

You want to draw some simple diagrams on your screen. Two examples are the house and female stick figure shown in Figure 3.4.

ANALYSIS

The house is formed by displaying a triangle without its base on top of a rectangle. The stick figure consists of a circular shape, a triangle, and a triangle without its base. We can draw both figures with four basic components:

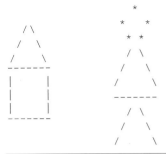

Figure 3.4   House and stick figure

- a circle
- a base line
- parallel lines
- intersecting lines

DESIGN

To create the stick figure, you can divide the problem into three subproblems.

INITIAL ALGORITHM

1. Draw a circle.

2. Draw a triangle.

3. Draw intersecting lines.

ALGORITHM REFINEMENTS

Because a triangle is not a basic component, you must refine Step 2:

Step 2 Refinement

2.1. Draw intersecting lines.

2.2. Draw a base line.

You can use a structure chart to show the relationship between the original problem and its subproblems (Figure 3.5). The original problem (Level 0) is in the darker color and its three subordinate subproblems are shown at Level 1. The subproblem "Draw a triangle" is also in color because it has its own subproblems (shown at Level 2).

The subproblems appear in both the algorithm and the structure chart. The algorithm, not the structure chart, shows the order in which you carry out each step to solve the problem. The structure chart simply illustrates the subordination of subproblems to each other and to the original problem.

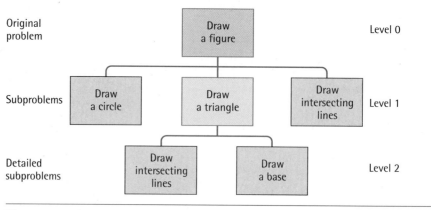

Figure 3.5   Structure chart for drawing a stick figure

EXERCISES FOR SECTION 3.3

Self–Check

1. Draw the structure chart for the subproblem of drawing a house (see Figure 3.4).

2. Draw the structure chart for the problem of drawing a rocket ship that consists of a triangle on top of a rectangle that is on top of a second rectangle. The bottom rectangle rests on a triangular base.

3. In which phase of the software development method do you apply top-down design to break the problem into subproblems?

3.4   Functions without Arguments

One way that programmers use top-down design in their programs is by designing their own functions. Often a programmer will write one function subprogram for each subproblem in the structure chart. In this section we show how to use and define your own functions, focusing on simple functions that have no arguments and return no value.

As an example of top-down design with functions, you could use the `main` function in Listing 3.6 to draw the stick figure. In that figure, the three algorithm steps are coded as calls to three C++ function subprograms. For example, the statement

```
// Draw a circle.
drawCircle();
```

Listing 3.6 Function prototypes and `main` function for drawing a stick figure

```
// Draws a stick figure (main function only)

#include <iostream>
using namespace std;

// Functions used . . .
void drawCircle();      // Draws a circle

void drawTriangle();    // Draws a triangle

void drawIntersect();   // Draws intersecting lines

void drawBase();        // Draws a horizontal line

int main()
{
    // Draw a circle.
    drawCircle();
    // Draw a triangle.
    drawTriangle();
    // Draw intersecting lines.
    drawIntersect();

    return 0;
}
```

in function `main` calls function `drawCircle` to implement the algorithm step *Draw a Circle*. We call function `drawCircle` just like we call the functions in library `cmath`. The empty parentheses after the function name indicate that `drawCircle` requires no arguments.

Function Call Statement (Function Without Arguments)

Form: fname();

Example: `drawCircle();`

Interpretation: The function fname is activated. After fname finishes execution, the program statement that follows the function call will be executed.

Function Prototypes

Just like other identifiers in C++, a function must be declared before it can be referenced. One way to declare a function is to insert a function prototype before the `main` function. A function prototype tells the C++ compiler the data type of the function, the function name, and information about the arguments that the function expects. The data type of a function is determined by the type of value returned by the function. In Listing 3.6, the prototype for `drawCircle` is written as:

```
void drawCircle();
```

void function
A function that does not return a value.

The reserved word `void` indicates that `drawCircle` is a **void function**— that is, its type is `void`—because it doesn't return a value. The empty parentheses after the function name indicate that `drawCircle` has no arguments.

Function Prototype (Function Without Arguments)

Form: ftype fname();

Example: `void skipThree();`

Interpretation: The identifier fname is declared to be the name of a function. The identifier ftype specifies the data type of the function result.

Note: ftype is **void** if the function does not return a value. The argument list `( )` indicates that the function has no arguments. The function prototype must appear before the first call to the function. We recommend you place all prototypes before function **main**.

Function Definitions

Although the prototype specifies the number of arguments a function takes and the type of its result, it doesn't specify the function operation. To do this, you need to provide a definition for each function subprogram similar to the definition of the `main` function. Listing 3.7 shows the definition for function `drawCircle`.

Listing 3.7   Function `drawCircle`

```cpp
// Draws a circle
void drawCircle()
{
   cout << "    *  " << endl;
   cout << " *    *" << endl;
   cout << "  * *  " << endl;
}
```

The function heading is similar to the function prototype in Listing 3.6 except that it doesn't end with a semicolon. The function body, enclosed in braces, consists of three output statements that cause the computer to display a circular shape. We omit the `return` statement because `drawCircle` doesn't return a result.

The function call statement

```
drawCircle();
```

causes the three output statements to execute. Control returns to the `main` function after the circle shape is displayed.

Function Definition (Function Without Arguments)

Syntax: ftype fname()
```
{
        local declarations
        executable statements
}
```

Example:
```
// Displays a block-letter H
void printH()
{
    cout << "**    **"    << endl;
    cout << "**    **"    << endl;
    cout << "******"      << endl;
    cout << "******"      << endl;
    cout << "**    **"     << endl;
    cout << "**    **"     << endl;
}
```

Interpretation: The function fname is defined. In the function heading, the identifier ftype specifies the data type of the function result. Notice that there are no semicolons after the function heading. The braces enclose the function body. Any identifiers that are declared in the optional local declarations are defined only during the execution of the function and can be referenced only within the function. The executable statements of the function body describe the data manipulation to be performed by the function.

Note: ftype is **void** if the function does not return a value. The argument list `()` indicates that the function has no arguments.

Each function body may contain declarations for its own variables. These variables are considered *local* to the function; in other words, they can be referenced only within the function. There will be more on this topic later.

The structure chart in Figure 3.5 shows that the subproblem *Draw a triangle* (Level 1) depends on the solutions to its subordinate subproblems *Draw intersecting lines* and *Draw a base* (both Level 2). Listing 3.8 shows how you can use top-down design to code function drawTriangle. Instead of using output statements to display a triangular pattern, the body of function drawTriangle calls functions drawIntersect and drawBase to draw a triangle.

Placement of Functions in a Program

Listing 3.9 shows the complete program with function subprograms. The subprogram prototypes precede the main function (after any #include directives) and the subprogram definitions follow the main function. The relative order of the function definitions doesn't affect their order of execution; that is determined by the order of execution of the function call statements.

PROGRAM STYLE   Use of Comments in Function Declarations and Definitions

Listing 3.9 includes several comments. A comment precedes each function and describes its purpose. The same comment follows the prototype declaration. For clarity, the right brace at the end of each function may be followed by a comment, such as

```
// end fname
```

identifying that function.

Order of Execution of Functions

The prototypes for the function subprograms appear before the main function, so the compiler processes the function prototypes before it translates the main function. The information in each prototype lets the compiler correctly translate a call to that function. The compiler translates a function call statement as a transfer of control to the function.

After compiling the main function, the compiler translates each function subprogram. During translation, when the compiler reaches the end of a function body, it inserts a machine language statement that causes a *transfer of control* back from the function to the calling statement.

Listing 3.8   Function drawTriangle

```
// Draws a triangle
void drawTriangle()
{
      drawIntersect();
      drawBase();
}
```

Listing 3.9 Program to draw a stick figure

```cpp
// File: stickFigure.cpp
// Draws a stick figure

#include <iostream>
using namespace std;

// Functions used . . .
void drawCircle();      // Draws a circle

void drawTriangle();   // Draws a triangle

void drawIntersect(); // Draws intersecting lines

void drawBase();        // Draws a horizontal line

int main()
{
    // Draw a circle.
    drawCircle();

    // Draw a triangle.
    drawTriangle();

    // Draw intersecting lines.
    drawIntersect();

    return 0;
}

// Draws a circle
void drawCircle()
{
    cout << "   *   " << endl;
    cout << " *   *" << endl;
    cout << "  * * " << endl;
}   // end drawCircle

// Draws a triangle
void drawTriangle()
{
    drawIntersect();
    drawBase();
}   // end drawTriangle
```

(continued)

Listing 3.9   Program to draw a stick figure (continued)

```
// Draws intersecting lines
void drawIntersect()
{
    cout << "   /\\   " << endl;
    cout << "  /  \\ " << endl;
    cout << " /    \\" << endl;
} // end drawIntersect

// Draws a horizontal line
void drawBase()
{
    cout << " _ _ _ _ _ _" << endl;
} // end drawBase
```

Figure 3.6 shows the main function and function drawCircle of the stick figure program in separate areas of memory. Although the C++ statements are shown in Figure 3.6, it is actually the object code corresponding to each statement that is stored in memory.

When we run the program, the first statement in the main function is the first statement executed (the call to drawCircle in Figure 3.6). When the computer executes a function call statement, it transfers control to the function that is referenced (indicated by the top arrow in Figure 3.6). The computer allocates any memory that may be needed for variables declared in the function and then performs the statements in the function body. After the last statement in function drawCircle is executed, control returns to the main function (indicated by the bottom arrow in Figure 3.6), and the computer releases any memory that was allocated to the function. After the return to the main function, the next statement is executed (the call to drawTriangle).

Advantages of Using Function Subprograms

There are many advantages to using function subprograms. Their availability changes the way an individual programmer organizes the solution to a

Figure 3.6   Flow of control between main function and subprogram programming problem. For a team of programmers working together on a large program, subprograms make it easier to apportion programming tasks: Each programmer will be responsible for a particular set of functions. Finally, subprograms simplify programming tasks because existing functions can be reused as the building blocks for new programs.

Procedural Abstraction

Function subprograms allow us to remove from the `main` function the code that provides the detailed solution to a subproblem. Because these details are provided in the function subprograms and not in the `main` function, we can write the `main` function as a sequence of function call statements as soon as we have specified the initial algorithm and before we refine any of the steps. We should delay writing the function for an algorithm step until we have finished refining that step. With this approach to program design, called **procedural abstraction**, we defer implementation details until we're ready to write an individual function subprogram. Focusing on one function at a time is much easier than trying to write the complete program all at once.

procedural abstraction
A programming technique in which the `main` function consists of a sequence of function calls and each function is implemented separately.

Reuse of Function Subprograms

Another advantage of using function subprograms is that functions can be executed more than once in a program. For example, function `drawInter-sect` is called twice in Listing 3.9 (once by `drawTriangle` and once by the `main` function). Each time `drawIntersect` is called, the list of output statements in `drawIntersect` is executed and a pair of intersecting lines is drawn. Without functions, the output statements that draw the lines would

---

EXAMPLE 3.4

Let's write a function (Listing 3.10) that displays instructions to a user of the program that computes the area and the circumference of a circle (see Listing 3.3). This simple function demonstrates one of the benefits of separating the statements that display user instructions from the **main** function body: Editing these instructions is simplified when they are separated from the code that performs the calculations.

If you place the prototype for function `instruct`

```
void instruct();
```

just before the **main** function, you can insert the function call statement

```
instruct();
```

as the first executable statement in the **main** function. The rest of the **main** function consists of the executable statements shown earlier. We show the output displayed by calling function `instruct` at the bottom of Listing 3.10.

Listing 3.10   Function instruct

```
// Displays instructions to user of area/circumference
// program

void instruct()
{
    cout << "This program computes the area and " << endl;
    cout << "circumference of a circle. " << endl << endl;
    cout << "To use this program, enter the radius of the "
         << endl;
    cout << "circle after the prompt" << endl << endl;
    cout << "Enter the circle radius: " << endl << endl;
    cout << "The circumference is computed in the same"
         << endl;
    cout << "units of measurement as the radius. The area "
         << endl;
    cout << "is computed in the same units squared."
         << endl << endl;
}   // end instruct
```

```
This program computes the area and
circumference of a circle.

To use this program, enter the radius of the
circle after the prompt

Enter the circle radius:

The circumference is computed in the same
units of measurement as the radius. The area
is computed in the same units squared.
```

be listed twice in the main function, thereby increasing the main function's length and the chance of error.

Finally, once you have written and tested a function, you can use it in other programs or functions. The functions in the stick figure program, for example, could easily be reused in programs that draw other diagrams.

Displaying User Instructions

The simple functions introduced in this section have limited capability. Without the ability to pass information into or out of a function, we can use functions only to display multiple lines of program output, such as instructions to a program user or a title page or a special message that precedes a program's results.

EXERCISES FOR SECTION 3.4

Self-Check

1. Assume that you have functions printH, printI, printM, and printO, each of which draws a large block letter (for example, printO draws a block letter O). What is the effect of executing the following main function?

```cpp
int main()
{
    printO();
    cout << endl;
    printH();
    skipThree(); // see Programming Exercise 1

    printH();
    cout << endl;
    printI();
    cout << endl;
    printM();
}
```

2. Draw a structure chart for a program with three function subprograms that displays POPS in a vertical column of block letters.

3. If you write a program followed by a collection of functions, do the functions execute in the order in which they are listed before the main function (the function prototypes), the order in which they are listed after the main function (the function definitions), or neither? If your answer is neither, what determines the order in which the functions execute?

4. What error message do you get when a function prototype is missing?

Programming

1. Write a function that skips three lines when it is called.

2. Write a function drawParallel that draws parallel lines and a function drawRectangle that uses drawParallel and drawBase to draw a rectangle.

3. Write a complete program for the problem described in Self-Check Exercise 2.

4. Rewrite the miles-to-kilometers conversion program shown in Figure 2.1, so that it includes a function that displays instructions to its user.

5. Show the revised program that calls function instruct for the circle area and circumference problem.

6. Write a `main` method that solves Self-Check Exercise 2 for Section 3.3. Assume you have functions `drawRectangle` (see Programming Exercise 2), `drawTriangle`, and `drawIntersect`.

3.5   Functions with Input Arguments

Programmers use functions like building blocks to construct large programs. Functions are more like Lego blocks (Figure 3.7) than the smooth-sided wooden blocks you might have used as a young child to demonstrate your potential as a budding architect. Your first blocks were big and did not link together, so buildings over a certain size would topple over. Legos, in contrast, have one surface with little protrusions and one surface with little cups. By placing the protrusions into the cups, you could build rather elaborate structures.

What does this have to do with programming? Simple functions such as `drawCircle` and `instruct` are like wooden blocks. They can display information on the screen, but they are not particularly useful. To be able to construct more interesting programs, we must provide functions with "protrusions" and "cups" so they can be easily interconnected.

The arguments of a function are used to carry information into the function subprogram from the main function (or from another function subprogram) or to return multiple results computed by a function subprogram. Arguments that carry information into the function subprogram are called **input arguments**; arguments that return results are called **output arguments**. We can also return a single result from a function by executing a `return` statement in the function body. We study functions with input arguments in this section and functions with output arguments in Chapter 6.

input arguments
Arguments that pass information into a function.

output arguments
Arguments that return results from a function.

Figure 3.7   Lego blocks

The use of arguments is a very important concept in programming. Arguments make function subprograms more versatile because they enable a function to manipulate different data each time it is called. For example, in the statement

```
rimArea = findArea(edgeRadius) - findArea(holeRadius);
```

each call to function `findArea` calculates the area of a circle with a different radius.

EXAMPLE 3.5

Function `drawCircleChar` (Listing 3.11) is an improved version of function `drawCircle` that enables the caller to specify the character drawn in the circle. When function `drawCircleChar` is called, the character that is its actual argument is passed into the function and is substituted for the formal parameter `symbol` (type `char`). The actual argument character is displayed wherever `symbol` appears in an output statement.
   The function call

```
drawCircleChar('*');
```

draws the stick figure head shown earlier in Figure 3.4. Figure 3.8 shows the execution of this function call. You can use the function call

```
drawCircleChar('#');
```

to display the same circle shape, but with the character # displayed instead of *.
   You must provide a prototype that declares `drawCircleChar` before function `main`. The prototype should indicate that `drawCircleChar` is type `void` (returns no result) and has an argument of type `char`. The prototype follows.

```
drawCircleChar(char);
```

You only need to specify the data type of the formal parameter, not its name, but you may specify the name if you like.

Listing 3.11   Function `drawCircleChar`

```
// Draws a circle using the character specified by symbol
void drawCircleChar(char symbol)
{
   cout << "   " << symbol << endl;
   cout << " " << symbol << "   " << symbol << endl;
   cout << "   " << symbol << " " << symbol << endl;
} // end drawCircle
```

Figure 3.8   Execution of `drawCircleChar('*')`

void Functions with Input Arguments

In the last section, we used `void` functions such as `instruct` and `drawCircle` to display several lines of program output. Recall that a `void` function does not return a result. The next example shows a new function, `drawCircleChar`, that has an input argument.

Functions with Input Arguments and a Single Result

Next we show how to write functions with input arguments that return a single result, as diagrammed in Figure 3.9. We can reference these functions in expressions just like the library functions described in Section 3.2.

Let's reconsider the problem of finding the area and circumference of a circle using functions with just one argument. Section 3.2 described functions `findCircum` and `findArea`, each of which has a single input argument (a circle radius) and returns a single result (the circumference or area). Listing 3.12 shows these functions.

Each function heading begins with the word `float`, indicating that the function result is a real number. Both function bodies consist of a single `return` statement. When either function executes, the expression in its `return` statement is evaluated and returned as the function result. If `PI` is the constant `3.14159`, calling function `findCircum` causes the expression `2.0 * 3.14159 * r` to be evaluated. To evaluate this expression, C++ substitutes the actual argument used in the function call for the formal parameter `r`.

For the function call below

```
radius = 10.0;
circum = findCircum(radius);
```

the actual argument, `radius`, has a value of `10.0`, so the function result is `62.8318` (`2.0 * 3.14159 * 10.0`). The function result is assigned to `circum`. Figure 3.10 shows the execution of this function call.

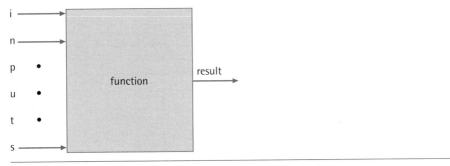

Figure 3.9   Function with input arguments and one result

Listing 3.12   Functions `findCircum` and `findArea`

```
// Computes the circumference of a circle with radius r.
// Pre:  r is defined and is > 0.
//       PI is a constant.
//       Library cmath is included.
float findCircum(float r)
{
     return (2.0 * PI * r);
}


// Computes the area of a circle with radius r.
// Pre:   r is defined and is > 0.
//       PI is a constant.
//       Library cmath is included.
float findArea(float r)
{
     return (PI * pow(r, 2));
}
```

The function call to `findArea`

```
area = findArea(radius);
```

causes C++ to evaluate the expression `3.14159 * pow(r, 2)`, where `pow` is a library function (part of `cmath`) that raises its first argument to the power indicated by its second argument (`pow(r, 2)` computes r2). When `radius` is `10.0`, `pow` returns `100.0` and `findArea` returns a result of `314.59`, which is assigned to `area`. This example shows that a user-defined function can call a C++ library function.

You must provide prototypes that declare these functions before function `main`. The prototypes should indicate that each function is type `float`

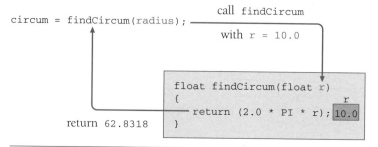

Figure 3.10 Execution of `circum = findCircum(radius);`

(returns a type `float` result) and has a formal parameter of type `float`. The prototypes follow.

```
float findArea(float);
float findCircum(float);
```

Like the function definition, the function prototype specifies the function type and its name. In the formal parameter list, you need to specify only the formal parameter types, not their names, but you can specify both. The function prototype, but not the heading, ends with a semicolon. Because function prototypes and function headings are so similar, we recommend that you write one of them first, and edit a copy of it (using your

---

Function Definition (Input Arguments and One Result)

Syntax: `// function interface comment`
`ftype fname(formal-parameter-declaration-list)`
`{`
  `local variable declarations`
  `executable statements`
`}`

Example: `// Finds the cube of its argument.`
`// Pre: n is defined.`
`int cube(int n)`
`{`
  `return (n * n * n);`
`} // end cube`

Interpretation: The function fname is defined. In the function heading, the identifier ftype specifies the data type of the function result. The formal-parameter-declaration-list, enclosed in parentheses, declares the type and name of each function parameter. Commas separate the parameters. Notice that there are no semicolons after the function heading. The braces enclose the function body. Any identifiers

---

that are declared in the optional local declarations are defined only during the execution of the function and can be referenced only within the function. The executable statements of the function body describe the data manipulation to be performed by the function in order to compute the result value. Execution of a **return** statement causes the function to return control to the statement that called it. The function returns the value of the expression following **return** as its result.

Note: ftype is **void** if the function does not return a value. The argument list **( )** indicates that the function has no arguments.

Function Prototype (With Parameters)

Form: ftype fname(formal-parameter-type-list);

Example: `int cube(int);`

Interpretation: The identifier fname is declared as the name of a function whose type is ftype. This declaration provides all the information that the C++ compiler needs to know to translate correctly all references to the function. The function definition will be provided after the **main** function. The formal-parameter-type-list enclosed in parentheses shows the data type of each formal parameter. Commas separate the data types. A semicolon terminates the prototype.

Note: C++ permits the specification of formal parameter names in function prototypes, as in

`int cube(int n);`

In this case, the heading of the function definition and the prototype should be identical except that the prototype ends with a semicolon.

---

word-processor) to create the other. Make sure you perform whatever editing operations are required—that is, remove (or add) a semicolon and remove (or add) the formal parameter names.

PROGRAM STYLE   Function Interface Comments

The comments that begin each function in Listing 3.12 contain all the information required in order to use the function. The function interface comments begin with a statement of what the function does. Then the line

`// Pre: r is defined.`

describes the **precondition**—the condition that should be true before the function is called. You may also want to include a statement describing the **postcondition**—the condition that must be true after the function

precondition
A condition assumed to be true before a function call.

postcondition
A condition assumed to be true after a function executes.

completes execution, if some details of this postcondition are not included in the initial statement of the function's purpose.

We recommend that you begin all function definitions in this way. The function interface comments provide valuable documentation to other programmers who might want to reuse your functions in a new program.

PROGRAM STYLE   Problem Inputs versus Input Parameters

Make sure you understand the distinction between *problem inputs* and *input parameters*. *Problem inputs* are variables that receive their data from the program user through execution of an input statement. *Input parameters* receive their data through execution of a function call statement. Beginning programmers sometimes make the mistake of attempting to read a data value for a function's input parameter in the function body. The data passed to an input parameter must be defined *before* the function is called, not *after*.

EXAMPLE 3.6

Function `scale` (Listing 3.13) multiplies its first argument (a real number) by 10 raised to the power indicated by its second argument (an integer). For example, the function call

    scale(2.5, 2)

returns the value `250.0` (2.5×10^2). The function call

    scale(2.5, -2)

returns the value `0.025` (2.5×10^{-2}).
In function `scale`, the statement

    scaleFactor = pow(10, n);

calls function `pow` to raise 10 to the power specified by the second formal parameter `n`. Local variable `scaleFactor`, defined only during the execution of the function, stores this value. The `return` statement defines the function result as the product of the first formal parameter, `x`, and `scaleFactor`.

Listing 3.14 shows a very simple `main` function written to test function `scale`. The output statement calls function `scale` and displays the function result after it is returned. The arrows drawn in Listing 3.14 show the information flow between the two actual arguments and formal parameters. To clarify the information flow, we omitted the function interface comment. The argument list correspondence is shown below.

Actual Argument	corresponds to	Formal Parameter
num1		x
num2		n

Functions with Multiple Arguments

Functions `findArea` and `findCircum` each have a single argument. We can also define functions with multiple arguments.

Listing 3.13   Function `scale`

```
// Multiplies its first argument by the power of 10
// specified by its second argument.
// Pre : x and n are defined and library cmath is
//       included.
float scale(float x, int n)
{
     float scaleFactor;  // local variable
     scaleFactor = pow(10, n);
     return (x * scaleFactor);
}
```

Listing 3.14   Testing function `scale`

```
// File: testScale.cpp
// Tests function scale.

#include <iostream>
#include <cmath>
using namespace std;

// Function prototype
float scale(float, int);

int main()
{
     float num1;
     int num2;
     // Get values for num1 and num2
     cout << "Enter a real number: ";
     cin >> num1;
     cout << "Enter an integer: ";
     cin >> num2;

     // Call scale and display result.
     cout << "Result of call to function scale is "
          << scale(num1, num2)     // actual arguments
          << endl;
     return 0;                     // information flow
}
float scale(float x, int n)        // formal parameters
```

(continued)

Listing 3.14   Testing function `scale` (continued)

```
{
        float scaleFactor;   // local variable
        scaleFactor = pow(10, n);
        return (x * scaleFactor);
}
```

```
Enter a real number: 2.5
Enter an integer: -2
Result of call to function scale is 0.025
```

Argument/Parameter List Correspondence

When using multiple-argument functions, you must be sure to include the correct number of arguments in the function call. Also, the order of the actual arguments used in the function call must correspond to the order of the formal parameters listed in the function prototype or heading.

Finally, if the function is to return meaningful results, assignment of each actual argument to the corresponding formal parameter must not cause any loss of information. Usually, you should use an actual argument of the same data type as the corresponding formal parameter, although this is not always essential. For example, the <cmath> library description indicates that both parameters of the function pow are of type double. Function scale calls pow with two actual arguments of type int. This call doesn't cause a problem because there is no loss of information when an int is assigned to a type double variable. If you pass an actual argument of type float or double to a formal parameter of type int, loss of the fractional part of the actual argument would likely lead to an unexpected function result. Next, we summarize these constraints on the **number**, **order**, and **type** (**not**) of input arguments.

Argument/Parameter List Correspondence

- The **number** of actual arguments used in a call to a function must be the same as the number of formal parameters listed in the function prototype.
- The **order** of arguments in the lists determines correspondence. The first actual argument corresponds to the first formal parameter, the second actual argument corresponds to the second formal parameter, and so on.
- Each actual argument must be of a data **type** that can be assigned to the corresponding formal parameter with no unexpected loss of information.

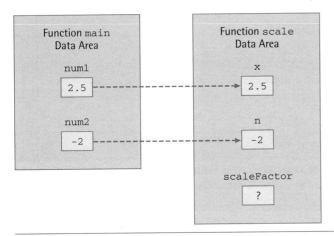

Figure 3.11 Data areas after call `scale(num1, num2);`

The Function Data Area

Each time a function call is executed, an area of memory is allocated for storage of that function's data. Included in the function data area are storage cells for its formal parameters and any local variables that may be declared in the function. The function data area is always lost when the function terminates; it is re-created empty (all values undefined) when the function is called again.

Figure 3.11 shows the `main` function data area and the data area for function `scale` after the function call `scale(num1, num2)` executes. The values 2.5 and −2 are passed into the formal parameters x and n, respectively. The local variable, `scaleFactor`, is initially undefined; the execution of the function body changes the value of this variable to 0.01.

The local variable `scaleFactor` can be accessed only in function `scale`. Similarly, the variables `num1` and `num2` declared in function `main` can be accessed only in function `main`. If you want a function subprogram to use the value stored in `num1`, you must provide `num1` as an actual argument when you call the function.

Testing Functions Using Drivers

A function is an independent program module, and as such it can be tested separately from the program that uses it. To run such a test, you should write a short **driver** function that defines the function arguments, calls the function, and displays the value returned. For example, the function `main` in Listing 3.14 acts as a driver to test function `scale`.

driver
A short function written to test another function by defining its arguments, calling it, and displaying its result.

EXERCISES FOR SECTION 3.5

Self-Check

1. Evaluate each of the following:
   a. `scale(2.55 + 5.23, 4 / 2)`
   b. `findCircum(3.0)`
   c. `findArea(2.0)`
   d. `scale(findArea(5.0), -1)`

2. Explain the effect of reversing the function arguments in the call to `scale` shown in Example 3.6—that is, `scale(num2, num1)`.

3. How does the use of function arguments make it possible to write larger, more useful programs?

4. Write the function prototypes for functions `drawCircleChar`, `findCircum`, and `findArea`.

5. What error message do you get if a function prototype has a different number of parameters than the function definition?

Programming

1. Revise the flat-washer program (Listing 3.4) to use function sub-programs `findArea`, `findRimArea`, `findUnitWeight`, and `instruct`. Show the complete program.

2. Write a function that calculates the elapsed time in minutes between a start time and an end time expressed as integers on a 24-hour clock (8:30 P.M. = 2030). You need to deal only with end times occurring later on the same day as the start time. Also write a driver program to test your function.

3. Assume your friend has solved Programming Exercise 2. Write another function that uses your friend's function to calculate the speed (km/h) one must average to reach a certain destination by a designated time. Function inputs include same-day departure and arrival times as integers on a 24-hour clock and the distance to the destination in kilometers. Also write a driver program to test your function.

3.6   Scope of Names

scope of a name
The region in a program where a particular meaning of a name is visible or can be referenced.

The **scope of a name** refers to the region in a program where a particular meaning of a name is visible or can be referenced. For example, we stated earlier that variable `num1` (declared in `main` in Listing 3.14) can be referenced only in function `main`, which means that that is its scope. Let's consider the names in the program outline shown in Listing 3.15. The identifiers `MAX` and `LIMIT` are defined as constants and their scope begins at their definition and continues to the end of the source file. This means that all three functions can access the constants `MAX` and `LIMIT`.

The scope of the function subprogram name funTwo begins with its prototype and continues to the end of the source file. This means that function funTwo can be called by functions one, main, and itself. The situation is different for function one because one is also used as a formal parameter name in function funTwo. Therefore, function one can be called by the main function and itself but not by function funTwo. This shows how you can use the same name for different purposes in different functions—generally not a good idea because it is confusing to human readers of the program, but C++ has no problem handling it.

All of the formal parameters and local variables in Listing 3.15 are visible only from their declaration to the closing brace of the function in which they are declared. For example, from the line that is marked with the comment // header 1 to the line marked // end one, the identifier anArg means an integer parameter in the data area of function one. From the line with the comment // header 2 through the line marked // end funTwo, this name refers to a character parameter in the data area of funTwo. In the rest of the file, the name anArg is not visible.

Listing 3.15   Outline of program for studying scope of names

```
void one(int anArg, double second);   // prototype 1

int funTwo(int one, char anArg);       // prototype 2

const int MAX = 950;
const int LIMIT = 200;

int main()
{
   int localVar;
   . . .
} // end main

void one(int anArg, double second)     // header 1
{
   int oneLocal;                       // local 1
   . . .
} // end one

int funTwo(int one, char anArg)        // header 2
{
   int localVar;                       // local 2
   . . .
} // end funTwo
```

Table 3.2 shows which identifiers are visible within each of the three functions

Table 3.2   Scope of Names in Listing 3.15

Name	Visible in One	Visible in funTwo	Visible in main
MAX	yes	yes	yes
LIMIT	yes	yes	yes
main	yes	yes	yes
localVar (in main)	no	no	yes
one (the function)	yes	no	yes
anArg (int parameter)	yes	no	no
second	yes	no	no
oneLocal	yes	no	no
funTwo	yes	yes	yes
one (formal parameter)	no	yes	no
anArg (char parameter)	no	yes	no
localVar (in funTwo)	no	yes	no

EXERCISES FOR SECTION 3.6

Self-Check

1. Develop a table similar to Table 3.2 for the identifiers declared in Listing 3.14.

2. Develop a table similar to Table 3.2 for the program below.

```
#include <iostream>
using namespace std;

const float PI = 3.14159;

// function prototypes
float findCircum(float);
float findArea(float);

int main()
{
    float radius;
    float circumf, area;
```

```
        cout << "Enter radius: ";
        cin >> radius;

        circumf = findCircum(radius);
        area = findArea(radius);

        cout << "For a circle with radius " << radius
             << ", area is " << area
             << ", circumference is " << circumf << endl;

        return 0;
}

float findCircum(float r)
{
        return (2.0 * PI * r);
}

float findArea(float r)
{
        return (PI * pow(r, 2));
}
```

3.7 Extending C++ through Classes: Using Class `string`

You have seen the advantages of procedural abstraction and the use of functions as program building blocks. C++ also facilitates **data abstraction** through its class feature, which enables users to define new data types and their associated operations. In this section we study the `string` class, which is part of the C++ standard library. In Chapter 10, we show how to define your own classes.

data abstraction Modeling real-world data using the data types available in a programming language or additional class types.

The `string` Class

In Section 2.3 we introduced the C++ `string` class, which defines a new data type `string` and many operators for `string` objects. Two attributes of a `string` object are the character sequence it stores and the length of that sequence. Some of the common operators you have seen so far (`<<`, `>>`, `=`, `+`) can be used with `string` objects. Listing 3.16 illustrates how we use these familiar operators and some new ones with `string` objects as operands.

Listing 3.16   Illustrating string operations

```cpp
// File: stringOperations.cpp
// Illustrates string operations

#include <iostream>
#include <string>
using namespace std;

int main()
{
    string firstName, lastName;  // inputs - first and
                                 //          last names
    string wholeName;            // output - whole name
    string greeting = "Hello ";  // output - a greeting
                                 //          string

    // Read first and last names.
    cout << "Enter your first name: ";
    cin >> firstName;
    cout << "Enter your last name: ";
    cin >> lastName;

    // Join names in whole name
    wholeName = firstName + " " + lastName;

    // Display results
    cout << greeting << wholeName << '!' << endl;
    cout << "You have " << (wholeName.length() - 1)
         << " letters in your name." << endl;

    // Display initials
    cout << "Your initials are " << firstName.at(0)
         << lastName.at(0) << endl;

    return 0;
}
```

```
Enter your first name: Caryn
Enter your last name: Jackson
Hello Caryn Jackson!
You have 12 letters in your name.
Your initials are CJ
```

Declaring `string` Objects

The declarations

```
string firstName, lastName;  // inputs - first and last
                             //          names
string wholeName;            // output - whole name
```

allocate storage for three `string` objects that initially contain empty strings (a string with zero characters). You can store new data in these strings through a string assignment or by reading a string value typed at the keyboard. You can also store data in a `string` object when you declare it. The statement

```
string greeting = "Hello ";  // output - a greeting string
```

stores the string "Hello" in the `string` object `greeting`.

Reading and Displaying `string` Objects

In Section 2.4, we saw that the extraction operator can be used with `string` operands. The statement

```
cin >> firstName;
```

reads keyboard data into `firstName`. It stores in `firstName` all data characters up to (but not including) the first blank or return. You must not enclose these characters in quotes. The statement

```
cout << greeting << wholeName << '!' << endl;
```

displays `string` objects `greeting` and `wholeName` followed by the character value `'!'`.

What if you want to read a data string that contains a blank? For example, you may want to read the characters `Van Winkle` into `lastName`. You can do this using the `getline` function. For example, the statement

```
getline(cin, lastName, '\n');
```

reads into `string` object `lastName` all characters typed at the keyboard (stream `cin`) up to (but not including) the character `'\n'`. The escape sequence `'\n'` is a text control character (see Table 2.5) and it represents the *newline* character. You enter this character at the keyboard by pressing RETURN or ENTER. (On some systems, you may need to press ENTER twice.)

You can specify another terminator character by changing the third argument. For example, use `'*'` as the third argument to make the symbol `*` the terminator character. In this case, you can type your data string over multiple lines, and it will not terminate until you enter the symbol `*`. All data characters entered, including any newline characters (but not the `*`), will be stored in the `string` object used as the second argument.

String Assignment and Concatenation

The assignment statement

```
wholeName = firstName + " " + lastName;
```

stores in `wholeName` the new string formed by joining the three strings that are operands of the operator +, which means to join, or *concatenate*, when its operands are strings. Notice that we insert a space between string objects `firstName` and `lastName` by joining the string value `" "`, not the character value `' '`. Remember to use quotes, not apostrophes, to enclose string values in C++ statements.

Operator Overloading

operator overloading
The ability of an operator to perform different operations depending on the data type of its operands.

Until now, the operator + has always meant addition, but now we see that it means concatenation when its operands are `string` objects. We use the term **operator overloading** to indicate that an operator's function may vary depending on its operands. Operator overloading is a very powerful concept because it allows C++ to give multiple meanings to a single operator; C++ can determine the correct interpretation of the operator from the way we use it.

Dot Notation: Calling Functions `length` and `at`

Listing 3.16 also uses member functions `length` and `at` from the `string` class. To call these functions (and most member functions), we use *dot notation*. Rather than passing an object as an argument to a member function, we write the name of the object, a dot (or period), and then the function to be applied to this object. The function reference

```
wholeName.length()
```

applies member function `length` (no arguments) to string object `wholeName`. This call to function `length` returns a value of 13 (`wholeName` contains the 13-character string `"Caryn Jackson"`); however, we subtract one before printing the result because of the blank character between the first and last names:

```
cout << "You have " << (wholeName.length() - 1)
     << " letters in your name." << endl;
```

The expression

```
firstName.at(0)
```

retrieves the character in `firstName` that is at position 0, where we number the characters from the left, starting with 0 for the first character, 1 for the second, and so on. By this numbering system, the last character in `string` object whole-Name (the letter n) is at position `wholeName.length()` - 1, or position 12.

Dot Notation

Syntax: object.function-call

Example: `firstName.at(0)`

Interpretation: The member function specified in the function-call is applied to object.

Note: The member function may change the attributes of object.

Member Functions for Word–Processing Operations

We would like to be able to perform on a `string` object all the operations that are available on most word processors. C++ provides member functions for searching for a string (`find`), inserting a string at a particular position (`insert`), deleting a portion of a string (`erase`), and replacing part of a string with another string (`replace`). We illustrate some simple examples of these functions next.

For the strings `firstName`, `lastName`, and `wholeName` in Listing 3.16, the expression

```
wholeName.find(firstName)
```

returns 0 (the position of the first character of "Caryn" in "Caryn Jackson") and the expression

```
wholeName.find(lastName)
```

returns 6 (the position of the first character of "Jackson" in "Caryn Jackson").

The first statement below inserts a string at the beginning of `string` object `wholeName` (at position 0) and the second statement inserts a string in the middle of `wholeName` (at new position 10).

```
wholeName.insert(0, "Ms. ");        // Change to
                                    // "Ms. Caryn Jackson"
wholeName.insert(10, "Heather ");   // Change to
                                    // "Ms. Caryn Heather
                                    //  Jackson"
```

Notice that member function `insert` changes the string stored in object `wholeName`.

You can use the following statement to change the middle name from Heather to Amy:

```
wholeName.replace(10, 7, "Amy");  // Change to
                                  // "Ms. Caryn Amy Jackson"
```

This statement means: start at position 10 of `wholeName` (at the letter `H`) and replace the next seven characters (`Heather`) with the string `"Amy"`. Finally, you can delete the new middle name altogether by using the statement

```
wholeName.erase(10, 4);   // Change back to
                          // "Ms. Caryn Jackson"
```

which means: start at position 10 and erase four characters (`Amy` and a space) from `string` object `wholeName`.

Assigning a Substring to a **string** Object

You can also store a *substring* (portion of a string) in another `string` object using member function `assign`. For example, if `title` is a `string` object, the statement

```
title.assign(wholeName, 0, 3);   // Store "Ms." in title
```

stores in `title` the first three characters of `wholeName`. The content of `wholeName` is not changed.

Table 3.3 summarizes the member functions described in this section.

Table 3.3   Some Member Functions for `string` Operations

Function	Purpose
`getline(cin, aString, '\n')`	Extracts data characters up to (but not including) the first newline character from stream `cin` and stores them in `aString`. The first newline character is extracted from `cin` but not stored in `aString`.
`aString.length()`	Returns the count of characters (an integer) in `aString`.
`aString.at(i)`	Returns the character in position `i` of `aString` where the leftmost character is at position 0 and the rightmost character is at position `aString.length() - 1`.
`aString.find(target)`	Returns the starting position (an integer) of string target in `aString`. If target is not in `aString`, returns a value that is outside the range of valid positions; that is, it returns a value < 0 or a value $\geq$ the length of `aString`.
`aString.insert(start, newString)`	Inserts `newString` at position `start` of `aString`.
`aString.replace(start, count, newString)`	Starting at position `start` of `aString`, replaces the next count characters with `newString`.
`aString.erase(start, count)`	Starting at position `start` of `aString`, removes the next count characters.
`aString.assign(oldString, start, count)`	Starting at position `start` of `oldString`, assigns to `aString` the next count characters.

EXERCISES FOR SECTION 3.7

Self-Check

1. Explain the effect of each of the following; assume a data line containing the characters `Jones***John Boy` is typed in.

   ```
   String name;
   cout << "name: ";
   getline(cin, name, '\n');
   int start = name.find("***");
   name.erase(start, 3);
   name.insert(start, ", ");
   cout << name << endl;
   ```

2. Trace each of the following statements:

   ```
   string author;
   author = "John";
   author = author + " Steinbeck";
   cout << author.length() << endl;
   cout << author.at(0) << author.at(4) << endl;
   ```

```
cout << author.at(author.length() - 1)
    << endl;
cout << author.find("n");
cout << author.find("nb");
author.insert(4, "ny");
author.replace(0, 6, "Jonathan");
author.erase(3, 5);
```

3. Write a statement that stores in wholeName the strings stored in firstName and lastName in the form *lastName, firstName.*

4. What happens if the first argument for insert is larger than the number of characters in the string? What happens if it is negative?

Programming

1. Write a program that reads three strings and displays the strings in all possible sequences, one sequence per output line. Display the symbol * between the strings on each line.

3.8 Introduction to Computer Graphics (Optional)

text mode
A display mode in which a C++ program displays only characters.

graphics mode
A display mode in which a C++ program draws graphics patterns and shapes in an output window.

In normal computer display mode (called **text mode**), we use cout to display lines of characters to the standard output device, or console. In Section 3.3, we showed how to write C++ functions for drawing simple stick figures using text mode. In several optional sections beginning with this one, we discuss another display mode (called **graphics mode**) that enables a C++ program to draw pictures or graphical patterns in an output window. To write graphics programs, you must learn how to use special graphics functions that enable you to draw lines and various geometric shapes (for example, rectangles, circles, ellipses) anywhere on your screen and color and shade them in different ways.

Several programming languages include graphics libraries. Although there is no standard graphics library for C++, several libraries have been developed for use with C++. We will study a simple graphics library called WinBGIm which is based on Borland Turbo Pascal Graphics, with the addition of mouse control. This library was developed by Professor Michael Main of the Computer Science Department, University of Colorado, Boulder. The principles we study will apply to other graphics libraries you may use in the future.

Composition of a Window

In text mode, you don't pay much attention to the position of each line of characters displayed on the screen. In graphics programming, you control the location of each line or shape that you draw in a window. Consequently, you must know your window size and how to reference the individual picture elements (called **pixels**) in a window.

pixel
A picture element on a computer screen

You can visualize a window as an x-y grid of pixels. Assume that your window has the dimensions 400 × 300. Figure 3.12 shows the coordinates for the four pixels at the corners. The pixel at the top-left corner has x-y coordinates (0, 0), and the pixel at the top-right corner has x-y coordinates (400, 0).

Notice the pixels in the y-direction are numbered differently from how we are accustomed. The pixel (0, 0) is at the top-left corner of the screen, and the y-coordinate values increase as we move down the screen. In a normal x-y coordinate system, the point (0, 0) is at the bottom-left corner.

Some Common Graphics Functions

A graphics program is a sequence of statements that call graphics functions to do the work. Listing 3.17 is a program that uses several key functions. The functions getmaxwidth and getmaxheight return the position of the last pixel in the X and Y-directions on your computer screen. Some typical screen dimensions are 640 × 480 for 14-inch screens and 1024 × 768 for 15- or 17-inch screens, but the largest window will be slightly smaller. Therefore, the statements

```
bigx = getmaxwidth();   // get largest x-coordinate.
bigy = getmaxheight();  // get largest y-coordinate.
initwindow(bigx, bigy,
    "Full screen window - press a character to close window");
```

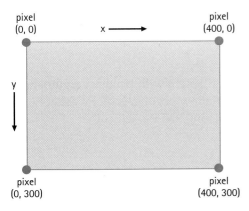

Figure 3.12   Referencing pixels in a window

Listing 3.17   Drawing intersecting lines

```cpp
// Draws intersecting lines
// File: lines.cpp

#include <graphics.h>
#include <iostream>

using namespace std;

int main()
{
    int bigX;                   // largest x-coordinate
    int bigY;                   // largest y-coordinate

    bigX = getmaxwidth();       // get largest x-coordinate
    bigY = getmaxheight();      // get largest y-coordinate
    initwindow(bigX, bigY,
            "Full screen window - press a key to close");

    // Draw intersecting lines
    line(0, 0, bigX, bigY);  // Draw white line from (0, 0) to (bigX, bigY)
    setcolor(LIGHTGRAY);     // Change color to gray
    line(bigX, 0, 0, bigY);  // Draw gray line from (bigX, 0) to (0, bigY)

    // Close screen when ready
    getch();                    // pause until user presses a key
    closegraph();               // close the window

    // Display window size in console
    cout << "Window size is " << bigX << " X " << bigY << endl;

    return 0;
}
```

```
Window size is 1018 × 736
```

pop up a window of maximum width and height with the third argument as the window label (see Figure 3.13). The window position is set by the optional fourth and fifth arguments. If they are missing, the top-left corner of the window is at (0, 0).

In the statements

```cpp
line(0, 0, bigx, bigy);  // Draw white line from(0, 0) to
                         //   (bigx, bigy)
setcolor(LIGHTGRAY);     // Change color to gray
line(bigx, 0, 0, bigy);  // Draw gray line from (bigx, 0)
                         //   to (0, bigy)
```

Figure 3.13 Window drawn by `lines.cpp`

the two calls to function `line` draw a pair of intersecting lines in this window. Method `setcolor` changes the drawing color from white (the default color) to gray for the second line. Then, the statements

```
getch();        // pause until user presses a character
closegraph();   // close the window
```

call the `getch` function (also part of `graphics.h`) to pause the program until the user presses a key. Once a key is pressed, or the user clicks on the close icon on the top right ⊠, the `closegraph` function closes the window. Finally, the statement beginning with `cout` displays the window size in the console window for normal text output.

Background Color and Foreground Color

In graphics mode, the computer displays all pixels continuously in one of 16 colors. The default color used to display a pixel is called the background color. Consequently, your initial display window appears empty because all its pixels

background color
The default color for all of the pixels in a display window.

foreground color
The new color of pixels that are part of a graphics object in a display window.

are displayed in the **background color.** When you draw a line or a shape, the pixels it contains stand out because they are changed to the **foreground color.**

Black and white are the default values for the background and foreground colors, respectively. The statements

```
setbkcolor(GREEN);   // GREEN is the background color.
setcolor(RED)        // RED is the foreground color.
```

reset the background color to GREEN and the foreground color to RED where GREEN and RED are color constants defined in `graphics.h`. You select a color constant from the list shown in Table 3.4, using either the constant name or its numeric value as a parameter (for example, RED or 4). Once you change the foreground or background color, it retains its new value until you change it again.

Drawing Rectangles

We use function `rectangle` to draw a rectangle in a window. The statement

```
rectangle(x1, y1, x2, y2);
```

draws a rectangle that has one diagonal with end points (x1, y1) and (x2, y2).

EXAMPLE 3.7

The program in Listing 3.18 draws a house (Figure 3.14). The program begins by defining the corner points of the house, where the roof is a pair of lines intersecting at point (x2, y2). The first call to `rectangle` draws the rest of the house, and the second call to `rectangle` draws the door. We drew the house in a window of size 640 × 500, with the top-left corner of the window at point (100, 50) of the screen.

Table 3.4   Color Constants

Constant	Value	Constant	Value
BLACK	0	DARKGRAY	8
BLUE	1	LIGHTBLUE	9
GREEN	2	LIGHTGREEN	10
CYAN	3	LIGHTCYAN	11
RED	4	LIGHTRED	12
MAGENTA	5	LIGHTMAGENTA	13
BROWN	6	YELLOW	14
LIGHTGRAY	7	WHITE	15

Listing 3.18   Drawing a house

```cpp
// File: house.cpp
// Draws a house

#include <graphics.h>

int main()
{
    // Define corners of house
    int x1 = 100; int y1 = 200;        // top-left corner
    int x2 = 300; int y2 = 100;        // roof peak
    int x3 = 500; int y3 = 200;        // top-right corner
    int x4 = 500; int y4 = 400;        // bottom-right corner
    int x5 = 325; int y5 = 400;        // bottom-right corner of door
    int x6 = 275; int y6 = 325;        // top-left corner of door

    initwindow(640, 500, "House - press a key to close", 100, 50);

    // Draw roof
    line(x1, y1, x2, y2);              // Draw line from (x1, y1) to (x2,y2)
    line(x2, y2, x3, y3);              // Draw line from (x2, y2) to (x3,y3)

    // Draw rest of house
    rectangle(x1, y1, x4, y4);

    // Draw door
    rectangle(x5, y5, x6, y6);

    getch();                           // pause until user presses a key
    closegraph();                      // close the window
    return 0;
}
```

Drawing Circles, Ellipses, and Arcs

We use function `circle` to draw a circle. The function call statement

```cpp
circle(x, y, radius);
```

draws a circle whose center is at (x, y). The third parameter is the circle radius.

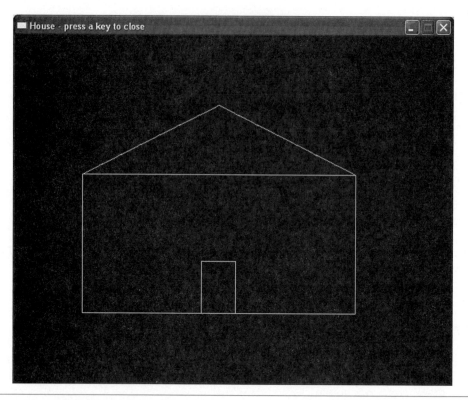

Figure 3.14   House drawn by `house.cpp`

Function `arc` draws an arc, or part of a circle. To draw an arc, you must specify its starting angle and ending angle in degrees. The statement

```
arc(x, y, 0, 180, radius)
```

draws the top half a circle with center at (x, y) (of 3.28). If you imagine a clock on the screen, 0 degrees is at 3 o'clock (horizontal direction), 30 degrees is at 2 o'clock, 60 degrees is at 1 o'clock, 90 degrees is at 12 o'clock (vertical direction), and so on.

Function `ellipse` draws an ellipse or a portion of an ellipse: the third argument is the start angle, the fourth argument is the end angle, the fifth argument is the horizontal radius, and the sixth argument is the vertical radius. The statement

```
ellipse(x, y, 0, 360, radius, 2 * radius);
```

draws a complete ellipse that is twice as high as it is wide.

EXAMPLE 3.8

The program in Listing 3.19 draws a happy face (Figure 3.15). It begins by completing an outer circle (radius `headRadius`), then it draws three smaller circles (radius `eyeNoseRadius`) representing the eyes and nose. Finally, it draws the smile as an arc from 210 degrees (8 o'clock) to 330 degrees (4 o'clock). The arc has the same center as the outer circle, but its radius is 75% as large:

```
smileRadius = int(0.75 * headRadius + 0.5);
                          // 3/4 of head radius
arc(midX, midY, 210, 330, smileRadius);
```

Note that this program uses functions `getmaxx` and `getmaxy` to determine the width and height of the drawing window, instead of `getmaxwidth` and `getmaxheight` which return the screen width and height. The statements

```
midX = getmaxx() / 2       // center head in x-direction
midY = getmaxy() / 2;      // center head in y-direction
```

use these functions to find the coordinates of the center of the window.

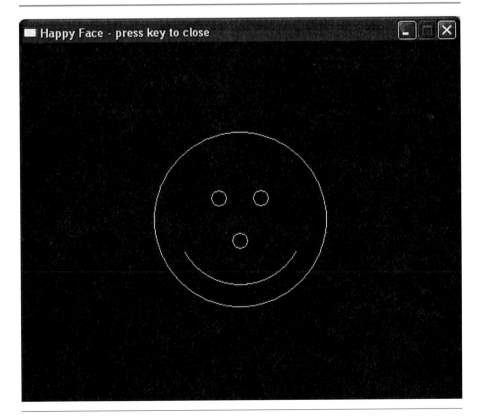

Figure 3.15   Happy face drawn by `happyFace.cpp`

Listing 3.19   Program to draw a happy face

```
// File: happyFace.cpp
// Draws a happy face

#include <graphics.h>

int main()
{
   int midX, midY;                           // coordinates of center point
   int leftEyeX, rightEyeX, eyeY;            // eye center points
   int noseX, noseY;                         // nose center point
   int headRadius;                           // head radius
   int eyeNoseRadius;                        // eye/nose radius
   int smileRadius;                          // smile radius
   int stepX, stepY;                         // x and y increments

   initwindow(500, 400, "Happy Face - press key to close");

   // Draw head
   midX = getmaxx() / 2;                     // center head in x-direction
   midY = getmaxy() / 2;                     // center head in y-direction
   headRadius = getmaxy() / 4;               // head will fill half the window
   circle(midX, midY, headRadius);           // draw head.

   // Draw eyes
   stepX = headRadius / 4;                   // x-offset for eyes
   stepY = stepX;                            // y-offset for eyes and nose
   leftEyeX = midX - stepX;                  // x-coordinate for left eye
   rightEyeX = midX + stepX;                 // x-coordinate for right eye
   eyeY = midY - stepY;                      // y-coordinate for both eyes
   eyeNoseRadius = headRadius / 10;
   circle(leftEyeX, eyeY, eyeNoseRadius);    // draw left eye
   circle(rightEyeX, eyeY, eyeNoseRadius);   // draw right eye

   // Draw nose
   noseX = midX;                                  // nose is centered in x direction
   noseY = midY + stepY;
   circle(noseX, noseY, eyeNoseRadius);

   // Draw smile
   smileRadius = int(0.75 * headRadius + 0.5);   // 3/4 of head radius
   arc(midX, midY, 210, 330, smileRadius);

   getch();
   closegraph();
   return 0;
}
```

PROGRAM STYLE   Writing General Graphics Programs

The program in Listing 3.19 is general and bases the happy face position and dimensions on the window dimensions as determined by getmaxx and getmaxy. If you change the window dimensions, the happy face will expand or shrink to fit. Conversely, the size of the house drawn by the program in Listing 3.18 is fixed and is independent of the window size. If the window is too small, part of the house may be missing. It is generally easier to draw figures with fixed dimensions; however, with a little practice you should be able to draw general graphics figures. To generalize the program in Listing 3.18, you could base the coordinates of the house corners on the window dimensions as follows (see Self-Check Exercise 4).

```
x1 = getmaxx() / 4;  y1 = getmaxy() / 2;  // top-left corner
x2 = getmaxx() / 2;  y2 = getmaxy() / 4;  // roof peak
```

Drawing Filled Figures

So far, all our graphics figures have been line drawings. To fill in sections of the screen using different colors and patterns, you would use function setfillstyle to specify the pattern and color. The function call statement

```
setfillstyle(SLASH_FILL, RED);
```

sets the fill pattern to red slashes until you change it through another call to setfillstyle. Table 3.5 shows the options for the first parameter in a call to setfillstyle. Use either the constant name or its value (for example, SLASH_FILL or 4) and any color constant in Table 3.4 as the second parameter.

Use function floodfill to actually fill in a portion of a diagram. The function call statement

```
floodfill(x, y, WHITE);
```

Table 3.5   Fill Pattern Constants

Constant	Value	Fill Pattern	Constant	Value	Fill Pattern
EMPTY_FILL	0	Background color	LTBKSLASH_FILL	6	\ \ \ (light)
SOLID_FILL	1	Solid color	HATCH_FILL	7	Hatch (light)
LINE_FILL	2	---	XHATCH_FILL	8	Crosshatch
LTSLASH_FILL	3	/ / / (light)	INTERLEAVE_FILL	9	Interleaving line
SLASH_FILL	4	/// (heavy)	WIDE_DOT_FILL	10	Dots (light)
BKSLASH_FILL	5	\\\ (heavy)	CLOSE_DOT_FILL	11	Dots (heavy)

fills with the current fill pattern an area on the screen that contains the point (x, y) and is bounded by white lines. If the point (x, y) is outside an area bounded by white lines, the exterior of the bounded figure is filled.

The floodfill function sometimes gives unexpected results and is a bit inefficient. As an alternative to drawing a rectangle and then filling it, function bar draws a filled rectangle. The function call statement

```
setfillstyle(SOLID_FILL, BLUE);
bar(x1, y1, x2, y2);
```

draws a filled rectangle that has a diagonal with end points (x1, y1) and (x2, y2).

EXAMPLE 3.8

We can insert the following program fragment at the end of the program in Listing 3.18 to paint the house (Figure 3.16).

```
// Paint the house
setfillstyle(HATCH_FILL, LIGHTGRAY);
floodfill(x2, y2 + 10, WHITE);      // Paint the roof
setfillstyle(LINE_FILL, WHITE);
floodfill(x2, y1 + 10, WHITE);      // Paint the house front
```

In the two calls to floodfill, we use x2, the midpoint in the X-direction, as the first parameter. The second parameter (the Y-coordinate) determines which section (roof or house front) to fill in. All boundary lines for the house are white (the default foreground color), so the third parameter is WHITE. The roof is painted in a gray hatch pattern, the house itself is painted in a white lined pattern.

The call to function bar below paints the door blue. It replaces the earlier call to function rectangle with the same arguments. Listing 3.20 shows the complete program.

```
setfillstyle(SOLID_FILL, BLUE);
bar(x5, y5, x6, y6);        // Draw blue door
```

PROGRAM PITFALL   Incorrect Order of Function Calls Draws Over Earlier Results

The order of statement execution is critical in all programs, but an incorrect order can cause strange results in graphics program. If you call function bar to paint the door blue before calling floodfill to paint the house front, floodfill will change the color of the pixels in the door to white, and it will not appear in the window.

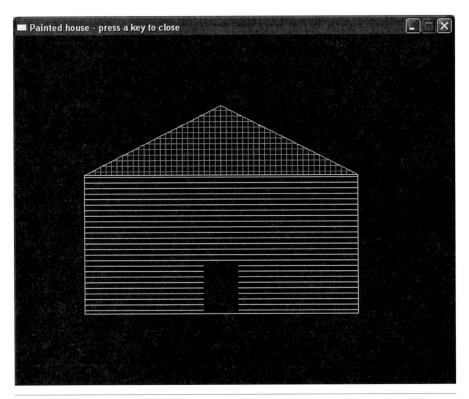

Figure 3.16 Painted house drawn by `paintedHouse.cpp`

Listing 3.20 Program to paint a house

```cpp
// File: paintedHouse.cpp
// Paints a house

#include <graphics.h>

int main()
{
    // Define corners of house
    int x1 = 100; int y1 = 200;        // top-left corner
    int x2 = 300; int y2 = 100;        // roof peak
    int x3 = 500; int y3 = 200;        // top-right corner
    int x4 = 500; int y4 = 400;        // bottom-right corner
    int x5 = 325; int y5 = 400;        // bottom-right corner of door
    int x6 = 275; int y6 = 325;        // top-left corner of door

    initwindow(640, 500, "House - press a key to close", 100, 50);
```

(continued)

Listing 3.20   Program to paint a house (continued)

```
// Draw roof
line(x1, y1, x2, y2);              // Draw line from (x1, y1) to (x2, y2)
line(x2, y2, x3, y3);              // Draw line from (x2, y2) to (x3, y3)

// Draw rest of house
rectangle(x1, y1, x4, y4);

// Paint the house
setfillstyle(HATCH_FILL, LIGHTGRAY);
floodfill(x2, y2 + 10, WHITE);          // Paint the roof
setfillstyle(LINE_FILL, WHITE);
floodfill(x2, y1 + 10, WHITE);          // Paint the house

setfillstyle(SOLID_FILL, BLUE);
bar(x5, y5, x6, y6);                    // Draw blue door

getch();
closegraph();
return 0;
}
```

Pie Slices and Filled Ellipses

Function `pieslice` draws a filled pie slice (section of a circle) and `fillellipse` draws a filled ellipse or circle. Insert the first statement below at the end of Listing 3.19 to change the happy face smile to a frown (replaces the original call to function `arc`). The last statement calls `pieslice` to draw an eyepatch over the pirate's right eye (Figure 3.17).

```
arc(midX, midY + headRadius, 65, 115, smileRadius / 2);
                              // Draw frown
setfillstyle(CLOSE_DOT_FILL, WHITE);
pieslice(midX, midY, 10, 60, smileRadius);
                              // Draw eye patch
```

The eye patch is a pie slice with radius `smileRadius` centered at point (`midX`, `midY`). The pie slice goes from 10 degrees to 60 degrees. The final program is shown in Listing 3.21.

You can use the `pieslice` and `bar` functions to draw pie charts and bar graphs (see Programming Project 13 at the end of the chapter). We describe how to display the message shown under the happy face next.

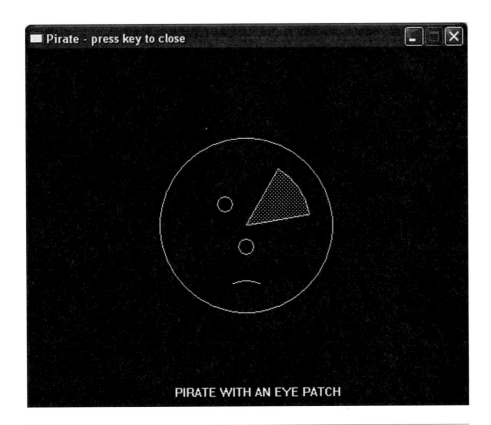

Figure 3.17 Pirate drawn by `pirate.cpp`

Listing 3.21 Program to draw a pirate

```
// File: pirate.cpp
// Draws a pirate

#include <graphics.h>

int main()
{
    int midX, midY;                        // coordinates of center point
    int leftEyeX, rightEyeX, eyeY;         // eye center points
    int noseX, noseY;                      // nose center point
    int headRadius;                        // head radius
    int eyeNoseRadius;                     // eye/nose radius
    int smileRadius;                       // smile radius
    int stepX, stepY;                      // x and y increments
```

(continued)

Listing 3.21   Program to draw a pirate (continued)

```
initwindow(500, 400, "Pirate - press key to close", 200, 150);

// Draw head
midX = getmaxx() / 2;                  // center head in x-direction
midY = getmaxy() / 2;                  // center head in y-direction
headRadius = getmaxy() / 4;            // head will fill half the window
circle(midX, midY, headRadius);        // draw head.

// Draw eyes
stepX = headRadius / 4;                // x-offset for eyes
stepY = stepX;                         // y-offset for eyes and nose
leftEyeX = midX - stepX;               // x-coordinate for left eye
rightEyeX = midX + stepX;              // x-coordinate for right eye
eyeY = midY - stepY;                   // y-coordinate for both eyes
eyeNoseRadius = headRadius / 10;
circle(leftEyeX, eyeY, eyeNoseRadius);   // draw left eye
circle(rightEyeX, eyeY, eyeNoseRadius);  // draw right eye

// Draw nose
noseX = midX;                          // nose is centered in x direction
noseY = midY + stepY;
circle(noseX, noseY, eyeNoseRadius);

// Draw frown
smileRadius = int(0.75 * headRadius + 0.5);   // 3/4 of head radius
arc(midX, midY + headRadius, 65, 115, smileRadius / 2);   // Draw frown

setfillstyle(CLOSE_DOT_FILL, WHITE);
pieslice(midX, midY, 10, 60, smileRadius);   // Draw eye patch

outtextxy(getmaxx() / 3, getmaxy() - 20, "PIRATE WITH AN EYE PATCH");

getch();
closegraph();
return 0;
}
```

Adding Text to Drawings

In graphics mode, you cannot use cout to display characters, but you must instead draw characters just as you draw other shapes. Fortunately, the graphics library provides a function that does this. The function call statement

```
outtextxy(getmaxx() / 3, getmaxy() - 20,
                      "PIRATE WITH AN EYE PATCH");
```

draws each character in a string (its third parameter) starting at the pixel whose
X-Y coordinates are specified by its first two parameters (see Figure 3.17). You
may see a warning message associated with `outtextxy` during program compilation. You can ignore it for now; we explain what it means in Section 9.12.

Table 3.6 shows the functions in the graphics library. With the exception
of `label` (in `init`) and `textString` (in `outtextxy`), all arguments are type

Table 3.6 Functions in Graphics Library

Function	Effect
`arc(x, y, stAng, endAng, r)`	draws an arc from angle `stAng` to `endAng` with center at (`x`, `y`) and radius `r`
`bar(x1, y1, x2, y2)`	draws a filled rectangle with a diagonal through points (`x1`, `y1`) and (`x2`, `y2`)
`circle(x, y, r)`	draws a circle with center at (`x`, `y`) and radius `r`
`closegraph()`	closes graphics mode
`ellipse(x, y, stAng, endAng, xRad, yRad)`	Draws an ellipse with center at (`x`, `y`) from `stAng` to `endAng` with `xRad` as horizontal radius and `yRad` as vertical radius
`fillellipse(x, y, xRad, yRad)`	Draws a filled ellipse with center at (`x`, `y`) with `xRad` as horizontal radius and `yRad` as vertical radius
`floodfill(x, y, border)`	fills with the current fill pattern the figure containing the point (`x`, `y`) and bounded by lines with color `border`
`getch()`	pauses the program until the user enters a character
`getmaxheight()`	returns the position of the last pixel in the y-direction in the screen
`getmaxwidth()`	returns the position of the last pixel in the x-direction in the screen
`getmaxx()`	returns the window width in pixels
`getmaxy()`	returns the window height in pixels
`initgraph(x, y, label)`	displays a window x pixels wide and y pixels high with the given `label` and top-left corner at (0, 0)
`initgraph(x, y, label, x0, y0)`	displays a window x pixels wide and y pixels high with the given `label` and top-left corner at (`x0`, `y0`)
`line(x1, y1, x2, y2)`	draws a line with end points (`x1`, `y1`) and (`x2`, `y2`)
`outtextxy(x, y, textString)`	draws the characters for `textString` starting at point (`x`, `y`)
`pieslice(x, y, stAng, endAng, r)`	draws a filled pie slice with center at (`x`, `y`) from angle `stAng` to `endAng` with radius `r`
`rectangle(x1, y1, x2, y2)`	draws a rectangle with a diagonal through points (`x1`, `y1`) and (`x2`, `y2`)
`setbkcolor(backColor)`	sets the background color to `backColor`
`setcolor(foreColor)`	sets the foreground color to `foreColor`
`setfillstyle(filPat, filCol)`	sets the fill pattern to `filPat` and the fill color to `filCol`

int. We will pass string literals as arguments corresponding to `label` and `textString`.

EXERCISES FOR SECTION 3.8

Self-Check

1. In Listing 3.21, what is the reason for basing the head radius on `getmaxy` and not `getmaxx`?

2. Describe or show the drawing produced by the following fragment. Assume a 640 × 480 palette.

```
circle(200, 50, 25);
line(200, 75, 100, 100);
line(200, 75, 300, 100);
pieslice(200, 75, 245, 295, 100);
line(200, 150, 100, 250);
line(200, 150, 300, 250);
bar(50, 250, 350, 300)
```

3. Write statements to add two windows to the second floor of the house in Figure 3.20.

4. Modify the program in Figure 3.20 so that it draws the house in the center of the screen and with the same relative size regardless of the actual palette dimensions.

Programming

1. Write the statements to draw a tennis racket in the appropriate place in the figure for Self-Check Exercise 2. At the end of a thin bar, draw a circle and fill it with a green crosshatch pattern.

2. Write a graphics program that draws a rocket ship consisting of a triangle (the cone) on top of a rectangle (the body). Draw a pair of intersecting lines under the rectangle. Fill the cone with a blue hatch pattern and the body with a red solid pattern.

3. Write a program that draws a pair of nested rectangles at the center of the screen, filling the inner rectangle in red and the outer rectangle in white. The outer rectangle should have a width 1/4 of the X-dimension and a height 1/4 of the Y-dimension of the screen. The height and width of the inner rectangle should be half that of the outer rectangle.

4. Write a program that draws a male and a female stick figure side-by-side.

3.9 Common Programming Errors

Remember to use a `#include` compiler directive for every standard library that your program accesses. If you're including a user-defined library, enclose the header file name in quotes, not angle brackets.

If you're using function subprograms, place their prototypes in the source file before the `main` function. Place the actual function definitions after the `main` function.

Syntax or run-time errors may occur when you use functions. The acronym **not** summarizes the requirements for argument list correspondence. Provide the required **n**umber of arguments and make sure the **o**rder of arguments is correct. Make sure that each function argument is the correct **t**ype or that conversion to the correct type will lose no information. For user-defined functions, verify that each argument list is correct by comparing it to the formal parameter list in the function heading or prototype. Also be careful when using functions that are undefined on some range of values. For example, if the argument for function `sqrt`, `log`, or `log10` is negative, a run-time error will occur. The following are additional errors to look for.

- *Semicolons in a function heading and prototype:* A missing semicolon at the end of a function prototype may cause a `"Statement missing ;"` or `"Declaration terminated incorrectly"` diagnostic. (A prototype is a declaration and must be terminated with a semicolon.) However, make sure you don't insert a semicolon after the function heading.

- *Wrong number of arguments:* If the number of arguments in a function call is not the same as the number in the prototype, your compiler may generate an error message such as the following:

```
Incorrect number of arguments in call to intPower(int, int).
```

As shown above, in most cases the error message lists the function prototype—`intPower(int, int)` in this case—to help you determine the exact nature of the error.

- *Argument mismatches:* Verify that each actual argument in a function call is in the right position relative to its corresponding formal parameter. You do this by comparing each actual argument to the type and description of its corresponding formal parameter in the function prototype. Remember, the actual argument name is not what's important; it's the positional correspondence that's critical.

C++ permits most type mismatches that you're likely to create and usually won't generate even a warning message. Instead, the compiler will perform a *standard conversion* on the actual argument, converting it to the type specified by the formal parameter. These conversions may produce incorrect results, which in turn can cause other errors during the execution of your program. If you pass a real number to a type char formal parameter, your compiler may generate a warning diagnostic such as

```
Float or double assigned to integer or character data type.
```

- *Function prototype and definition mismatches:* The compiler will not detect type mismatches between a function prototype and the function definition, but they might be detected by the linker program for your C++ system.

```
undefined symbol intPower(int, int) in module square.
```

This message may be caused by a missing function definition or by the use of a function prototype that doesn't match the function definition. If the parameters in a function prototype don't match those in the definition, the linker assumes that the prototype refers to a different function, one for which there is no definition.

- *Return statement errors:* All functions that you write, except for type void functions, should terminate execution with a return statement that includes an expression indicating the value to be returned. The data type of the value returned should match the type specified in the function heading. Make sure that you don't omit the expression (or even worse, the entire return statement). If you forget to specify a return value when one is expected, you'll see a message such as

```
Return value expected.
```

or

```
Function should return a value . . .
```

If you specify a return value for a void function, you'll see a message such as

```
Function cannot return a value . . .
```

- *Missing object name in call to a member function:* If you omit the object name and dot when attempting to apply a member function to an object, you'll get an error message such as

```
Call to undefined function
```

Because the object name is missing, the compiler can't determine the class library in which the function is defined and assumes the function definition is missing.

■ *Missing #include line or incorrect library name in #include:* If you forget to include a library header file or write the wrong header (for example, <cmath> instead of <string>), you'll see multiple error messages because the compiler will not be able to access the symbols and functions defined in that library. The error messages will tell you that symbols and functions from that library are undefined. A similar error occurs if you omit the using namespace std; statement.

■ *Argument mismatch in a call to a member function:* If you have argument type mismatches or an incorrect number of arguments in a call to a member function, you'll get an error message such as

```
Could not find a match for getline(string, char)
```

This message is displayed if you call function getline with a string and char argument instead of a stream, string, and char argument.

■ *Logic errors in your program—testing a program and checking your results:* Many errors, such as the incorrect specification of computations (in writing mathematical formulas) may go undetected by the compiler, yet produce incorrect results. For example, if you're given the formula

$$y = 3k^2 - 9k + 7$$

to program, and you write the C++ code

```
y = 9 * pow(k, 2) 2 3 - k + 7
```

(accidentally reversing the coefficients 9 and 3), no error will be detected by the compiler. As far as the compiler is concerned, no mistake has been made—the expression is perfectly legal C++ code.

Separately Testing Function Subprograms

There is usually just one way to find logic errors, and that's by testing your program using carefully chosen *test data samples* and verifying, for each sample, that your answer is correct. Such testing is a critical part of the programming process and cannot be omitted.

As we proceed through the text, we will have more to say about testing strategies. We discussed one testing strategy that involves breaking down a problem into subproblems, writing the solutions to the subproblems using separate functions, and then separately testing these functions with short driver functions. This strategy can help simplify the testing process and make it easier for you to perform a more thorough test of your entire program.

Chapter Review

1. Develop your program solutions from existing information. Use the system documentation derived from applying the software development method as the initial framework for the program.

   - Edit the data requirements to obtain the `main` function declarations.
   - Use the refined algorithm as the starting point for the executable statements in the `main` function.

2. If a new problem is an extension of a previous one, modify the previous program rather than starting from scratch.

3. Use C++ library functions to simplify mathematical computations through the reuse of code that has already been written and tested. Write a function call (consisting of the function name and arguments) to activate a library function. After the function executes, the function result is substituted for the function call.

4. Use a structure chart to show subordinate relationships between subproblems.

5. Utilize modular programming by writing separate function subprograms to implement the different subproblems in a structure chart. Ideally, your `main` function will consist of a sequence of function call statements that activate the function subprograms.

6. You can write functions without arguments and results to display a list of instructions to a program user or to draw a diagram on the screen. Use a function call consisting of the function name followed by an empty pair of parentheses `()` to activate such a function.

7. Write functions that have input arguments and that return a single result to perform computations similar to those performed by library functions. When you call such a function, each actual argument value is assigned to its corresponding formal parameter.

8. Place prototypes (similar to function headings) for each function subprogram before the `main` function, and place the function definitions after the `main` function in a source file. Use `()` to indicate that a function has no parameters. List only the formal parameter types, not their names, in the prototype. Use a semicolon after the prototype but not after the function heading.

9. You can use the standard `string` class and its member functions to process textual data. Insert the compiler directive `#include <string>` and the statement `using namespace std;` in your program. You should use dot notation to apply a member function to an object (*object.function-call*).

Summary of New C++ Constructs

Construct	Effect
Function Prototype `void display();`	Prototype for a function that has no arguments and returns no result.
`float average(float, float);`	Prototype for a function with two type `float` input arguments and a type `float` result.
Function Call `display();`	Calls void function `display`, causing it to begin execution. When execution is complete, control returns to the statement in the calling function that immediately follows the call.
`x = average(2, 6.5) + 3.0;`	Calls function `average` with actual arguments 2 and 6.5. When execution is complete, adds 3.0 to the function result and stores the sum in variable x.
Member Function Call Using Dot Notation `cout << wholeName.at(0);`	Calls `string` member function at, applying it to object `wholeName`. Displays the first character in `wholeName`.

Function Definition
`// Displays a diamond of stars`
`void display()`
`{`
`    cout << "    *    " << endl;`
`    cout << "   * *   " << endl;`
`    cout << "  *   *  " << endl;`
`    cout << " *     * " << endl;`
`    cout << "  *   *  " << endl;`
`    cout << "   * *   " << endl;`
`    cout << "    *    " << endl;`
 	
`} // end display`
	Definition of a function that has no arguments and returns no result.

`// Computes average of two integers`
`float average(float, float)`
`{`
	Definition of a function with two type `float` input arguments and a type `float` result.

`    return (m1 + m2) / 2.0;` `} // end average`	Returns a type `float` result.

Quick-Check Exercises

1. Each function in a program executes exactly once. True or false?

2. State the order of declarations used in a program source file.

3. What is the difference between an actual argument and a formal parameter? How is correspondence between arguments and parameters determined?

4. Can you use an expression for a formal parameter or for an actual argument? If so, for which?

5. What is a structure chart? Explain how a structure chart differs from an algorithm.

6. What does the function below do?

```
void nonsense(char c, char d)
{
    cout << "*****" << endl;
    cout << c << "!!!" << d << endl;
    cout << "*****" << endl;
} // end nonsense
```

7. Given the function nonsense from Exercise 6, describe the output that's produced when the following lines are executed.

```
nonsense('a', 'a');
nonsense('A', 'Z');
nonsense('!', '!');
```

8. Explain what dot notation is and how you use it.

9. Trace the statements below:

```
string flower = "rose";
flower = flower + " of Sharon";
cout << flower.at(0) << flower.at(8) << endl;
cout << flower.find("s") << " " << flower.find("S")
<< endl;
flower.replace(5, 2, "from");
flower.erase(0, 4);
flower.insert(0, "thorn");
```

10. Explain the role of a function prototype and a function definition. Which comes first? Which must contain the formal parameter names? Which ends with a semicolon?

11. Write the following equation as a C++ statement using functions exp, log, and pow:

$$y = (e^{n \ln b})^2$$

Review Questions

1. Discuss the strategy of divide and conquer.

2. Provide guidelines for the use of function interface comments.

3. Briefly describe the steps you would take to derive an algorithm for a given problem.

4. The diagram that shows the algorithm steps and their interdependencies is called a _____.

5. What are three advantages of using functions?

6. A C++ program is a collection of one or more _____, one of which must be named _____.

7. When is a function executed? What is the difference between a function prototype and its definition? Which comes first?

8. Is the use of functions a more efficient use of the programmer's or the computer's time? Explain your answer.

9. Write a program that reads into a string object a name with three blanks between the first and last names. Then extract the first and last names and store them in separate string objects. Write a function subprogram that displays its string argument two times. Call this function to display the first name four times and then to display the last name six times.

10. Write a program that reads into a string object your name with the symbol * between first and last names. Then extract your first and last names and store them in separate string objects. Write a function subprogram that displays its string argument three times. Call this function to display your first name three times and then to display your last name three times.

Programming Projects

1. Add one or more of your own unique functions to the stick figure program presented in Section 3.2. Create several more pictures combining the drawCircle, drawIntersect, drawBase, and drawParallel functions with your own. Make any modifications to these functions that you need in order to make the picture components fit nicely.

2. Write functions that display each of your initials in block letter form. Use these functions to display your initials.

3. Write three functions, one that displays a circle, one that displays a rectangle, and one that displays a triangle. Use these functions to write a complete C++ program from the following outline:

```
int main()
{
    // Draw circle.
    // Draw triangle.
```

```
    // Draw rectangle.
    // Display 2 blank lines.
    // Draw triangle.
    // Draw circle.
    // Draw rectangle.

    return 0;
}
```

4. Write a computer program that computes the duration of a projectile's flight and its height above the ground when it reaches the target. As part of your solution, write and call a function that displays instructions to the program user.

Problem Constant

```
G = 32.17        // gravitational constant
```

Problem Inputs

```
float theta      // input - angle (radians) of elevation
float distance   // input - distance (ft) to target
float velocity   // input - projectile velocity (ft/sec)
```

Problem Outputs

```
float time       // output - time (sec) of flight
float height     // output - height at impact
```

Relevant Formulas

$$time = \frac{distance}{velocity \times cos\,(theta)}$$

$$height = velocity \times sin(theta) \times time - \frac{g \times time^2}{2}$$

Try your program on these data sets.

Inputs	Data Set 1	Data Set 2
Angle of elevation	0.3 radian	0.71 radian
Velocity	800 ft/sec	1,600 ft/sec
Distance to target	11,000 ft	78,670 ft

5. Write a program that takes a positive number with a fractional part and rounds it to two decimal places. For example, 32.4851 would round to 32.49, and 32.4431 would round to 32.44.

6. Four track stars entered the mile race at the Penn Relays. Write a program that will read the last name and the race time in minutes and seconds for one runner and compute and print the speed in feet per

second and in meters per second after the runner's name. (Hints: There are 5280 feet in one mile, and one kilometer equals 3281 feet; one meter is equal to 3.281 feet.) Test your program on each of the times below.

Name	Minutes	Seconds
Deavers	3	52.83
Jackson	3	59.83
Smith	4	00.03
Rivera	4	16.22

Write and call a function that displays instructions to the program user. Write two other functions, one to compute the speed in meters per second and the other to compute the speed in feet per second.

7. A cyclist coasting on a level road slows from a speed of 10 miles/hr to 2.5 miles/hr in one minute. Write a computer program that calculates the cyclist's constant rate of deceleration and determines how long it will take the cyclist to come to rest, given an initial speed of 10 miles/hr. (Hint: Use the equation

$$a = (v_f - v_i) / t,$$

where a is acceleration, t is time interval, v_i is initial velocity, and v_f is the final velocity.) Write and call a function that displays instructions to the program user and another function that computes and returns the deceleration given v_f, v_i, and t.

8. In shopping for a new house, you must consider several factors. In this problem the initial cost of the house, estimated annual fuel costs, and annual tax rate are available. Write a program that will determine the total cost after a five-year period for each set of house data below. You should be able to inspect your program output to determine the "best buy."

Initial House Cost	Annual Fuel Cost	Tax Rate
$175,000	$2500	0.025
$200,000	$2800	0.025
$210,000	$2050	0.020

To calculate the house cost, add the fuel cost for five years to the initial cost, then add the taxes for five years. Taxes for one year are computed by multiplying the tax rate by the initial cost. Write and call a function that displays instructions to the program user and another function that computes and returns the house cost given the initial cost, the annual fuel cost, and the tax rate.

9. Write a program that reads a string containing exactly four words (separated by * symbols) into a single string object. Next, extract each word from the original string and store each word in a string object. Then concatenate the words in reverse order to form another string. Display both the original and final strings. (Hint: To extract the words, you should use the `find` member function to find each symbol *, assign the characters up to the * to one of the four string objects, and then remove those characters from the original string.)

10. Write a program to take a depth (in kilometers) inside the earth as input data; compute and display the temperature at this depth in degrees Celsius and Fahrenheit. The relevant formulas are

Celsius = 10 × (*depth*) + 20   (*Celsius temperature at depth in km*)
Fahrenheit = 1.8 × (*Celsius*) + 32

Include two functions in your program. Function `celsiusAtDepth` should compute and return the Celsius temperature at a depth measured in kilometers. Function `toFahrenheit` should convert a Celsius temperature to Fahrenheit.

11. The ratio between successive speeds of a six-speed gearbox (assuming that the gears are evenly spaced to allow for whole teeth) is

$$\sqrt[3]{M/m}$$

where M is the maximum speed in revolutions per minute and m is the minimum speed. Write a function `speedsRatio` that calculates this ratio for any maximum and minimum speeds. Write a `main` function that prompts for maximum and minimum speeds (rpm), calls `speedsRatio` to calculate the ratio, and displays the results.

12. Write a program that calculates and displays the volume of a box and the surface area of a box. The box dimensions are provided as input data. The volume is equal to the area of the base times the height of the box. Define and call a function `rectangleArea` to calculate the area of each rectangle in the box.

13. For any integer $n > 0$, $n!$ is defined as the product $n \times n - 1 \times n - 2 \ldots \times 2 \times 1$. 0! is defined to be 1. It is sometimes useful to have a closed-form definition instead; for this purpose, an approximation can be used. R.W. Gosper proposed the following such approximation formula:

$$n! \approx n^n e^{-n} \sqrt{\left(2n + \frac{1}{3}\right)\pi}$$

Create a program that prompts the user to enter an integer n, uses Gosper's formula to approximate $n!$, and then displays the result. The message displaying the result should look something like this:

```
5! equals approximately 119.97003
```

Your program will be easier to debug if you use some intermediate values instead of trying to compute the result in a single expression. If you are not getting the correct results, then you can compare the results of your intermediate values to what you get when you do the calculations by hand. Use at least two intermediate variables—one for $2n + \frac{1}{3}$ and one for $\sqrt{(2n + \frac{1}{3})\pi}$. Display each of these intermediate values to simplify debugging. Be sure to use a named constant for PI, and use the approximation 3.14159265. Test the program on non-negative integers less than 8.

14. Write a program that calculates the speed of sound (a) in air of a given temperature T (°F). Formula to compute the speed in ft/sec:

$$a = 1086\sqrt{\frac{5T + 297}{247}}$$

Be sure your program does not lose the fractional part of the quotient in the formula shown. As part of your solution, write and call a function that displays instructions to the program user.

15. After studying the population growth of Gotham City in the last decade of the twentieth century, we have modeled Gotham's population function as

$$P(t) = 52.966 + 2.184t$$

where t is years after 1990, and P is population in thousands. Thus, $P(0)$ represents the population in 1990, which was 52.966 thousand people. Write a program that defines a function named `population` that predicts Gotham's population in the year provided as an input argument. Write a program that calls the function and interacts with the user as follows:

```
Enter a year after 1990> 2015
Predicted Gotham City population for 2010 (in thousands):
107.566
```

Graphics Projects

16. Use graphics functions in programs that draw a rocket ship (triangle over rectangle over intersecting lines), a male stick figure (circle over rectangle over intersecting lines), and a female stick figure standing on the head of a male stick figure.

17. Redo Programming Project 2 using graphics mode.

18. Read in five values that represent the monthly amount spent on budget categories: food, clothing, transportation, entertainment, and rent. Write a program that displays a bar graph showing these values. In a bar graph, the length of each bar is proportional to the value it represents. Use a different color for each bar. (Hint: Multiply each value by the scale factor `maxy()` / `maxExpense`, where `MaxExpense` is the largest possible expense.

19. Redo Programming Project 18 using a pie chart. For the pie chart, the arc length of each section should be proportional to the amount it represents. Use a different fill pattern and color for each section.

20. Redo Programming Project 18 drawing a line graph. The first line should begin at the height representing the first budget category value and end at the height representing the second budget category value; the second line should begin at the height representing the second budget category value and end at the height representing the third budget category value; and so on.

Answers to Quick–Check Exercises

1. False; a function is only executed when it is called. It can execute more than once or not at all.

2. We declare function prototypes before function `main`. Next comes function `main` followed by any other function definitions. Within each function, we declare any local constants and variables that are defined only during the execution of that function.

3. An actual argument is listed in a function call; a formal parameter is used inside the function body to describe the function operation. When a function call executes, the value of each actual argument is passed into the corresponding formal parameter. Correspondence is determined by relative position in the lists of arguments and parameters (that is, the first actual argument corresponds to the first formal parameter, and so on).

4. An actual argument can be an expression but not a formal parameter.

5. A structure chart is a diagram used to show an algorithm's subproblems and their interdependence, so it shows the hierarchical relationship between subproblems. An algorithm lists the sequence in which subproblems are performed.

6. It would display a line of five stars, followed by a line showing the first argument, three exclamation points, and the second argument, followed by a line of five stars.

7. It displays the following:

```
*****
a!!!a
*****
*****
A!!!Z
*****
*****
!!!!!
*****
```

8. In dot notation, you write an object name, a dot, and a member function name. You use dot notation to apply the member function to the object that precedes the dot.

9. Allocate a `string` object `flower` and initialize it to `"rose"`.
   Change `flower` to `"rose of Sharon"`.
   Display `rS`.
   Display `2 8`.
   Change `flower` to `"rose from Sharon"`.
   Change `flower` to `" from Sharon"`.
   Change `flower` to `"thorn from Sharon"`.

10. A function prototype gives the C++ compiler enough information to translate each call to the function. The function definition provides a complete description of the function operation and is translated into machine language by the compiler. The prototype comes first; the definition must contain formal parameter names; the prototype ends with a semicolon.

11. `y = pow(exp(n * log(b)), 2);`

Mark Hall

Mark Hall is an expert on compilers. He works at Microsoft as the software architect for the Visual C++ compiler. Before that he was a computer scientist at Pyramid Technology. He received his B.S. in computer science from the College of William and Mary and his Ph.D. from the University of Colorado.

How did you decide to study computer science?
I remember filling out my college application in the kitchen of my parents' house. The application asked, "in what field do you expect to pursue a career?" I was a hopeless tinkerer as a kid, and when I saw the "computer design" option, I checked the box without hesitation. Of course, there was no checkbox for "software design" at that time, and I wouldn't have checked it if there was one, because I had no idea what value software could possibly have. I was thinking purely hardware. In fact, my first week in an introductory programming course was quite a struggle for me. I was a math major in high school, and I just couldn't fathom what $x = x + 1$ could possibly mean. Then one night I was in the card punch room in the basement of the math building, and a little voice said, "You dummy, that's assignment, not equality," and the true nature of computers was revealed to me. I was shocked! Until then I thought computers were sophisticated, but you had to instruct them to do even the simplest task. The real

sophistication was in the software. When I realized you could get from $x = x + 1$ to the video game Galaxians on the same piece of hardware, I knew my career would be in software. I was hooked. I could tinker in software to my heart's delight and build anything I wanted.

In my fourth year of college I took the first compiler course offered at my school. The fact that a compiler was a software program that read other software programs, *including itself*, was totally mind-blowing. Then, one fateful day we studied DeRemer's thesis on constructing LR(k) parsers, and when the professor built the parse states for a grammar on the board, my jaw just hung open. I kept saying, "No way!" I've been working in the compiler field ever since.

Describe your work at Microsoft.
Every day is basically a balancing act between standard's conformance, bugs, new features, and platform support. Customers rightfully want it all, and they think Microsoft is big enough to deliver it all. But it's actually pretty

difficult to hire and retain gifted compiler developers. It really has to be in your blood, because it isn't the most glamorous or hip software job at Microsoft (just think about Xbox, for example). Plus, our product offers so much functionality. Just compiling the language is challenging, but when you add in all the visualization tools like IntelliSense, wizards, designers, browsers, and debuggers, you're talking about many millions of lines of code. At the end of the day, we try to maximize the overall customer benefit of our work.

Lately I've been very busy thinking about the productivity enhancements we want to deliver to C++ programmers over the next decade. The C++ developer is a precious commodity. The vast majority of all revenue in the software business derives from programs written in C++. Fortunately, we have many great ideas for enhancing the development process. The great thing about Microsoft is how the company wants you to make the big, long-term bets. That's why I like working here.

What is the most challenging part of your job?

I'd say the most difficult part of the job for me is making the hard tradeoffs needed to ship the product. We have limited resources, competitive pressures, and changing markets, so we never get to implement all of the features or fix all the bugs we want to. This is frustrating, but at some point the customer needs the product and the access it provides to the new platform features.

Do you have any advice about programming in C++?

Yes. My advice is, "Don't be afraid to program in C++." C++ has gotten a bad rap for being too complex. But some of that complexity is useful. I have attended many design meetings for technology frameworks that ironically are more complex than they need to be because the implementation language lacked features available in C++. Let's face it: software is an intellectual pursuit. If you're solving hard problems in software, you need a sophisticated tool. Hammers and screwdrivers are simple, and you can probably build a car with them, but why would you want to? And remember: you don't always have to use all the power of C++ to solve every problem, nor should you. It's quite easy to write simple, easy-to-read code in C++.

How do you see Visual C++ evolving over the next few years?

I see a lot of productivity enhancements coming. Visualization and code analysis tools will become much more powerful and precise. This will happen because the compiler itself will fundamentally change from a monolithic program to a set of services that are available to everyone. That will spawn an unprecedented ecology of C++ development tools. I think the language itself will evolve in response to the demand for new and better tools.

Selection Structures: `if` and `switch` Statements

Chapter Objectives

- To become familiar with the 3 kinds of control structures: sequence, selection, repetition and to understand compound statements
- To learn how to compare numbers, characters, and strings
- To learn how to use the relational, equality, and logical operators to write expressions that are type bool (true or false)
- To learn how to write selection statements with one and two alternatives using the if statement
- To learn how to implement decisions in algorithms using the `if` statement
- To understand how to select among more than two alternatives by nesting `if` statements
- To learn how to use the switch statement as another technique for selecting among multiple alternatives

THIS BOOK TEACHES a disciplined approach that results in programs that are easy to read and less likely to contain errors. An important element of this technique is the use of top-down design to divide an algorithm into individual steps. We can use a small number of control structures to code the individual algorithm steps.

At this point, we've used just one of these control mechanisms, sequence. In this chapter and the next, we'll introduce two other important control structures: selection and repetition.

This chapter will also show how to use the C++ if and switch statements to select one group of statements for execution from several alternative groups. These control statements will allow a program to evaluate its data and to select a path of execution to follow based on the data. The chapter also discusses conditions and logical expressions, which the `if` statement relies on.

4.1   Control Structures

control structure
A combination of individual instructions into a single logical unit with one entry point and one exit point that regulates the flow of execution in a program.

Control structures regulate the flow of execution in a program or function, combining individual instructions into a single logical unit with one entry point and one exit point. There are three categories of control structures for controlling execution flow: (1) *sequence*, (2) *selection*, and (3) *repetition*. Until now, we've been using only sequential flow. A **compound statement,** written as a group of statements bracketed by { and }, is used to specify sequential control.

compound statement
A group of statements bracketed by { and } that are executed sequentially.

```
{
    statement₁;
    statement₂;
        .
        .
        .
    statementₙ;
}
```

Sequential flow means that each statement is executed in sequence, starting with *statement₁*, followed by *statement₂*, and so on through *statementₙ*.

selection control
A control structure that chooses among alternative program statements.

This chapter describes how to write algorithms and programs that use **selection control,** a control structure that enables the program to execute one of several alternative statements or groups of statements. With selection control, flow doesn't necessarily follow from one statement to the next as in sequential control, but may skip some statements and execute others based on selection criteria.

4.2   Logical Expressions

In C++, the primary selection control structure is the `if` statement. We can use an `if` statement to select from several alternative executable statements. For example, the `if` statement

```
if (weight > 100.00)
   shipCost = 10.00;
else
   shipCost = 5.00;
```

selects one of the two assignment statements listed by testing the condition `weight > 100.00`. If the condition is true (`weight` is greater than `100.00`), it selects the statement `shipCost = 10.00;`. If the condition is false (`weight` is not greater than `100.00`), it selects the statement `shipCost = 5.00;`. It is never possible for both assignment statements to execute after testing a particular condition.

In order to write `if` statements, we must first understand how to write the conditions that the `if` statement relies on to make a selection.

Logical Expressions Using Relational and Equality Operators

A program selects among alternative statements by testing the value of key variables. In C++, **logical expressions**, or **conditions**, are used to perform such tests. Each logical expression has two possible values, `true` or `false`. Such an expression is called a condition because it establishes a criterion for either executing or skipping a group of statements.

logical expression (condition) An expression that is either true or false.

Most conditions that we use to perform comparisons will have one of these forms:

variable   relational-operator   variable
variable   relational-operator   constant
variable   equality-operator   variable
variable   equality-operator   constant

Table 4.1 lists the relational and equality operators. Be careful not to confuse the assignment operator (single =) with the equality operator (double ==).

Table 4.1   Relational and Equality Operators

Operator	Meaning	Type
<	less than	relational
>	greater than	relational
<=	less than or equal to	relational
>=	greater than or equal to	relational
==	equal to	equality
!=	not equal to	equality

EXAMPLE 4.1

Table 4.2 shows some sample conditions in C++. Each condition is evaluated assuming these variable and constant values:

x	power	maxPower	y	item	minItem	momOrDad
-5	1024	1024	7	1.5	-999.0	'm'

Table 4.2   Sample Conditions

Operator	Condition	English Meaning	Value
<=	x <= 0	x less than or equal to 0	true
<	power < maxPower	power less than `maxPower`	false
>=	x >= y	x greater than or equal to y	false
>	item > minItem	item greater than `minItem`	true
==	momOrDad == 'm'	momOrDad equal to 'm'	true
!=	num != sentinel	num not equal to `sentinel`	false

Logical Expressions Using Logical Operators

With the three logical operators—`&&` (and), `||` (or), `!` (not)—we can form more complicated conditions or compound logical expressions. Examples of logical expressions formed with the `&&` (and) and `||` (or) operators are

```
(salary < minSalary) || (dependents > 5)
(temperature > 90.0) && (humidity > 0.90)
```

The first logical expression determines whether an employee is eligible for special scholarship funds. It evaluates to `true` if *either* the condition

```
(salary < minSalary)
```

or the condition

```
(dependents > 5)
```

is true. The second logical expression describes an unbearable summer day, with temperature and humidity both in the nineties. The expression evaluates to true only when *both* conditions are true.

The operands of `||` and `&&` are themselves logical expressions and each has a type `bool` value (`true` or `false`). The compound logical expression also has a type `bool` value. None of the parentheses used in these expressions are required; they are used here just for clarity.

The third logical operator, `!` (not), has a single type `bool` operand and yields the **logical complement, or negation,** of its operand (that is, if the variable `positive` is `true`, `!positive` is `false` and vice versa). The logical expression

```
winningRecord && (!probation)
```

manipulates two bool variables (`winningRecord, probation`). A college team for which this expression is true has a winning record and is not on probation, so it may be eligible for the postseason tournament. Note that the expression

```
(winningRecord == true) && (probation == false)
```

is logically equivalent to the one above; however, the first one is preferred because it's more concise and more readable.

Simple expressions such as

```
x == y
x < y
```

can be negated by applying the unary operator `!` to the entire expression.

```
!(x == y)
!(x < y)
```

However, using the logical complement of the relational operator often works just as well in these situations:

```
x != y
x >= y
```

The best time to use the `!` operator is when you want to reverse the value of a long or complicated logical expression that involves many operators. For example, expressions such as

```
(salary < minSalary) || (numberDependents > 5)
```

are most easily negated by enclosing the entire expression in parentheses and preceding it with the `!` operator.

```
!((salary < minSalary) || (numberDependents > 5))
```

logical complement (negation) The logical complement of a condition has the value true when the condition's value is false; the logical complement of a condition has the value false when the condition's value is true.

Table 4.3 shows that the `&&` operator (and) yields a true result only when both its operands are true. Table 4.4 shows that the `||` operator (or) yields a false result only when both its operands are false. The `not` operator `!` has a single operand; Table 4.5 shows that the `not` operator yields the logical complement, or negation, of its operand (that is, if `flag` is `true`, `!flag` is `false` and vice versa). Remember to use logical operators only with logical expressions.

Operator Precedence

The precedence of an operator determines its order of evaluation in an expression. Table 4.6 shows the precedence from highest to lowest of all C++ operators you've seen so far. The unary operators (including `!`) have the highest precedence followed by the arithmetic, relational, equality operators, and then the binary logical operators. To prevent errors and to clarify the meaning of expressions, use parentheses freely.

Table 4.3   `&&` Operator

Operand$_1$	Operand$_2$	Operand$_1$ `&&` Operand$_2$
true	true	true
true	false	false
false	true	false
false	false	false

Table 4.4   `||` Operator

Operand$_1$	Operand$_2$	Operand$_1$ `||` Operand$_2$
true	true	true
true	false	true
false	true	true
false	false	false

Table 4.5   `!` Operator

Operand	`!`Operand
true	false
false	true

Table 4.6 Operator Precedence

Operator	Precedence	Description
`!, +, -`	Highest	Logical not, unary plus, unary minus
`*, /, %`		Multiplication, division, modulus
`+, -`		Addition, subtraction
`<, <=, >=, >`		Relational inequality
`==, !=`		Equal, not equal
`&&`		Logical and
`||`		Logical or
`=`	Lowest	Assignment

The expression

```
x < min + max
```

involving the `float` variables `x`, `min`, and `max` is interpreted correctly in C++ as

```
x < (min + max)
```

because + has higher precedence than <. The expression

```
min <= x && x <= max
```

is also correct, but providing the extra parentheses

```
(min <= x) && (x <= max)
```

makes the expression clearer.

Because ! has higher precedence than ==, C++ incorrectly interprets the expression

```
!x == y
```

as

```
(!x) == y
```

To avoid this error, insert the parentheses where needed:

```
!(x == y)
```

EXAMPLE 4.2

Expressions 1 to 4 below contain different operands and operators. Each expression's value is given in the corresponding comment, assuming `x`, `y`, and `z` are type `float`, `flag` is type `bool`, and the variables have the values:

x	y	z	flag
3.0	4.0	2.0	false

1. `!flag`   `// !false is true`
2. `x + y / z <= 3.5`   `// 5.0 <= 3.5 is false`
3. `!flag || (y + z >= x - z)`   `// true || true is true`
4. `!(flag || (y + z >= x - z))`   `// !(false || true) is false`

Figure 4.1 shows the evaluation tree and step-by-step evaluation for expression 3.

Writing Conditions in C++

To solve programming problems, you must convert conditions expressed in English to C++. Many algorithm steps require testing to see if a variable's value is within a specified range of values. For example, if `min` represents the lower bound of a range of values and `max` represents the upper bound (`min` is less than `max`), the expression

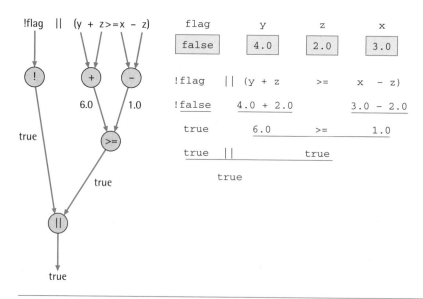

Figure 4.1   Evaluation tree and step-by-step evaluation of `!flag || (y + z >= x - z)`

```
(min <= x) && (x <= max)
```

tests whether x lies within the range min through max, inclusive. In Figure 4.2, this range is shaded. The expression is true if x lies within this range and false if x is outside the range.

min   max   x

Figure 4.2   Range of true values for (min <= x) && (x <= max)

EXAMPLE 4.3

Table 4.7 shows some English conditions and their corresponding C++ expressions. Each expression is evaluated assuming x is 3.0, y is 4.0, and z is 2.0.

The first logical expression shows the C++ code for the English condition "x and y are greater than z." You may be tempted to write this as

```
x && y > z       // invalid logical expression
```

However, if you apply the precedence rules to this expression, you quickly see that it doesn't have the intended meaning. Also, the type float variable x is an invalid operand for the logical operator &&.

The third logical expression shows the C++ code for the mathematical relationship $z \le x \le y$. The boundary values, 2.0 and 4.0, are included in the range of x values that yield a true result.

The last table entry shows a pair of logical expressions that are true when x is outside the range bounded by z and y. We get the first expression in the pair by complementing the expression just above it. The second expression states that x is outside the range if z is larger than x or x is larger than y. In

Table 4.7   English Conditions as C++ Expressions

English Condition	Logical Expression	Evaluation
x and y are greater than z	(x > z) && (y > z)	true && true is true
x is equal to 1.0 or 3.0	(x == 1.0) || (x == 3.0)	false || true is true
x is in the range z to y, inclusive	(z <= x) && (x <= y)	true && true is true
x is outside the range z to y	!(z <= x && x <= y)	!(true && true) is false
	(z > x) || (x > y)	false || false is false

Figure 4.3, the shaded areas represent the values of x that yield a true result. Both y and z are excluded from the set of values that yield a true result.

Figure 4.3   Range of true values for `(z > x) || (x > y)`

Comparing Characters and Strings

In addition to comparing numbers, it's also possible to compare characters and strings of characters using the relational and equality operators. Several examples of such comparisons are shown in Table 4.8.

In writing such comparisons, you can assume that both the uppercase and lowercase letters appear in alphabetical order, and that the *digit characters* are ordered as expected: `'0' < '1' < '2' < . . . < '9'`. For the relationships among other characters (such as `'+'`, `'<'`, `'!'`, etc.) or between two characters not in the same group (for example, `'a'` and `'A'`, or `'B'` and `'b'`, or `'c'` and `'A'`), see Appendix A.

If you include library `string`, you can compare `string` objects (see the last four examples in Table 4.8). C++ compares two strings by comparing corresponding pairs of characters in each string, starting with the leftmost pair. The result is based on the relationship between the first pair of different characters (for example, for `"acts"` and `"aces"`, the result depends on characters t and e). The last comparison involves a string (`"aces"`) that begins with a shorter *substring* (`"ace"`). The substring `"ace"` is considered less than the longer string `"aces"`. We'll say more about character comparisons in Chapter 7.

Table 4.8   Examples of Comparisons

Expression	Value
`'a' < 'c'`	true
`'X' <= 'A'`	false
`'3' > '4'`	false
`('A' <= ch) && (ch <= 'Z')`	true if ch contains an uppercase letter; otherwise false
`"XYZ" <= "ABC"`	false (X <= A)
`"acts" > "aces"`	true (t > e)
`"ace" != "aces"`	true (strings are different)
`"ace" < "aces"`	true (shorter string is smaller)

Boolean Assignment

Assignment statements can be written to assign a type `bool` value to a `bool` variable. If same is type `bool`, the statement

    same = true;

assigns the value `true` to same. Since assignment statements have the general form

    variable = expression;

you can use the statement

    same = (x == y);

to assign the value of the logical expression (x == y) to same. The value of same is `true` when x and y are equal; otherwise, same is `false`.

EXAMPLE 4.4

The following assignment statements assign values to two type `bool` variables, inRange and isLetter. Variable inRange gets `true` if the value of n is between −10 and 10; variable isLetter gets `true` if ch is an uppercase or a lowercase letter.

    inRange = (n > -10) && (n < 10);
    isLetter = (('A' <= ch) && (ch <= 'Z')) ||
               (('a' <= ch) && (ch <= 'z'));

The expression in the first assignment statement is `true` if n satisfies both conditions listed (n is greater than 210 and n is less than 10); otherwise, the expression is `false`. The expression in the second assignment statement uses the logical operators &&, ||. The first subexpression (before ||) is `true` if ch is an uppercase letter; the second subexpression (after ||) is true if ch is a lowercase letter. Consequently, isLetter gets `true` if ch is either an uppercase or lowercase letter; otherwise, isLetter gets `false`.

EXAMPLE 4.5

The statement below assigns the value `true` to even if n is an even number:

    even = (n % 2 == 0);

Because all even numbers are divisible by 2, the remainder of n divided by 2 (the C++ expression n % 2) is 0 when n is an even number. The expression in parentheses above compares the remainder to 0, so its value is `true` when the remainder is 0 and its value is `false` when the remainder is nonzero.

Writing `bool` Values

Most logical expressions appear in control structures, where they determine the sequence in which C++ statements execute. You'll rarely have a need to read `bool` values as input data or display `bool` values as program results. If necessary, however, you can display the value of a `bool` variable using the output operator `<<`. If `flag` is `false`, the statement

```
cout << "The value of flag is " << flag;
```

displays the line

```
The value of flag is 0
```

If you need to read a data value into a type `bool` variable, you can represent the data as an integer; use 0 for `false` and 1 for `true`.

Using Integers to Represent Logical Values

Earlier C++ compilers did not implement type `bool`. Instead they used the `int` data type to model type `bool` data. Internally C++ uses the integer value 0 to represent `false` and any nonzero integer value (usually 1) to represent `true`. A logical expression that evaluates to 0 is considered false; a logical expression that evaluates to nonzero is considered true.

EXERCISES FOR SECTION 4.2

Self-Check

1. Assuming `x` is 15 and `y` is 10, what are the values of the following conditions?

    a. `x != y`   **b.** `x < y`   **c.** `x >= (y - x)`   **d.** `x == (y + x - y)`

2. Evaluate each expression below if a is 10, b is 12, c is 8, and `flag` is false.

    a. `(c == (a * b)) || !flag`

    b. `(a != 7) && flag || ((a + c) <= 20)`

    c. `!(b <= 12) && (a % 2 == 0)`

    d. `!((a < 5) || (c < (a + b)))`

3. Evaluate the following logical expressions. Assume `x` and `y` are type `float` and `p`, `q`, and `r` are type `bool`. The value of `q` is `false`. Why is it not necessary to know the value of `x`, `y`, `p`, `q`, or `r`?

    a. `x < 5.1 || x >= 5.1 || y != 0`

    b. `p && q || q && r`

4. Draw evaluation trees for the following:

   a. `a == (b + a - c)`

   b. `(c == (a + b)) || !flag`

   c. `(a <> 7) && (c >=6) || flag`

   d. `!flag && a > b || c < d`

Programming

1. Write a logical expression that is true for each of the following conditions.

   a. gender is `'m'` or `'M'` and age is greater than or equal to 62 or gender is `'f'` or `'F'` and age is greater than or equal to 65.

   b. water is greater than 0.1 and also less than 1.5.

   c. year is divisible by 4 but not divisible by 100. (Hint: use %.)

   d. speed is not greater than 55.

   e. temp below freezing and windSpeed over 20 knots

2. Write logical assignment statements for the following:

   a. Assign true to between if n is in the range -k and +k, inclusive; otherwise, assign a value of false.

   b. Assign true to lowercase if ch is a lowercase letter; otherwise, assign a value of false.

   c. Assign true to isDigit if next is a digit character ('0' through '9', inclusive).

   d. Assign true to divisor if m is a divisor of n; otherwise assign a value of false.

   e. Assign true to isLeapYear if year is divisible by 400 or if year is divisible by 4 but not by 100. For example, 2000 is a leap year, 2004 is a leap year, 2008 is a leap year . . . but 2100 is not a leap year. Every fourth century is a leap year (2000, 2400, 2800, and so on).

   f. Assign true to isOp if ch is one of the characters `+, -, *, /, %`.

4.3   Introduction to the `if` Control Statement

You now know how to write a C++ expression that is the equivalent of a question such as "is x an even number?" Next, we need to investigate a way to use the value of the expression to select a course of action. In C++, the if statement is the primary selection control structure.

`if` Statement with Two Alternatives

The `if` statement

```
if (gross > 100.00)
    net = gross - tax;
else
    net = gross;
```

selects one of the two assignment statements listed. It selects the statement immediately following the condition (`gross > 100.00`) if the condition is true (that is, `gross` is greater than `100.00`); it selects the statement following the reserved word `else` if the logical expression is false (that is, `gross` is not greater than `100.00`). It is never possible for both statements to execute after testing a particular condition. You must always enclose the condition in parentheses, but must not place a semicolon after the condition.

flowchart
A diagram that shows the step-by-step execution of a control structure

Figure 4.4 provides a **flowchart**—a diagram that uses boxes and arrows to show the step-by-step execution of a control structure—for the `if` control statement above. A diamond-shaped box in a flowchart represents a decision. There's always one path into a decision and there are two paths out (labeled true and false).

The figure shows that the condition (`gross > 100.00`) enclosed in the diamond-shaped box is evaluated first. If the condition is true, program control follows the arrow labeled true, and the assignment statement in the rectangle on the right is executed. If the condition is false, program control

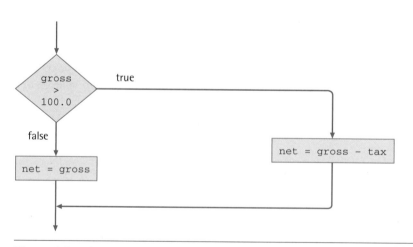

Figure 4.4   Flowchart of `if` statement with two alternatives

follows the arrow labeled false, and the assignment statement in the rectangle on the left is executed.

if Statement with Dependent Statement

The if statement above has two alternatives, but only one will be executed for a given value of gross. Example 4.6 illustrates that an if statement can also have a single alternative that is executed only when the condition is true.

EXAMPLE 4.6

The if statement below has one dependent statement that is executed only when x is not equal to zero. It causes **product** to be multiplied by x; the new value is saved in **product**, replacing the old value. If x is equal to zero, the multiplication is not performed. Figure 4.5 shows a flowchart for this if statement.

```
// Multiply product by a non zero x only.
if (x != 0)
      product = product * x;
```

---

if Statement Conditions with Characters and Strings

The if statements in the next few examples evaluate conditions with character or string operands.

In all our examples so far, the true and false alternatives of an if statement consist of a single C++ statement. In the next section, we'll see how to write true and false tasks consisting of more than one statement.

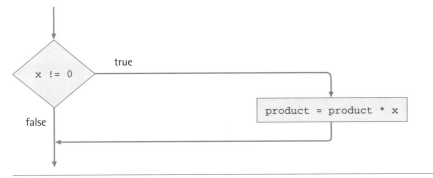

Figure 4.5 Flowchart of if statement with a dependent statement

EXAMPLE 4.7

The `if` statement below has two alternatives. It displays either `"Hi Mom"` or `"Hi Dad"` depending on the character stored in variable `momOrDad` (type `char`).

```
if (momOrDad == 'm')
    cout << "Hi Mom" << endl;
else
    cout << "Hi Dad" << endl;
```

EXAMPLE 4.8

The `if` statement below has one dependent statement; it displays the message `"Hi Mom"` only when `momOrDad` has the value `'m'`. Regardless of whether or not `"Hi Mom"` is displayed, the message `"Hi Dad"` is always displayed.

```
if (momOrDad == 'm')
    cout << "Hi Mom" << endl;
cout << "Hi Dad" << endl;
```

EXAMPLE 4.9

The `if` statement below displays the result of a string search operation. If the search string is found, the position is printed; otherwise, a message is printed indicating that the search string was not found. The call to `string` member function `find` (see Table 3.3) returns to `posTarget` (type `int`) the starting position in `testString` (type `string`) of `target` (type `string`). If `target` is not found, `find` returns a value that is not in the allowable range (0 through $k-1$ where k is the length of `testString`). The if statement tests whether the value returned to `posTarget` is in range before reporting the search result. If `testString` is `"This is a string"` and `target` is `"his"`, the `if` statement would display `his found at position 1`.

```
posTarget = testString.find(target);
if ((0 <= posTarget) && (posTarget < testString.length()))
    cout << target << " found at position " << posTarget
        << endl;
else
    cout << target << " not found!" << endl;
```

EXAMPLE 4.10

The next `if` statement replaces one substring (`target`) with another (`newString`). If `target` is found in `testString`, function `find` returns the position of `target`. The condition will be true and the **true task** (following the condition) of the `if` statement replaces it with `newString`. Recall that the three arguments of `string` member function `replace` (see Table 3.3) are the starting position of the string to be replaced (`posTarget`), the number of characters to be removed (`target.length()`), and the replacement string (`newString`). If `testString` is `"This is a string"`, `target` is `"his"`, and `newString` is `"here"`, `testString` will become `"There is a string"`. If the condition is false, the **false task** (following the word `else`) displays a message.

true task
Statement(s) after the condition that execute when the condition is true.

false task
Statement(s) after `else` that execute when the condition is false.

```
posTarget = testString.find(target);
if ((0 <= posTarget) && (posTarget < testString.length()))
    testString.replace(posTarget, target.length(),
                       newString);
else
    cout << target << " not found - no replacement!" << endl;
```

Format of the `if` Statement

In all the `if` statement examples, *statement*$_T$ and *statement*$_F$ are indented. If you use the word `else`, enter it on a separate line, aligned with the word `if`. The format of the `if` statement makes its meaning apparent. Again, this is done solely to improve program readability; the format used makes no difference to the compiler.

`if` Statement with Dependent Statement

Form: `if` (*condition*)
            statement$_T$

Example: `if (x > 0.0)`
            `positiveProduct = positiveProduct * x;`

Interpretation: If the *condition* evaluates to true, then *statement*$_T$ is executed; otherwise, it is skipped.

---

if Statement with Two Alternatives

Form: `if` (*condition*)
                 statement$_T$
             `else`
                 statement$_F$

Example: `if (x >= 0.0)`
                 `cout << "Positive" << endl;`
             `else`
                 `cout << "Negative" << endl;`

Interpretation: If the *condition* evaluates to true, then *statement$_T$* is executed and *statement$_F$* is skipped; otherwise, *statement$_T$* is skipped and *statement$_F$* is executed.

EXERCISES FOR SECTION 4.3

Self–Check

1. What does the following fragment in part a display when x is 10? When x is 20? What does the fragment in part b display?

   a. ```
       if (x < 12)
           cout << "less" << endl;
       else
           cout << "done" << endl;
       ```

   b.  ```
       var1 = 15.0;
       var2 = 25.12;
       if (2 * var1 >= var2)
           cout << "O.K." << endl;
       else
           cout << "Not O.K." << endl;
       ```

2. What value is assigned to x for each segment below when y is 10.0?

   a. ```
       x = 20.0;
       if (y != (x - 10.0))
           x = x - 10.0;
       else
           x = x / 2.0;
       ```

   b.  ```
       if (y < 5.0 && y >= 0.0)
           x = 5 + y;
       else
           x = 2 - y;
       ```

3. Trace the execution of the if statement in Example 4.10 for the values of target and newString below. For each part, assume testString is "Here is the string" before the if statement executes.
   a. target is "the", newString is "that"
   b. target is "Here", newString is "There"
   c. target is "Where", newString is "There"

Programming

1. Write C++ statements to carry out the steps below.

   a. Store the absolute difference of x and y in result, where the absolute difference is (x - y) or (y - x), whichever is positive. Don't use the abs or fabs function in your solution.
   b. If x is zero, add 1 to zeroCount. If x is negative, add x to minusSum. If x is greater than zero, add x to plusSum.

2. Write your own absolute value function that returns the absolute value of its input argument.

3. Write an if statement that stores the value of a + b in result if the character stored in op is '+'; otherwise, it stores −1.0 in result. Variables a, b, and result are type float.

4. Write an if statement that displays the value of a / b if b is not zero; otherwise, it displays the message quotient not defined.

4.4 if Statements with Compound Alternatives

So far, we've seen if statements in which only one statement executes in either the true case or the false case. You may also write if statements that execute a series of steps by using compound statements, statements bracketed by { }. When the symbol { follows the condition or the keyword else, the C++ compiler either executes or skips all statements through the matching }. Assignment statements, function call statements, or even other if statements may appear in these alternatives.

EXAMPLE 4.11

Suppose you're a biologist studying the growth rate of fruit flies. The if statement

```
if (popToday > popYesterday)
{
    growth = popToday - popYesterday;
    growthPct = 100.0 * growth / popYesterday;
    cout << "The growth percentage is " << growthPct;
}
```

computes the population growth from yesterday to today as a percentage of yesterday's population. The compound statement after the condition executes only when today's population is larger than yesterday's. The first assignment computes the increase in the fruit fly population, and the second assignment converts it to a percentage of the original population, which is displayed.

EXAMPLE 4.12

As the manager of a clothing boutique, you want to keep records of your financial transactions, which can be either payments you make for goods received or deposits made to your checking account. Payments are designated by a `transactionType` value of `'c'`. The true task in the `if` statement below processes a payment; the false task processes a deposit. In both cases, an appropriate message is printed and the account balance is updated. Both the true and false statements are compound statements.

```
if (transactionType == 'c')
{   // process check
    cout << "Check for $" << transactionAmount << endl;
    balance = balance - transactionAmount;
}
else
{   // process deposit
    cout << "Deposit of $" << transactionAmount << endl;
    balance = balance + transactionAmount;
}
```

PROGRAM STYLE   Writing `if` Statements with Compound True or False Statements

Each `if` statement in this section contains at least one compound statement bracketed by { }. The placement of the braces is a stylistic preference. Your instructor may want the opening { at the end of the same line as the condition. The closing } of a compound `if` may also appear on the same line as the `else`:

```
} else {
```

Some programmers prefer to use braces even when the statement following `if` or `else` is a single statement. This way all `if` statements look the same, and there will be no danger of forgetting braces when needed. Whichever style you choose, be consistent in its use.

Tracing an `if` Statement

A critical step in program design is to verify that an algorithm or C++ statement is correct before you spend extensive time coding or debugging it.

Often a few extra minutes spent in verifying the correctness of an algorithm saves hours of coding and testing time.

A **hand trace**, or **desk check**, is a careful, step-by-step simulation on paper of how the computer executes the algorithm or statement. The results of this simulation should show the effect of each step's execution using data that are relatively easy to process by hand. We illustrate this next.

hand trace (desk check)
The step-by-step simulation of an algorithm's execution.

EXAMPLE 4.13

In many programming problems you must order a pair of data values in memory so that the smaller value is stored in one variable (say, x) and the larger value in another (say, y). The next if statement rearranges any two values stored in x and y so that the smaller number is in x and the larger number is in y. If the two numbers are already in the proper order, the compound statement is not executed.

```
if (x > y)
{                 // exchange values in x and y
    temp = x;     // store original value of x in temp
    x = y;        // store original value of y in x
    y = temp;     // store original value of x in y
}
```

Although the values of x and y are being switched, an additional variable, temp, is needed to store a copy of one of these values. Variables x, y, and temp should all be the same data type.

Table 4.9 traces the execution of this if statement when x is 12.5 and y is 5.0. The table shows that temp is initially undefined (indicated by ?). Each line of the table shows the part of the if statement that is being executed, followed by its effect. If any variable gets a new value, its new value is shown on that line. If no new value is shown, the variable retains its previous value. The last value stored in x is 5.0, and the last value stored in y is 12.5.

The trace in Table 4.9 shows that 5.0 and 12.5 are correctly stored in x and y when the condition is true. To verify that the if statement is correct, you should select other data that cause the condition to evaluate to false. Also, you should verify that the statement is correct for special situations. For example, what would happen if x were equal to y? Would the statement still provide the correct result? To complete the hand trace, you would need to show that the algorithm handles this special situation properly.

In tracing each case, you must be careful to execute the statement step-by-step exactly as the computer would execute it. Often programmers assume how a particular step will be executed and don't explicitly test each condition and trace each step. A trace performed in this way is of little value.

Table 4.9 Step-by-Step Hand Trace of `if` Statement

Statement Part	x	y	temp	Effect
	12.5	5.0	?	
`if (x > y)`				12.5 > 5.0 is true
`{`				
`  temp = x;`			12.5	Store x in temp
`  x = y;`	5.0			Store original y in x
`  y = temp;`		12.5		Store original x in y
`}`				

EXERCISES FOR SECTION 4.4

Self-Check

1. Insert braces where needed below to avoid syntax or logic errors. Indent as needed to improve readability. The last statement should execute regardless of the value of x or y.

```
if (x > y)

x = x + 10.0;
cout << "x bigger than y" << endl;

else

    y = y + 10.0;
cout << "x smaller than y" << endl;
cout << "x is " << x
        << "y is " << y << endl;
```

2. What would be the syntax error in Self-Check Exercise 1?

3. What would be the effect of placing braces around the last three statements in Self-Check Exercise 1?

4. Correct the following `if` statement:

```
if (num1 < 0)
{
    product = num1 * num2 * num3;
    cout << "Product is " << product << endl;
else
    sum = num1 + num2 + num3;
    cout << "Sum is " << sum << endl;
}
```

Programming

1. Write an `if` statement that assigns to `ave` the average of a set of n numbers when n is greater than 0. If n is not greater than 0, assign 0 to `ave` and display an error message. The average should be computed by dividing `total` by n.

2. Write an interactive program that contains a compound `if` statement and may be used to compute the area of a square (area = side^2) or triangle (area = $1/2 \times$ base $\times$ height) after prompting the user to type the first character of the figure name (`t` or `s`).

4.5 Decision Steps in Algorithms

Algorithm steps that select from a choice of actions are called **decision steps.** The algorithm in the following case contains decision steps to compute an employee's gross and net pay after deductions. The decision steps are coded as `if` statements.

decision step
An algorithm step that selects one of several alternatives.

case study **Payroll Problem with Functions**

STATEMENT

Your company pays its hourly workers once a week. An employee's pay is based upon the number of hours worked (to the nearest half hour) and the employee's hourly pay rate. Weekly hours exceeding 40 are paid at a rate of time and a half. Employees who earn over $100 a week must pay union dues of $15 per week. Write a payroll program that will determine the gross pay and net pay for an employee.

ANALYSIS

The problem data include the input data for hours worked and hourly pay, and two required outputs: gross pay and net pay. There are also several constants: the union dues ($15), the minimum weekly earnings before dues must be paid ($100), the maximum hours before overtime must be paid (40), and the overtime rate (1.5 times the usual hourly rate). With this information, we can begin to write the data requirements for this problem. We can model all data using the `float` data types.

DATA REQUIREMENTS

Problem Constants

```
MAX_NO_DUES = 100.00      // maximum earnings (dollars) without
                          // paying union dues
```

```
DUES = 15.00              // union dues (dollars) to be paid
MAX_NO_OVERTIME = 40.0    // maximum hours without overtime pay
OVERTIME_RATE = 1.5       // time and a half for overtime
```

Problem Input

```
float hours    // hours worked
float rate     // hourly rate
```

Problem Output

```
float gross    // gross pay
float net      // net pay
```

PROGRAM DESIGN

The problem solution requires that the program read the hours worked and the hourly rate before performing any computations. After reading these data, we need to compute and then display the gross pay and net pay.

The structure chart for this problem (Figure 4.6) shows the decomposition of the original problem into five subproblems. We'll write three of the subproblems as functions. For these three subproblems, the corresponding function name appears under its box in the structure chart.

We added to the structure chart *data flow* information that shows the input and output of each program step. The structure chart shows that the step *enter data* provides values for hours and rate as its output (data flow arrow points up). Similarly, the step *compute gross pay* uses hours and rate as input to the function (data flow arrow points down) and provides gross as the function output.

We can now write the initial algorithm.

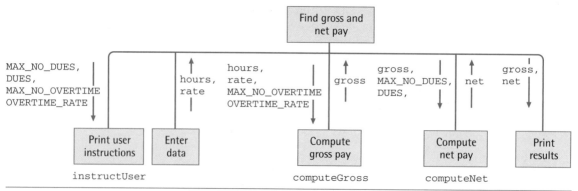

Figure 4.6   Structure chart for payroll problem

INITIAL ALGORITHM

1. Display user instructions (function `instructUser`).

2. Enter hours worked and hourly rate.

3. Compute gross pay (function `computeGross`).

4. Compute net pay (function `computeNet`).

5. Display gross pay and net pay.

We now focus on the three lower-level functions listed in parentheses in the algorithm. We begin by defining the interfaces between these functions and the main function.

ANALYSIS AND DESIGN FOR **INSTRUCTUSER** (ALGORITHM STEP 1)

In our analysis of the lower-level functions, we'll assume that the constant identifiers `MAX_NO_DUES`, `DUES`, `MAX_NO_OVERTIME`, and `OVERTIME_RATE` are declared before function `main`. This makes them **global constants,** which means that their values can be referenced in all functions without the need to pass them as arguments.

global constant
A constant declared before function `main` that can be referenced in all functions.

INTERFACE FOR `instructUser`

Input Arguments

(none)

Function Return Value

(none—a void function)
This function simply displays a short list of instructions and information about the program for the user. The information includes the values of the four program constants and other information to ensure that the user has an overview of what the program does and how the user should enter the input data.

ANALYSIS AND DESIGN FOR **COMPUTEGROSS** (ALGORITHM STEP 3)

The function `computeGross` needs to know the hours worked and the hourly rate for the employee. It also needs the values of the constants (`MAX_NO_OVERTIME` and `OVERTIME_RATE`) involved in determining the employee's gross pay.

INTERFACE FOR `computeGross`

Input Arguments

| `float hours` | // number of hours worked |
| `float rate` | // hourly pay rate (dollars) |

Function Return Value

```
float gross
```

FORMULA

Gross pay = Hours worked × Hourly pay

To compute gross pay, we first need to determine whether any overtime pay is due. If there is, we should compute regular pay and overtime pay and return their sum. If not, we simply compute gross pay as the product of hours and rate. We list the local data needed and refine the algorithm step (Step 3) as a *decision step*.

Local Data for `computeGross`

```
float gross          // gross pay (dollars)
float regularPay     // pay for first 40 hours of work
float overtimePay    // pay for hours in excess of 40 (dollars)
```

Algorithm for `computeGross`

3.1. If the hours worked exceeds 40.0 (max hours before overtime)

> **3.1.1.** Compute `regularPay`.
>
> **3.1.2.** Compute `overtimePay`.
>
> **3.1.3.** Add `regularPay` to `overtimePay` to get `gross`.

Else

> **3.1.4.** Compute `gross` as hours * rate.

The decision step above is expressed in **pseudocode**—a mixture of English and C++ reserved words that is used to describe algorithm steps. In the pseudocode above, we use indentation and the reserved words `if` and `else` to show the flow of control.

pseudocode
A mixture of English and C++ reserved words that is used to describe an algorithm step.

ANALYSIS AND DESIGN FOR `COMPUTENET` (STEP 4)

Once we have the gross pay (returned by `computeGross`), we can compute net pay. The constants representing the union dues cutoff value ($100) and the dues ($15) are required as well as the value of gross salary.

INTERFACE FOR `computeNet`

Input Arguments

```
float gross          // gross pay (dollars)
```

Function Return Value

```
float net            // net pay (dollars)
```

FORMULA

```
net pay = gross pay − deductions
```

Next, we list the local data needed for `computeNet` and refine the algorithm step (Step 4).

Local Data for `computeNet`
`float net`   // net pay (dollars)

Algorithm for `computeNet`

4.1. If the gross pay is larger than $100.00
    4.1.1.   Deduct the dues of $15 from gross pay.
  Else
    4.1.2.   Deduct no dues.

IMPLEMENTATION

We now write the main function along with the prototypes for the lower-level functions (see Listing 4.1).

TESTING

To test this program, we need to be sure that all possible alternatives work properly. For example, to test function `computeNet`, we need three sets of data, one for the `if` (gross salary greater than $100), one for the `else` (gross salary less than $100), and one for the pivotal point (gross salary exactly $100). Listing 4.2 shows program output from a sample run.

Listing 4.1   Payroll problem with functions

```
// File: payrollFunctions.cpp
// Computes and displays gross pay and net pay given an hourly
//     rate and number of hours worked. Deducts union dues of $15
//     if gross salary exceeds $100; otherwise, deducts no dues.

#include <iostream>
using namespace std;

// Functions used    . . .
void instructUser();
float computeGross(float, float);
float computeNet(money);

const float MAX_NO_DUES = 100.00;      // max earnings before dues (dollars)
const float dues = 15.00;              // dues amount (dollars)
const float MAX_NO_OVERTIME = 40.0;    // max hours before overtime
const float OVERTIME_RATE = 1.5;       // overtime rate
```

(continued)

Listing 4.1   Payroll problem with functions (continued)

```
int main ()
{
    float hours;            // input: hours worked
    float rate;             // input: hourly pay rate (dollars)
    float gross;            // output: gross pay (dollars)
    float net;              // output: net pay (dollars)

    // Display user instructions.
    instructUser();
    // Enter hours and rate.
    cout << "Hours worked: ";
    cin >> hours;
    cout << "Hourly rate: $";
    cin >> rate;

    // Compute gross salary.
    gross = computeGross(hours, rate);

    // Compute net salary.
    net = computeNet(gross);

    // Print gross and net.
    cout << "Gross salary is $" << gross << endl;
    cout << "Net salary is $" << net << endl;

    return 0;
}

// Displays user instructions
void instructUser()
{
    cout << "This program computes gross and net salary." << endl;
    cout << "A dues amount of " << DUES << " is deducted for" << endl;
    cout << "an employee who earns more than " << MAX_NO_DUES << endl
         << endl;
    cout << "Overtime is paid at the rate of " << OVERTIME_RATE << endl;
    cout << "times the regular rate for hours worked over "
         << MAX_NO_OVERTIME endl << endl;
    cout << "Enter hours worked and hourly rate" << endl;
    cout << "on separate lines after the prompts." << endl;
```

(continued)

Listing 4.1   Payroll problem with functions (continued)

```
      cout << "Press <return> after typing each number." << endl << endl;
}   // end instructUser

// Find the gross pay
float computeGross
   (float hours,                    // IN: number of hours worked
    float rate)                     // IN: hourly pay rate (dollars)
{

   // Local data . . .
   float gross;              // RESULT: gross pay (dollars)
   float regularPay;         // pay for first 40 hours
   float overtimePay;        // pay for hours in excess of 40

   // Compute gross pay.
   if (hours > MAX_NO_OVERTIME)
   {
      regularPay = MAX_NO_OVERTIME * rate;
      overtimePay = (hours - MAX_NO_OVERTIME) * OVERTIME_RATE * rate;
      gross = regularPay + overtimePay;
   }
   else
      gross = hours * rate;

   return gross;
}   // end computeGross

// Find the net pay
float computeNet
   (float gross)             // IN: gross salary (dollars)
{
   // Local data . . .
   float net;                // RESULT: net pay (dollars)

   // Compute net pay.
   if (gross > MAX_NO_DUES)
      net = gross - DUES;    // deduct dues amount
   else
      net = gross;           // no deductions

   return net;
} // end computeNet
```

Listing 4.2   Sample run of payroll program with functions

```
This program computes gross and net salary.
A dues amount of $15.00 is deducted for
an employee who earns more than $100.00

Overtime is paid at the rate of 1.5
times the regular rate on hours worked over 40

Enter hours worked and hourly rate
on separate lines after the prompts.
Press <return> after typing each number.

Hours worked: 50
Hourly rate: $6
Gross salary is $330
Net salary is $315
```

PROGRAM STYLE   Global Constants Enhance Readability and Maintenance

The four program constants used in this case are not essential. We could just as easily have placed the constant values (40.0, 1.5, 100.00, and 15.00) directly in the code. For example, we could have written the decision in `computeNet` as

```
if (gross > 100.00)
    net = gross - 15.00;   // deduct amount dues
else
    net = gross;           // no deductions
```

However, the use of constant identifiers rather than constant values has two advantages. First, the original `if` statement is easier to understand because it uses descriptive names such as MAX_NO_DUES rather than numbers, which have no intrinsic meaning. Second, a program written with constant identifiers is much easier to maintain than one written with constant values. For example, if we want to use different constant values in the payroll program in Listing 4.1, we need to change only the constant declarations. However, if we had inserted constant values directly in the `if` statement, we'd have to change the `if` statement and any other statements that manipulate or display the constant values.

The constants have global scope, which means that any function can reference them. Although you must not give variables global scope, you can give constants global scope because the value of a constant, unlike a variable, cannot be changed in a lower-level function. If a constant is used by more than one function, you should declare it as a global constant. The alternatives would be to pass it as an argument to each function or to duplicate its definition in each function. Giving it global scope shortens argument lists and ensures that all functions have the same value for the constant.

A Reminder About Identifier Scope

Notice that identifier gross is declared as a local variable in functions main and computeGross, and as a formal argument in function computeNet. The scope of each declaration is the function that declares it. To establish a connection between these independent declarations of the identifier gross, we use argument list correspondence or the function return mechanism. The variable gross in function main is passed as an actual argument (corresponding to formal argument gross) in the call to computeNet. Function computeGross returns as its result the value of its local variable gross; the statement in function main that calls computeGross

```
gross = computeGross(hours, rate );
```

assigns the function result to main's local variable gross.

Adding Data Flow Information to Structure Charts

In Figure 4.6, we added data flow information to the structure chart showing the input and output of each of the top-level problem solution steps. The data flow information is an important part of the program documentation. It shows what program variables are processed by each step and the manner in which these variables are processed. If a step gives a new value to a variable, then the variable is considered an *output of the step.* If a step displays a variable's value or uses it in a computation without changing its value, the variable is considered an *input of the step.* For example, the step "compute net pay" consists of a function that processes variables gross and net. This step uses the value of the variable gross, as well as the constants MAX_NO_DUES and DUES (its inputs) to compute net (its output).

Figure 4.6 also shows that a variable may have different roles in different subproblems of the structure chart. When considered in the context of the original problem statement, hours and rate are problem inputs (data supplied by the program user). However, when considered in the context of the subproblem "enter data," the subproblem's task is to deliver values for hours and rate to the main function, so they're considered outputs from this step.

When considered in the context of the subproblem "compute gross pay," the subproblem's task is to use `hours` and `rate` to compute a value of `gross`, so they're considered inputs to this step. In the same way, the role of the variables `gross` and `net` changes as we go from step to step in the structure chart.

Commentary—The Software Development Method

The sequence of steps taken to solve the payroll problem with functions follows exactly the process outlined for the software development method presented in Chapter 1:

1. Analyze the problem statement to be sure that the problem specification is clear and complete.

2. Identify the relevant problem data including constants, input data, and output requirements as well as their data types.

3. Use top-down design to develop your solution. Break the main problem into simpler, smaller subproblems that can be solved with separate functions. Construct the structure chart, showing the data flow between modules and an algorithm that shows the sequence of steps required for the problem solution.

4. Refine your subproblems starting with an analysis similar to Step 1 above.

Once Steps 1 through 4 have been completed, you can write the main function and the prototypes for the lower-level functions. Next, design each of the subproblems following Steps 1 through 4, as was done for the main function. The layered approach to software design will enable you to focus first on the description of the data elements to be modeled and the data types that are most natural for modeling these elements.

This approach will also help you manage more complex problems by breaking them down into simpler, more easily solvable components. You'll see the benefits of this approach more clearly as problems become more complicated and you're able to build a complex system out of independent and reusable components that are relatively easy to understand and modify.

EXERCISES FOR SECTION 4.5

Self-Check

1. What are the benefits of using constant identifiers instead of literals in a program?

2. List three benefits of using the software design method applied in solving the payroll problem.

3. List all changes that would have to be made to the payroll program in Listing 4.1 if the union dues amount were changed from $15 to $25.

4. The input arguments to function computeGross included the employee's hourly rate, hours worked, overtime rate, and the maximum number of hours that could be worked without overtime. Should we have also included the union dues amount and the maximum earnings before union dues had to be paid? Why or why not?

Programming

1. Describe all modifications that would be required in the analysis, design, implementation, and testing of the payroll program if the problem statement were changed to include the requirement to deduct 18 percent in federal income tax if earnings exceeded $250.

2. Write function readHours that reads in hours worked and returns the value entered and function readRate that reads in hourly pay rate and returns the value entered.

3. Write function printResults that displays in a meaningful way the values of its two arguments that represent gross pay and net pay.

4. Modify the program in Listing 4.1 to use the functions in Programming Exercises 2 and 3.

4.6 Checking the Correctness of an Algorithm

As we said earlier, verifying the correctness of an algorithm is a critical step in algorithm design and can save hours of coding and testing time.

In Section 4.4, we simulated the execution of an if statement that switches the values of two variables. We now trace the execution of the refined algorithm for the payroll problem solved in the last section.

Refined Algorithm
1. Display user instructions.

2. Enter hours worked and hourly rate.

3. Compute gross pay.

    3.1. If the hours worked exceed 40.0 (max hours before overtime)

        3.1.1. Compute regularPay.

        3.1.2. Compute overtimePay.

        3.1.3. Add `regularPay` to `overtimePay` to get gross.

    Else

        3.1.4. Compute gross as hours * rate.

  4. Compute net pay.

    4.1. If `gross` is larger than $100.00

        4.1.1. Deduct the dues of $15.00 from gross pay.

    Else

        4.1.2. Deduct no dues.

  5. Display gross and net pay.

In Table 4.10, each step is listed at the left in the order of its execution. The last column shows the effect of each step. If a step changes the value of a variable, then the table shows the new value. If no new value is shown, the variable retains its previous value. For example, the table shows that step 2 stores the data values `30.0` and `10.00` in the variables `hours` and `rate`; gross and net are still undefined (indicated by ? in the first table row).

    The trace in Table 4.10 shows that `300.0` and `285.0` are stored in gross and net and then displayed. To verify that the algorithm is correct, you'd need to select other data that cause the two conditions to evaluate to different combinations of their values. Since there are two conditions and each has two possible values (`true` or `false`), there are two times two, or four, different combinations that should be tried. An exhaustive hand trace of the algorithm would show that it works for all combinations.

    Besides the four cases discussed above, you should verify that the algorithm works correctly for unusual data. For example, what would happen if hours were `40.0` (value of `MAX_NO_OVERTIME`) or if gross were `100.0` (value of `MAX_NO_DUES`)? Would the algorithm still provide the correct

Table 4.10 Trace of Algorithm for Payroll Problem

Algorithm Step	hours	rate	gross	net	Effect
	?	?	?	?	
2. Enter hours and rate	30.0	10.00			Reads the data
3.1. If hours > 40.0					hours > 40 is false
3.1.4. gross gets hours * rate			300.0		Compute gross as hours * rate
4.1. If gross > $100.00					gross > 100.00 is true
4.1.1. Deduct the dues of $15				285.0	Deduct the dues of $15.00
5. Display gross and net					Displays 300.00 and 285.00

result? To complete the hand trace, you'd need to show that the algorithm handles these special situations properly.

In tracing each case, you must be careful to execute the algorithm exactly as the computer would execute it. Don't assume how a particular step will execute.

EXERCISES FOR SECTION 4.6

Self-Check

1. Provide sample data that cause both conditions in the payroll problem to be true and trace the execution for these data.

2. If hours is greater than MAX_NO_OVERTIME and gross is less than MAX_NO_DUES, which assignment steps in the algorithm would be performed? Provide a trace.

4.7 Nested if Statements and Multiple-Alternative Decisions

Until now, we used if statements to implement decisions involving up to two alternatives. In this section, we use **nested if statements** (one if statement inside another) to code decisions with several alternatives.

nested if statement
An if statement with another if statement as its true task or its false task.

EXAMPLE 4.14

The following nested if statement has three alternatives. It increases one of three variables (numPos, numNeg, or numZero) by one depending on whether x is greater than zero, less than zero, or equal to zero, respectively. The boxes show the logical structure of the nested if statement: the second if statement is the **false** task following the **else** of the first if statement.

```
if (x > 0)
        numPos = numPos + 1;
else
        if (x < 0)
                numNeg = numNeg + 1;
        else // x equals 0
                numZero = numZero + 1;
```

The execution of the nested `if` statement proceeds as follows: the first condition `(x > 0)` is tested; if it is true, `numPos` is incremented and the rest of the `if` statement is skipped. If the first condition is false, the second condition `(x < 0)` is tested; if it is true, `numNeg` is incremented; otherwise, `numzero` is incremented. It's important to realize that the second condition is tested only when the first condition is false.

Table 4.11 traces the execution of this statement when x is −7. Because `x > 0` is false, the second condition is tested.

Table 4.11   Trace of `if` Statement in Example 4.14 for `x = -7`

Statement Part	Effect
`if (x > 0)`	−7 > 0 is false
`else`	
`if (x < 0)`	−7 < 0 is true
`numNeg = numNeg + 1;`	add 1 to `numNeg`

Comparison of Nested `if` Statements and a Sequence of `if` Statements

Beginning programmers sometimes prefer to use a sequence of `if` statements rather than a single nested `if` statement. For example, the previous `if` statement is rewritten as the following sequence of `if` statements.

```
// Less efficient sequence of if statements
if (x > 0)
    numPos = numPos + 1;
if (x < 0)
    numNeg = numNeg + 1;
if (x == 0)
    numZero = numZero + 1;
```

Although this sequence is logically equivalent to the original, it's neither as readable nor as efficient. Unlike the nested `if`, the sequence doesn't show clearly that exactly one of the three assignment statements is executed for a particular x. It's less efficient because all three of the conditions are always tested. In the nested `if` statement, only the first condition is tested when x is positive.

Writing a Nested `if` as a Multiple-Alternative Decision

Nested `if` statements can become quite complex. If there are more than two alternatives and indentation is not consistent, it may be difficult to determine the logical structure of the `if` statement. For example, in the following nested `if` statement

```
if (condition₁)
    // statement₁
    . . .
    if (condition₂)
        // statement₂
    . . .
else
    // statement₃
    . . .
```

does the `else` match up with the first `if` as shown by the identation or with the second `if`? The answer is the second `if` because an `else` is always associated with the closest `if` without an `else`. In the situation discussed in Example 4.14 in which each false task (except the last) is followed by an `if` and matching `else`, you can code the nested `if` as the *multiple-alternative decision* described next.

Multiple-Alternative Decision Form

Form:
```
if (condition₁)
    statement₁;
else if (condition₂)
    statement₂;
        .
        .
        .
else if (conditionₙ)
    statementₙ;
else
    statementₑ;
```

Example:
```
// Increment numPos, numNeg, or numZero
// depending on x.
if (x > 0)
    numPos = numPos + 1;
else if (x < 0)
    numNeg = numNeg + 1;
else // x == 0
    numZero = numZero + 1;
```

Interpretation: The conditions in a multiple-alternative decision are evaluated in sequence until a true condition is reached. If a condition is true, the statement following it is executed and the rest of the multiple-alternative decision is skipped. If a condition is false, the statement following it is skipped and the next condition is tested. If all conditions are false, then *statementₑ* following the last **else** is executed.

EXAMPLE 4.15

Suppose you want to match exam scores to letter grades for a large class of students. The following table describes the assignment of grades based on each exam score.

Exam Score	Grade Assigned
90 and above	A
80 to 89	B
70 to 79	C
60 to 69	D
Below 60	F

The multiple-alternative decision in function `displayGrade` (Listing 4.3) displays the letter grade assigned according to this table. If a student has an exam score of 85, the last three conditions would be true; however, a grade of B would be assigned because the first true condition is `(score >= 80)`.

Listing 4.3   Function `displayGrade`

```
// Displays the letter grade corresponding to an exam
// score assuming a normal scale.
void displayGrade(int score)        // IN: exam score
{
    if (score >= 90)
       cout << "Grade is A" << endl;
    else if (score >= 80)
       cout << "Grade is B" << endl;
    else if (score >= 70)
       cout << "Grade is C" << endl;
    else if (score >= 60)
       cout << "Grade is D" << endl;
    else
       cout << "Grade is F" << endl;
}
```

Order of Conditions

When more than one condition in a multiple-alternative decision is true, only the task following the first true condition is executed. Therefore, the order of the conditions can affect the outcome.

Writing the decision as follows would be incorrect. All passing scores (60 or above) would be incorrectly categorized as a grade of D because the first condition would be true and the rest would be skipped.

```
// incorrect grade assignment
if (score >= 60)
    cout << "Grade is D" << endl;
else if (score >= 70)
    cout << "Grade is C" << endl;
else if (score >= 80)
    cout << "Grade is B" << endl;
else if (score >= 90)
    cout << "Grade is A" << endl;
else
    cout << "Grade is F" << endl;
```

The order of conditions can also have an effect on program efficiency. If we know that low exam scores are much more likely than high scores, it would be more efficient to test first for scores below 60, next for scores below 70, and so on (see Programming Exercise 3 at the end of this section).

EXAMPLE 4.16

You could use a multiple-alternative if statement to implement a decision table that describes several alternatives. Let's assume that you're an accountant setting up a payroll system for a small firm having five different ranges for salaries up to $150,000, as shown in Table 4.12. Each table line shows the base tax amount (column 2) and tax percentage (column 3) for a particular salary range (column 1). Given a salary, you can calculate the tax by adding the base tax for that salary range to the product of the percentage of excess and the amount of salary over the minimum salary for that range.

For example, the second line of the table specifies that the tax due on a salary of $20,000.00 is $2,250.00 plus 16 percent of the excess salary over $15,000.00 (that is, 16 percent of $5,000.00, or $800.00). Therefore, the total tax due is $2,250.00 plus $800.00, or $3,050.00.

The if statement in function computeTax (Listing 4.4) implements the tax table. If the value of salary is within the table range (0.00 to 150,000.00), exactly one of the statements assigning a value to tax will be executed. Table 4.13 shows a hand trace of the if statement when salary is $20,000.00. You can see that the value assigned to tax, $3050.00, is correct. Remember not to include symbols such as the dollar sign or commas in a float literal.

Table 4.12   Decision Table for Example 4.16

Range	Salary	Base Tax	Percentage of Excess
1	0.00 to 14,999.99	0.00	15
2	15,000.00 to 29,999.99	2250.00	16
3	30,000.00 to 49,999.99	4650.00	18
4	50,000.00 to 79,999.99	8250.00	20
5	80,000.00 to 150,000.00	14,250.00	25

Listing 4.4   Function `computeTax`

```
// Compute the tax due based on a tax table
float computeTax(float salary)    // IN: salary amount
{
    if (salary < 0.00)
        tax = -1;
    else if (salary < 15000.00)            // first range
        tax = 0.15 * salary;
    else if (salary < 30000.00)            // second range
        tax = (salary - 15000.00) * 0.16 + 2250.00;
    else if (salary < 50000.00)            // third range
        tax = (salary - 30000.00) * 0.18 + 4650.00;
    else if (salary < 80000.00)            // fourth range
        tax = (salary - 50000.00) * 0.20 + 8250.00;
    else if (salary <= 150000.00)          // fifth range
        tax = (salary - 80000.00) * 0.25 + 14250.00;
    else
        tax = -1;

    return tax;
}
```

Table 4.13   Trace of `if` Statement in Listing 4.4 for salary equals $20000.00

Statement Part	salary	tax	Effect
	20000.00	?	
`if (salary < 0.00)`			20000.00 < 0.00 is false
`else if (salary < 15000.00)`			20000.00 < 15000.00 is false
`else if (salary < 30000.00)`			20000.00 < 30000.00 is true
`tax = (salary - 15000.00)`			Evaluates to 5000.00
`* 0.16`			Evaluates to 800.00
`+ 2250.00`		3050.00	Evaluates to 3050.00

PROGRAM STYLE Validating the Value of Variables

If you validate the value of a variable before using it in computations, you can avoid processing invalid or meaningless data. Instead of computing an incorrect tax amount, function computeTax returns −1.0 (an impossible tax amount) if the value of salary is outside the range covered by the table (0.0 to 150,000.00). The first condition sets tax to −1.0 if salary is negative. All conditions evaluate to false if salary is greater than 150000.00, so the task following else sets tax to −1.0. The function calling computeTax should display an error message if the value returned to it is −1.0.

Short-Circuit Evaluation of Logical Expressions

When evaluating logical expressions, C++ uses a technique called **short-circuit evaluation.** This means that evaluation of a logical expression stops as soon as its value can be determined. For example, if the value of (single == 'y') is false, then the logical expression

short-circuit evaluation Stopping evaluation of a logical expression as soon as its value can be determined.

```
(single == 'y') && (gender == 'm') && (age >= 18)
```

must be false regardless of the value of the other conditions (that is, false && (. . .) must always be false). Consequently, there's no need to continue to evaluate the other conditions when (single == 'y') evaluates to false.

EXAMPLE 4.17

If x is zero, the if condition

```
if ((x != 0.0) && (y / x > 5.0))
```

is false because (x != 0.0) is false, and false && (. . .) must always be false. Thus there's no need to evaluate the subexpression (y / x > 5.0) when x is zero. In this case, the first subexpression guards the second and prevents the second from being evaluated when x is equal to 0. However, if the subexpressions were reversed, the expression

```
if ((y / x > 5.0) && (x != 0.0))
```

would cause a "division by zero" run-time error when the divisor x is zero. Therefore, the order of the subexpressions in this condition is critical.

EXERCISES FOR SECTION 4.7

Self-Check

1. Trace the execution of the nested `if` statements in Listing 4.4 for a salary of $135,000.

2. What would be the effect of reversing the order of the first two `if` statements in Listing 4.4?

3. Evaluate the expressions below, with and without short-circuit evaluation, if x equals 6 and y equals 7.

   a. `((x > 10) && (y / x <= 10))`
   b. `((x <= 10) || (x / (y - 7) > 3))`

4. Write pseudo code for the following: if the transaction is a deposit, add the transaction amount to the balance and display the new balance; else, if the transaction is a withdrawal and the transaction amount is less than or equal to the balance, deduct the transaction amount from the balance and display the new balance; else, if the transaction is a withdrawal but the amount is greater than the balance, deduct a PENALTY amount (a constant) from the balance and display a "withdrawal exceeds balance" warning message; else display an "illegal transaction" message.

5. Write pseudo code for the following: if `ch1` is one of the arithmetic operators, set `isOp` to `true`; otherwise, if `ch1` and `ch2` are both | or both &, set `isOp` to `true`; otherwise, set `isOp` to `false`.

Programming

1. Implement the decision table below using a nested `if` statement. Assume that the grade point average is within the range 0.0 through 4.0.

Grade Point Average	Transcript Message
0.0 to 0.99	Failed semester—registration suspended
1.0 to 1.99	On probation for next semester
2.0 to 2.99	(no message)
3.0 to 3.49	Dean's list for semester
3.5 to 4.0	Highest honors for semester

2. Implement the solution to Self-Check Exercise 4 using a string to represent the transaction type.

3. Rewrite the `if` statement for Example 4.15 using only the relational operator < in all conditions.

4. The Air Force has asked you to write a program to label supersonic aircraft as military or civilian. Your program is to be given the plane's observed speed in kilometers per hour (km/h) and its estimated length in meters.

For planes traveling in excess of 1100 km/h, you'll label those longer than 52 meters "civilian" and those shorter as "military". For planes traveling at slower speeds, you'll issue an "aircraft type unknown" message.

5. Write a type bool function that returns the value of isOp based on Self-Check Exercise 5.

6. Write a function that returns the value of a + b if op is +, a − b if op is −, and so on for '*', '/', and '%'. Parameters a, b are type int and op is type char.

4.8 The switch Control Statement

The switch control statement may also be used in C++ to select one of several alternatives. The switch statement is especially useful when the selection is based on the value of a single variable or a simple expression (called the switch *selector*). The value of this expression may be of type int, char, or bool, but not of type float or string.

EXAMPLE 4.18

The switch statement

```
switch (momOrDad)
{
   case 'M': case 'm':
      cout << "Hello Mom - Happy Mother's Day" << endl;
      break;
   case 'D': case 'd':
      cout << "Hello Dad - Happy Father's Day" << endl;
      break;
}
```

behaves the same way as the if statement below when the character stored in momOrDad is one of the four letters listed (M, m, D, or d).

```
if ((momOrDad == 'M') || (momOrDad == 'm'))
   cout << "Hello Mom - Happy Mother's Day" << endl;
else if ((momOrDad == 'D') || (momOrDad == 'd'))
   cout << "Hello Dad - Happy Father's Day" << endl;
```

The message displayed depends on the value of the **switch** selector momOrDad (type char). If the **switch** selector value is 'M' or 'm', the first message is displayed. If the switch selector value is 'D' or 'd', the second message is displayed. The character constants 'M', 'm' and 'D', 'd' are called *case labels*.

Once a particular case label statement has been executed, the reserved word **break** causes control to be passed to the first statement following the **switch** control statement.

---

switch Statement

Form: `switch` (*selector*)
　　　　　`{`
　　　　　　`case` label$_1$: *statements*$_1$;
　　　　　　　　　　`break;`
　　　　　　`case` label$_2$: *statements*$_2$;
　　　　　　　　　　`break;`

　　　　　　　　　·
　　　　　　　　　·
　　　　　　　　　·

　　　　　　`case` label$_n$: *statements*$_n$;
　　　　　　　　　　`break;`
　　　　　　`default`: *statements*$_d$; // *optional*
　　　　　`}`

Example: // *Display a musical note*
　　　　　`switch (musicalNote)`
　　　　　`{`
　　　　　　`case 'c':`
　　　　　　　`cout << "do";`
　　　　　　　`break;`
　　　　　　`case 'd':`
　　　　　　　`cout << "re";`
　　　　　　　`break;`
　　　　　　`case 'e':`
　　　　　　　`cout << "mi";`
　　　　　　　`break;`
　　　　　　`case 'f':`
　　　　　　　`cout << "fa";`
　　　　　　　`break;`
　　　　　　`case 'g':`
　　　　　　　`cout << "sol";`
　　　　　　　`break;`
　　　　　　`case 'a':`
　　　　　　　`cout << "la";`
　　　　　　　`break;`
　　　　　　`case 'b':`
　　　　　　　`cout << "ti";`
　　　　　　　`break;`
　　　　　　`default:`
　　　　　　　`cout << "An invalid note was read."`
　　　　　　　　`<< endl;`
　　　　　`}`

> **Interpretation:** The *selector* expression is evaluated and compared to each of the `case` labels until a match is found. The selector expression should be an integral type (for example, `int`, `char`, `bool`, but not `float` or `string`). Each *label* is a single, constant value, and each one must have a different value from the others. When a match between the value of the *selector* expression and a `case` *label* is found, the statements following the case *label* are executed until a `break` statement is encountered. Then the rest of the `switch` statement is skipped.
>
> If no case *label* matches the *selector*, the entire switch body is skipped unless it contains a `default` label. If there is a `default` label, the statements following the `default` are executed. The statements following a `case` *label* may be one or more C++ statements, which means that you don't need to make multiple statements into a single compound statement using braces.

EXAMPLE 4.19

The `switch` statement in Listing 4.5 finds the average life expectancy of a standard lightbulb based on the bulb's wattage. Since the value of the variable `watts` controls the execution of the `switch` statement, `watts` must have a value before the statement executes. Case labels `40` and `60` have the same effect (also, case labels `75` and `100`).

Listing 4.5   `switch` statement to determine life expectancy of a lightbulb

```cpp
// Determine average life expectancy of a standard
// lightbulb.
switch (watts)
{
    case 25:
        life = 2500;
        break;
    case 40:
    case 60:
        life = 1000;
        break;
    case 75:
    case 100:
        life = 750;
        break;
    default:
        life = 0;
}
```

Proper Use of break

Don't forget to use the reserved word break at the end of a statement sequence in a switch statement. If the break is omitted, then execution will continue, or *fall through*, to the next statement sequence. This is usually an error in logic.

Comparison of Nested if Statements and the switch Statement

You can use a nested if statement, which is more general than the switch statement, to implement any multiple-alternative decision. The switch statement is more readable in many contexts and should be used whenever practical. Case labels that contain type float values or strings are not permitted.

You should use the switch statement when each label set contains a reasonable number of case labels (a maximum of ten). However, if the number of values is large, use a nested if. You should use a default label in a switch statement wherever possible. The discipline of trying to define a default will help you to consider what will happen if the value of your switch statement's selector expression falls outside the range of your set of case labels.

Using a switch Statement to Select Alternative Functions

Instead of placing lengthy statement alternatives in the body of a switch, you should consider moving this code to a function. This leads to a very common use for the switch statement: selecting a particular function from a group of possible choices.

EXAMPLE 4.20

Assume the type char variable editOp contains a data value (D, I, or R) that indicates the kind of text edit operation to be performed on string object textString. We use the switch statement in function edit (Listing 4.6) to call a function that performs the selected operation, passing textString as a function argument. Each function returns the modified string as its result. The modified string is assigned to textString and is returned by function edit.

Using this structure, we place the code for each edit operation in a separate function. These functions might prompt the user for specific information, such as a substring to insert, replace, or delete, and perform all necessary operations on this data (by calling member functions from the string class).

Listing 4.6   String editing function edit

```
// Perform string editing function.
string edit(string textString,         // IN: string to edit
            char editOp)                // IN: edit operation
{
    switch (editOp)
    {
      case 'D': case 'd':               // Delete a substring
         textString = doDelete(textString);
         break;
      case 'I': case 'i':               // Insert a substring
         textString = doInsert(textString);
         break;
      case 'R': case 'r':               // Replace a substring
         textString = doReplace(textString);
         break;
      case 'Q': case 'q' :              // Quit editing
         cout << "All done!" << endl;
         break;
      default:
         cout << "An invalid edit code was entered." << endl;
    }
    return textString;

} //end edit
```

Program decomposition into separate components is the key here. The details of how our string is processed can be written without affecting the simple *control code* in the switch statement.

EXERCISES FOR SECTION 4.8

Self-Check

1. What will be printed by the following carelessly constructed switch statement if the value of color is 'R'? Fix the error in this statement.

```
switch (color)
{
case 'R': case 'r':
   cout << "red" << endl;
case 'B': case 'b':
   cout << "blue" << endl;
case 'Y': case 'y':
   cout << "yellow" << endl;
}
```

If `color` were type `string`, could you use `"Red"` and `"red"` as `case` labels for the first selection? Explain your answer.

2. Write an `if` statement that corresponds to the `switch` statement below.

```
switch (x > y)
{
    case 1 :
        cout << "x greater" << endl;
        break;
    case 0 :
        cout << "y greater or equal" << endl;
        break;
}
```

3. Why can't we rewrite our nested `if` statement examples from Section 4.7 using `switch` statements?

4. Why is it preferable to include a `default` label in a `switch` statement?

5. What would be the effect of omitting the first `break` statement in Listing 4.5? Would this be a syntax error, run-time error, or logic error?

Programming

1. Write a `switch` statement that prints a message indicating whether nextCh (type `char`) is an operator symbol (+, −, *, /, %), a punctuation symbol (comma, semicolon, parenthesis, brace, bracket), or a digit. Your statement should print the category selected. Include a `default` label.

2. Write a nested `if` statement equivalent to the `switch` statement described in Programming Exercise 1.

3. Implement the solution to Self-Check Exercise 4 of Section 4.7 using a type `char` variable for the transaction type. Assume `'d'` or `'D'` indicates a deposit and `'w'` or `'W'` indicates a withdrawal. Use a `switch` statement.

4. Use a `switch` statement in a function that returns the value of a + b if op is `'+'`, a − b if op is `'-'`, and so on for `'*'`, `'/'`, and `'%'`. Parameters a and b are type `int` and op is type char.

4.9 Common Programming Errors

Common errors using `if` statements involve writing the condition incorrectly and failure to enclose compound statements in braces. A common error for `switch` statements is omitting a `break` statement.

- *Parentheses:* For the most part, the defined precedence levels of C++ will prevent you from making a syntax error when writing conditions. But they will also allow you to do things you may not intend. The rule of thumb is, when in doubt, use parentheses.

■ *Operators:* You can use the logical operators, `&&`, `||`, and `!`, only with logical expressions. Remember that the C++ operator for equality is the double symbol `==`. Don't mistakenly use the assignment operator (single `=`) in its place. Your logical expression will probably compile, but the logic will be incorrect.

■ *Compound statements:* Don't forget to bracket a compound statement used as a true or false task in an `if` control statement with braces. If the `{ }` bracket is missing, only the first statement will be considered part of the task. This could lead to a syntax error—or, worse, a logic error that could be very difficult to find. In the following example, the `{ }` bracket around the true task is missing. The compiler assumes that only the statement

```
sum = sum + x;
```

is part of the true task of the `if` control statement. This creates a "misplaced else" syntax error. Of course, the correct thing to do is to enclose the compound statement in braces.

```
if (x > 0)                        // missing { }
    sum = sum + x;
    cout << "Greater than zero" << endl;
else
    cout << "Less than zero" << endl;
```

■ *Nested `if` statement:* When writing a nested `if` statement, try to select the conditions so that the multiple-alternative form shown in Section 4.7 can be used. If the conditions are not mutually exclusive (that is, if more than one condition may be true), the most restrictive condition should come first.

■ `switch` *statements:* When using a `switch` statement, make sure the `switch` selector and `case` labels are of the same type (`int`, `char`, or `bool` but not `float`). If the selector evaluates to a value not listed in any of the `case` labels, the `switch` statement will fall through without any action being taken. For this reason, it's often wise to guard the `switch` with a `default` label. This way you can ensure that the `switch` executes properly in all situations. Be very careful in your placement of the `break` statements. Missing `break` statements will allow control to fall through to the next case label.

Chapter Review

1. Control structures are used to control the flow of statement execution in a program. The compound statement is a control structure for sequential execution.

2. Selection control structures are used to represent decisions in an algorithm and pseudocode is used to write them in algorithms. Use the `if` statement or `switch` statement to code decision steps in C++.

3. Expressions whose values indicate whether certain conditions are true can be written

- using the relational operators (`<`, `<=`, `>`, `>=`) and equality operators (`==`, `!=`) to compare variables and constants.
- using the logical operators (`&&` (and), `||` (or), `!` (not)) to form more complex conditions.

4. Data flow information in a structure chart indicates whether a variable processed by a subproblem is used as an input or an output, or as both. An input provides data that are manipulated by the subproblem, and an output returns a value copied from an input device or computed by the subproblem. The same variable may be an input to one subproblem and an output from another.

5. A hand trace of an algorithm verifies whether it is correct. You can discover errors in logic by carefully hand tracing an algorithm. Hand tracing an algorithm before coding it as a program will save you time in the long run.

6. Nested `if` statements are common in C++ and are used to represent decisions with multiple alternatives. Programmers use indentation and the multiple-alternative decision form when applicable to enhance readability of nested `if` statements.

7. The `switch` statement implements decisions with several alternatives, where the alternative selected depends on the value of a variable or expression (the *selector* expression). The *selector* expression can be type `int`, `bool`, or `char`, but not type `double` or `string`.

Summary of New C++ Constructs

Construct	Effect
`if` Control Statement	
With Dependent Statement	
`    if (y != 0)`	Divides x by y only if y is nonzero.
`        result = x / y;`	
Two Alternatives	
`    if (x >= 0)`	If x is greater than or equal to 0, display the message
`        cout << x << " is positive"`	`"is positive"`; otherwise, display the message
`            << endl;`	`"is negative"`.
`    else`	
`        cout << x << " is negative"`	
`            << endl;`	

Summary of New C++ Constructs (continued)

Construct	Effect

Several Alternatives

```
if (x < 0)
{
    cout << "Negative" << endl;
    absX = -x;
}
else if (x == 0)
{
    cout << "Zero" << endl;
    absX = 0;
}
else
{
    cout << "Positive" << endl;
    absX = x;
}
```

One of three messages is printed, depending on whether x is negative, positive, or zero. absX is set to represent the absolute value or magnitude of x.

switch Statement

```
switch (nextCh)
{
    case 'A': case 'a':
        cout << "Excellent" << endl;
        break;
    case 'B': case 'b':
        cout << "Good" << endl;
        break;
    case 'C': case 'c':
        cout << "Fair" << endl;
        break;
    case 'D': case 'd':
    case 'F': case 'f':
        cout << "Poor, student is"
             << " on probation"
             << endl;
        break;
    default :
        cout << "Invalid grade."
             << endl;
}
```

Prints one of five messages based on the value of nextCh (type char). If nextDh is 'D', 'd' or 'F', 'f', the student is put on probation.

Quick-Check Exercises

1. An `if` statement implements a(n) _____ in an algorithm or program.

2. What is a compound statement?

3. A `switch` statement is often used instead of _____.

4. What values can a logical expression have?

5. Are the conditions `(x != y)` and `!(x == y)` logically equivalent or different? Explain your answer.

6. A hand trace is used to verify that a(n) _____ is correct.

7. Correct the syntax errors below.

```
if x > 25.0
    y = x
    cout << x << y << endl;
else
    y = z;
    cout << y << z << endl;
```

8. What value is assigned to `fee` by the `if` statement below (a) when speed is 50? (b) When speed is 51? (c) When speed is 15? (d) When speed is 130?

```
if (speed > 35)
    fee = 20;
else if (speed > 50)
    fee = 40;
else if (speed > 75)
    fee = 60;
```

9. Can you implement the `if` statement for question 8 as a `switch` statement? If yes, what are the advantages or disadvantage of doing it?

10. Answer Exercise 8 for the `if` statement below. Which `if` statement is correct?

```
if (speed > 75)
    fee = 60;
else if (speed > 50)
    fee = 40;
else if (speed > 35)
    fee = 20;
else
    fee = 0;
```

11. What output line(s) are displayed by the statements below (a) when grade is `'W'`? (b) When grade is `'C'`? (c) When grade is `'c'`? (d) When grade is `'P'`?

```
switch (grade)
{
    case 'A':
        points = 4;
        break;
    case 'B':
        points = 3;
        break;
    case 'C':
        points = 2;
        break;
    case 'D':
        points = 1;
        break;
    case 'F':
    case 'I':
    case 'W':
        points = 0;
        break;
}
if (('A' <= grade) && (grade <= 'D'))
    cout << "Passed, points earned = " << points << "."
        << endl;
else
    cout << "Failed, no points earned." << endl;
```

12. Explain the difference between the statements on the left and the statements on the right below. For each of them, what is the final value of x if the initial value of x is 0?

```
if (x >= 0)              if (x >= 0)
    x = x + 1;               x = x + 1;
else if (x >= 1)         if (x >= 1)
    x = x + 2;               x = x + 2;
```

13. a. Evaluate the expression below when x is 25:

```
true  &&  (x % 10 >= 0)  &&  (x / 10 <= 3)
```

  b. Is either pair of parentheses required? Is the constant true required?

  c. Write the complement of the expression.

Review Questions

1. Making a decision between two alternatives is usually implemented with a(n) _____ statement in C++.

2. How does a relational operator differ from a logical operator?

3. What is short-circuit logical evaluation? What are its benefits?

4. Trace the following program fragment and indicate which function will be called if a data value of 35.5 is entered.

```
cout << "Enter a temperature: ";
cin >> temp;
if (temp > 32.0)
    notFreezing();
else
    iceForming();
```

5. Write a nested `if` statement to display a message indicating the educational level of a student based on his or her number of years of schooling (0, none; 1 through 6, elementary school; 7 through 8, middle school; 9 through 12, high school; 13 through 16, college; greater than 16, graduate school). Print a message to indicate bad data as well.

6. Write a `switch` statement to select an operation based on the value of inventory. Increment `totalPaper` by `paperOrder` if inventory is `'b'` or `'c'`; increment `totalRibbon` by 1 if inventory is `'e'`, `'f'`, or `'d'`; increment `totalLabel` by `labelOrder` if inventory is `'a'` or `'x'`. Do nothing if inventory is `'m'`. Display an error message if inventory is any other value.

7. Implement a decision structure for the following computation:
   - If your taxable income is less than or equal to $15,000, pay no taxes.
   - If your taxable income is greater than $15,000 but less than or equal to $44,000, pay taxes at a rate of 20 percent on the amount in excess of $15,000.
   - If your taxable income is greater than $44,000 but less than or equal to $68,150, pay taxes at the rate of 22 percent on the first $44,000 and 28 percent on the amount in excess of $44,000.
   - If your taxable income is greater than $68,150 but less than or equal to $121,300, pay taxes at the rate of 28 percent on the first $58,150 and 31 percent on the amount in excess of $58,150.
   - If your taxable income is greater than $121,300 but less than or equal to $263,750, pay taxes at the rate of 31 percent on the first $121,300 and 36 percent on the amount in excess of $121,300.
   - If your taxable income is greater than $263,750, pay taxes at a rate of 36 percent on the first $263,750 and 39.6 percent on the amount in excess of $263,750.

8. Write a type bool function that returns true if its argument (a year) is a leap year. A leap year occurs every fourth year. Not every century is a leap year; every *fourth* century is a leap year. This means that 1900 is not a leap year, 2000 is a leap year, and 2100 is not a leap year.

Programming Projects

1. Write functions to draw a circle, square, and triangle. Write a program that reads a letter c, s, or T and, depending on the letter chosen, draws either a circle, square, or triangle.

2. Write a program that reads in four words (as character strings) and displays them in increasing as well as in decreasing alphabetic sequence.

3. Write a program that reads in a room number, its capacity, and the size of the class enrolled so far and prints an output line showing the classroom number, capacity, number of seats filled, number of seats available, and a message indicating whether the class is filled. Call a function to display the following heading before the first output line:

```
Room    Capacity    Enrollment    Empty Seats    Filled/
                                                 Not Filled
```

Display each part of the output line under the appropriate heading. Test your program with the following classroom data:

Room	Capacity	Enrollment
426	25	25
327	18	14
420	20	15
317	100	90

4. Write a program that displays a "message" consisting of three block letters where each letter is an X or an O. The program user's data determines whether a particular letter will be an X or O. For example, if the user enters the three letters XOX, the block letters X, O, and X will be displayed.

5. Write a program to simulate a state police radar gun. The program should read an automobile speed and print the message "speeding" if the speed exceeds 55 mph.

6. While spending the summer as a surveyor's assistant, you decide to write a program that transforms compass headings in degrees (0 to 360) to compass bearings. A compass bearing consists of three

items: the direction you face (north or south), an angle between 0 and 90 degrees, and the direction you turn before walking (east or west). For example, to get the bearing for a compass heading of 110.0 degrees, you would first face due south (180 degrees) and then turn 70.0 degrees east (180.0 − 110.0). Be sure to check the input for invalid compass headings.

7. Write a program that interacts with the user like this:

```
(1) Carbon monoxide
(2) Hydrocarbons
(3) Nitrogen oxides
(4) Nonmethane hydrocarbons
Enter pollutant number>> 2
Enter number of grams emitted per mile>> 0.35
Enter odometer reading>> 40112
Emissions exceed permitted level of 0.31 grams/mile.
```

Use the table of emissions limits below to determine the appropriate message.

	First Five Years or 50,000 Miles	Second Five Years or Second 50,000 Miles
carbon monoxide	3.4 grams/mile	4.2 grams/mile
hydrocarbons	0.31 grams/mile	0.39 grams/mile
nitrogen oxides	0.4 grams/mile	0.5 grams/mile
nonmethane hydrocarbons	0.25 grams/mile	0.31 grams/mile

8. The New Telephone Company has the following rate structure for long-distance calls:

- The regular rate for a call is $0.10 per minute.
- Any call started at or after 6:00 P.M. (1800 hours) but before 8:00 A.M. (0800 hours) is discounted 50 percent.
- Any call longer than 60 minutes receives a 15 percent discount on its cost (after any other discount is subtracted).
- All calls are subject to a 4 percent federal tax on their final cost.

Write a program that reads the start time for a call based on a 24-hour clock and the length of the call. The gross cost (before any discounts or tax) should be printed, followed by the net cost (after discounts are deducted and tax is added). Use separate functions to print instructions to the program user and to compute the net cost.

9. Write a program that will calculate and print out bills for the city water company. The water rates vary, depending on whether the bill is for home use, commercial use, or industrial use. A code of h means home

use, a code of c means commercial use, and a code of i means industrial use. Any other code should be treated as an error. The water rates are computed as follows:

- Code h: $5.00 plus $0.0005 per gallon used
- Code c: $1000.00 for the first 4 million gallons used and $0.00025 for each additional gallon
- Code i: $1000.00 if usage does not exceed 4 million gallons; $2000.00 if usage is more than 4 million gallons but does not exceed 10 million gallons; and $3000.00 if usage exceeds 10 million gallons

Your program should prompt the user to enter an account number (type int), the code (type char), and the gallons of water used (type float). Your program should echo the input data and print the amount due from the user.

10. Write a program to control a bread machine. Allow the user to input the type of bread as w for White and s for Sweet. Ask the user if the loaf size is double and if the baking is manual. The program should fail if the user inputs are invalid. The following table is a time chart for the machine used for each bread type. Print a statement for each step. If the loaf size is double, increase the baking time by 50 percent. If baking is manual, stop after the loaf-shaping cycle and instruct the user to remove the dough for manual baking. Use a function to print program instructions.

Time Chart for Making Bread

Operation	White Bread	Sweet Bread
Primary kneading	15 mins	20 mins
Primary rising	60 mins	60 mins
Secondary kneading	18 mins	33 mins
Secondary rising	20 mins	30 mins
Loaf shaping	2 seconds	2 seconds
Final rising	75 mins	75 mins
Baking	45 mins	35 mins
Cooling	30 mins	30 mins

11. Write a function that returns the digit value (an integer) corresponding to the letter passed to it as an argument based on the encoding on your telephone handset. For example, if the argument is the letter a, b, or c (uppercase or lowercase), your function should return the digit 2. If the argument is not one of the letters of the alphabet, return a value of −1. Write a program that tests your function. Implement two versions of the function: one using a switch statement and one using a nested if statement. Write a program that tests your functions.

12. Write a function `dayNumber` that returns the day number (1 to 366) in a year for a date that is provided as input data. Your function should accept the month (1 through 12), day, and year as integers. As an example, January 1, 1994 is day 1. December 31, 1993 is day 365. December 31, 1996 is day 366 since 1996 is a leap year. A year is a leap year if it's divisible by four, except that any year divisible by 100 is a leap year only if it's also divisible by 400. Write and use a second function that returns true if its argument, a year, is a leap year.

13. Write a program that reads in two dates (using three integers for each) and displays a message showing the date that comes first. Use the following algorithm: `if` the first date's year is smaller, it comes first; `else if` the second date's year is smaller, it comes first; `else` check the month to determine which date comes first in a similar way. If the months are the same, check the day.

14. Write a function that uses Euclid's algorithm to calculate the greatest common divisor of its two integer arguments where both arguments are positive and the first argument should be greater than or equal to the second. For example, `euclid(10, 2)` is 2, `euclid(20, 12)` is 4. Euclid's algorithm (`int euclid(int m, int n)`) for finding the greatest common divisor of m and n follows:

```
if (m is less than n)    // the arguments are in the
                         // wrong order
   return the result of euclid(n, m)   // reverse the
                                       // arguments
else if (n divides m)  // n is a divisor of m
   return n
else
   return euclid(n, remainder of m divided by n)
```

The above algorithm is called a recursive algorithm because function `euclid` calls itself (a legal operation in C++). If the first condition is true, the arguments need to be reversed before the greatest common divisor can be found by recalling function `euclid`. If the second condition is true, the smaller argument, n, must be the divisor we're seeking. Otherwise, the result can be determined by recalling function `euclid` to find the greatest common divisor of n and the remainder of m divided by n. Verify that this algorithm works for the examples shown in the first paragraph. Then write this function and test it out.

15. Keith's Sheet Music needs a program to implement its music teacher's discount policy. The program is to prompt the user to enter the purchase total and to indicate whether the purchaser is a teacher. The store plans to give each customer a printed receipt, so your

program is to create a nicely formatted file called `receipt.txt`. Music teachers receive a 10% discount on their sheet music purchases unless the purchase total is $100 or higher. In that case, the discount is 12%. The discount calculation occurs before addition of the 5% sales tax. Here are two sample output files—one for a teacher and the other for a nonteacher.

```
Total purchases                    $122.00
Teacher's discount (12%)             14.64
Discounted total                    107.36
Sales tax (5%)                        5.37
Total                              $112.73

Total purchases                    $ 24.70
Sales tax (5%)                        1.25
Total                              $ 26.15
```

16. Write a program that calculates the user's body mass index (BMI) and categorizes it as underweight, normal, overweight, or obese, based on the following table from the United States Centers for Disease Control:

BMI	Weight Status
Below 18.5	Underweight
18.5–24.9	Normal
25.0–29.9	Overweight
30.0 and above	Obese

To calculate BMI based on weight in pounds (*wt_lb*) and height in inches (*ht_in*), use this formula (rounded to tenths):

$$\frac{703 \times wt\_lb}{ht\_in^2}$$

Prompt the user to enter weight in pounds and height in inches.

17. Chatmore Wireless offers customers 600 weekday minutes for a flat rate of 39.99. Night (8 P.M. to 7 A.M.) and weekend minutes are free, but additional weekday minutes cost 0.40 each. There are taxes of 5.25% on all charges. Write a program that prompts the user to enter the number of weekday minutes, night minutes, and weekend minutes used and calculates the monthly bill and average cost of a minute before taxes. The program should display with labels all the input data, the pretax bill and average minute cost, the taxes, and the total bill. Store all monetary values as whole cents (rounding the taxes and average minute cost), and divide by 100 for display of results.

18. The table below shows the normal boiling points of several substances. Write a program that prompts the user for the observed boiling point of a substance in °C and identifies the substance if the observed boiling point is within 5% of the expected boiling point. If the data input is more than 5% higher or lower than any of the boiling points in the table, the program should output the message `Substance unknown`.

Substance	Normal Boiling Point (°C)
Water	100
Mercury	357
Copper	1187
Silver	2193
Gold	2660

Your program should define and call a function `inXperCent` that takes as parameters a reference value `ref`, a data value `data`, and a percentage value `x` and returns 1 meaning true if `data` is within `x % of ref`— that is, $(ref - x\% * ref) \le data \le (ref + x\% * ref)$. Otherwise `inXperCent` would return zero, meaning false. For example, the call `inXperCent (357, 323, 10)` would return true, since 10% of 357 is 35.7, and 323 falls between 321.3 and 392.7.

Answers to Quick–Check Exercises

1. decision

2. a block that combines one or more statements into a single statement

3. nested `if` statements or a multiple-alternative `if` statement

4. true or false

5. They are logically equivalent because they always have the same logical value.

6. algorithm

7.
```
if (x > 25.0)
{
    y = x;
    cout << x << y << endl;
}
else
{
    y = z;
    cout << y << z << endl;
}
```

8. 20, 20, undefined, 20

9. You could use speed as a *selector* expression, but it would be impractical because the list of case labels would be very long.

10. 20, 40, 0, 60; this one

11. **a.** when grade is `'W'`: `Failed, no points earned.`

   b. when grade is `'C'`: `Passed, points earned = 2.`

   c. when grade is `'c'`: `Failed, no points earned.`

   d. when grade is `'P'`: `Failed, no points earned.`

12. A nested if statement is on the left; a sequence of if statements is on the right. x becomes 1 on the left; x becomes 3 on the right.

13. **a.** true, remainder is 5 and quotient is 2.

   b. no, no

   c. Removing false and unnecessary parentheses: `!(x % 10 > 0 && x % 10 <= 3)`

chapter five

Repetition and Loop Statements

Chapter Objectives

- To understand why repetition is an important control structure in programming
- To learn about loop control variables and the three steps needed to control loop repetition
- To learn how to use the C++ for, while, and do-while statements for writing loops and when to use each statement type
- To learn how to accumulate a sum or a product within a loop body
- To learn common loop patterns such as counting loops, sentinel-controlled loops, flag-controlled loops, and menu-driven loops
- To understand nested loops and how the outer loop control variable and inner loop control variable are changed in a nested loop
- To learn how to debug programs using a debugger
- To learn how to debug programs by adding diagnostic output statements

IN THE PROGRAMS YOU'VE WRITTEN so far, the statements in the program body execute only once. But in most commercial software that you're likely to use, you can repeat a process many times. For example, when using an editor program or a word processor, you can move the cursor to a program line and perform as many edit operations as you need to.

Repetition, you'll recall, is the third type of program control structure (*sequence, selection, repetition*), and the repetition of steps in a program is called a **loop**. In this chapter we describe when to use loops in programs and common loop patterns in programming. We also describe three C++ loop control statements: while, for, and `do-while`. In addition to explaining how to write loops using each statement, we describe the advantages of each and explain when it's best to use each one. Like `if` statements, loops can be nested, and this chapter demonstrates how to write and use nested loops in your programs.

5.1   Counting Loops and the `while` Statement

loop
A control structure that repeats a group of statements in a program.

loop body
The statements that are repeated in a loop.

Just as the ability to make decisions is an important programming tool, so too is the ability to specify repetition of a group of operations. For example, a company that has seven employees will want to repeat the gross pay and net pay computations in its payroll program seven times, once for each employee. The **loop body** contains the statements to be repeated.

Writing out a solution to a specific problem can help you create a general algorithm to solve similar problems. After solving the sample case, ask yourself some of the following questions to determine whether loops will be required in the general algorithm:

1. Were there any steps I repeated as I solved the problem? If so, which ones?

2. If the answer to question 1 is yes, did I know in advance how many times to repeat the steps?

3. If the answer to question 2 is no, how did I know how long to keep repeating the steps?

Your answer to the first question indicates whether your algorithm needs a loop and what steps to include in the loop body if it does need one. Your answers to the other questions will help you determine which loop structure to choose for your solution.

counter-controlled loop (counting loop)
A loop whose repetition is managed by a loop control variable whose value represents a count.

loop control variable
A variable that is used to regulate how many times a loop should be repeated.

The loop shown in pseudocode below is called a **counter-controlled loop** (or **counting loop**) because its repetition is managed by a **loop control variable** whose value represents a count. A counter-controlled loop follows the following general format:

Counting Loop
Set *loop control variable* to an initial value of 0.
`while` *loop control variable* < *final value*
     . . .
     Increase *loop control variable* by 1.

We use a counter-controlled loop when we can determine prior to loop execution exactly how many loop repetitions will be needed to solve the problem. This number should appear as the *final value* in the `while` condition.

The `while` Statement

Listing 5.1 shows a program fragment that computes and displays the gross pay for seven employees. The loop body is the compound statement that starts on the third line. The loop body gets an employee's payroll data and computes and displays that employee's pay. After seven weekly pay amounts are displayed, the statement following the loop body executes and displays the message `All employees processed`.

The three colored lines in Listing 5.1 control the looping process. The first statement

```
countEmp = 0;            // no employees processed yet
```

stores an initial value of 0 in the variable `countEmp`, which represents the count of employees processed so far. The next line evaluates the condition `countEmp < 7`. If the condition is true, the compound statement for the loop body executes, causing a new pair of data values to be read and a new pay to be computed and displayed. The last statement in the loop body,

```
countEmp = countEmp + 1;   // increment count of employees
```

adds 1 to the current value of `countEmp`. After executing the last step in the loop body, control returns to the line beginning with `while`, and the condition is reevaluated for the next value of `countEmp`. The loop body executes once for each value of `countEmp` from 0 to 6. Eventually, `countEmp` becomes 7, and the condition evaluates to false. When this happens, the loop body is not executed and control passes to the display statement that follows the loop body.

Listing 5.1   Program fragment with a loop

```
countEmp = 0;                 // no employees processed yet
while (countEmp < 7)          // test the count of employees
{
    cout << "Hours: ";
    cin >> hours;
    cout << "Rate : $";
    cin >> rate;
    pay = hours * rate;
    cout << "Weekly pay is " << pay << endl;
    countEmp = countEmp + 1;  // increment count of
                              // employees
}
cout << "All employees processed" << endl;
```

loop repetition condition
The condition that is evaluated to determine whether to execute the loop body (condition is true) or to exit from the loop (condition is false).

The logical expression following the reserved word `while` is called the **loop repetition condition**. The loop is repeated when this condition is true. We say that the loop is *exited* when this condition is false.

The flowchart in Figure 5.1 summarizes what we've explained so far about `while` loops. In the flowchart, the expression in the diamond-shaped box is evaluated first. If that expression is true, the loop body is executed, and the process is repeated. The `while` loop is exited when the expression becomes false. If the loop repetition condition is false when it's first tested, then the loop body is not executed at all.

Make sure you understand the difference between the `while` statement in Listing 5.1 and the `if` statement:

```
if (countEmp < 7)
{
      . . .
}
```

In an `if` statement, the compound statement after the condition executes at most only once. In a `while` statement, the compound statement (loop body) may execute more than once.

Syntax of the `while` Statement

In Listing 5.1, variable `countEmp` is the loop control variable because its value determines whether or not the loop body is repeated. The loop control variable `countEmp` must be (1) *initialized*, (2) *tested*, and (3) *updated* for the loop to execute properly. Each step is summarized as follows:

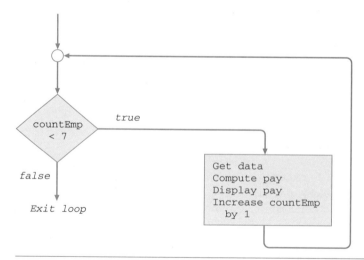

Figure 5.1   Flowchart for a `while` loop

1. *Initialize:* `countEmp` is set to a starting value of 0 (initialized to 0) before the `while` statement is reached.

2. *Test:* `countEmp` is tested before the start of each loop repetition (called an *iteration* or a *pass*).

3. *Update:* `countEmp` is updated (its value increases by 1) during each iteration.

Similar steps must be performed for every `while` loop. Without the initialization, the initial test of `countEmp` is meaningless. The updating step ensures that the program progresses toward the final goal (`countEmp >= 7`) during each repetition of the loop. If the loop control variable is not updated, the loop will execute "forever." Such a loop is called an **infinite loop**.

infinite loop
A loop that executes forever.

`while` Statement

Form: `while` (loop repetition condition)
           statement;

Example: `// display n asterisks`
          `countStar = 0;`
          `while (countStar < n)`
          `{`
              `cout << "*";`
              `countStar = countStar + 1;`
          `}`

Interpretation: The *loop repetition condition* (a condition to control the loop process) is tested; if it's true, the *statement* (loop body) is executed and the *loop repetition condition* is retested. The *statement* is repeated as long as (while) the *loop repetition condition* is true. When this condition is tested and found to be false, the `while` loop is exited and the next program statement after the while statement is executed.

Notes: If the *loop repetition condition* evaluates to false the first time it's tested, *statement* is not executed.

EXERCISES FOR SECTION 5.1

Self-Check

1. What will happen in the execution of the loop in Listing 5.1

   a. if the update statement

   `countEmp = countEmp + 1;`

   is omitted?

    b. if the initialization statement

```
countEmp = 0;
```

      is omitted?

2. Predict the output of this program fragment:

```
i = 0;
while (i < 7)
{
    cout << i - 1 << i
        << -i + 1 << endl;
    i = i + 1;
}
```

3. What does this program fragment display for an input of 11?

```
cin >> n;
ev = 0;
sum = 0;
while (ev < n)
{
    cout << ev;
    sum = sum + ev;
    ev = ev + 2;
}
cout << ev << "*** " << sum << endl;
```

4. How many times is the loop body below repeated? What is displayed during each repetition of the loop body?

```
x = 3;
count = 0;
while (count < 3)
{
    x = x * x;
    cout << x << endl;
    count = count + 1;
}
```

5. Answer the previous exercise if the last statement in the loop is

```
count = count + 2;
```

Programming

1. Write a while loop that displays each integer from 1 to 5 together with its square and cube. Display all three values for each integer on a separate line.

2. Write a program fragment that produces the output below. Hint: If n is the number in the first column, the number in the second column is 2 to the power n.

```
0    1
1    2
2    4
3    8
4    16
5    32
6    64
```

3. Write a program fragment that displays a string two times on line 1, four times on line 2, six times on line 3, and so on.

4. Write a function `powerOfTwo` with a parameter n that uses a loop to compute 2^n and returns its value.·

5.2   Accumulating a Sum or Product in a Loop

Loops often accumulate a sum or a product by repeating an addition or multiplication operation, as will be demonstrated in Examples 5.1 and 5.2.

EXAMPLE 5.1

The program in Listing 5.2 has a `while` loop similar to the loop in Listing 5.1. Besides displaying each employee's weekly pay, it computes and displays the company's total payroll. Prior to loop execution, the statements

```
totalPay = 0.0;
countEmp = 0;
```

initialize both `totalPay` and `countEmp` to zero, where `countEmp` is the counter variable. Here `totalPay` is an accumulator variable, and it accumulates the total payroll value. Initializing `totalPay` is critical; if you omit this step, your final total will be off by whatever value happens to be stored in `totalPay` when the program begins execution.

In the loop body, the assignment statement

```
totalPay = totalPay + pay;          // add next pay
```

adds the current value of `pay` to the sum being accumulated in `totalPay`. Consequently, the value of `totalPay` increases with each loop repetition. Table 5.1 traces the effect of repeating this statement for the three values of pay shown in the sample run.

Listing 5.2   Program to compute company payroll

```cpp
// File: computePay.cpp
// Computes the payroll for a company

#include <iostream>
using namespace std;
int main()
{
    int numberEmp;          // input - number of employees
    int countEmp;           // counter - current employee number
    float hours;            // input - hours worked
    float rate;             // input - hourly rate
    float pay;              // output - weekly pay
    float totalPay;         // output - company payroll

    // Get number of employees from user.
    cout << "Enter number of employees: ";
    cin >> numberEmp;

    // Process payroll for all employees.
    totalPay = 0.0;
    countEmp = 0;
    while (countEmp < numberEmp)
    {

        cout << "Hours: ";
        cin >> hours;
        cout << "Rate : $";
        cin >> rate;
        pay = hours * rate;
        cout << "Pay is $" << pay << endl << endl;
        totalPay = totalPay + pay;        // add next pay
        countEmp = countEmp + 1;
    }
    cout << "Total payroll is $" << totalPay << endl;
    cout << "All employees processed." << endl;

    return 0;
}
```

```
Enter number of employees: 3
Hours: 50
Rate : $5.25
Pay is $262.5
```

(continued)

Listing 5.2   Program to compute company payroll (continued)

```
Hours:  6
Rate :  $5
Pay is $30
Hours:  15
Rate :  $7
Pay is $105
Total payroll is $397.5
All employees processed.
```

Table 5.1   Trace of Three Repetitions of the Loop in Listing 5.2

Statement	Hours	Rate	Pay	totalPay	countEmp	Effect
	?	?	?	0.0	0	
countEmp < numberEmp						true
cin >> hours;	50.0					get hours
cin >> rate;		5.25				get rate
pay = hours * rate;			262.5			compute pay
totalPay = totalPay				262.5		add to
+ pay;						totalPay
countEmp = countEmp					1	increment
+ 1;						countEmp
countEmp < numberEmp						true
cin >> hours;	6.0					get hours
cin >> rate;		5.0				get rate
pay = hours * rate;			30.0			compute pay
totalPay = totalPay				292.5		add to
+ pay;						totalPay
countEmp = countEmp					2	increment
+ 1;						countEmp
countEmp < numberEmp						true
cin >> hours;	15.0					get hours
cin >> rate;		7.0				get rate
pay = hours * rate;			105.0			compute pay
totalPay = totalPay				397.5		add pay to
+ pay;						totalPay
countEmp = countEmp					3	increment
+ 1;						countEmp

PROGRAM STYLE   Writing General Loops

Because the loop in Listing 5.1 uses the loop repetition condition `countEmp`
`< 7`, it processes exactly seven employees. The loop in Listing 5.2 is more
general. It uses the loop repetition condition `countEmp < numberEmp` so it
can process any number of employees. The number of employees to be

processed must be read into variable `numberEmp` before the `while` statement executes. The loop repetition condition compares the number of employees processed so far (`countEmp`) to the total number of employees (`numberEmp`).

Multiplying a List of Numbers

In a similar way, we can use a loop to accumulate a product, as shown in the next example.

EXAMPLE 5.2

The next loop multiplies data items as long as the product remains less than 10,000. It displays the product calculated so far before asking for the next data value. The product so far is updated on each iteration by executing the statement

```
product = product * item;        // Update product
```

Loop exit occurs when the value of **product** is greater than or equal to 10,000. Consequently, the loop body does not display the last value assigned to product.

```
// Multiply data while product remains less than 10000
product = 1;
while (product < 10000)
{
    cout << product << endl;      // display product so far
    cout << "Enter data item: ";
    cin >> item;
    product = product * item;     // Update product
}
```

conditional loop
A loop that repeats the processing of data while a specified condition is true.

This is an example of a **conditional loop**—a loop that repeats the processing of data while a specified condition is true as indicated by its pseudocode below.

Conditional Loop

1. Initialize the *loop control variable.*
2. `while` a condition involving the loop control variable is true
    3. Continue processing.
    4. Update the loop control variable.

For the product computation loop, the loop control variable is `product`, which is initialized to 1. The loop repetition condition is that `product` is less than 10,000, and the steps of the loop body make up the processing mentioned in pseudocode Step 3. We discuss conditional loops in Section 5.4.

Compound Assignment Operators

We've seen several assignment statements of the form

$$variable = variable\ op\ expression;$$

where *op* is a C++ arithmetic operator. These include increments and decrements of loop counters

```
countEmp = countEmp + 1;
time = time - 1;
```

as well as statements accumulating a sum or computing a product in a loop, such as

```
totalPay = totalPay + pay;
product = product * item;
```

C++ provides special assignment operators that enable a more concise notation for statements of this type. For the operations +, -, *, /, and %, C++ defines the compound *op=* assignment operators +=, -=, *=, /=, and %=. A statement of the form

$$variable\ op = expression;$$

is an alternative way of writing the statement

$$variable = variable\ op\ (expression);$$

Table 5.2 shows some examples using compound assignment operators.

Table 5.2   Compound Assignment Operators

Statement with Simple Assignment Operator	Equivalent Statement with Compound Assignment Operator
`countEmp = countEmp + 1;`	`countEmp += 1;`
`time = time - 1;`	`time -= 1;`
`totalTime = totalTime + time;`	`totalTime += time;`
`product = product * item;`	`product *= item;`
`n = n * (x + 1);`	`n *= (x + 1);`

EXERCISES FOR SECTION 5.2

Self-Check

1. What output values are displayed by the `while` loop below for a data value of 5? Of 6? Of 7? In general, what does this loop display?

```
cout << "Enter an integer: ";
cin >> x;
product = 1;
count = 0;
while (count < 4)
{
    cout << product << endl;
    product *= x;
    count += 1;
}
```

2. Answer Self-Check Exercise 1 if the order of the first two statements in the loop body is reversed.

3. The following segment needs some revision. Insert braces where needed, indent properly, and correct the errors. The corrected segment should read five integers and display their sum.

```
count = 0;
while (count <= 5)
cout << "Enter data item: ";
cin >> item;
item += sum;
count += 1;
cout << count << " data items were added;" << endl;
cout << "their sum is " << sum << endl;
```

4. Write equivalents for the following statements using compound assignment operators.

```
r = r % 10;          s = s / 5;
z = z + x + 1;       g = g * n + 4;
q = q - r * m;       t = t + (u % v);
m = m - (n + p);
```

Programming

1. Write a loop that produces the output below (hint: each number in the right column is the sum of all values in the left column up to that point):

```
i    sum
0    0
1    1
2    3
3    6
4    10
5    15
6    21
```

2. Write a program fragment that computes 1 + 2 + 3 + ... + (n - 1) + n using a loop, where n is a data value. Follow the loop with an if statement that compares this value to (n * (n + 1)) / 2 and displays a message that indicates whether the values are the same or different. What message do you think will be displayed?

5.3 The **for** Statement

C++ provides the **for** statement as another form for implementing loops, especially for counting loops. The loops we've seen so far are typical of most repetition structures in that they have three loop control components:

- *initialization* of the loop control variable,
- *testing* the loop repetition condition, and
- *updating* the loop control variable.

An important feature of the **for** statement in C++ is that it supplies a designated place for each of these three components. A **for** statement implementation of the loop from Listing 5.2 is shown in Listing 5.3.

Listing 5.3   Using a **for** statement in a counting loop

```cpp
// Process payroll for all employees.
totalPay = 0.0;
for (countEmp = 0;                 // initialization
     countEmp < numberEmp;         // test
     countEmp += 1)                // update
{
    cout << "Hours: ";
    cin >> hours;
    cout << "Rate : $";
    cin >> rate;
    pay = hours * rate;
    cout << "Pay is $" << pay << endl << endl;
    totalPay += pay;               // accumulate total pay
}
cout << "Total payroll is $" << totalPay << endl;
cout << "All employees processed." << endl;
```

The effect of this `for` statement is exactly equivalent to the execution of the comparable `while` loop in the earlier program (Listing 5.2). Because the `for` statement's heading

```
for (countEmp = 0;          // initialization
     countEmp < numberEmp;  // test
     countEmp += 1)         // update
```

combines the three loop control steps of initialization, testing, and update in one place, separate steps to initialize and update `countEmp` must not appear elsewhere. The `for` statement can be used to count up or down by any interval.

`for` Statement

Form: `for` (*initialization expression;*
              loop repetition condition;
              update expression)
              statement;

Example: `// Display N asterisks.`
              `for (countStar = 0;`
              `     countStar < N;`
              `     countStar += 1)`
              `   cout << '*';`

Interpretation: First, the initialization expression is executed. Then, the *loop repetition condition* is tested. If it's true, the *statement* is executed, and the *update expression* is evaluated. Then the *loop repetition condition* is retested. The *statement* is repeated as long as the *loop repetition condition* is true. When this condition is tested and found to be false, the **for** loop is exited, and the next program statement after the **for** statement is executed.

Caution: Although C++ permits the use of fractional values for counting loop control variables of type **float**, we strongly discourage this practice. Counting loops with type **float** control variables may not execute the same number of times on different computers.

PROGRAM STYLE   Formatting the `for` Statement

For clarity, we often place each expression of the `for` heading on a separate line. If all three expressions are very short, we may place them together on one line. Here is an example:

```
// Display nonnegative numbers < max
for (i = 0; i < max; i += 1)
    cout << i << endl;
```

The body of the for loop is indented. If the loop body is a compound statement or if we're using a style in which we bracket all loop bodies, we place the opening brace on a separate line after the for heading and terminate the statement by placing the closing brace on a separate line. The braces should align with the "f" of for.

Increment and Decrement Operators

The counting loops that we've discussed so far have all included assignment statements of the form

```
counter = counter + 1;
```

or

```
counter += 1;
```

We can also implement this assignment as

```
counter++;
```

or

```
++counter;
```

using the C++ increment operator. The increment operator ++ takes a single variable as its operand. The **side effect** of applying the ++ operator is that the value of its operand is incremented by one. Frequently, ++ is used just for this side effect, as in the following loop in which the variable counter is to run from 0 up to (but not including) limit:

> side effect
> A change in the value of a variable as a result of carrying out an operation.

```
for (counter = 0; counter < limit; counter++)
    . . .
```

The *value* of the expression in which the ++ operator is used depends on the position of the operator. When the ++ is placed immediately in front of its operand (*prefix increment*), the value of the expression is the variable's value *after* incrementing. When the ++ comes immediately after the operand (*postfix increment*), the expression's value is the value of the variable *before* it's incremented. For example, the second statement below

```
m = 3;
n = m++;
```

assigns 3 to n and then increments m (new value of m is 4). Conversely, the second statement below

```
m = 3;
n = ++m;
```

increments m before the assignment to n (m and n are both 4).

You should avoid using the increment and decrement (--) operators in complex expressions in which the variables to which they are applied appear more than once. C++ compilers are expected to exploit the commutativity and associativity of various operators in order to produce efficient code. For example, the next code fragment may assign y the value 13 (2 * 5 + 3) in one implementation and the value 18 (3 * 5 + 3) in another.

```
x = 5;
i = 2;
y = i * x + ++i;
```

A programmer must not depend on side effects that will vary from one compiler to another.

EXAMPLE 5.3

Function `factorial` (Listing 5.4) computes the factorial of an integer represented by the formal parameter n. The loop body executes for *decreasing values* of i from n through 2, and each value of i is incorporated in the accumulating product (n × (n-1) × ... × 3 × 2). Loop exit occurs when i is 1.

PROGRAM STYLE   Localized Declarations of Variables

The example that follows illustrates the use of a localized variable declaration—the loop control variable i. Because for loop control variables often have meaning only inside the loop, we can declare these

Listing 5.4   Function to compute factorial

```
// Computes factorial (n!)
// Pre: n is greater than or equal to zero
int factorial(int n)
{
    int product;      // accumulator for product computation
    product = 1;
    // Computes the product n x (n-1) x (n-2) x  . . .  x2
    for (int i = n; i > 1; i--)
      product = product * i;
    // Returns function result
    return product;
}
```

variables at the point of first reference—in the for loop header. A loop control variable declared this way can be referenced only inside the loop body.

EXAMPLE 5.4

The for statement shown next displays the characters in firstName, one character per line. It illustrates the use of the string functions length and at. If firstName is Jill, the loop displays the letters J, i, l, l on separate lines. The loop repeats exactly firstName.length() times.

```
string firstName;
cout << "Enter your first name: ";
cin >> firstName;
for (int posChar = 0; posChar < firstName.length();
     posChar++)
   cout << firstName.at(posChar) << endl;
```

Increments and Decrements Other than One

We've seen for statement counting loops that count up by one and down by one. Now we'll use a loop that counts down by five to display a Celsius-to-Fahrenheit conversion table.

EXAMPLE 5.5

The table displayed by the program in Listing 5.5 shows temperature conversions from 10 degrees Celsius to 25 degrees Celsius because of the values of the constants CBEGIN (10) and CLIMIT (-5). The loop update step celsius -= CSTEP decreases the value of the counter celsius by five after each repetition. Loop exit occurs when celsius becomes less than CLIMIT, so loop exit occurs when the value of celsius is 210. The last value of celsius displayed in the program output is 25.

Listing 5.5   Converting Celsius to Fahrenheit

```
// File: temperatureTable.cpp
// Conversion of celsius to fahrenheit temperature

#include <iostream>
#include <iomanip>
using namespace std;
```

(continued)

Listing 5.5   Converting Celsius to Fahrenheit (continued)

```
int main()
{
    const int CBEGIN = 10;
    const int CLIMIT = -5;
    const int CSTEP = 5;
    float fahrenheit;

    // Display the table heading.
    cout << "Celsius" << " Fahrenheit" << endl;

    // Display the table.
    for (int celsius = CBEGIN;
             celsius >= CLIMIT;
             celsius -= CSTEP)
    {
        fahrenheit = 1.8 * celsius + 32.0;
        cout << setw(5) << celsius
             << setw(15) << fahrenheit << endl;
    }

    return 0;
}
```

```
Celsius    Fahrenheit
     10         50.00
      5         41.00
      0         32.00
     -5         23.00
```

Displaying a Table of Values

The program in Listing 5.5 displays a table of output values. The output state before the loop displays a string that forms the table heading. Within the loop body, the output statement

```
cout << setw(5) << celsius
     << setw(15) << fahrenheit << endl;
```

displays a pair of output values each time it executes. The items in color above are **manipulators**—member functions of the class iomanip. Manipulators can precede one or more output list items and they control the format or appearance of these items when they are displayed. The manipulator setw(5) causes the next output value (value of celsius) to be displayed using five character positions on the screen. If a number has less than five characters, blanks appear before the number. If a number requires more than

manipulators
Member functions of class iomanip that control the format of input/output list items.

five characters to be displayed correctly, the extra characters will be displayed. The manipulators in the above output statement align the output values for `celsius` and `fahrenheit` in columns under the appropriate heading. We describe manipulators in more detail in Section 8.5.

EXERCISES FOR SECTION 5.3

Self-Check

1. Trace the execution of the loop that follows for n = 10. Show values of odd and sum after the update of the loop counter for each iteration.

```
sum = 0;
for (odd = 1;
     odd < n;
     odd += 2)
{
   sum = sum + odd;
   cout << setw(3) << odd << setw(6) << sum << endl;
}
cout << "Sum of positive odd numbers less "
     << "than " << n << " is " << sum << endl;
```

2. Rewrite the loop in Exercise 1 using a `while` statement.

3. Given the constant definitions of Listing 5.5 (repeated here)

```
const int CBEGIN = 10;
const int CLIMIT = -5;
const int CSTEP = 5;
```

indicate what values of `celsius` would appear in the conversion table displayed if the `for` loop header of Listing 5.5 were rewritten as shown:

a.   for (celsius = CLIMIT;
           celsius >= CBEGIN;
           celsius += CSTEP)

b.   for (celsius = CLIMIT;
           celsius <= CBEGIN;
           celsius += CSTEP)

c.   for (celsius = CLIMIT;
           celsius <= CSTEP;
           celsius += CBEGIN)

d.   for (celsius = CSTEP;
           celsius >= CBEGIN;
           celsius += CLIMIT)

3. What is the least number of times that the body of a `while` loop can be executed? The body of a `for` loop?

4. Assume `i` is 3 and `j` is a. What is the value assigned to variables `m`, `n`, and `p` and what is the value of `i` and `j` after each statement below executes?

```
n = ++i * -j;
m = i + j-;
p = i + j;
```

5. Rewrite the code shown in Exercise 4 so the effect is equivalent but no increment/decrement operator appears in an expression with another arithmetic operator. (Hint: the first statement should be ++i;.)

6. What errors do you see in the following fragment? Correct the code so it displays all multiples of 5 from 0 through 100.

```
for mult5 = 0;
mult5 < 100;
mult5 += 5;
cout << mult5 << endl;
```

7. **a.** Trace the following program fragment:

```
j = 10;
for  (int i = 5; i > 0 ; i-)
{
    cout << setw(3) << i << setw(5) << j;
    j -= 2;
}
```

b. Rewrite the previous program fragment so that it produces the same output but displays `i` in the first five columns and `j` in the next five columns.

Programming

1. Write a loop that displays a table of angle measures along with their sine and cosine values. Assume that the initial and final angle measures (in degrees) are available in `initDegree` and `finalDegree` (type `int` variables), and that the change in angle measure between table entries is given by `stepDegree` (also a type `int` variable). Remember that the `cmath` library's `sin` and `cos` functions take arguments that are in radians. Write this loop using a `for` statement and a `while` statement.

2. Write a program to display a centimeter-to-inches conversion table. The smallest and largest number of centimeters in the table are input values. Your table should give conversions in 10-centimeter intervals. One inch equals 2.54 cm.

3. Write a function that return x^n where x is a type `float` parameter and n is a type `int` parameter. Use a loop. The function should work for negative values as well. (Hint: $x^{-n} = 1/x^n$).

5.4 Conditional Loops

In many programming situations, you won't be able to determine the exact number of loop repetitions before loop execution begins. The number of repetitions may depend on some aspect of the data that is not known in advance but that usually can be stated by a condition. Like the counting loops we considered earlier, a conditional loop typically has three parts that control repetition: (1) initialization, (2) testing of a loop repetition condition, and (3) an update. The general form for a conditional loop is the following:

> Conditional Loop
>
> Initialize the loop control variable.
> `while` a condition involving the loop control variable is true
>   Continue processing.
>   Update the loop control variable.

For example, if we're getting the number of employees of a company, we want to continue reading data until a positive number or zero is entered. Another way of saying this is "We want to continue reading numbers as long as all previous data for number of employees were negative." Clearly, the loop repetition condition is

$$\textit{number of employees} < 0$$

Because it makes no sense to test this condition unless number of employees has a meaning, getting this value must be the initialization step. We still need to identify the update action—the statement that, if left out, would cause the loop to repeat infinitely. Getting a new number of employees within the loop body is just such a step. Since we've found these three essential loop parts, we can write this validating input loop in pseudocode:

> Prompt for number of employees.
> Read number of employees.
> `while` number of employees < 0
>   Display a warning and another prompt.
>   Read number of employees.

This loop can be implemented easily using the C++ `while` statement:

```cpp
cout << "Enter number of employees: ";
cin >> numEmp;                    // initialization
while (numEmp < 0)                // test
{
    cout << "Negative number invalid; try again: ";
    cin >> numEmp;                // update
}
```

At first, it may seem odd that the initialization and update steps are identical. In fact, this is very often the case for loops performing input operations in situations where the number of input values is not known in advance.

A Loop with a Decreasing Loop Control Variable

We study another conditional loop in the next case study. In this example, the loop repetition condition involves testing whether the value of the loop control variable has dropped below a critical point. The value of the loop control variable decreases during each iteration.

case study   Monitoring Oil Supply

PROBLEM

We want to monitor the amount of oil remaining in a storage tank at the end of each day. The initial supply of oil in the tank and the amount taken out each day are data items. Our program should display the amount left in the tank at the end of each day and it should also display a warning when the amount left is less than or equal to 10 percent of the tank's capacity. At this point, no more oil can be removed until the tank is refilled.

ANALYSIS

Clearly, the problem inputs are the initial oil supply and the amount taken out each day. The outputs are the oil remaining at the end of each day and a warning message when the oil left in the tank is less than or equal to 10 percent of its capacity.

DATA REQUIREMENTS

Problem Constant

```
CAPACITY = 10000          // tank capacity
MINPCT = 0.10             // minimum percent
```

Problem Inputs

```
float supply              // initial oil supply
```
Each day's oil use

Problem Output

```
float oilLevel            // final oil amount
```
Each day's oil supply
A warning message when the oil
supply is less than minimum

Program Variable

```
float minOil              // minimum oil supply
```

FORMULAS

Minimum oil supply is 10 percent of tank's capacity

DESIGN

We list the major steps next.

INITIAL ALGORITHM

1. Get the initial oil supply.

2. Compute the minimum oil supply.

3. Compute and display the amount of oil left each day.

4. Display the oil left and a warning message if necessary.

We'll implement Step 3 using function `monitorOil`. The function's analysis and design follows.

ANALYSIS FOR `MONITOROIL`

Function `monitorOil` must display a table showing the amount of oil left at the end of each day. To accomplish this, the function must read each day's usage and deduct that amount from the oil remaining. The function needs to receive the initial oil supply and the minimum oil supply as inputs (arguments) from the main function.

FUNCTION INTERFACE FOR MONITOROIL
Input Parameters

```
float supply          // initial oil supply
float minOil          // minimum oil supply
```

Output
Returns the final oil amount

Local Data

```
float usage           // input from user - Each day's oil use
float oilLeft         // output to user - Each day's oil supply
```

DESIGN OF `MONITOROIL`

The body of `monitorOil` is a loop that displays the oil usage table. We can't use a counting loop because we don't know in advance how many days it will take to bring the supply to a critical level. We do know the initial supply of oil, and we know that we want to continue to compute and display the amount of oil remaining (`oilLeft`) as long as the amount of oil remaining does not fall below the minimum. So the loop control variable must be `oilLeft`. We need to initialize `oilLeft` to the initial supply and to repeat the loop as long as `oilLeft > minOil` is true. The update step should deduct the daily usage (a data value) from `oilLeft`.

INITIAL ALGORITHM FOR MONITOROIL

1. Initialize `oilLeft` to `supply`.

2. `while (oilLeft > minOil)`

    2.1. Read in the daily usage.

    2.2. Deduct the daily usage from `oilLeft`.

    2.3. Display the value of `oilLeft`.

IMPLEMENTATION

Listing 5.6 shows the program. Notice that function `monitorOil` performs three critical steps that involve the loop control variable `oilLeft`.

- *Initialize* `oilLeft` to the initial supply before loop execution begins.
- *Test* `oilLeft` before each execution of the loop body.
- *Update* `oilLeft` (by subtracting the daily usage) during each iteration.

TESTING

To test the program, try running it with a few samples of input data. One sample should bring the oil level remaining to exactly 10 percent of the capacity. For example, if the capacity is 10,000 gallons, enter a final daily usage amount that brings the oil supply to 1,000 gallons and see what happens. Also, verify that the program output is correct when the initial oil supply is below 10 percent of the capacity, as discussed next.

Zero Iteration Loops

The body of a `while` loop is not executed if the loop repetition test fails (evaluates to false) when it's first reached. You should always verify that a program still generates the correct results for zero iteration loops. If the value read into `supply` is less than 10 percent of the tank's capacity, the loop body in Listing 5.6 would not execute and the main function would display only the line below.

```
The oil left in the tank is less than 1000 gallons.
```

PROGRAM STYLE   Performing Loop Processing in a Function Subprogram

In Listing 5.6, function `monitorOil` contains a `while` loop that performs the major program task—monitoring the oil remaining in a tank. This program structure is fairly common and quite effective. Placing all loop processing in a function subprogram simplifies the main function.

Listing 5.6 Program to monitor oil supply

```cpp
// File: oilSupply.cpp
// Displays daily usage and amount left in oil tank.
#include <iostream>
using namespace std;

float monitorOil(float, float);

int main()
{
    const float CAPACITY = 10000;      // tank capacity
    const float MINPCT = 10.0;         // minimum percent

    float supply;              // input - initial oil supply
    float oilLeft;             // output - oil left in tank
    float minOil;              // minimum oil supply

    // Get the initial oil supply.
    cout << "Enter initial oil supply: ";
    cin >> supply;

    // Compute the minimum oil supply.
    minOil = CAPACITY * (MINPCT / 100.0);

    // Compute and display the amount of oil left each day.
    oilLeft = monitorOil(supply, minOil);

    // Display a warning message if supply is less than minimum
    cout << endl << oilLeft << " gallons left in tank." << endl;
    if (oilLeft < minOil)
        cout << "Warning - amount of oil left is below minimum!"
             << endl;

    return 0;
}

// Computes and displays the amount of oil left each day.
// Pre: initial supply and minimum amount are calculated.
// Returns the amount of oil left at end of last day.

float monitorOil(float supply, float minOil)
{
    // Local data ...
    float usage;               // input from user - Each day's oil use
```

(continued)

Listing 5.6   Program to monitor oil supply (continued)

```
    float oilLeft;      // Amount left each day

    oilLeft = supply;
    while (oilLeft > minOil)
    {
        cout << "Enter amount used today: ";
        cin >> usage;
        oilLeft -= usage;
        cout << "After removal of " << usage << " gallons, ";
        cout << "number of gallons left is " << oilLeft
            << endl << endl;
    }

    return oilLeft;
}
```

```
Enter initial oil supply: 7000
Enter amount used today: 1000
After removal of 1000 gallons, number of gallons left is 6000

Enter amount used today: 4000
After removal of 4000 gallons, number of gallons left is 2000

Enter amount used today: 1500
After removal of 1500 gallons, number of gallons left is 500

500 gallons left in tank
Warning - amount of oil left is below minimum!
```

More General Conditional Loops

Often the loop repetition condition in a conditional loop contains the logical operator && (and). For example, if we know that the oil tank is always refilled after 14 days, we might want to use the loop heading

```
while ((oilLeft > minOil) && (numDays < 14))
```

in function monitorOil. In this case, loop repetition continues only if both relations are true, so loop exit will occur if either one becomes false.

The loop repetition condition uses oilLeft and numDays as loop control variables, so each variable should be initialized before loop entry and update in the loop body. We should initialize numDays to 0 and increment it by one in the loop body.

EXERCISES FOR SECTION 5.4

Self-Check

1. Provide an example of data that would cause function monitorOil to return without executing the body of the loop.

2. **a.** Correct the syntax and logic of the code that follows so that it displays all multiples of 3 from 0 through 60, inclusive:

```
sum = 0;
while (sum < 60) ;
    sum += 3;
    cout << sum << endl;
```

   b. Rewrite the above fragment using a for loop. Is this a counting loop? Explain your answer.

3. What output is displayed if this list of data is used for the program in Listing 5.6?

```
5000
4000.5
550.25
```

4. How would you modify the program in Listing 5.6 so that it also determines the number of days (numDays) before the oil supply drops below the minimum? Which is the loop control variable, oilLeft or numDays or both?

5. Trace the execution of the following loop for data values of 5, 4, 10, –5. Are all the data values read in?

```
cin >> n;
while (n > 0 && pow(2, n) < 1000)
{
    cout << setw(2) << n << setw(8) << pow(2, n) << endl;
    cin >> n;
}
```

Programming

1. There are 900 people in a town whose population increases by 10 percent (a data item) each year. Write a loop that displays the annual population and determines how many years (countYears) it will take for the population to pass 20,000. Verify that your program works if the population doubles each year (an increase of 100%).

2. Rewrite the payroll program (Listing 5.2), moving the loop processing into a function subprogram. Return the total payroll amount as the function result.

3. Rewrite function `monitorOil` to allow the tank to have oil added to it as well as removed.

5.5 Loop Design and Loop Patterns

In this section, we look more carefully at loop design issues and illustrate some common loop patterns you're likely to encounter in programming. First we summarize the thought processes that went into the design of the loop in Listing 5.6. The comment

```
// Compute and display the amount of oil left each day.
```

that precedes the call to function `monitorOil` in the main function is a good summary of the purpose of the loop. The columns labeled "Answers" and "Implications ..." in Table 5.3 represent one problem solver's approach to the loop design.

Table 5.3   Problem-Solving Questions for Loop Design

Question	Answer	Implications for the Algorithm
What are the inputs?	Initial supply of oil (`supply`) Amounts removed (`usage`)	Input variables needed: `supply` `usage`
		Value of `supply` must be input once, but amounts used are entered many times.
What are the outputs?	Current amount of oil	Values of `oilLeft` are displayed.
Is there any repetition?	Yes. Program repeatedly	Program variable `oilLeft` is needed.
	1. gets amount used 2. subtracts the amount used from the amount left 3. checks to see whether the amount left has fallen below the minimum.	
Do I know in advance how many times steps will be repeated?	No	Loop will not be controlled by a `counter`.
How do I know how long to keep repeating the steps?	As long as current supply not less than or equal to minimum	The loop repetition condition is `oilLeft > minOil`

Sentinel-Controlled Loops

Many programs with loops read one or more data items each time the loop body is repeated. Often we don't know how many data items the loop should process when it begins execution. Therefore, we must find some way to signal the program to stop reading and processing data.

One way to do this is to instruct the user to enter a unique data value, called a **sentinel value**, after the last data item. The loop repetition condition tests each data item and causes loop exit when the sentinel value is read. Choose the sentinel value carefully; it must be a value that could not normally occur as data.

sentinel value
A data item entered after the last actual data item, used to cause loop exit.

A loop that processes data until the sentinel value is entered has the following form:

> **Sentinel-Controlled Loop**
> 1. Read the first data item.
> 2. while the sentinel value has not been read
>   3. Process the data item.
>   4. Read the next data item.

Note that this loop, like other loops we've studied, has an *initialization* (Step 1), a *loop repetition condition* (Step 2), and an *update* (Step 4). Step 1 gets the first data item; Step 4 gets all the other data items and then tries to obtain one more item. This attempted extra input permits entry (but not processing) of the sentinel value. For program readability, we usually name the sentinel by defining a constant.

EXAMPLE 5.6

A program that calculates the sum of a collection of exam scores is a candidate for using a sentinel value. If the class is large and attendance varies, the instructor may not know the exact number of students who took the exam being graded. The program should work regardless of class size. The following statements (a and b) must be true for a sentinel-controlled loop that accumulates the sum of a collection of exam scores where each data item is read into the variable **score**. The sentinel value must not be included in the sum.

a. **sum** is the total of all scores read so far.
b. **score** contains the sentinel value just after loop exit.

From statement (a) we know that we must add each score to **sum** in the loop body, and that **sum** must initially be zero in order for its final value to be correct. From statement (b) we know that loop exit must occur after the sentinel value is read into **score**.

A solution is to read the first score as the initial value of **score** before the loop is reached and then to perform the following steps in the loop body:

- Add score to sum.
- Read the next score.

The algorithm outline for this solution is shown next.

Sentinel-Controlled Loop for Processing Exam Scores
1. Initialize sum to zero.
2. Read first score.
3. while score is not the sentinel
   4. Add score to sum.
   5. Read next score.

Beginning programmers sometimes try to cut down on the number of Read operations by reversing the order of Steps 4 and 5 above and deleting Step 2. We show this incorrect sentinel loop pattern next.

Incorrect Sentinel Loop for Processing Exam Scores
1. Initialize sum to zero.
2. while score is not the sentinel
   3. Read score.
   4. Add score to sum.

There are two problems associated with this strategy. Because there's no initializing input statement, the initial test of score is meaningless. Also, consider the last two iterations of the loop. On the next-to-last iteration, the last data value is copied into score and added to the accumulating sum; on the last iteration, the attempt to get another score obtains the sentinel value. However, this fact will not cause the loop to exit until the loop repetition condition is tested again. Before this happens, the sentinel is added to sum. For these reasons, it's important to set up sentinel-controlled loops using the recommended structure: one input to get the loop going (the *initialization* input), and a second to keep it going (the *updating* input).

The program in Listing 5.7 uses a while loop to implement the correct sentinel-controlled loop shown earlier. It calls function displayGrade (see again Listing 4.3) to display the grade for each score. Besides summing the scores, the program also computes and displays the average, as discussed in the next section.

Let's check what happens when there are no data items to process. In this case, the sentinel value would be entered after the first prompt. Loop

Listing 5.7   A sentinel-controlled loop

```cpp
// File: sumScores.cpp
// Accumulates the sum of exam scores.

#include <iostream>
using namespace std;

void displayGrade(int);              // See Listing 4.3

int main()
{
    const int SENTINEL = -1;         // sentinel value
    int score;                       // input - each exam score
    int sum;                         // output - sum of scores
    int count;                       // output - count of scores
    int average;                     // output - average score

    // Process all exam scores until sentinel is read
    count = 0;
    sum = 0;
    cout << "Enter scores one at a time as requested." << endl;
    cout << "When done, enter " << SENTINEL << " to stop." << endl;
    cout << "Enter the first score: ";
    cin >> score;
    while (score != SENTINEL)
    {
      sum += score;
      count++;
      displayGrade(score);
      cout << endl<< "Enter the next score: ";
      cin >> score;
    }

    cout << endl << endl;
    cout << "Number of scores processed is " << count << endl;
    cout << "Sum of exam scores is " << sum << endl;

    // Compute and display average score.
    if (count > 0)
    {
        average = sum / count;
        cout << "Average score is " << average;
    }
```

(continued)

Listing 5.7   A sentinel-controlled loop (continued)

```
    return 0;
}


// Insert function displayGrade here. (See Listing 4.3).
```

```
Enter scores one at a time as requested.
When done, enter -1 to stop.
Enter the first score: 85
Grade is B
Enter the next score : 33
Grade is F
Enter the next score : 77
Grade is C
Enter the next score : -1
Number of scores processed is 3
Sum of exam scores is 195
Average score is 65
```

exit would occur right after the first and only test of the loop repetition condition, so the loop body would not execute. The variables sum and count would remain zero. Also, the average would not be calculated or displayed.

Calculating an Average

The program in Listing 5.7 calculates the average exam score as well as the sum. This happens because an extra variable, count, has been added to keep track of the number of scores processed. We initialize count to 0 before entering the loop and use the statement

```
    count++;
```

in the loop body to increment count after each exam score is processed. Notice that count has no role in loop control—the loop repetition condition tests the loop control variable score, not count.

After loop exit, the value of sum is the sum of scores and the value of count is the number of scores processed, so we can divide sum by count to get the average. Notice that this division takes place only when count is nonzero.

Flag-Controlled Loops

Type bool variables are often used as *flags* to control the execution of a loop. The value of the flag is initialized (usually to false) prior to loop entry and is redefined (usually to true) when a particular event occurs inside the loop. A **flag-controlled loop** executes as long as the anticipated event has not yet occurred.

flag-controlled loop A loop whose repetition condition is a type bool variable that is initialized to one value (either false or true) and reset to the other value when a specific event occurs.

Flag-Controlled Loop

1. Set the flag to false.
2. while the flag is false
   3. Perform some action.
   4. Reset the flag to true if the anticipated event occurred.

EXAMPLE 5.7

Function getDigit (Listing 5.8) has no arguments and returns a type char value. It scans the data characters entered at the keyboard and returns the first digit character in the data. For example, if the user has typed in the data line Abc$34%, the character returned would be 3. The statement

```
ch = getDigit();
```

stores the character returned by getDigit in ch (type char).

Function getDigit uses the local variable digitRead as a flag to indicate whether a digit character has been read. Because no characters are read before the loop executes, it initializes digitRead to false. The while loop continues to execute as long as digitRead is false because this means that the event "digit character read" has not yet occurred. Therefore, the loop repetition condition is (!digitRead), because this condition is true when digitRead is false. Inside the loop body, the type bool assignment statement

```
digitRead = (('0' <= nextChar) && (nextChar <= '9'));
```

assigns a value of true to digitRead if the character just read into nextChar is a digit character (within the range '0' through '9', inclusive); otherwise, digitRead remains false. If digitRead becomes true, loop exit occurs and the last character read into nextChar is returned as the function result.

Function getDigit is a bit different from other functions you've seen. Instead of returning a value that has been computed, it returns a value that was read as a data item. This is perfectly reasonable, and we'll see more examples of problem data items being returned as function outputs in the next section and in Chapter 6.

Listing 5.8   Function `getDigit`

```
// Returns the first digit character read
// Pre: The user has entered a line of data
char getDigit()
{

    char nextChar;          // user input - next data character
    bool digitRead;         // status flag - set true
                            // when digit character is read

    digitRead = false;      // no digit character read yet
    while (!digitRead)
    {
        cin >> nextChar;
        digitRead = (('0' <= nextChar) && (nextChar <= '9'));
    }

    return nextChar;        // return first digit character
}
```

EXERCISES FOR SECTION 5.5

Self-Check

1. In Listing 5.7, how would program execution change if we made the assignment statement (`sum += score;`) the last statement in the loop body?

2. You can use a `for` statement to implement a sentinel-controlled loop. The initialization and update steps would be input operations. Show the loop in Listing 5.4 as a `for` statement. Make sure you do not use count for loop control.

3. a. What would happen if the type `bool` assignment statement

      `digitRead = (('0' <= nextChar) && (nextChar <= '9'));`

      was accidentally omitted from the loop in Listing 5.8?

   b. What is the value of each relational expression in the preceding assignment statement if the value of `nextChar` is `'2'`? If the value of `nextChar` is `'a'`?

   c. Replace the assignment statement with an `if` statement that assigns a value of true or false to `digitRead`.

4. What value of count would the program in Listing 5.7 display when the user enters the sentinel value as the first data item? What would happen when the program attempted to compute the average?

Programming

1. Modify the counter-controlled loop in Listing 5.2 so that it's a sentinel-controlled loop. Use a negative value of hours as the sentinel.

2. Write a program segment that allows the user to enter values and displays the number of positive and negative values entered. Use 0 as the sentinel value.

3. Write a while loop that displays all powers of an integer, n, less than a specified value, MAXPOWER. On each line of a table, show the power (0, 1, 2, ...) and the value of the integer n raised to that power.

4. Write a loop that reads in a collection of words and builds a sentence out of all the words by appending each new word to the string being formed. For example, if the three words This, is, one are entered, your sentence would be "This", then "This is", and finally "This is one". Exit your loop when a sentinel word is entered.

5. Write a flag-controlled loop that continues to read pairs of integers until it reads a pair with the property that the first integer in the pair is the same as the second. If the integers are stored in variables m and n, your loop should display each value of m, n, m–n, and n–m.

5.6 The do-while Statement

The do-while statement is used to specify a conditional loop that executes at least once. In the do-while statement, the loop repetition test is specified at the bottom of the loop, so the test cannot be made until at least one execution of the loop body has been completed.

We can use a do-while statement to implement a **data-validation loop**—a loop that continues to prompt and read data until a valid data item is entered. Because the user must enter at least one data item before validation can occur, the do-while is a convenient loop structure.

data-validation loop
A loop that continues to execute until it reads a valid data item.

Data-Validation Loop

do
    Prompt for and read a data item
while data item is not valid.

As an example, we can use the following do-while loop to ensure that the value read into numEmp (number of employees) is valid (greater than or equal to zero). The loop continues to prompt for and read data until the user enters a number that is not negative. Loop exit occurs when the condition `numEmp < 0` is false.

```
do
{
    cout << "Enter number of employees: ";
    cin >> numEmp;
} while (numEmp < 0);
```

---

do-while Statement

Form: do
        statement;
    while (*expression*);

Example: do
```
{
    cout << "Enter a digit character: ";
    cin >> ch;
} while ((ch < '0') || (ch > '9'));
```

Interpretation: After each execution of the *statement*, the *expression* is evaluated. If the *expression* is true, the (loop body) is repeated. If the *expression* is false, loop exit occurs and the next program statement is executed.

EXAMPLE 5.8

Function `getIntRange` in Listing 5.9 contains a data-validation loop that continues to read numbers until the user enters a number within a specified range. The function parameters, `min` and `max`, specify the bounds of the range and are included in the range. The loop repetition condition

```
((nextInt < min) || (nextInt > max))
```

is true if `nextInt` is either less than the lower limit or greater than the upper limit. Otherwise, `nextInt` must be in the desired range.

Listing 5.9   Function `getIntRange`

```
// Returns the first integer in the range min through max
// Pre: min <= max
int getIntRange(int min, int max)   // range boundaries
{
    int nextInt;        // next number read
```

(continued)

Listing 5.9   Function getIntRange (continued)

```
        // Enter data until a number between min and max is read.
        do
        {
            cout << "Enter a number between " << min
                 << " and " << max << ": ";
            cin >> nextInt;
        } while ((nextInt < min) || (nextInt > max));
        return nextInt;

    }
```

EXAMPLE 5.9

A do-while statement is often used to control a menu-driven program that displays a list of choices from which the program user selects a program operation. For example, the menu displayed for a text editing program (see Example 4.20) might look like this:

```
List of edit operations:
D - Delete a substring.
F - Find a string.
I - Insert a string.
R - Replace a substring.
Q - Quit
Enter D, F, I, R, or Q as your selection:
```

The main control routine for such a program would implement the pseudocode that follows.

> do
> > Display the menu.
> > Read the user's choice.
> > Perform the user's choice.
> > Display the edited string.
> while the choice is not Quit.

Listing 5.10 shows the main function. For each iteration, function displayMenu displays the menu and reads and performs the user's choice. Function edit (Listing 4.6) is called with actual arguments textString and choice. Function edit carries out the action specified by the choice value (a character in the list D, F, I, R, or Q). For any other value of choice, edit does nothing but return control to the loop. Notice that the loop continues to execute for all values of choice except Q (value of SENTINEL). Therefore, if the user enters an invalid value (one not in the menu), function edit should not change textString and the user gets another chance to enter a correct value.

Listing 5.10   main function for text editor program

```cpp
// file textEditor.cpp
// main function to test menu
#include <iostream>
#include <string>
using namespace std;

// Insert function subprogram prototypes here.

int main()
{
    const char SENTINEL = 'Q';
    char choice;            // input - edit operation
    string textString;      // input/output - string to edit

    cout << "Enter string to edit: ";
    getline(cin, textString);

    do
    {
        displayMenu();            // display the menu & prompt
        cin >> choice;
        textString = edit(textString, choice);  // edit
                                                 // string
        cout << "New string is " << textString << endl;
    } while (choice != SENTINEL);

    return 0;
}

// Insert function subprograms here.
```

EXAMPLE 5.10

The program in Listing 5.11 uses a `do-while` loop to find the largest value in a sequence of data items. The variable `itemValue` is used to hold each data item, and the variable `largestSoFar` is used to save the largest data value encountered. Within the loop, the `if` statement

```cpp
if (itemValue > largestSoFar)
    largestSoFar = itemValue;     // save new largest number
```

redefines the value of `largestSoFar` if the current data item is larger than all previous data values.

The variable `minValue`, which represents the smallest integer value, serves two purposes in the program shown in Listing 5.11. By initializing `largestSoFar` to `minValue` before loop entry, we ensure that the condition (`itemValue > largestSoFar`) will be true during the first loop repetition. Thus the first data item will be saved as the largest value so far. We're also using `minValue` as a sentinel because it's unlikely to be entered as a data item for a program that is finding the largest number in a sequence. We include the library `limits`, which defines `INT_MIN` in the program shown in Listing 5.11. Because `INT_MIN` is system dependent, your system may display a different value of `INT_MIN`.

Listing 5.11   Finding the largest value

```cpp
// File: largest.cpp
// Finds the largest number in a sequence of integer values

#include <iostream>
#include <limits>              // needed for INT_MIN
using namespace std;

int main()
{

    int itemValue;       // input - each data value
    int largestSoFar;    // output - largest value so far
    int minValue;        // the smallest integer

    // Initialize largestSoFar to the smallest integer.
    minValue = INT_MIN;
    largestSoFar = minValue;

    // Save the largest number encountered so far.
    cout << "Finding the largest value in a sequence: " << endl;
    do
    {

        cout << "Enter an integer or " << minValue << " to stop: ";
        cin >> itemValue;
        if (itemValue > largestSoFar)
            largestSoFar = itemValue;                // save new largest number
    } while (itemValue != minValue);

    cout << "The largest value entered was " << largestSoFar
        << endl;

    return 0;
}
```

(continued)

Listing 5.11   Finding the largest value (continued)

```
Finding the largest value in a sequence:
Enter an integer or -2147483648 to stop: -999
Enter an integer or -2147483648 to stop: 500
Enter an integer or -2147483648 to stop: 100
Enter an integer or -2147483648 to stop: -2147483648
The largest value entered was 500
```

EXERCISES FOR SECTION 5.6

Self-Check

1. What output is produced by the following do-while loop (m is type int)?

```
m = 10;
do
{
    cout << m << endl;
    m = m - 2;
} while (m > 0);
```

2. Redo Exercise 1 for an initial value of m = 11.

3. Rewrite the loop repetition condition in Listing 5.10 so that loop exit occurs after the user enters either q or Q or 10 edit operations have been performed.

4. Rewrite the loop in Self-Check Exercise 1 as a while loop.

5. Rewrite the loop in Self-Check Exercise 1 using for statement.

Programming

1. Modify function getIntRange so that it uses a flag-controlled loop instead of a do-while.

2. Modify the loop in the largest score program so that it uses a while loop.

3. **a.** Write a while loop that prompts a user for a score between 0 and 100 inclusive and continues to repeat the prompt until a valid entry is provided.

   b. Write a do-while loop that prompts a user for a score between 0 and 100 inclusive and continues to read data until a valid entry is provided.

   c. Do you prefer version (a) or (b) of these loops? Justify your answer.

5.7   Review of `while`, `for`, and `do-while` Loops

C++ provides three loop control statements: `while`, `for`, and `do-while`. The `while` loop executes as long as its loop repetition condition is true; the `do-while` loop executes in a similar manner except that the statements in the loop body are always performed at least once. Normally, we use a `for` loop to implement counting loops. In a `for` loop, we can specify the three loop control steps—initialization, testing, and update—together in the loop heading. Table 5.4 describes when to use each of these three loop forms.

Although we tend to rely on the `while` statement to write most conditional loops, experienced C++ programmers often use the `for` statement instead. Because the format of a `for` statement heading is

```
for (initialization; loop-repetition test; update)
```

all the `while` loops in this chapter can be written using `for` statements. To do this, you simply move the loop control steps to the locations indicated above. For example, we could write the sentinel-controlled loop for Listing 5.7 using the `for` statement heading

```
for (cin >> score; score != SENTINEL; cin >> score)
```

This clearly shows that the initialization and update steps for a sentinel-controlled loop are the same.

It's relatively easy to rewrite a `do-while` loop as a `while` loop (or a `for` loop) by inserting an initialization step that makes the loop-repetition condition true the first time it's tested. However, not all `while` loops can be conveniently expressed as `do-while` loops; a `do-while` loop will always execute at least once, but a `while` loop body may be skipped entirely. For this reason, a `while` loop is preferred over a

Table 5.4   Three Loop Forms

`while`	Most commonly used when repetition is not counter controlled; condition test precedes each loop repetition; loop body may not be executed at all
`for`	Used to implement a counting loop; also convenient for other loops with simple initialization and update steps; condition test precedes the execution of the loop body
`do-while`	Convenient when at least one repetition of the loop body is required

do-while loop unless it's clear that at least one loop iteration must always be performed.

As an illustration of the three loop forms, a simple counting loop is written in Listing 5.12. (The dotted lines represent the loop body.) The for loop is the best to use in this situation. The do-while loop must be nested in an if statement to prevent it from being executed when startValue is greater than stopValue. For this reason, the do-while version of a counting loop is least desirable.

In Listing 5.12, the expression

```
count++;
```

is used in all three loops to update the loop control variable count. count will be equal to stopValue after the loops are executed; count will remain equal to startValue if these loops are skipped.

Listing 5.12 Comparison of three loop forms

```
while loop
count = startValue;
while (count < stopValue)
{

    .. . . .
    count++;
}  // end while
```

```
for loop
for (count = startValue; count < stopValue; count++)
{

    .. . . .
} // end for
```

```
do-while loop
count = startValue;
if (startValue < stopValue)
    do
    {
        .. . . .
        count++;
    } while (count < stopValue);
```

EXERCISES FOR SECTION 5.7

Self-Check

1. What does the `while` statement below display? Rewrite it as a `for` statement and as a do-while statement.

```
num = 5;
while (num <= 50)
{
    cout << num << endl;
    num += 5;
}
```

2. What does the `for` statement below display? Rewrite it as a `while` statement and as a do-while statement.

```
for (n = 3; n > 0; n--)
    cout << n << " cubed is " << pow (n, 3) << endl;
```

3. When would you make use of a do-while loop rather than a `while` loop in a program?

Programming

1. Write a program fragment that ignores any negative integer values read as data and finds the sum of only the positive numbers. Write two versions: one using do-while and one using `while`. Loop exit should occur after a sequence of three negative values is read.

2. Write a program fragment that could be used as the main control loop in a menu-driven program for updating an account balance (D = deposit, W = withdrawal, Q = quit). Assume that functions `processWithdrawal` and `processDeposit` already exist and are called with the actual argument `balance`. Prompt the user for a transaction code (D, W, or Q) and call the appropriate function.

3. Write a program that displays the value of each triplet of items entered as data; for example, for the data + 5 3.5, it should display the line: 5 + 3.5 = 8.5. The program should terminate when q or Q is the first item of a triplet.

5.8 Nested Loops

We've used nested `if` statements in earlier programs and now show that it's also possible to nest loops. Nested loops consist of an outer loop with one or more inner loops. Each time the outer loop is repeated, the inner loops are reentered, their loop control components are reevaluated, and all required iterations are performed.

EXAMPLE 5.11

Listing 5.13 shows a sample run of a program with two nested **for** loops. The outer loop is repeated four times (**for** i equals 0, 1, 2, 3). Each time the outer loop is repeated, the statement

```
cout << "Outer" << setw(7) << i << endl;
```

displays the string **"Outer"** and the value of i (the outer loop control variable). Next, the inner loop is entered, and its loop control variable, j, is reset to 0. The inner loop repeats exactly i times. Each time the inner loop body is executed, the statement

```
cout << " Inner" << setw(10) << j << endl;
```

displays the string **"Inner"** and the value of j.

The outer loop control variable i determines the number of repetitions of the inner loop, which is perfectly valid. However, it's best not to use the same variable as the loop control variable of both an outer and inner **for** loop in the same nest.

EXAMPLE 5.12

The program in Listing 5.14 displays the multiplication table. The first **for** loop displays the table heading. The nested loops display the table body. The outer loop control variable

```
for (int rowVal = 0; rowVal < 10; rowVal++)
```

sets the value for each row of the table. The inner loop control variable

```
for (int colVal = 0; colVal < 11; colVal++)
```

cycles through each of the column values (0 through 10). Inside the inner loop, the statement

```
cout << setw(3) << rowVal * colVal;
```

displays each item in the table body as the product of a row value times a column value. The output statement

```
cout << endl;
```

follows the inner loop and terminates the row of values displayed by that loop.

Listing 5.13   Nested for loop program

```cpp
// File: nestedLoops.cpp
// Illustrates a pair of nested for loops

#include <iostream>
#include <iomanip>
using namespace std;

int main()
{
    // Display heading
    cout << setw(12) << "i" << setw(6) << "j" << endl;
    for (int i = 0; i < 4; i++)
    {
        cout << "Outer" << setw(7) << i << endl;
        for (int j = 0; j < i; j++)
            cout << "Inner" << setw(10) << j << endl;
    }  // end outer loop

    return 0;
}
```

```
                i       j
Outer           0
Outer           1
    Inner               0
Outer           2
    Inner               0
    Inner               1
Outer           3
    Inner               0
    Inner               1
    Inner               2
```

EXERCISES FOR SECTION 5.8

Self-Check

1. In Listing 5.14, how many times does the line

   ```cpp
   cout << setw(3) << rowVal * colVal;
   ```

   execute? How many times does the line that follows it execute? How would you change the program to display the addition table?

Listing 5.14   Displaying the multiplication table

```
// File: multiplication.cpp
// Displays the multiplication table

#include <iostream>
#include <iomanip>
using namespace std;

int main()
{

    // Display table heading
    cout << "    ";
    for (int colHead = 0; colHead < 11; colHead++)
        cout << setw(3) << colHead;
    cout << endl;
    cout << " -----------" << endl;

    // Display table, row-by-row
    for (int rowVal = 0; rowVal < 10; rowVal++)
    {
        cout << setw(3) << rowVal << ' ';

        // Display all columns of current row
        for (int colVal = 0; colVal < 11; colVal++)
            cout << setw(3) << rowVal * colVal;
        cout << endl;
    }

    return 0;
}
```

```
   | 0  1  2  3  4  5  6  7  8  9 10
   _____
0  | 0  0  0  0  0  0  0  0  0  0  0
1  | 0  1  2  3  4  5  6  7  8  9 10
2  | 0  2  4  6  8 10 12 14 16 18 20
3  | 0  3  6  9 12 15 18 21 24 27 30
4  | 0  4  8 12 16 20 24 28 32 36 40
5  | 0  5 10 15 20 25 30 35 40 45 50
6  | 0  6 12 18 24 30 36 42 48 54 60
7  | 0  7 14 21 28 35 42 49 56 63 70
8  | 0  8 16 24 32 40 48 56 64 72 80
9  | 0  9 18 27 36 45 54 63 72 81 90
```

2. What do the following program segments display, assuming m is three and n is five? Trace each loop's execution, showing the values of the loop control variables when each display statement executes.

a.
```
for (int i = 0; i < n; i++)
{
    for (int j = 0; j < i; j++)
        cout << "*";
    cout << endl;
}  // end for i
```

b.
```
for (int i = m; i > 0; i--)
{
    for (int j = n; j > 0; j--)
        cout << "*";
    cout << endl;
}  // end for i
```

3. Show the output displayed by the following nested loops:

```
for (int i = 0; i < 2; i++)
{
    cout << "Outer" << setw(5) << i << endl;
    for (int j = 0; j < 3; j++)
        cout << " Inner" << setw(3) << i <<
                << setw(3) << j << endl;
    for (int k = i; k >= 0; k-)
        cout << " Inner" << setw(3) << i
                << setw(3) << k << endl;
} // end for i
```

Programming

1. Write nested loops that display the output below.

```
0
0 1
0 1 2
0 1 2 3
0 1 2 3 4
```

2. Write nested loops that display the output below.

```
0 1 2 3 4
1 2 3 4
2 3 4
3 4
4
```

3. Write a program that displays the pattern below.

```
        *
       ***
      *****
     *******
    *********
     *******
      *****
       ***
        *
```

5.9 Debugging and Testing Programs

Section 2.8 described several categories of errors: syntax, link, run-time, and logic errors. Sometimes the cause of a run-time error or the source of a logic error is apparent and the error can be fixed easily. Often, however, the error is not obvious and you may spend considerable time and energy locating it.

The first step in locating a hidden error is to examine the program output to determine which part of the program is generating incorrect results. Then you can focus on the statements in that section of the program to determine which are at fault. We describe two ways to do this.

Using a Debugger

Modern Integrated Development Environments (IDEs) include features to help you debug a program while it's executing. In this section, we describe these features in a general way. Specific details for Microsoft Visual C++ and Borland C++ Builder are provided in Appendixes F and G.

You can use a debugger to observe changes in variables as the program executes. Debuggers enable you to single-step through a program, or to execute it statement-by-statement. Before starting execution, you indicate to the IDE that you want to debug or trace the program's execution. You place the names of variables you wish to trace in a **watch window**. As each program statement executes, the value of each variable in the watch window is updated. The program pauses and you can inspect the changes. When you're ready, you instruct the IDE to execute the next statement. With single-step execution, you can validate that loop control variables and other important variables (for example, accumulators) are incremented as expected during each iteration of a loop. You can also check that input variables contain the correct data after each input operation.

watch window
A window listing the variables that are traced during debugging.

Usually you want to trace each statement in a program. However, when you reach a library function call, you should select the "step over" option, which executes the function as a single unit instead of tracing through the individual statements in the C++ library code for that function. For the same reason, you should also select the "step over" option when you reach an input or output statement.

You may not want to single-step through all the statements in your program. You can place the cursor at a specific line and then select "Run to cursor". When the program pauses, you then check the variables in the watch window to see if their values are correct.

You can also divide your program into segments by setting *breakpoints,* a feature that is like a fence between two segments of a program. You should set a breakpoint at the end of each major algorithm step. Then instruct the debugger to execute all statements from the last breakpoint up to the next breakpoint. When the program stops at a breakpoint, you can examine the variables in the watch window to determine whether the program segment has executed correctly. If it has, you'll want to execute through to the next breakpoint. If it hasn't, you'll want to single-step through that segment.

Debugging without a Debugger

If you cannot use a debugger, insert extra **diagnostic output statements** to display intermediate results at critical points in your program. For example, you should display the values of variables affected by each major algorithm step before and after the step executes. By comparing these results, you may be able to determine which segment of your program contains bugs. For example, if the loop in Listing 5.7 is not computing the correct sum, you might want to insert an extra diagnostic statement, as shown in the second line of the loop below.

diagnostic output statement An output statement that displays intermediate results during debugging.

```
cin >> score;
while (score != SENTINEL)
{
    sum += score;
    cout << "***** score is " << score << " and sum is "
        << sum << endl;
    cout << "Enter the next score : ";
    cin >> score;
}
```

The diagnostic output statement displays the current value of score and each sum that is accumulated. This statement displays a string of asterisks at the beginning of an output line. This makes it easier to identify diagnostic output in the debugging runs and to locate the diagnostic `cout` statements in the source program.

Be careful when inserting extra diagnostic output statements. Sometimes you must add braces if a single statement inside an `if` or `while` statement becomes a compound statement when you add a diagnostic output statement.

Once you think you have located an error, you'll want to take out the extra diagnostic statements. You can turn the diagnostic statements into comments by prefixing them with the double slash (`//`). If errors appear again in later testing, you can remove the slashes to get more debugging information.

Off-by-One Errors

A fairly common logic error in programs with loops is a loop that executes one more time or one less time than required. If a sentinel-controlled loop performs an extra repetition, it may erroneously process the sentinel value along with the regular data.

If a loop performs a counting operation, make sure that the initial and final values of the loop control variable are correct and that the loop repetition condition is right. For example, the loop body below executes n + 1 times instead of n times. If you want the loop body to execute n times, change the loop repetition condition to `count < n`.

```
for (int count = 0; count <= n; count++)
    sum += count;
```

loop boundaries
Initial and final values of a loop control variable.

Often you can determine whether a loop is correct by checking the **loop boundaries**—that is, the initial and final values of the loop control variable. For a counting loop, carefully evaluate the initialization step, substitute this value everywhere the counter variable appears in the loop body, and verify that it makes sense as a beginning value. Then choose a value for the counter that still causes the loop repetition condition to be true but that will make this condition false after one more evaluation of the update expression. Check the validity of this boundary value wherever the counter variable appears. As an example, in the `for` loop,

```
k = 1;
sum = 0;
for (int i = -n; i < n - k; i++)
    sum += (i * i);
```

check that the first value of the counter variable `i` is supposed to be `-n` and that the last value is supposed to be n - 2. Next, check that the assignment statement

```
sum += (i * i);
```

is correct at these boundaries. When i is -n, sum gets the value of n2. When i is n - 2, the value of (n - 2)2 is added to the previous sum. As a final check, pick some small value of n (for example, 2) and trace the loop execution to see that it computes sum correctly for this case.

Testing

After you've corrected all errors and the program appears to execute as expected, you should test the program thoroughly to make sure that it works. If the program contains a decision statement, check all paths through this statement. Make enough test runs to verify that the program works properly for representative samples of all possible data combinations. We discuss testing again in Section 6.5.

EXERCISES FOR SECTION 5.9

Self-Check

1. In the subsection entitled "Off-by-One Errors," add debugging statements to the first for loop to show the value of the loop control variable at the start of each repetition. Also, add debugging statements to show the value of sum at the end of each loop repetition.

5.10   Loops in Graphics Programs (Optional)

You can form many interesting geometric patterns on your screen by using a loop in a graphics program to repeatedly draw similar shapes. Each shape can have a different size, color, fill pattern, and position. Using a loop, you can also draw a sequence of frames to move an object across the screen.

EXAMPLE 5.13

The program in Listing 5.15 draws a "quilt" consisting of nested filled rectangles (see Figure 5.2). It first draws a large black bar which fills the output window. Each subsequent bar is centered inside the previous one, overwriting its pixels in a new color, so only a border from the previous rectangle remains on the screen.

Before switching to graphics mode, the program prompts the user to specify the number of bars. The statements

```
stepX = width / (2 * numBars);      // x increment
stepY = height / (2 * numBars);     // y increment
```

Figure 5.2   Nested rectangles for a quilt pattern

define the change in **x** and **y** values for the corners of each bar and are computed so that there will be room to display all the bars.

In the **for** loop, the statements

```
foreColor = i % 16;                    // 0 <= foreColor <= 15
setcolor(foreColor);
setfillstyle(i % 12, foreColor);       // set fill style.
bar(x1, y1, x2, y2);                    // draw a bar.
```

set the foreground color to one of 16 colors, based on the value of loop control variable **i**. Similarly, function **setfillstyle** sets the fill pattern to one of 12 possible patterns. After each bar is drawn, the statements

```
x1 = x1 + stepX; y1 = y1 + stepY; // change top left
x2 = x2 - stepX; y2 = y2 - stepY; // change bottom right
```

change the top-left corner (point **x1, y1**) and the bottom-right corner (point **x2, y2**) for the next bar, moving them closer together. For interesting effects, try running this program with different values assigned to **stepX** and **stepY**.

Listing 5.15   Program to draw a quilt

```cpp
// File: quilt.cpp
// Draws a set of nested rectangles

#include <graphics.h>
#include <iostream>

using namespace std;

int main()
{
    int x1, y1, x2, y2;          // coordinates of corner points
    int stepX, stepY;            // change in coordinate values
    int foreColor;               // foreground color
    int numBars;                 // number of bars
    int width, height;           // screen width and height

    cout << "Enter number of bars: ";
    cin >> numBars;

    width = getmaxwidth();
    height = getmaxheight();

    initwindow(width, height, "Quilt");

    // Set corner points of outermost bar and
    // set increments for inner bars
    x1 = 0;         y1 = 0;            // top left corner
    x2 = width;     y2 = height;       // bottom right corner
    stepX = width / (2 * numBars);     // x increment
    stepY = height / (2 * numBars);    // y increment

    // Draw nested bars
    for (int i = 1; i <= numBars; i++)
    {
        foreColor = i % 16;            // 0 <= foreColor <= 15
        setcolor(foreColor);
        setfillstyle(i % 12, foreColor);   // Set fill style
        bar(x1, y1, x2, y2);               // Draw a bar
        x1 = x1 + stepX; y1 = y1 + stepY;  // Change top left corner
        x2 = x2 - stepX; y2 = y2 - stepY;  // Change bottom right
    }
    getch();      // pause

    closegraph();
    return 0;
}
```

Animation

Loops are used in graphics programs to create animation. In graphics animation, motion is achieved by displaying a series of frames in which the object is in a slightly different position from one frame to another, so it appears that the object is moving. Each frame is displayed for a few milliseconds. This is analogous to the flip-books you may had as a child, in which objects were drawn in slightly different positions on each page of the book. As you flipped the pages, the object moved.

The program in Listing 5.16 draws a ball that moves around the screen like the ball in a pong game. It starts moving down the screen and to the

Listing 5.16   Program to draw a moving ball

```cpp
// File animate.cpp
// Draws a ball that moves around the screen like in pong

#include <graphics.h>

using namespace std;

int main()
{
    const int PAUSE = 10;             // delay between frames
    const int DELTA = 5;              // change in x or y value
    const int RADIUS = 30;            // ball radius
    const int COLOR = RED;

    int width;                        // width of screen
    int height;                       // height of screen
    int x; int y;                     // center of ball
    int stepX;                        // increment for x
    int stepY;                        // increment for y

    // Open a full-screen window with double buffering
    width = getmaxwidth();
    height = getmaxheight();
    initwindow(width, height, "Pong - close window to quit", 0, 0, true);

    x = RADIUS;          y = RADIUS;     // Start ball at top-left corner
    stepX = DELTA; stepY = DELTA;        // Move down and to the right
```
                                                                    (continued)

Listing 5.16   Program to draw a moving ball (continued)

```
// Draw the moving ball
while (true) {
    // Clear the old frame and draw the new one.
    clearviewport();
    setfillstyle(SOLID_FILL, COLOR);
    fillellipse(x, y, RADIUS, RADIUS);   // Draw the ball

    // After drawing the frame, swap the buffers
    swapbuffers();
    delay(PAUSE);

    // If ball is too close to a window boundary, change its direction
    if (x <= RADIUS)        // Is ball too close to left/right edge?
        stepX = DELTA;      // At left edge, move right
    else if (x >= width - RADIUS)
        stepX = -DELTA;     // At right edge, move left

    if (y <= RADIUS)        // Is ball too close to top/bottom?
        stepY = DELTA;      // At top, move down
    else if (y >= height - RADIUS)
        stepY = -DELTA;     // At bottom, move up

    // Move the ball
    x = x + stepX;
    y = y + stepY;
}

closegraph();
return 0;
}
```

right until it reaches a "wall" (a window edge) and then reverses its x- or y-direction depending on which wall it hit.

Animation programs use a technique called double buffering to reduce the screen flicker and make the motion seem smoother. In **single buffering** (the default situation), a single memory area (or **buffer**) is used to hold the frame that will be shown next on the screen. After the buffer is filled, its bytes are sent to the graphics hardware for display. When

single buffering
The default case in which only one buffer is allocated.

buffer
An area of memory where data to be displayed or printed is temporarily stored.

double buffering
a technique used in graphics programming to reduce display flicker by allocating two buffers: the second buffer is filled while the ontents of the first buffer is displayed and then the roles of each buffer are reversed.

done, the bytes for the next frame are loaded into the buffer. In **double buffering**, while the bytes in the first buffer are being sent to the graphics display, the second buffer is being filled with the bytes for the next frame. Then, the contents of the second buffer are sent to the graphics hardware, while the first buffer is being filled. The extra buffer enables the screen display to be refreshed more frequently, resulting in less flicker between transitions. In `graphics.h`, double buffering is turned on by setting the sixth argument for `initwindow` to `true`.

```
initwindow(width, height, "Pong - close window to quit", 0,
0, true);
```

Because the `while` loop condition is always true (the `bool` constant `true`), the loop executes "forever," or until the user closes the window. The loop begins by clearing the window for the new frame (function `clearviewport`). Next, it draws the ball in the new frame (stored in the second buffer). Then the buffers are swapped (function `swapbuffers`) and there is a delay of 10 milliseconds while the ball is displayed in its new position.

```
swapbuffers();
delay(PAUSE);
```

The `if` statements change the direction of motion when the ball reaches an edge. For example, in the statement below, the first condition is true if the current x position is closer to the left edge than the radius of the ball. In that case, the ball should move to the right (`stepX` is positive).

```
if (x <= RADIUS)    // Is ball too close to left/right edge
    stepX = DELTA;       // At left edge, move right
else if (x >= width - RADIUS)
    stepX = -DELTA;      // At right edge, move left
```

The second condition is true if the x position of the ball is to too close to the right edge, so the ball should move to the left (`stepX` is negative). The assignment statements at the end of the loop compute the position of the ball for the next frame.

Figure 5.3 shows a trace of the ball as it bounces around the screen. This was obtained by removing the call to `clearviewport`. In the actual display, only one ball would be drawn at a time. Table 5.5 shows the new graphics functions introduced in this section.

Figure 5.3   Trace of the moving ball

Table 5.5   Functions in Graphics Library

Function Prototype	Effect
void clearviewport()	Clears the active viewport. The current window is the default viewport.
void delay(int)	The program pauses for the number of milliseconds specified by its argument.
swapbuffers()	Swaps the buffers if double buffering is turned on.

EXERCISES FOR SECTION 5.10

Self-Check

1. What would be drawn by the following fragment?

```
radius = 20;
x = radius;      y = getmaxy() / 2;
for (int i = 1; i <= 10; i++)
{
    color = i % 16;
    setcolor(color);
    setfillstyle(HATCH_FILL, color);
```

```
        fillellipse(x, y, radius, radius);
        x = x + radius;
        getch();      // pause for user entry
    }
```

2. Experiment with the animation program by removing the call to `clearviewport`. What happens? Also what happens if you eliminate double buffering by removing the call to `swapbuffers`? How does changing the value of `PAUSE` affect the animation?

Programming

1. Write a program that draws an archery target with alternating black and white circles.

2. Modify the program in Self-Check Exercise 1 so the ball moves continuously back and forth in a horizontal direction.

5.11 Common Programming Errors

Beginners sometimes confuse `if` and `while` statements because both statements contain a parenthesized condition. Always use an `if` statement to implement a decision step and a `while` or `for` statement to implement a loop.

The syntax of the `for` statement header is repeated.

```
for (initialization expression; loop repetition condition;
    update expression)
```

Remember to end the initialization expression and the loop repetition condition with semicolons. Do not put a semicolon before or after the closing parenthesis of the `for` statement header. A semicolon after this parenthesis would have the effect of ending the `for` statement without making execution of the loop body dependent on its condition.

- *Omitting braces* A common mistake in using `while` and `for` statements is to forget that the structure assumes that the loop body is a single statement. Remember to use braces around a loop body consisting of multiple statements. Some C++ programmers always use braces around a loop body, even if it contains just one statement. Keep in mind that your compiler ignores indentation, so a loop defined as shown (with braces around the loop body left out)

```
while (x > xbig)
    x -= 2;
    xbig++;
```

really executes as

```
while (x > xbig)
    x -= 2;              // only this statement is repeated
xbig++;
```

■ *Omitting a closing brace* The C++ compiler can easily detect that there is something wrong with code in which a closing brace has been omitted for a compound statement. However, the error message noting the symbol's absence may be far from the spot where the brace belongs, and other error messages often appear as a side effect of the omission. When compound statements are nested, the compiler will associate the first closing brace encountered with the innermost structure. Even if it is the terminator for this inner structure that is left out, the compiler may complain about the outer structure. In the example that follows, there's no closing brace at the end of the body of the inner `while` statement. But the compiler will associate the closing brace in the last line with the inner loop, and then assume that the code that follows (not shown) is part of the outer loop. The message about the missing brace will not appear until much later in the program source code.

```
sum = 0;
for (int i = 0; i < 9; i++)
{
    for (int j = 0; j < i, j++)
    {
        sum += j;
        cout << j << endl;
    cout << i << endl;
} // end for i
```

■ *Infinite loop* Be sure to verify that a loop's repetition condition will eventually become false (0); otherwise, an infinite loop may result. Be especially careful if you use tests for inequality to control the repetition of a loop. The following loop is intended to process all transactions for a bank account while the balance is positive:

```
cin >> balance;
while (balance != 0.0)
{
    cout << "Next check amount: ";
    cin >> check;
    balance -= check;
}
```

If the bank balance goes from a positive to a negative amount without being exactly 0.0, the loop will not terminate (an infinite loop). This loop is safer:

```
cin >> balance;
while (balance > 0.0)
```

```
    {
        cout << "Next check amount: ";
        cin >> check;
        balance -= check;
    }
```

- *Misuse of = for ==* One common cause of a nonterminating loop is the use of a loop repetition condition in which an equality test is mistyped as an assignment operation. Consider the following loop that expects the user to type the letter Y to continue and anything else to quit:

```
do
{
    . . .
    cout << "Continue execution - Y(Yes)/N(No): ";
    cin >> choice;
} while (choice = 'Y');        // should be: choice == 'Y';
```

This loop will compile but will cause a warning message such as "Pos-sible incorrect assignment". If you run the program, the assignment statement will execute after each loop repetition. Its value (a positive integer) will be considered true, so the loop will not exit regardless of the letter typed in.

- *Bad sentinel value* If you use a sentinel-controlled loop, remember to provide a prompt that tells the program's user what value to enter as the sentinel. Make sure that the sentinel value cannot be confused with a normal data item and is not processed in the loop body.

- *Using do-while instead of while* A do-while always executes at least once. Use a do-while only when there's no possibility of zero loop iterations. If you find yourself adding an if statement to patch your code with a result like this

```
if (condition₁)
    do
    {
        . . .
    } while (condition₁);
```

replace the segment with a while or for statement. Both statements automatically test the loop repetition condition before executing the loop body.

- *Incorrect use of compound assignment* Do not use increment, decrement, or compound assignment operators in complex expressions. At best, such usage leads to expressions that are difficult to read, and at worst, to expressions that produce varying results in different implementations of C++.

- *Incorrect use of increment and decrement operators* Be sure that the operand of an increment or decrement operator is a variable and that this variable is referenced after executing the increment or decrement operation. Without a subsequent reference, the operator's side effect of changing the value of the variable is pointless. Do not use a variable twice in an expression in which it is incremented/decremented. Applying the increment/decrement operators to constants or expressions is illegal.

Chapter Review

1. A loop is used to repeat steps in a program. Two kinds of loops occur frequently in programming: counting loops and sentinel-controlled loops. For a counting loop, the number of iterations required can be determined before the loop is entered. For a sentinel-controlled loop, repetition continues until a special data value is read. The pseudocode for each loop form follows.

   Counter-Controlled Loop
   Set *loop control variable* to an initial value of 0.
   `while` *loop control variable* < *final value*

      . . .
      Increase *loop control variable* by 1.

   Sentinel-Controlled Loop
   Read the first data item.
   `while` the sentinel value has not been encountered
      Process the data item.
      Read the next data item.

2. Pseudocode forms were introduced for two other kinds of loops:

   General Conditional Loop
   Initialize the loop control variable.
   `while` a condition involving the loop control variable is still true
      Continue processing.
      Update the loop control variable.

   Data-Validation Loop
   `do`
      Prompt for and read a data item
   `while` data item is not valid.

3. C++ provides three statements for implementing loops: `while`, `for`, and `do-while`. Use `for` to implement counting loops and `do-while` to implement loops that must execute at least once, such as data validation loops for interactive programs. Use `while` or `for` to code other conditional loops, using whichever implementation is clearer.

4. In designing a loop, the focus should be on both loop control and loop processing. For loop processing, make sure that the loop body contains steps that perform the operation that must be repeated. For loop control, you must provide steps that initialize, test, and update the loop control variable. Make sure that the initialization step leads to correct program results when the loop body is not executed (zero-iteration loop).

Summary of New C++ Constructs

Construct	Effect

while Statement
 	
``cpp
sum = 0;
while (sum <= maxSum)
{
    cout << "Next integer: ";
    cin >> nextInt;
    sum += nextInt;
}
``
	A collection of input data items is read and their sum is accumulated in sum. The process stops when the accumulated sum exceeds maxSum.

Counting for Statement
 	
``cpp
for (int currentMonth = 0;
     currentMonth < 12;
     currentMonth++)
{
     cin >> monthSales;
     yearSales += monthSales;
}
``
	The loop body is repeated 12 times. For each month, the value of monthSales is read and added to yearSales.

Counting for Loop with a Negative Step
 	
``cpp
for (volts = 20;
     volts >= -20;
     volts -= 10)
{
     current = volts / resistance;
     cout << setw(5) << volts
          << setw(10) << current
          << endl;
}
``
	For values of volts equal to 20, 10, 0, –10, –20, the loop computes value of current and displays volts and current.

Sentinel-Controlled while Loop
 	
``cpp
product = 1;
cout << "Enter -999 to quit: ";
cout << "Enter first number: "
cin >> dat;
while (dat != -999)
{
    product *= dat;
    cout << "Next number: ";
    cin >> dat;
}
``
	Computes the product of a list of numbers. The product is complete when the user enters the sentinel value (–999).

Data Validation do–while Loop
 	
``cpp
do
{
    cout << "Positive number < 10: ";
    cin >> num;
} while (num < 1 && num >= 10);
``
	Repeatedly displays prompt and stores a number in num until user enters a number that is in range 1 through 9.

Summary of New C++ Constructs (continued)

Construct	Effect

Flag-Controlled while Loop
`divisible = false;`
`while (!divisible)`
`{`
`   cout << "Enter an integer: ";`
`   cin >> n;`
`   divisible = ((n % 2 == 0) ||`
`                (n % 3 == 0));`
`}`
	Continues to read in numbers until a number that is divisible by 2 or by 3 is read.

Increment / Decrement `z = ++j * k--;`	Stores in z the product of the incremented value of j and the current value of k. Then k is decremented.
Compound Assignment `ans *= (a - b);`	Assigns to ans the value of ans * (a - b).

Quick-Check Exercises

1. A loop that continues to process input data until a special value is entered is called a _____ loop.

2. It's an error if a `for` loop body never executes. (True/False)

3. The sentinel value is always the last value added to a sum being accumulated in a sentinel-controlled loop. (True/False)

4. Which loop form (`for, do-while, while`)

   a. executes at least one time?
   b. should be used to implement a sentinel loop?
   c. should be used to implement a counting loop?
   d. should be used to implement a menu-controlled loop?

5. What does the following segment display?

   ```
   product = 1;
   counter = 2;
   while (counter < 5)
       product *= counter;
       counter++;
   cout << product;
   ```

6. What does the segment of Exercise 5 display if the two statements that are indented are in braces?

7. For the program segment below:

   ```
   for (int i = 0; i < 9; i++)
   {
       for (int j = 0; j <= i; j++)
   ```

```
            cout << setw(4) << (i * j);
        cout << endl;
}
```

a. How many times does the first cout statement execute?
b. How many times does the second cout statement execute?
c. What is the last value displayed?

8. If the value of m is 5 and n is 3, what is the value of the following expression?

```
m++ * --n
```

9. What are the values of m and n after the expression in Exercise 8 executes?

10. What does the following code segment display? Try each of these inputs: 345, 82, 6. Then describe the action of the code.

```
cout << "Enter a positive integer: ";
cin >> num;
do
{
    cout << num % 10;
    num /= 10;
} while (num > 0);
cout << endl;
```

Review Questions

1. How does a sentinel value differ from a program flag as a means of loop control?

2. For a sentinel value to be used properly when reading in data, how many input statements should there be and where should the input statements appear?

3. Write a program to read a collection of employee data (hours and rate) entered at the terminal and to calculate and display the gross pay for each employee. Your program should stop when the user enters a sentinel value of –0 for hours.

4. Hand trace the program below given the following data:

```
4 2 8 4 1 4 2 1 9 3 3 1 -22 10 8 2 3 3 4 5
// File: Slope.cpp
// Calculates the slope of a line

#include <iostream>
using namespace std;

int main()
{
```

```
    const float SENTINEL = 0.0;
    float slope;
    float y2, y1, x2, x1;

    cout << "Enter 4 numbers: " << endl;
    cout << "The program terminates if the last two";
    cout << " numbers are the same." << endl;
    cout << "Numbers entered will be in the order: "
            << "y2, y1, x2, x1." << endl << endl;
    cout << "Enter four numbers: ";
    cin >> y2 >> y1 >> x2 >> x1;

    while ((x2 - x1) != SENTINEL)
    {
        slope = (y2 - y1) / (x2 - x1);
        cout << "Slope is " << slope << endl;
        cout << "Enter 4 more numbers: ";
        cin >> y2 >> y1 >> x2 >> x1;
    }

    return 0;
}
```

5. Rewrite the while loop appearing in Exercise 4 as a
   a. do-while loop.
   b. flag-controlled loop.

6. Consider the following program segment:

```
count = 0;
for (i = 0; i < n; i++)
{
    cin >> x;
    if (x % i == 0)
        count++;
}
```

   a. After loop exit, what does the value of count represent.
   b. Write a while loop equivalent to the for loop.
   c. Write a do-while loop equivalent to the for loop.

7. Write a do-while loop that repeatedly prompts for and reads data until a value in the range 0 through 15 inclusive is entered.

8. Write a program that will find the product of a collection of data values. Your program should ignore any negative data and should terminate when a zero value is read.

Programming Projects

1. Write a program that reads a collection of positive and negative numbers and multiplies only the positive integers. Loop exit should occur when three consecutive negative values are read.

2. The greatest common divisor (gcd) of two integers is the largest integer that divides both numbers. Write a program that inputs two numbers and implements the following approach to finding their gcd. We'll use the numbers 252 and 735. First, we find the remainder of the larger number divided by the other.

$$
\begin{array}{r}
2 \\
252 \overline{)735} \\
504 \\
\hline
231
\end{array}
$$

Now we calculate the remainder of the old divisor divided by the remainder found.

$$
\begin{array}{r}
1 \\
231 \overline{)252} \\
231 \\
\hline
21
\end{array}
$$

We repeat this process until the remainder is zero.

$$
\begin{array}{r}
11 \\
21 \overline{)231} \\
21 \\
\hline
21 \\
21 \\
\hline
0
\end{array}
$$

The last divisor (21) is the gcd.

3. Write a program to find the largest, smallest, and average values in a collection of n numbers where the value of n will be the first data item read.

4. **a.** Write a program to read in a collection of exam scores ranging in value from 0 to 100. Your program should display the category of each score. It should also count and display the number of outstanding scores (90 to 100), the number of satisfactory scores (60 to 89), and the number of unsatisfactory scores (0 to 59).

   b. Modify your program so that it also displays the average score at the end of the run.

   c. Modify your program to ensure that each score is valid (in the range 0 to 100).

5. Write a program to process weekly employee time cards for all employees of an organization. Each employee will have three data items: the employee's name, the hourly wage rate, and the number of hours worked during a given week. Employees are to be paid time-and-a-half for all hours worked over 40. A tax amount of 3.625 percent of gross salary will be deducted. The program output should show each employee's name, gross pay, and net pay, and should also display the total net and gross amounts and their averages. Use zzzzzz as a sentinel value for name.

6. Write a menu-driven savings account transaction program that will process the following sets of data:

Group 1

```
I   1234   1054.07
W             25.00
D            243.35
W            254.55
Z
```

Group 2

```
I   5723   2008.24
W             15.55
Z
```

Group 3

```
I   2814    128.24
W             52.48
D             13.42
W             84.60
Z
```

Group 4

```
I   7234     7.77
Z
```

Group 5

```
I   9367    15.27
W            16.12
D            10.00
Z
```

Group 6

```
I   1134   12900.00
D           9270.00
Z
```

The first record in each group contains the code (I) along with the account number and its initial balance. All subsequent transaction records show the amount of each withdrawal (W) and deposit (D) made for that account, followed by a sentinel value (Z). Display the account number and its balance after processing each record in the group. If a balance becomes negative, display an appropriate message and take whatever corrective steps you deem proper. If there are no transactions for an account, display a message stating this. A transaction code (Q) should be used to allow the user to quit program execution.

7. Suppose you own a soft drink distributorship that sells Coca-Cola (ID number 1), Pepsi (ID number 2), Canada Dry (ID number 3), and Hires (ID number 4) by the case. Write a program to do the following:

a. Read in the case inventory for each brand at the start of the week.

b. Process all weekly sales and purchase records for each brand.

c. Display the final inventory.

Each transaction will consist of two data items. The first will be the brand identification number (an integer). The second will be the amount purchased (a positive integer) or the amount sold (a negative integer). You can assume that you always have sufficient foresight to prevent depletion of your inventory for any brand.

8. Revise the previous project to make it a menu-driven program. The menu operations supported by the revised program should be as follows:

(E)nter inventory

(P)urchase soda

(S)ell soda

(D)isplay inventory

(Q)uit program

Negative quantities should no longer be used to represent goods sold.

9. Write a simple arithmetic expression translator that reads in expressions such as 25.5 + 34.2 and displays their value. Each expression has two numbers separated by an arithmetic operator. (Hint: Use a switch statement with the operator symbol (type char) as a selector to determine which arithmetic operation to perform on the two numbers. For a sentinel, enter an expression with zero for both operands.)

10. Complete the text editor program (Listings 4.6 and 5.10). You need to write only function displayMenu and the function subprograms called by function edit.

11. Bunyan Lumber Company needs to create a table of the engineering properties of its lumber. The dimensions of the wood are given as the base and the height in inches. Engineers need to know the following information about lumber:

$$\text{cross-sectional area: } base \times height$$

$$\text{moment of intertia: } \frac{base \times height^3}{12}$$

$$\text{section modulus: } \frac{base \times height^2}{6}$$

The owner makes lumber with base sizes of 2, 4, 6, 8, and 10 inches. The height sizes are 2, 4, 6, 8, 10, and 12 inches. Produce a table with appropriate headings to show these values and the computed engineering properties. The first part of the table's outline follows.

Lumber Size	Cross-Sectional Area Inertia	Moment of Modulus	Section
2 × 2			
2 × 4			
2 × 6			
2 × 8			
2 × 10			
2 × 12			
4 × 2			
4 × 4			
.			
.			
.			

12. Write a program that reads in a collection of strings and displays each string read with the vowels removed. For example, if the data strings are:

```
hat
dog
kitten
*** (sentinel)
```

the output would be:

```
ht
dg
kttn
```

Write and call a function `removeVowel` with prototype

```
string removeVowel(string);
```

that returns its argument string with the vowels removed.

13. Write a loop that reads a collection of words and builds a sentence out of all the words by appending each new word to the string being formed. For example, if the three words "This", "is", and "one." are entered, your sentence would be "This", then "This is", and finally "This is one." Exit your loop when a word that ends with a period is entered or the sentence being formed is longer than 20 words or contains more than 100 letters. Do not append a word if it was previously entered.

14. A prime number is a number that is divisible only by itself and 1. Write a program that asks a user for an integer value and then displays all prime numbers less than or equal to that number. For example, if the user enters 17, the program should display:

```
Prime numbers less than or equal to 17:
2
3
5
```

```
7
11
13
17
```

15. **a.** Write a program to process a collection of daily high temperatures. Your program should count and print the number of hot days (high temperature 85 or higher), the number of pleasant days (high temperature 60–84), and the number of cold days (high temperature less than 60). It should also display the category of each temperature. Test your program on the following data:

```
55  62   68   74   59   45   41   58   60   67   65   78   82   88   91
92  90   93   87   80   78   79   72   68   61   59
```

b. Modify your program to display the average temperature (a real number) at the end of the run.

16. Write a program to process weekly employee time cards for all employees of an organization. Each employee will have three data items: an identification number, the hourly wage rate, and the number of hours worked during a given week. Each employee is to be paid time and a half for all hours worked over 40. A tax amount of 3.625 percent of gross salary will be deducted. The program output should show the employee's number and net pay. Display the total payroll and the average amount paid.

17. The pressure of a gas changes as the volume and temperature of the gas vary. Write a program that uses the Van der Waals equation of state for a gas,

$$\left(P + \frac{an^2}{V^2}\right)(V - bn) = nRT$$

to display in tabular form the relationship between the pressure and the volume of n moles of carbon dioxide at a constant absolute temperature (T). P is the pressure in atmospheres, and V is the volume in liters. The Van der Waals constants for carbon dioxide are $a = 3.592$ $L^2 \cdot atm/mol^2$ and $b = 0.0427$ L/mol. Use 0.08206 L$\cdot$atm/mol$\cdot$K for the gas constant R. Inputs to the program include n, the Kelvin temperature, the initial and final volumes in milliliters, and the volume increment between lines of the table. Your program will output a table that varies the volume of the gas from the initial to the final volume in steps prescribed by the volume increment. Here is a sample run:

```
Please enter at the prompts the number of moles of carbon
dioxide, the absolute temperature, the initial volume in
milliliters, the final volume, and the increment volume
between lines of the table.

Quantity of carbon dioxide (moles)> 0.02
Temperature (kelvin)> 300
```

```
Initial volume (milliliters)> 400
Final volume (milliliters)> 600
Volume increment (milliliters)> 50
```

Output File

```
0.0200 moles of carbon dioxide at 300 kelvin

Volume (ml)      Pressure (atm)
   400               1.2246
   450               1.0891
   500               0.9807
   550               0.8918
   600               0.8178
```

18. A concrete channel to bring water to Crystal Lake is being designed. It will have vertical walls and be 15 feet wide. It will be 10 feet deep, have a slope of .0015 feet/foot, and a roughness coefficient of .014. How deep will the water be when 1,000 cubic feet per second is flowing through the channel? To solve this problem, we can use Manning's equation

$$Q = \frac{1.486}{N} AR^{2/3}S^{1/2}$$

where Q is the flow of water (cubic feet per second), N is the roughness coefficient (unitless), A is the area (square feet), S is the slope (feet/foot), and R is the hydraulic radius (feet).

The hydraulic radius is the cross-sectional area divided by the wetted perimeter. For square channels like the one in this example,

Hydraulic radius = depth × width/(2.0 × depth + width)

To solve this problem, design a program that allows the user to guess a depth and then calculates the corresponding flow. If the flow is too little, the user should guess a depth a little higher; if the flow is too high, the user should guess a depth a little lower. The guessing is repeated until the computed flow is within 0.1 percent of the flow desired.

To help the user make an initial guess, the program should display the flow for half the channel depth. Note the example run:

```
At a depth of 5.0000 feet, the flow is 641.3255 cubic
feet per second.

Enter your initial guess for the channel depth
when the flow is 1000.0000 cubic feet per second
Enter guess> 6.0

Depth: 6.0000 Flow: 825.5906 cfs Target: 1000.0000 cfs
Difference: 174.4094 Error: 17.4409 percent
Enter guess> 7.0
```

```
Depth: 7.0000 Flow: 1017.7784 cfs Target: 1000.0000 cfs
Difference: -17.7784 Error: -1.7778 percent
Enter guess> 6.8
```

Graphics Projects

19. Draw a series of circles along one diagonal of a window. The circles should be different colors and each circle should touch the one above and below it.

20. Redo Programming Project 19 but this time draw a series of squares along the other diagonal as well.

21. Draw a simple stick figure and move it across the screen.

22. Redo Programming Project 19 but this time draw a single circle that moves down a diagonal.

23. Redo Programming Project 20 with a single circle and square moving along each diagonal.

Answers to Quick-Check Exercises

1. sentinel-controlled loop

2. False

3. False; the sentinel should not be processed.

4. a. `do-while`   b. `while`   c. `for`

5. Nothing; the loop executes "forever" because only one statement is repeated.

6. The value of $1 \cdot 2 \cdot 3 \cdot 4 \cdot 5$ (or 24).

7. a. $1 + 2 + 3 + ... + 9 + 10$ (or 45)   b. 9   c. 64

8. 10 (product of 5 times 2)

9. m is 6 (incremented after the multiplication), n is 2(decremented before the multiplication)

10.
```
Enter a positive integer: 345
543
Enter a positive integer: 82
28
Enter a positive integer: 6
6
```

The code displays the digits of an integer in reverse order.

Mike Weisert

Mike Weisert is currently the ScopeTools engineering manager at Wind River, where he is responsible for creating dynamic debugging and analysis tools for embedded system programmers. After Weisert was acquired twice by Wind River, once while at Integrated Systems and once at RTI, Inc, he started to focus on analysis tools that go beyond the common debugger. Before moving to Integrated Systems, Weisert helped develop successful C and C++ products at Borland International. One such example is Turbo C, for which Weisert developed the user interface. Turbo C offered C programmers an integrated development environment (providing an editor and compiler options) for the first time.

What is your educational background?
Science, math, and art were my passions in college, though my degree was in business. My computer education began with a Sinclair ZX-80 computer that my dad gave me in high school.

I was fascinated with the interaction between computers and people. So, my degree in business administration led me to study how computers could increase productivity for people in business environments by making programmers more efficient.

How did you become interested in computer science?
I found the puzzles of computer science more entertaining than any other discipline. I was pleasantly surprised when I found that the skills I learned were in high demand and that people would pay me to do what I liked to do.

What was your first job in the computer industry? What did it entail?
I started in a C programming position on a project that was canceled two months after I started on it. Welcome to business and the Silicon Valley. My software career began in earnest as a technical support engineer at Borland International in 1985 because of my experience with Modula-2 [a programming language developed by Niklaus Wirth and released in 1980]. After three months of answering questions about hard-sector floppies, configuration files, and Pascal programming, I turned in my resignation to take an Ada programming position. However, I was convinced to stay at Borland as a Modula-2 programmer.

I proceeded to develop software in Modula-2. Following techniques I learned in school, such as stepwise refinement and structured programming, I developed a graphics package for single-board computers and helped develop a CPM-based development tool. Later, I had the luck to build development tools for BASIC and C. The first product to ship out of this effort was Turbo C 1.0. Integration and automation of the development tool were forever altered. The user interfaces for Turbo Basic, Turbo C, and Turbo Pascal became known as IDEs, or Integrated Development Environments.

What is a typical day like for you?
My day generally starts early at home on the phone in front of my laptop. Engineering managers meet to discuss dependencies, or review open issues in a bug board. After the commute to Silicon Valley, I check in with engineers and make sure everyone has what they need to do their job. Depending on which part of the development cycle we are in, I'm either translating marketing requirements into engineering tasks or I'm reviewing defect reports to decide which problems will be addressed in the next release. The fun part of my day is when we discuss new designs and how we can implement them.

Do you have any advice for students learning C++?
C++ has become a staple in many programmers' toolboxes. Learn the concepts, especially virtual, and don't wed yourself to just one language. With the advent of networks and wireless devices, software programs are becoming bigger than just one program running on one device. So, learn the difference between C and C++ and plan on using the right language for the job.

How do you see C++ evolving over the next few years?
C++ is a very complete language with templates and exceptions. Evolution of the language will be small. Most changes affecting programmers will revolve around the standard libraries; for example, to handle things such as concurrency driven by the trend toward multi core processors.

What kind of project are you currently working on?
I manage a development team of seven engineers building ScopeTools. This suite of tools includes a memory leak detector, a statistical profiler, a data monitor and graphing tool, and a code coverage tool. These tools are now built in the context of the Eclipse open source IDE project, which allows different companies to share a common platform and integrate their programming tools along side tools from other vendors. Besides the normal development of the "next version" of ScopeTools, we have started a project to work with the open source community to define standards for Analysis tools. The aim is to define interfaces and data structures that will decouple data sources from data viewers (always a noble goal). This would allow one vendor's data collection code to work with another vendors filtering and graphing viewers.

What do you enjoy most about working on a software development team?
The ability to build something bigger than one person alone can create, and organizing an effort to build a shared vision. When I manage to have a team deliver a finished product, I feel accomplished.

Modular Programming

Learning Objectives

- To learn how to return function results through a function's arguments
- To understand the differences between call-by-value and call-by-reference
- To understand the distinction between input, inout, and output parameters and when to use each kind
- To learn how to modularize a program system and pass information between system modules (functions)
- To understand how to document the flow of information using structure charts
- To learn testing and debugging techniques appropriate for a program system with several modules

A CAREFULLY DESIGNED PROGRAM that has been constructed using functions has many of the properties of a stereo system. Each stereo component is an independent device that performs a specific operation. Electronic audio signals move back and forth over wires linking the stereo components. Plugs on the back of the stereo receiver are marked as inputs or outputs. Wires attached to the input plugs carry electronic signals into the receiver, where receiver sends new electronic signals through the output plugs to the speakers or back to the cassette deck for recording. You can connect the components and listen to your favorite music without knowing what electronic parts each component contains or how it works.

In Chapter 3 you learned how to write the separate components—the functions—of a program. The functions correspond to the individual steps in a problem solution. You also learned how to provide inputs to a function and how to return a single output. In this chapter you complete your study of functions, learning how to connect the functions to create a program system—an arrangement of separate modules that pass information from one to the other.

6.1   Value and Reference Parameters

At this point we know how to write functions that return up to one result. In this section, we'll learn how to write functions that use output parameters to return more than one result.

EXAMPLE 6.1

Function `computeSumAve` at the bottom of Listing 6.1 has four parameters: two for input (`num1` and `num2`) and two for output (`sum` and `average`). The symbol `&` (ampersand) in the function header indicates that the parameters `sum` and `average` are output parameters. The function computes the sum and average of its inputs but doesn't display them. Instead, these values are assigned to formal parameters `sum` and `average` and returned as function results to the `main` function that displays them.

The function call

```
computeSumAve(x, y, sum, mean);
```

sets up the argument correspondence below.

Actual Argument	Corresponds to formal parameter
x	num1 (input)
y	num2 (input)
sum	sum (output)
mean	average (output)

The values of `x` and `y` are passed into the function when it's first called. These values are associated with formal input parameters `num1` and `num2`. The statement

```
sum = num1 + num2;
```

stores the sum of the function inputs in the calling function variable `sum` (the third actual argument). The statement

```
average = sum / 2.0;
```

divides the value stored in the calling function variable `sum` by `2.0` and stores the quotient in the calling function variable `mean` (the fourth actual argument).

Listing 6.1 Function to compute sum and average

```cpp
// File: computeSumAve.cpp
// Tests function computeSumAve.

#include <iostream>
using namespace std;

// Function prototype
void computeSumAve(float, float, float&, float&);

int main()
{
    float x,          // input - first number
          y,          // input - second number
          sum,        // output - their sum
          mean;       // output - their average

    cout << "Enter 2 numbers: ";
    cin >> x >> y;

    // Compute sum and average of x and y
    computeSumAve(x, y, sum, mean);

    // Display results
    cout << "Sum is " << sum << endl;
    cout << "Average is " << mean << endl;

    return 0;
}

// Computes the sum and average of num1 and num2.
// Pre: num1 and num2 are assigned values.
// Post: The sum and average of num1 and num2 are
//       computed and returned as function outputs.
void computeSumAve
    (float num1,          // IN -   values used in
     float num2,          //         computation
     float& sum,          // OUT - sum of num1 and num2
     float& average)      // OUT - average of num1 and num2
{
    sum = num1 + num2;
    average = sum / 2.0;
} // end computeSumAve
```

```
Enter 2 numbers: 8 10
Sum is 18
Average is 9
```

Figure 6.1 shows the main function data area and function computeSumAve's data area after the function call but before the execution of computeSumAve begins; Figure 6.2 shows these data areas just after computeSumAve finishes execution. The execution of computeSumAve sets the values of calling function variables sum and mean to 18.0 and 9.0, respectively. We explain how this happens next.

Call-by-Value and Call-by-Reference Parameters

In C++, you insert the symbol & immediately following the type of a formal parameter to declare an output parameter. Therefore, in function computeSumAve in Listing 6.1, the formal parameters sum and average are output parameters, and num1 and num2 are input parameters.

call by-value
An argument-passing mechanism in which the value of an actual argument is stored in the called function's data area.

The compiler uses the information in the parameter declaration list to set up the correct *argument-passing mechanism* for each function parameter. For parameters used only as input, C++ uses **call-by-value** because the *value* of the argument is copied to the called function's data area and there's no further connection between the formal parameter and its corresponding actual argument. In Figures 6.1 and 6.2, the dashed arrows pointing to num1 and num2 indicate this situation. The top dashed arrow shows that the value of the

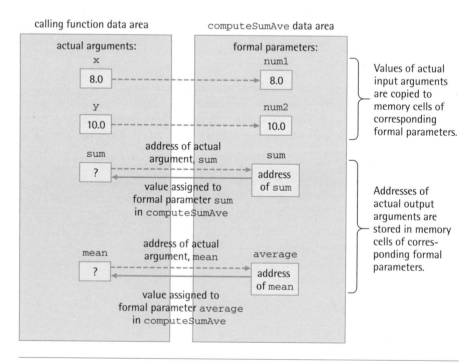

Figure 6.1   Data areas after call to computeSumAve (before execution)

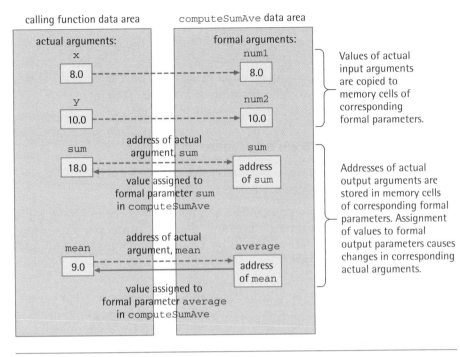

Figure 6.2 Data areas after execution of `computeSumAve`

actual argument x is passed to the formal parameter `num1` in function `computeSumAve`.

For output parameters, C++ uses **call-by-reference**. For *reference parameters*, the compiler stores in the called function's data area the memory *address* of the actual variable that corresponds to each reference parameter. Through this address, the called function can access the actual argument in the calling function, which enables the called function to modify the actual argument value or to use it in a computation. In Figure 6.2, a dashed arrow and a solid arrow connect a reference parameter in `computeSumAve` with its corresponding actual argument in the calling function. The dashed arrow in color shows that the address of variable `mean` in the calling function is passed to formal parameter `average` in `computeSumAve`; the solid arrow in color shows that the value assigned to formal parameter `average` in `computeSumAve` is actually stored in variable `mean` in the calling function.

Remember to place the & (for reference parameters) in the formal parameter list only, not in the actual argument list. Also, you must insert &s in the function prototype to indicate that the third and fourth formal parameters are reference parameters:

```
void computeSumAve(float, float, float&, float&);
```

call-by-reference
An argument-passing mechanism in which the address of an actual argument is stored in the called function's data area.

`void` Functions Can Return Results

Beginning programmers are sometimes confused by the fact that `compute-SumAve` is declared as a `void` function but still returns results to the calling function. By declaring `computeSumAve` as `void`, we're only telling C++ that it doesn't return a value through execution of a `return` statement. But `computeSumAve` is still permitted to return results through its output parameters.

When to Use a Reference or a Value Parameter

How do you decide whether to use a reference parameter or a value parameter? Here are some rules of thumb:

input parameter
A parameter used to receive a data value from the calling function.

output parameter
A parameter used to return a result to the calling function.

input/output (inout) parameter
A parameter that receives a data value from the calling function and returns a value to it.

- If information is to be passed into a function and doesn't have to be returned or passed out of the function, then the formal parameter representing that information should be a value parameter (for example, `num1` and `num2` in Figure 6.1). A parameter used in this way is called an **input parameter**.

- If information is to be returned to the calling function through a parameter, then the formal parameter representing that information must be a reference parameter (`sum` and `average` in Figure 6.1). A parameter used in this way is called an **output parameter**.

- If information is to be passed into a function, perhaps modified, and a new value returned, then the formal parameter representing that information must be a reference parameter. A parameter used in this way is called an **input/output parameter** (or **inout parameter**).

Although we make a distinction between output parameters and input/output parameters, C++ does not. Both must be specified as reference parameters (using the ampersand), so that the address of the corresponding actual argument is stored in the called function data area when the function is called. For an input/output parameter (as well as for an input parameter), we assume there are some meaningful data in the actual argument before the function executes; for an output parameter, we make no such assumption.

PROGRAM STYLE   Writing Formal Parameter Lists

In Listing 6.1, the formal parameter list

```
(float num1,          // IN - values used
 float num2,          //       in computation
 float& sum,          // OUT - sum of num1 and num2
 float& average)      // OUT - average of num1 and num2
```

is written on four lines to improve program readability. The value parameters are on the first two lines with comments that document their use as input parameters. The reference parameters are on the next two lines followed by comments that document their use as function outputs

Generally, we follow this practice in writing formal parameter lists. We list input parameters first, input/output parameters next, and output parameters last.

Comparison of Value and Reference Parameters

Table 6.1 summarizes what we've learned so far about value and reference parameters.

Protection Afforded by Value Parameters

Reference parameters are more versatile than value parameters because their values can be used in a computation as well as changed by the function's execution. Why not make all parameters, even input parameters, reference parameters? The reason is that value parameters offer some protection for data integrity. Because copies of value parameters are stored locally in the called function data area, C++ protects the actual argument's value and prevents it from being erroneously changed by the function's execution. For example, if we insert the statement

```
num1 = -5.0;
```

at the end of function `computeSumAve`, the value of formal parameter `num1` will be changed to -5.0, but the value stored in x (the corresponding actual argument) will still be 8.0.

Table 6.1 Comparison of Value and Reference Parameters

Value Parameters	Reference Parameters
• Value of corresponding actual argument is stored in the called function.	• Address of corresponding actual argument is stored in the called function.
• The function execution cannot change the actual argument value.	• The function execution can change the actual argument value.
• Actual argument can be an expression, variable, or constant.	• Actual argument must be a variable.
• Formal parameter type must be specified in the formal parameter list.	• Formal parameter type must be followed by & in the formal parameter list.
• Parameters are used to store the data passed to a function (input parameters).	• Parameters are used to return outputs from a function (output parameters) or to change the value of a function argument (input / output parameters).

If you forget to declare a formal output parameter as a reference parameter (using the ampersand), then its value (not its address) will be passed to the function when it's called. The argument value is stored locally, and any change to its value will not be returned to the calling function. This is a very common error in parameter usage.

Argument/Parameter List Correspondence Revisited

We first discussed argument/parameter list correspondence in Section 3.5. We used the acronym **not** to indicate that an argument list used in a function call must agree with the called function's parameter list in **n**umber, **o**rder, and **t**ype. We repeat these three rules below and add one more.

Argument/Parameter List Correspondence

- **Number:** The number of actual arguments used in a call to a function must be the same as the number of formal parameters listed in the function prototype.
- **Order:** The order of arguments in the lists determines correspondence. The first actual argument corresponds to the first formal parameter, the second actual argument corresponds to the second formal parameter, and so on.
- **Type:** Each actual argument must be of a data type that can be assigned to the corresponding formal parameter with no unexpected loss of information.
- For reference parameters, an actual argument must be a variable. For value parameters, an actual argument may be a variable, a constant, or an expression.

The last rule states that you can use expressions (or variables or constants) as actual arguments corresponding to value parameters but not to reference parameters. For example, the function call

```
computeSumAve(x + y, 10, mySum, myAve);
```

calls `computeSumAve` to compute the `sum` (returned in `mySum`) and the `average` (returned in `myAve`) of the expression `x + y` and the integer `10`.

Only variables can correspond to reference parameters, so `mySum` and `myAve` must be declared as type `float` variables in the calling function. This restriction is imposed because an actual argument corresponding to a formal reference parameter may be modified when the called function executes; it makes no sense to allow a function to change the value of either a constant or an expression.

EXAMPLE 6.2

Listing 6.2 shows the outline of a **main** function and a lower-level function called **test**.
    The prototype for function **test** shows that **test** has two type **int** value parameters (a and b), two type **float** reference parameters (c and d), and one type **char** reference parameter (e). You could use any of the following function calls in the **main** function:

```
test(m + 3, 10, x, y, next);
test(m, -63, y, x, next);
test(35, m * 10, y, x, next);
```

In each call above, the first two arguments are type **int** variables, constants, or expressions; the next two arguments are type **float** variables; the last parameter is a type **char** variable (**next**). Table 6.2 shows the correspondence specified by the first argument list.

Listing 6.2   Functions main and test

```
// Functions used . . .
void test(int, int, float&, float&, char&);

int main()
{ . . .
  float x, y;
  int m;
  char next;
  . . .
}

void test(int a, int b,              // IN
          float& c, float& d, char& e) // OUT
{
  . . .
}  // end test
```

Table 6.2   Argument/Parameter Correspondence for test(m + 3, 10, x, y, next)

Actual Argument	Formal Parameter	Description
m + 3	a	int, value
10	b	int, value
x	c	float, reference
y	d	float, reference
next	e	char, reference

Table 6.3   Invalid Function Calls

Function Call	Error
`test(30, 10, m, 19, next);`	The constant 19 cannot correspond to reference parameter d. Note that the integer m would be converted to floating point by the compiler.
`test(m, 19, x, y);`	Not enough actual arguments.
`test(m, 10, 35, y, 'E');`	Constants 35 and `'E'` cannot correspond to reference parameters.
`test(m, 3.3, x, y, next);`	This is legal; however, the type of 3.3 is not an integer so the fractional part will be lost.
`test(30, 10, x, x + y, next);`	Expression x + y cannot correspond to a reference parameter.
`test(30, 10, c, d, e);`	c, d, and e are not declared in the `main` function.

All the function calls in Table 6.3 contain errors. The last function call points out an error often made in using functions. The last three actual argument names (c, d, e) are the same as their corresponding formal parameters. However, they are not declared as variables in the `main` function, so they cannot be used as actual arguments.

When writing relatively long argument lists such as those in this example, be careful not to transpose two actual arguments. If you transpose arguments, you may get a syntax error. If no syntax rule is violated, the function execution will probably generate incorrect results.

EXERCISES FOR SECTION 6.1

Self-Check

1. The function definitions below are from Example 6.2.

```
int main()
{
    float x, y;
    int m;
    char next;
    . . .
}
void test(int a, int b,                 // IN
          float& c, float& d, char& e)   // OUT
{
    . . .
} // end test
```

For each argument list below, provide a table similar to Table 6.2 if the argument list is correct. Otherwise, indicate the reason(s) the argument list would not be correct.

```
test(m, -63, y, x, next);
test(35, m * 10, y, x, next);
test(m, m, x, m, 'a');
```

2. Correct the syntax errors in the prototype parameter lists below.

```
(int&, int&; float)
(value int, char x, y)
(float x + y, int account&)
```

3. Assume that you've been given the following declarations:

```
// Functions used ...
void massage (float&, float&, int);

    // Local data ...
    const int MAX = 32767;

    float x, y, z;
    int m, n;
```

Determine which of the following function calls are invalid and indicate why. If any standard conversions are required, indicate which one(s) and specify the result of the conversion.

a. `massage(x, y, z);`

b. `massage(x, y, 8);`

c. `massage(y, x, n);`

d. `massage(m, y, n);`

e. `massage(25.0, 15, x);`

f. `massage(x, y, m+n);`

g. `massage(a, b, x);`

h. `massage(y, z, m);`

i. `massage(y+z, y-z, m);`

j. `massage(z, y, x);`

k. `massage(x, y, m, 10);`

l. `massage(z, y, MAX);`

4. Trace the execution of the program in Listing 6.1 for the data items 5, 3.5.

Programming

1. Write a function that accepts a real number as input and returns its whole and fractional parts as outputs. For example, if the input is –5.32, the function outputs should be the integer –5 and the real value –0.32.

2. Write a function that accepts an input argument consisting of two words with a space between them and returns each word through its two output parameters. All three parameters should be type `string`. If the input argument has only one word, the second output parameter should store the string `""`.

3. Write a function that accepts a real number as input and returns the largest integer that is smaller than the real number and the smallest integer that is larger than the real number. (Hint: Use cmath functions `floor` and `ceil`.)

4. Write a function that has two input parameters, x and y, and two output parameters, `small` and `big`. The function should return the smaller of its inputs through `small` and the larger through `big`.

6.2   Functions with Output and Input Parameters

In previous examples, we passed information to a function through its input parameters and returned a result from a function through its output parameters. In this section, we study three functions that have only output or inout (input/output) parameters.

EXAMPLE 6.3

Function `getFrac` in Listing 6.3 reads a common fraction typed in by a user and returns the numerator and denominator through two type `int` output parameters. For example, if the user types in 4 / 7, the function returns 4 through `numerator` and 7 through `denominator`. The `main` function calls `getFrac` to read a fraction and then displays the fraction read.

This example illustrates a curious phenomenon. Notice that function `getFrac`'s outputs (numerator and denominator) are actually data items that are entered at the keyboard. Although this seems strange at first, it's a fairly common occurrence in programming. It illustrates that data elements in a program system can have different purposes in different modules. For example, numerator and denominator are output parameters of function `getFrac` and return their values to `main` program variables num and denom. In the `main` function, the values of num and denom are considered problem inputs because they are entered by the program user.

Listing 6.3 Testing function `getFrac`

```
// File: testGetFrac
// Test function getFrac

#include <iostream>
using namespace std;

void getFrac(int&, int&);

int main()
{
    int num,            // input - fraction numerator
        denom;          // input - fraction denominator

    cout << "Enter a common fraction "
         << "as 2 integers separated by a slash: ";

    getFrac(num, denom);

    cout << "Fraction is " << num
         << " / " << denom << endl;

    return 0;
}

// Reads a fraction.
// Pre: none
// Post: Returns fraction numerator through numerator
//       Returns fraction denominator through denominator
void getFrac(int& numerator,          // OUT
             int& denominator)        // OUT
{
    char slash;                       // temporary storage for slash
    cin >> numerator >> slash >> denominator;
}
```

```
Enter a fraction as 2 integers separated by a slash: 3 / 4
Fraction is 3 / 4
```

Similarly, if we wrote a function to display the fraction, we'd have to pass the fraction's numerator and denominator values to the display function through its input parameters. The display function would then display its inputs on the screen. In this case, the numerator and denominator are problem outputs, but they are inputs to the display function.

EXAMPLE 6.4

In this example, we illustrate multiple calls to a function. Function `readFracProblem` in Listing 6.4 reads a problem involving two common fractions. A sample problem would be 2/4 + 5/6 . The function outputs would be the numerator and denominators of both fractions and the operation as a character ('+' for the sample). Function `readFracProblem` calls `getFrac` twice. Programming Project 10 at the end of this chapter describes a program that uses `readFracProblem`.

Notice that the data for a fraction numerator (or denominator) has different names in each function. We use the name `numerator` in function `getFrac`, and we use the names `num1` and `num2` in function `getFracProblem`. The parameter `numerator` in `getFrac` corresponds to parameter `num1` in the first call and parameter `num2` in the second. If we use the statement

```
readFracProblem(n1, d1, n2, d2, op);
```

to call `readFracProblem`, argument `n1` will receive the value returned through `num1` and argument `n2` will receive the value returned through `num2`. Table 6.4 summarizes the argument/parameter list correspondence.

Listing 6.4   Function `readFracProblem`

```
// Reads a fraction problem
// Pre: none
// Post: Returns first fraction through num1, denom1
//       Returns second fraction through num2, denom2
//       Returns operation through op
void readFracProblem(
    int& num1, int& denom1,              // OUT - 1st fraction
    int& num2, int& denom2,              // OUT - 2nd fraction
    char& op)                            // OUT - operator
{
    getFrac(num1, denom1);
    cin >> op;
    getFrac(num2, denom2);
}
```

Table 6.4   Argument/Parameter Correspondence for `readFracProblem(n1, d1, n2, d2, op);`

Actual Argument	readFracProblem Parameter	getFrac Parameter
n1	num1	numerator (in first call)
d1	denom1	denominator (in first call)
n2	num2	numerator (in second call)
d2	denom2	denominator (in second call)

EXAMPLE 6.5

In this example, we illustrate multiple calls to a function with inout parameters. The `main` function in Listing 6.5 reads three data values into num1, num2, and num3 and rearranges the data so that they are in increasing sequence, with the smallest value in num1. The three calls to function `order` perform an operation known as **sorting**.

Each time that function `order` executes, the smaller of its two argument values is stored in its first actual argument and the larger is stored in its second actual argument. Therefore, the first function call

sorting
Rearranging data values so they are in an ordered sequence.

```
order(num1, num2);        // order the data in num1 & num2
```

stores the smaller of num1 and num2 in num1 and the larger in num2. In the sample run shown, num1 is 7.5 and num2 is 9.6, so these values are not changed by the function execution. However, the function call

```
order(num1, num3);        // order the data in num1 & num3
```

switches the values of num1 (initial value is 7.5) and num3 (initial value is 5.5). Table 6.5 traces the `main` function execution.

The body of function `order` is based on the `if` statement from Example 4.13. The function heading

```
void order(float& x, float& y)   // INOUT - numbers to sort
```

identifies x and y as inout (input/output) parameters because the function uses the current actual argument values as inputs and may return new values.

During the execution of the second function call

```
order(num1, num3);        // order the data in num1 & num3
```

the formal parameter x contains the address of the actual argument num1, and the formal parameter y contains the address of actual argument num3. In testing the condition

```
(x > y)
```

the variable corresponding to x (num1) has value 7.5 and the variable corresponding to y (num3) has value 5.5 so the condition is true. Executing the first assignment statement in the true task

```
temp = x;
```

causes 7.5 to be copied into the local variable `temp`. Figure 6.3 shows a snapshot of the values in memory immediately after execution of this assignment statement.

Execution of the next assignment statement

```
x = y;
```

replaces the 7.5 in the variable corresponding to **x** (num1) with the value (5.5) of the variable corresponding to **y** (num3). The final assignment statement

```
y = temp;
```

copies the contents of the temporary variable (7.5) into the variable corresponding to **y** (num3). This completes the swap of values.

Listing 6.5   Function to order three numbers

```
// File: sort3Numbers.cpp
// reads three numbers and sorts them in ascending order

#include <iostream>
using namespace std;

// Functions used . . .
// Sorts a pair of numbers
void order(float&, float&);   // INOUT - numbers to sort

int main()
{

    float num1, num2, num3;   // user input - numbers to sort

    // Read 3 numbers.
    cout << "Enter 3 numbers to sort: "
    cin >> num1 >> num2 >> num3;

    // Sort them.
    order(num1, num2);            // order data in num1 & num2
    order(num1, num3);            // order data in num1 & num3
    order(num2, num3);            // order data in num2 & num3

    // Display results.
    cout << "The three numbers in order are:" << endl;
    cout << num1 << " " << num2 << " " << num3 << endl;

    return 0;
}

// Sorts a pair of numbers represented by x and y
// Pre: x and y are assigned values.
// Post: x is the smaller of the pair and y is the larger.
void order(float& x, float& y)          // INOUT - numbers to sort
{
```

(continued)

Listing 6.5 Function to order three numbers (continued)

```
    // Local data . . .
    float temp;              // storage for number in x

    // Compare x and y, exchange values if not in order.
    if (x > y)
    {                        // exchange the values in x and y
        temp = x;            // store old x in temp
        x = y;               // store old y in x
        y = temp;            // store old x in y
    }
}  // end order
```

```
Enter 3 numbers to sort: 7.5 9.6 5.5
The three numbers in order are:
5.5 7.5 9.6
```

Table 6.5 Trace of Program to Sort Three Numbers

Statement	num1	num2	num3	Effect
cin >> num1 >> num2 >> num3;	7.5	9.6	5.5	Enters data
order(num1, num2);				No change
order(num1, num3);	5.5		7.5	Switches num1 and num3
order(num2, num3);		7.5	9.6	Switches num2 and num3
cout << num1 << num2 << num3				Displays 5.5, 7.5, 9.6
<< endl;				

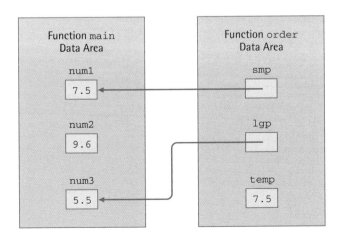

Figure 6.3 Data areas after temp = x; for call order(num1, num3);

EXERCISES FOR SECTION 6.2

Self-Check

1. Examine the functions below and answer the questions after function sumDiff.

```
#include <iostream>
using namespace std;

void sumDiff(int, int, int&, int&)

int main()
{
    int w, x, y, z;

    x = 5;   y = 3;   z = 7;   w = 9;
    cout << "   x   y   z   w " << endl;
    cout << "   " << x << "   " << y << "   " << z
         << "   " << w << endl;

    sumDiff(x, y, z, w);
    cout << " " << x << " " << y << " " << z
         << " " << w << endl;

    sumDiff(y, x, w, z);
    cout << " " << x << " " << y << " " << z
         << " " << w << endl;

    sumDiff(y, x, y, x);
    cout << " " << x << " " << y << " " << z
         << " " << w << endl;

    sumDiff(z, w, y, x);
    cout << " " << x << " " << y << " " << z
         << " " << w << endl;

    return 0;
}

void sumDiff(
    int num1, int num2,          // IN:
    int& num3, int& num4)        // INOUT:
{
    num3 = num1 + num2;
    num4 = num1 - num2;
}  // end sumDiff
```

a. Show the output displayed by function show in the form of a table of values for w, x, y, and z.

b. Briefly describe what function sumDiff computes. Include a description of how the input and input/output parameters to sumDiff are used.

c. Write the preconditions and postconditions for function sumDiff.

2. **a.** Refer to Listing 6.5 and trace the execution of the three function calls

```
order(num3, num2);
order(num3, num1);
order(num2, num1);
```

for the data sets: 15 20 4 and 4 15 20.

b. What is the effect of this sequence of calls?

3. Write an algorithm for a function addFrac that computes and returns through its two outputs the sum of two fractions passed as its inputs.

Programming

1. Write the function sumDiff in Self-Check Exercise 1 as two separate functions sum and diff that take two input arguments. Function sum performs the addition, and function diff performs the subtraction. Rewrite the main function to use sum and diff to compute the same results as before.

2. Write function doFrac that returns a string representing a common fraction given its numerator and denominator as input arguments and also returns the decimal value of the function. If the input arguments are 1 and 4, the string should be "1/4" and the decimal value should be 0.25. Make sure you don't use integer division to calculate the decimal value (1 / 4 is 0 using integer division).

3. Write and test a function multiplyFrac that has four inputs representing the numerator and denominator of two fractions. The function should return the numerator and denominator of their product fraction.

4. Write and test the function for Self-Check Exercise 3.

6.3 Stepwise Design with Function

Using argument lists to pass information to and from functions improves problem-solving skills. If the solution to a subproblem cannot be written easily using just a few C++ statements, code it as a function. The case study demonstrates stepwise design of programs using functions.

case study   General Sum and Average Problem

PROBLEM

You have been asked to accumulate a sum and to average a list of data values using functions. Because these tasks surface in many problems, design a general set of functions you can reuse in other programs.

ANALYSIS

Let's look again at the loop in Figure 5.2, which computed a company's total payroll. We can use a similar loop here to sum a collection of data values. To compute an average, divide a sum by the total number of items, being careful not to perform this division if the number of items is zero.

DATA REQUIREMENTS

Problem Input

int numItems	*// number of data items*
the data items	

Problem Output

float sum	*// accumulated sum of data items*
float average	*// average of all data items*

FORMULA

Average = Sum of data / number of data items

DESIGN

INITIAL ALGORITHM

1. Read the number of items.

2. Read the data items and compute the sum of the data (computeSum).

3. Compute the average of the data (computeAve).

4. Print the sum and the average (printSumAve).

The structure chart in Figure 6.4 documents the data flow between the main problem and its subproblems. We'll implement each step as a separate function; the label under a step denotes the name of the function implementing that step.

Figure 6.4 clarifies the data flow between the main function and each subordinate function. All variables whose values are set by a function are *function outputs* (indicated by an arrow pointing out of the function). All variables whose values are used in a computation but are not changed by a function are *function inputs* (indicated by an arrow pointing into the function). The role of each variable depends on its usage in a function and changes from step to step in the structure chart.

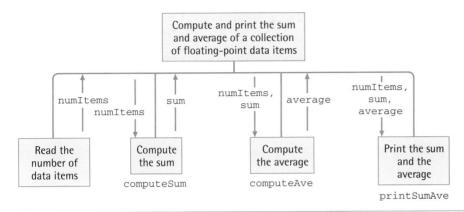

Figure 6.4 Structure chart for general sum and average problem

Because the step "Read the number of data items" defines the value of numItems, this variable is an output of this step. Function computeSum needs the value of numItems to know how many data items to read and sum; consequently, numItems is an input to function computeSum. The variable sum is an output of function computeSum but is an input to functions computeAve and printSumAve. The variable average is an output of function computeAve but is an input to function printSumAve.

IMPLEMENTATION

Using the data flow information in the structure chart, you can write the main function even before refining the algorithm. Follow the approach described in Section 3.1 to write function main. Begin by converting the data requirements shown earlier into local declarations for function main. Declare all the variables that appear in the structure chart in the main function, because they store data passed to a function or results returned from a function. Omit the declaration for a variable that stores the individual data items, since it doesn't appear in the structure chart. However, remember to declare this variable later in the function that uses it (computeSum). Next, move the initial algorithm into the main function body, writing each algorithm step as a comment.

To complete the main function (see Listing 6.6), code each algorithm step *in-line* (as part of the main program code) or as a function call. Code the data entry step in-line because it consists of a simple prompt and data entry operation.

The data flow information in Figure 6.4 tells you the actual arguments to use in each function call. It also tells you the name of the main program variable that will hold the function result. For example, use the assignment statement

```
sum = computeSum(numItems);
```

Listing 6.6   Main function for general sum and average problem

```cpp
// File: computeSumAve.cpp
// Computes and prints the sum and average of a collection of data.

#include <iostream>
using namespace std;

// Functions used . . .
// Computes sum of data
float computeSum
    (int);              // IN - number of data items

// Computes average of data
float computeAve
    (int,               // IN - number of data items
     float);            // IN - sum of data items

// Prints number of items, sum, and average
void printSumAve
    (int,               // IN - number of data items
     float,             // IN - sum of the data
     float);            // IN - average of the data

int main()
{
    int numItems;       // input - number of items to be added
    float sum;          // output - accumulated sum of data
    float average;      // output - average of data being processed

    // Read the number of items to process.
    cout << "Enter the number of items to process: ";
    cin >> numItems;

    // Compute the sum of the data.
    sum = computeSum(numItems);

    // Compute the average of the data.
    average = computeAve(numItems, sum);

    // Print the sum and the average.
    printSumAve(numItems, sum, average);

    return 0;
}

// Insert definitions for functions computeSum, computeAve,
// and printSumAve here.
```

to call `computeSum` and set the value of `sum`. In this call, `numItems` is passed as an input argument to function `computeSum` and the function result (determined by the `return` statement) is assigned to `sum`. Similarly, use the statement

```
average = computeAve(numItems, sum);
```

to call `computeAve`. Finally, use the statement

```
printSumAve(numItems, sum, average);
```

to call `printSumAve`, which has three input parameters and returns no result.

ANALYSIS FOR COMPUTESUM

In specifying the data requirements for `computeSum`, begin with the function interface information. This function is given the number of items to be processed as an input parameter (`numItems`). It's responsible for reading and computing the sum of this number of values. This sum is then returned using the `return` statement.

FUNCTION INTERFACE FOR COMPUTESUM

Input Parameters

`int numItems`   *// number of items to process*

Output Parameters

(none)

Function Return Value

the sum (`float`) of the data items processed

Besides a variable to store the sum, `computeSum` needs two more local variables: one for storing each data item (`item`) and one for loop control (`count`).

Local Data

`float item`   *// Contains each data item as it is read in*
`float sum`   *// Used to accumulate the sum of data read in*
`int count`   *// The number of data items processed so far*

DESIGN OF COMPUTESUM

The loop control steps must ensure that the correct number of data items are read and summed. Since you know the number of items to sum beforehand (`numItems`), use a counting loop. Use these steps to write the algorithm for `computeSum`; Listing 6.7 shows the code for `computeSum`.

INITIAL ALGORITHM FOR COMPUTESUM

1. Initialize `sum` to zero.

2. For each value of `count` from 0, as long as `count < numItems`

Listing 6.7   Function computeSum

```
// Computes sum of data.
// Pre:  numItems is assigned a value.
// Post: numItems data items read; their sum is stored in sum.
// Returns: Sum of all data items read if numItems >= 1;
//          otherwise, 0.

float computeSum
   (int numItems) // IN: number of data items
{
   // Local data  . . .
   float item;       // input: contains current data item
   float sum;        // output: used to accumulate sum of data
                     //         read in

   // Read each data item and accumulate it in sum.
   sum = 0.0;
   for (int count = 0; count < numItems; count++)
   {
      cout << "Enter a number to be added: ";
      cin >> item;
      sum += item;
   }  // end for

   return sum;
}  // end computeSum
```

2.1. Read in a data item.

2.2. Add the data item to sum.

3. Return sum.

ANALYSIS FOR **COMPUTEAVE** AND **PRINTSUMAVE**

Both computeAve and printSumAve are relatively straightforward. We list their interface information and algorithms next. Neither function requires any local data, but both algorithms include a test of numItems. If numItems isn't positive, it makes no sense to compute or display the average of the data items.

FUNCTION INTERFACE FOR **COMPUTEAVE**

Input Parameters

int numItems	// the number of data items to be processed
float sum	// the sum of all data processed

Output Parameters

(none)

Function Return Value

the average of all the data (`float`)

DESIGN OF `computeAve`

INITIAL ALGORITHM

1. If the number of items is less than 1

    1.1. display "invalid number of items" message.

    1.2. return a value of 0.

2. Return the value of the sum divided by `numItems`.

FUNCTION INTERFACE FOR **PRINTSUMAVE**

Input Parameters

```
int numItems      // the number of data items to be processed
float sum         // the sum of all data processed
float average     // the average of all the data
```

Output Parameters

(none)

DESIGN OF `printSumAve`

INITIAL ALGORITHM

1. If the number of items is positive

    1.1. Display the number of items and the sum and average of the data.

    Else

    1.2. Display "invalid number of items" message.

IMPLEMENTATION OF `computeAve` AND `printSumAve`

The implementation of the `computeAve` and `printSumAve` functions is shown in Listings 6.8 and 6.9.

TESTING

The program that solves the general `sum` and `average` problem consists of four separate functions. In testing the complete program, you should make sure that `sum` and `average` are displayed correctly when `numItems` is positive and that a meaningful diagnostic is displayed when `numItems` is zero or negative. Listing 6.10 shows a sample run of the complete program system.

Listing 6.8   Function computeAve

```
// Computes average of data
// Pre: numItems and sum are defined; numItems must be
//       greater than 0.
// Post: If numItems is positive, the average is computed
//       as sum / numItems;
// Returns: The average if numItems is positive;
// otherwise, 0.

float computeAve
    (int numItems,            // IN: number of data items
     float sum)               // IN: sum of data
{
    // Compute the average of the data.
    if (numItems < 1)         // test for invalid input
    {
        cout << "Invalid value for numItems = " << numItems
            << endl;
        cout << "Average not computed." << endl;
        return 0.0;           // return for invalid input
    } // end if

    return sum / numItems;
}   // end computeAve
```

Listing 6.9   Function printSumAve

```
// Prints number of items, sum, and average of data
// Pre: numItems, sum, and average are defined.
// Post: Displays numItems, sum and average if numItems > 0.

void printSumAve
    (int numItems,            // IN: number of data items
     float sum,               // IN: sum of the data
     float average)           // IN: average of the data
{
    // Display results if numItems is valid.
    if (numItems > 0)
    {
        cout << "The number of items is " << numItems << endl;
        cout << "The sum of the data is " << sum << endl;
        cout << "The average of the data is " << average << endl;
    }
```

(continued)

Listing 6.9 Function printSumAve (continued)

```
        else
        {
            cout << "Invalid number of items = " << numItems << endl;
            cout << "Sum and average are not defined." << endl;
            cout << "No printing done. Execution terminated." << endl;
        }  // end if
}  // end printSumAve
```

Listing 6.10 Sample run of general sum and average problem

```
Enter the number of items to process:  3
Enter a number to be added:  5
Enter a number to be added:  6
Enter a number to be added:  17
The number of items is 3
The sum of the data is 28.00
The average of the data is 9.3333
```

Multiple Declarations of Identifiers in a Program

The identifiers sum and numItems are declared as variables in the main function and as formal parameters in the three subordinate functions. From the discussion of scope of names (see Section 3.6), you know that each of these declarations has its own scope, and the scope for each formal parameter is the function that declares it. The argument lists associate the main function variable sum with each of the other identifiers named sum. The value of variable sum (in function main) is initially defined when function computeSum finishes execution because variable sum is assigned the function result. This value is passed into function computeAve because variable sum corresponds to computeAve's input parameter sum, and so on.

To avoid the possible confusion of seeing the identifier sum in multiple functions, we could have introduced different names in each function (for example, total, mySum). But the program is easier to read if the name sum is used throughout to refer to the sum of the data values. Make sure that you remember to link these separate uses of identifier sum through argument list correspondence.

PROGRAM STYLE   Use of Functions for Relatively Simple Algorithm Steps

All but the first step of the general sum and average problem are performed by separate functions. Even though it was relatively easy to implement the step for computing the average, we used a function (computeAve) rather than writing the code inline in the main function. We want to encourage the use of separate functions even for relatively easy-to-implement algorithm steps. This helps you keep the details of these steps separate and hidden and makes the program system easier to debug, test, and even modify at some future date. Also, you may be able to reuse this function later. From this point on, your main functions should consist primarily of a sequence of function calls.

PROGRAM STYLE   Cohesive Functions

Function computeSum only computes the sum. It doesn't read in the number of data items (Step 1 of the main function), nor does it display the sum of the data (role of function printSumAve).

Functions that perform a single operation are called *functionally cohesive*. It's good programming style to write such single-purpose, highly cohesive functions, as this helps to keep each function relatively compact and easy to read, write, and debug. You can determine whether a function is highly cohesive from the comment describing what the function does. If the comment consists of a short sentence or phrase with no connectives such as "and" or "or," then the function should be highly cohesive. If more than one or two connectives or separate sentences are needed to describe the purpose of a function, this may be a hint that the function is doing too many things and should be further decomposed into subfunctions.

EXERCISES FOR SECTION 6.3

Self-Check

1. Function computeAve returns a single value using a return statement. Rewrite this function to return this result through an output parameter. Why is this not as good a solution as the one used in the case study?

2. Draw the before and after data areas for the main function and revised computeAve (see Self-Check Exercise 1) assuming computeAve is called with sum equal to 150.0 and numItems equal to 8.

3. Draw the main function and printSumAve data areas given the data value assumptions in Self-Check Exercise 2.

4. Consider the three functions `computeSum`, `computeAve`, and `printSumAve` as though the code to validate the value of the parameter `numItems` had been omitted. For each of these functions, describe what would happen now that the function would be allowed to proceed with its work even if `numItems` were zero or negative.

5. Design an algorithm for `readNumItems` that uses a loop to ensure that the user enters a positive value. The loop should continue reading numbers until the user enters a positive number.

Programming
1. Implement the solution to Self-Check Exercise 5.

6.4 Using Objects with Functions

C++ provides two ways that you can use functions to modify objects.

1. You can use dot notation to apply a member function to an object (also called "sending the object a message"). The member function may modify one or more data attributes of the object to which it is applied.

2. You can pass an object as an argument to a function.

We illustrate both approaches in the next example.

EXAMPLE 6.6

Listing 6.11 shows function `moneyToNumberString`, which has a single inout argument of type `string`. This function removes a dollar sign and any commas that appear in its argument string. For example, if the argument string passed to the function is `"-$5,405,123.65"`, the argument string will be changed to `"-5405123.65"` by the function execution.

The `if` statement checks for the presence of a `$`. If the argument string begins with a `$`, the true task removes it. The `else` clause removes only the `$` from a string that begins with the substring `"-$"`. Next, the `while` loop removes all commas from the argument string, starting with the leftmost one. If a comma is found, the loop repetition condition is true, so the comma is removed and the next one is searched for. The loop repetition condition fails when there are no commas left in the argument string. We will say more about objects as arguments in Chapter 10.

Listing 6.11   Testing function `moneyToNumberString`

```cpp
// File: moneyToNumberTest.cpp
// Tests function moneyToNumberString
#include <string>
#include <iostream>
using namespace std;

// Function prototype
void moneyToNumberString(string&);

int main()
{
    string mString;                 // input - a"money"string

    cout << "Enter a dollar amount with $ and commas: ";
    cin >> mString;

    moneyToNumberString(mString);

    cout << "The dollar amount as a number is " << mString
         << endl;

    return 0;
}

// Removes the $ and commas from a money string.
// Pre: moneyString is defined and may contain commas and
//      begin with $ or -$.
// Post: $ and all commas are removed from moneyString.
void moneyToNumberString
   (string& moneyString) // INOUT - string with possible $ and commas
{
    // Local data . . .
    int posComma; // position of next comma

    // Remove $ from moneyString
    if (moneyString.at(0) == '$')              // Starts with $ ?
        moneyString.erase(0, 1);               // Remove $
    else if (moneyString.find("-$") == 0)      // Starts with -$ ?
        moneyString.erase(1, 1);               // Remove $

    // Remove all commas
    posComma = moneyString.find(",");          // Find first ,
```

(continued)

Listing 6.11 Testing function `moneyToNumberString` (continued)

```
    while (posComma >= 0 &&
           posComma < moneyString.length())    // Is posComma valid ?
    {
        moneyString.erase(posComma, 1);        // Remove ,
        posComma = moneyString.find(",");      // Find next ,
    }
}   // end moneyToNumberString
```

```
Enter a dollar amount with $ and commas: -$5,405,123.65
The dollar amount as a number is -5405123.65
```

EXERCISES FOR SECTION 6.4

Self-Check

1. Trace the execution of function `moneyToNumberString` for the data value shown in Listing 6.11. Show all values assigned to `posComma`.

Programming

1. Write a function `compress` that removes all blanks from its string argument. If the argument is `"  this  Is  One"` it should be changed to `"thisIsOne"`.

2. Write a function `doRemove` that removes the first occurrence of a substring (an input argument) from a second argument string (input/output).

6.5 Debugging and Testing a Program System

As the number of statements in a program system grows, the possibility of error also increases. If we keep each function to a manageable size, the likelihood of error increases much more slowly. It's also easier to read and test each function.

Just as you can simplify the overall programming process by writing a large program as a set of independent functions, you can simplify testing and debugging if you test in stages as the program evolves. Two kinds of testing are used: top-down testing and bottom-up testing. You should use a combination of these methods to test a program and its functions.

Top-Down Testing and Stubs

Though a single programmer or a programming team may be developing a program system, not all functions will be ready at the same time. It's still

top-down testing
The process of testing flow of control between a main function and its subordinate functions.

stub
A function with a heading and a minimal body used in testing flow of control.

possible to test the overall flow of control between the main program and its level-1 functions and to test and debug the level-1 functions that are complete. Testing the flow of control between a main function and its subordinate functions is called **top-down testing**.

Because the main function calls all level-1 functions, we need for all functions that are not yet coded a substitute called a **stub**—a function heading followed by a minimal body, which should display a message identifying the function being executed and should assign simple values to any outputs. Listing 6.12 shows a stub for function computeSum that could be used in a test of the main function in Listing 6.6. The stub arbitrarily returns a value of 100.0, which is reasonable data for the remaining functions to process. Examining the program output tells us whether the main function calls its level-1 functions in the required sequence and whether data flows correctly between the main function and its level-1 functions.

Bottom–Up Testing and Drivers

unit test
A test of an individual function.

When a function is completed, it can be substituted for its stub in the program. However, we often perform a preliminary **unit test** of a new function before substitution because it's easier to locate and correct errors when dealing with a single function rather than with a complete program system. We can perform such a unit test by writing a short driver function to call it.

It isn't a good idea to spend a lot of time creating an elegant driver function, because it will be discarded as soon as the new function is tested. A driver function should contain only the declarations and executable statements necessary to test a single function. A driver should begin by reading or assigning values to all input arguments and to input/output arguments.

Listing 6.12   Stub for function computeSum

```
// Computes sum of data - stub
// Pre: numItems is assigned a value.
// Post: numItems data items read; their sum is stored in sum.
// Returns: Sum of all data items read if numItems >= 1;
//    otherwise 0.0.
float computeSum
   (int numItems)        // IN - number of data items

{
    cout << "Function computeSum entered" << endl;
    return 100.0;
}  // end computeSum stub
```

Next comes the call to the function being tested. After calling the function, the driver should display the function results. Listing 6.13 shows a driver for the completed function computeSum. Since we have no need to save the function result, we inserted the function call directly in the output statement.

Once you're confident that a function works properly, you can substitute it for its stub in the program system. The process of separately testing individual functions before inserting them in a program system is called **bottom-up testing**. Tests of the entire system are called **system integration tests**.

By following a combination of top-down and bottom-up testing, a programming team can be fairly confident that the complete function system will be relatively free of errors when it's finally put together. Consequently, the final debugging sessions should proceed quickly and smoothly.

bottom-up testing
The process of separately testing individual functions of a program system.

system integration tests
Testing a system after replacing all its stubs with functions that have been pretested.

Debugging Tips for Program Systems

The following suggestions will prove helpful when debugging a program system.

1. Carefully document each function parameter and local variable using comments as you write the code. Also describe the function's purpose using comments.

2. Create a trace of execution by displaying the function name as you enter it.

3. Trace or display the values of all input and input/output parameters upon entry to a function. Check that these values make sense.

Listing 6.13 A driver to test computeSum

```cpp
int main()
{

    int n;
    // Keep calling computeSum and displaying the result.
    do
    {
        cout << "Enter number of items or 0 to quit: ";
        cin >> n;
        cout << "The sum is " << computeSum(n) << endl;
    } while (n != 0);

    return 0;
}   // end driver
```

4. Trace or display the values of all function outputs after returning from a function. Verify that these values are correct by hand computation. Make sure you declare all input/output and output parameters as reference parameters (using the & symbol).

5. Make sure that the function stub assigns a value to each output parameter.

You should plan for debugging as you write each function rather than adding debugging statements later. Include any output statements that you might need to help determine that the function is working. When you're satisfied that the function works as desired, you can remove these debugging statements. In Section 5.9, it was suggested that you turn them into comments.

Another way to "turn debugging off and on" is to introduce a type bool flag called DEBUG. First, make each debugging statement a dependent statement that executes only if DEBUG is true.

```
if (DEBUG)
    cout << "***** score is " << score << " and sum is "
         << sum << endl;
```

To "turn on debugging," insert the statement

```
const bool DEBUG = true;
```

before your main function, making it visible in all your functions. Setting the debugging flag to true causes the debugging statements to execute. To "turn off debugging," set the constant DEBUG to false instead of true.

Identifier Scope and Watch Window Variables

You can use a debugger to trace values passed into a function's input arguments and to trace the values returned by a function. The values displayed in the Watch window are determined by the normal scope rules for identifiers. Consequently, a function's local variables and formal parameters will be considered undefined until that function begins execution. Upon exit from the function, its local variables and formal parameters will again become undefined.

Black–Box Versus White–Box Testing

black-box (or specification-based) testing
A testing process that assumes the tester has no knowledge of the code; the tester must compare a function or the system's performance with its specification.

There are two basic ways to test a completed function or system: (1) black-box testing and (2) white-box testing. In **black-box** (or **specification-based**) **testing**, we assume that the program tester has no information about the code inside the function or system. The tester's job is to verify that the function or system meets its specifications. For For each function, the tester must ensure that its postconditions are satisfied whenever its preconditions are met.

Because the tester cannot look inside the function or system, the tester must prepare sufficient sets of test data to verify that the system output is correct for all valid input values. The tester should also find out whether the function or system will crash for invalid data. The tester should especially check the *boundaries* of the system, or particular values where the system performance changes. For example, a boundary for a payroll program would be the value of hours worked that triggers overtime pay. Black-box testing is most often done by a special testing team or by program users.

In **white-box** (or **glass-box**) **testing**, the tester has full knowledge of the code for the function or system and must ensure that each section of code has been thoroughly tested. For a selection statement (if or switch), this means checking all possible paths through the selection statement. The tester must determine that the correct path is chosen for all possible values of the selection variable, taking special care at the boundary values where the path changes.

white box (or glass box) testing
A testing process that assumes the tester knows how the system is coded and requires checking all possible execution paths.

For a repetition statement, the tester must make sure that the loop always performs the correct number of iterations and that the number of iterations isn't off by one. Also, the tester should verify that the computations inside the loop are correct at the boundaries—that is, for the initial and final values of the loop control variable. Finally, the tester should make sure that the function or system still meets its specification when a loop executes zero times and that under no circumstances can the loop execute forever.

EXERCISES FOR SECTION 6.5

Self-Check

1. Show the output you'd expect to see for the sum and average program (Listing 6.6) using the stub in Listing 6.12 when numItems is 10.

2. Write a driver program to test function computeAve.

3. Explain the difference between black-box and white-box testing, between bottom-up and top-down testing, between unit tests and system integration tests.

4. Explain the difference between stubs and drivers. Which would be more useful in bottom-up testing? Which would be more useful in top-down testing?

5. Compare function prototypes and stubs. How are they similar, and how are they different?

Programming

1. Write a driver function to test function computeAve.

2. Rewrite the driver in Listing 6.13 using a while statement.

6.6   Recursive Functions (Optional)

C++ allows a function to call itself. A function that calls itself is a *recursive function*. Sometimes it's simpler to implement a repeated operation using recursion instead of iteration. A recursive function calls itself repeatedly, but with different argument values for each call.

Just as we did for a loop, we need to identify a situation (called a **stopping case**) that stops the recursion; otherwise, the function will call itself forever. Usually a recursive function has the following form:

stopping case
An alternative task in a recursive function that leads to no further recursive calls.

Template for a Recursive Function

1. If the stopping case is reached
          1.1. Return a value for the stopping case
       Else
          1.2. Return a value computed by calling the function again with
               different arguments.

The `if` statement tests whether the stopping case has been reached. When it is reached, the recursion stops and the function returns a value to the caller. If the stopping case isn't reached, the function calls itself again with different arguments. The arguments in successive calls should bring us closer and closer to reaching the stopping case.

In this section we describe a recursive function that returns an integer value representing the factorial of its argument. The *factorial of n* is the product of all positive integers less than or equal to n and is written in mathematics as $n!$. For example, 4! is the product $4 \times 3 \times 2 \times 1$ or 24. We provide a recursive definition for $n!$ next.

$$n! = 1 \qquad \text{for } n = 0 \text{ or } 1$$
$$n! = n \times (n-1)! \qquad \text{for } n > 1$$

We can translate this definition into pseudocode using the template shown earlier:

1. If n is 0 or 1
          1.1. Return 1
       Else
          1.2. Return $n \times (n-1)!$

Listing 6.14 shows function `factorial` rewritten as a recursive function. The stopping case is reached when n is less than or equal to 1. When n is greater than 1, the statement

```
return n * factorial(n-1);
```

executes, which is the C++ form of the second formula. The expression part of this statement contains a valid function call, `factorial(n-1)`, which calls function `factorial` with an argument that is 1 less than the current argument. This function call is a *recursive call*. If the argument in the initial call to `factorial` is 3, the following chain of recursive calls occurs:

```
factorial(3) → 3 * factorial(2) → 3 * (2 * factorial(1))
```

In the last call above, n is equal to 1, so the statement

```
return 1;
```

executes, stopping the chain of recursive calls.

When it finishes the last function call, C++ must return a value from each recursive call, starting with the last one. This process is called **unwinding the recursion**. The last call was `factorial(1)` and it returns a value of 1. To find the value returned by each call for n greater than 1, multiply n by the value returned from `factorial(n-1)`. Therefore, the value returned from `factorial(2)` is 2 * the value returned from `factorial(1)` or 2; the value returned from `factorial(3)` is 3 * the value returned from `factorial(2)` or 6 (see Figure 6.5).

unwinding the recursion
The process of returning a value from each recursive call.

For comparison purposes, Listing 6.15 shows an iterative factorial function that uses a loop to accumulate partial products in local variable `productSoFar`. The `for` statement repeats the multiplication step when n is greater than 1. If n is 0 or 1, the `for` loop body doesn't execute, so `productSoFar` retains its initial value of 1. After loop exit, the last value of `productSoFar` is returned as the function result.

Listing 6.14   Recursive function factorial
_____

```
// Pre: n is >= 0
// Returns: The product 1 * 2 * 3 * . . . * n for n > 1;
//             otherwise 1.

int factorial(int n)
{
    if (n <= 1)
        return 1;
    else
        return n * factorial(n-1);
}
```
_____

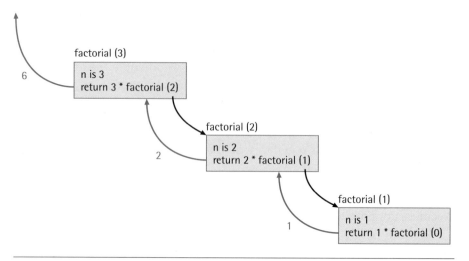

Figure 6.5 Unwinding the recursion

Listing 6.15 Iterative factorial function

```
// Pre: n is >= 0
// Returns: The product 1 * 2 * 3 * . . . * n for n > 1;
//          otherwise 1.
int factorial(int n)
{

    int productSoFar;           // output: accumulated product

    // Initialize accumulated product
    productSoFar = 1;

    // Perform the repeated multiplication for i > 1.
    for (int i = n; i > 1; i--)
       productSoFar = productSoFar * i;

       return productSoFar;
}
```

EXERCISES FOR SECTION 6.6

Self-Check

1. Trace the execution of function `factorial` when n is 5.

2. Show the chain of recursive calls to function `mystery` when m is 5 and n is 3. What do you think `mystery` does?

```
int mystery(int m, int n)
{
    if (n == 1) then
        return m;
    else
        return m * mystery(m, n-1);
}
```

3. Complete the recursive definition of function gcd which computes the greatest common divisor of two integers (gcd(20, 15) is 5).

```
// precondition: m is greater than or equal to n
int gcd(int m, int n)
{
    if (n > m)
        return gcd(__, __);     //exchange arguments
    else if (m % n == 0)
        return __;              //the result is known
    else
        return gcd(__, __);     //find gcd of n and
                                //remainder of m / n
}
```

Programming

1. Write a recursive function that, given an input value of n, computes:

```
n + n-1 + . . . + 2 + 1.
```

2. Write a function c(n, r) that returns the number of different ways r items can be selected from a group of n items. The mathematical formula for c(n, r) follows. Test c(n, r) using both the recursive and the nonrecursive versions of function factorial.

$$c(n, r) = \frac{n!}{r!(n - r)!}$$

6.7 Common Programming Errors

Many opportunities for error arise when you use functions with parameter lists, so be extremely careful. Proper use of parameters is difficult for beginning programmers to master, but it's an essential skill. One obvious pitfall is not ensuring that the actual argument list has the same number of items as the formal parameter list. Each actual input argument must be of a type that can be assigned to its corresponding formal parameter. An actual output argument or inout argument should be the same data type as the corresponding formal parameter. Let's now look at two specific errors that can occur with reference parameters.

- *Parameter inconsistencies with call-by-reference parameters:* In Chapter 3, we indicated that argument/parameter inconsistencies involving character, integer, and floating-point data usually don't cause even a warning message from the compiler. However, such inconsistencies will cause a warning message if they occur when using reference parameters.

  For example, if `initiate` has the prototype

  ```
  void initiate(char &);
  ```

  and `sum` is type `float`, the call

  ```
  initiate(sum);
  ```

  will result in a compiler warning such as

  ```
  "Temporary used for parameter 1 in call to 'initiate
  (char &)'"
  ```

  Even though this is only a warning, it does indicate a possible error. Check the function call carefully to ensure that you're passing the correct argument.

- *Forgetting to use an & with call-by-reference parameters:* Make sure you remember to use an `&` in the function prototype and function header (but not the call) before each output or inout parameter. Forgetting the `&` doesn't cause an error message; however, C++ will treat the formal parameter as call-by-value instead of call-by-reference. Therefore, any change made to the parameter by the called function will not be returned to the calling function.

Chapter Review

1. Functions provide a mechanism for separating and hiding the details for each component of a program system. The use of functions makes it possible to carry this separation through from the problem analysis and program design stages to the implementation of a program in C++.

2. Parameters enable a programmer to pass data to functions and to return multiple results from functions. The parameter list provides a highly visible communication path between a function and its calling program. Using parameters enables a function to process different data each time it executes, thereby making it easier to reuse the function in other programs.

3. Parameters may be used for input to a function, for output or sending back results, and for both input and output. An input parameter is used only for passing data into a function. The actual argument corresponding

to an input parameter may be an expression or a constant. The parameter's declared type should be the same as the type of the argument.

4. C++ uses call-by-value for input parameters and call-by-reference for output and inout (input/output) parameters. For call-by-value, the actual argument's value is passed to the function when it's called; for call-by-reference, the actual argument's address is passed to the function when it's called. C++ uses the symbol & after the parameter type to indicate a reference parameter in a function prototype and in a function definition but not in a function call.

5. Output and inout parameters must be able to access variables in the calling function's data area, so the actual argument corresponding to an output or inout parameter must be a variable. The parameter's declared type should be the same as the type of the data.

Summary of New C++ Constructs

Construct	Effect
Function Prototype `void doIt (float, char, float&, char&);`	Prototype for a function having two input and two output parameters.

Function Definition
<pre>void doIt
   (float x,   // IN
    char op,   // IN
    float& y,   // OUT
    char& sign)   // OUT
{
   switch(op)
   {
     case '+':
        y = x + x;
        break;
     case '*':
        y = x * x;
        break;
   }
   if (x >= 0.0)
      sign = '+';
   else
      sign = '-';
} // end doIt</pre>
	x and op are input parameters that contain valid values passed in from the calling function. The memory cells corresponding to the output parameters y and sign are undefined upon entrance to function doIt, but they contain valid values that are passed back to the calling function upon exit.

Function Call Statement `doIt(-5.0, '*', p, mySign);`	Calls function doIt. -5.0 is passed into x and '*' is passed into op. 25.0 is returned to p, and '-' is returned to mySign.

Quick-Check Exercises

1. Actual arguments appear in a function _____; formal parameters appear in a function _____ and function _____. Formal parameters are optional in a function _____.

2. Constants and expressions may be used as actual arguments corresponding to formal parameters that are _____ parameters.

3. In a function header, _____ parameters used for function output are designated by using the symbol _____ placed _____ the parameter type.

4. A _____ must be used as an actual argument corresponding to a call-by-reference formal parameter. You can use an _____ as an actual argument corresponding to a call-by-value parameter.

5. For _____ parameters, the argument's address is stored in the called function data area for the corresponding formal parameter. For _____ parameters, the argument's value is stored in the called function data area for the corresponding formal parameter.

6. If a function returns all its results (type `double`) through its formal parameters, what would the type of the function be?

7. Is a driver or a stub used to allow an upper-level function to be tested before all lower-level functions are complete?

8. Does a testing team use white-box or black-box testing?

9. What output lines are displayed by the program below?

```cpp
void silly(int);

int main()
{
    int x,  y;
    // Do something silly.
    x = 8;  y = 5;
    silly(x);
    cout << x << ", " << y << endl;
    silly(y); // values here
    cout << x << ", " << y << endl;

    return 0;

}
void silly(int x)
{
    int y;

    y = x;
```

```
    x *= 2;
    cout << x << ", " << y << endl;
} // end silly
```

10. Answer Quick-Check Exercise 9 if silly's parameter is a reference parameter.

11. In what ways can a function return values to its caller?

Review Questions

1. Write the prototype for a function named pass that has two integer parameters. The first parameter should be a value parameter and the second a reference parameter.

2. Write a function called letterGrade with a type int input parameter called score. The function should return through an output parameter (grade) the appropriate letter grade using a straight scale (90 to 100 is an A; 80 to 89 is a B; 70 to 79 is a C; 60 to 69 is a D; and 0 to 59 is an F). Return through a second output parameter a plus symbol if the student just missed the next higher grade by one or two points (for example, if a student got an 88 or 89, the second output parameter should be '+'). If the student just made the grade (for example, got a grade of 80 or 81), return a '−' for the second output parameter. The second output parameter should be blank if the student did not just miss or just make the grade.

3. Would you write a function that computes a single numeric value as a non-void function that returns a result through a return statement or as a void function with one output parameter? Explain your choice.

4. Explain the allocation of memory cells when a function is called. What is stored in the called function's data area for an input parameter? What is stored for an output parameter? What is stored for an inout parameter?

5. Write a driver program to test the function that you wrote for Review Question 2.

6. What are the two kinds of reference parameters? Explain the differences between them.

7. Sketch the data areas of functions main and silly as they appear immediately before the return from the first call to silly in Quick-Check Exercise 9 as modified in 10.

8. Present arguments against these statements:
   a. It's foolish to use function subprograms because a program written with functions has many more lines than the same program written without functions.
   b. The use of function subprograms leads to more errors because of mistakes in using argument lists.

Programming Projects

1. A hospital supply company wants to market a program to assist with the calculation of intravenous rates. Design and implement a program that interacts with the user as follows:

```
INTRAVENOUS RATE ASSISTANT

Enter the number of the problem you wish to solve.
      GIVEN A MEDICAL ORDER IN              CALCULATE RATE IN
(1) ml/hr & tubing drop factor               drops / min
(2) 1 L for n hr                             ml / hr
(3) mg/kg/hr & concentration in mg/ml        ml / hr
(4) units/hr & concentration in units/ml   ml / hr
(5) QUIT

Problem=> 1
Enter rate in ml/hr=> 150
Enter tubing's drop factor(drops/ml)=> 15
The drop rate per minute is 38.

Enter the number of the problem you wish to solve.
      GIVEN A MEDICAL ORDER IN              CALCULATE RATE IN
(1) ml/hr & tubing drop factor               drops / min
(2) 1 L for n hr                             ml / hr
(3) mg/kg/hr & concentration in mg/ml        ml / hr
(4) units/hr & concentration in units/ml   ml / hr
(5) QUIT

Problem=> 2
Enter number of hours=> 8
The rate in milliliters per hour is 125.

Enter the number of the problem you wish to solve.
      GIVEN A MEDICAL ORDER IN              CALCULATE RATE IN
(1) ml/hr & tubing drop factor               drops / min
(2) 1 L for n hr                             ml / hr
(3) mg/kg/hr & concentration in mg/ml        ml / hr
(4) units/hr & concentration in units/ml   ml / hr
(5) QUIT

Problem=> 3
Enter rate in mg/kg/hr=> 0.6
Enter patient weight in kg=> 70
Enter concentration in mg/ml=> 1
The rate in milliliters per hour is 42.
```

```
Enter the number of the problem you wish to solve.
      GIVEN A MEDICAL ORDER IN            CALCULATE RATE IN
(1) ml/hr & tubing drop factor              drops / min
(2) 1 L for n hr                            ml / hr
(3) mg/kg/hr & concentration in mg/ml       ml / hr
(4) units/hr & concentration in units/ml    ml / hr
(5) QUIT

Problem=> 4
Enter rate in units/hr=> 1000
Enter concentration in units/ml=> 25
The rate in milliliters per hour is 40.

Enter the number of the problem you wish to solve.
      GIVEN A MEDICAL ORDER IN            CALCULATE RATE IN
(1) ml/hr & tubing drop factor              drops / min
(2) 1 L for n hr                            ml / hr
(3) mg/kg/hr & concentration in mg/ml       ml / hr
(4) units/hr & concentration in units/ml    ml / hr
(5) QUIT

Problem=> 5
```

Implement the following functions:

getProblem—Displays the user menu, then inputs and returns as the function value the problem number selected.

getRateDropFactor—Prompts the user to enter the data required for problem 1, and sends this data back to the calling module via output parameters.

getKgRateConc—Prompts the user to enter the data required for problem 3, and sends this data back to the calling module via output parameters.

getUnitsConc—Prompts the user to enter the data required for problem 4, and sends this data back to the calling module via output parameters.

figDropsMin—Takes rate and drop factor as input parameters and returns drops/min (rounded to the nearest whole drop) as function value.

figMlHr—Takes as an input parameter the number of hours over which one liter is to be delivered and returns ml/hr (rounded) as function value.

byWeight—Takes as input parameters rate in mg/kg/hr, patient weight in kg, and concentration of drug in mg/ml and returns ml/hr (rounded) as function value.

byUnits—Takes as input parameters rate in units/hr and concentration in units/ml, and returns ml/hr(rounded) as function value.

(Hint: Use a sentinel-controlled loop. Call getProblem once before the loop to initialize the problem number and once again at the end of the loop body to update it.)

2. The table below summarizes three commonly used mathematical models of nonvertical straight lines.

Mode	Equation	Given
Two-point form	$m = \dfrac{y_2 - y_1}{x_2 - x_1}$	$(x_1, y_1), (x_2, y_2)$
Point-slope form	$y - y_1 = m(x - x_1)$	$m, (x_1, y_1)$
Slope-intercept form	$y = mx + b$	m, b

Design and implement a program that permits the user to convert either two-point form or point-slope form into slope-intercept form. Your program should interact with the user as follows:

```
Select the form that you would like to convert to slope-
intercept form:
1) Two-point form (you know two points on the line)
2) Point-slope form (you know the line's slope and one point)
=> 2

Enter the slope=> 4.2
Enter the x-y coordinates of the point separated by a
space=> 1 1

Point-slope form
   y - 1.00 = 4.20(x - 1.00)

Slope-intercept form
   y = 4.20x - 3.20

Do another conversion (Y or N) => Y

Select the form that you would like to convert to slope-
intercept form:
1) Two-point form (you know two points on the line)
2) Point-slope form (you know the line's slope and one
point)
=> 1

Enter the x-y coordinates of the first point separated by a
space=> 4 3
```

```
Enter the x-y coordinates of the second point separated by a
space=> -2 1

Two-point form

        (1.00 - 3.00)
m =  _____
        (-2.00 - 4.00)

Slope-intercept form

    y = 0.33x + 1.66

Do another conversion (Y or N)=> N
```

Implement the following functions:

getProblem—Displays the user menu, then inputs and returns as the function value the problem number selected.

get2Pt—Prompts the user for the x-y coordinates of both points, inputs the four coordinates, and returns them to the calling function through output parameters.

getPtSlope—Prompts the user for the slope and x-y coordinates of the point, inputs the three values, and returns them to the calling function through output parameters.

slopeIntcptFrom2Pt—Takes four input parameters, the x-y coordinates of two points, and returns through output parameters the slope (*m*) and y-intercept (*b*).

intcptFromPtSlope—Takes three input parameters, the x-y coordinates of one point and the slope, and returns as the function value the y-intercept.

display2Pt—Takes four input parameters, the x-y coordinates of two points, and displays the two-point line equation with a heading.

displayPtSlope—Takes three input parameters, the x-y coordinates of one point and the slope, and displays the point-slope line equation with a heading.

displaySlopeIntcpt—Takes two input parameters, the slope and y-intercept, and displays the slope-intercept line equation with a heading.

3. The trustees of a small college are considering voting a pay raise for their 12 faculty members. They want to grant a 2.5-percent pay raise; however, before doing so, they want to know how much this will cost. Write a program that will print the pay raise for each faculty member and the total amount of the raises. Also, print the total faculty payroll before and after the raise. Test your function for the salaries:

$52,500	$64,029.50	$56,000	$53,250
$65,500	$42,800	$45,000.50	$68,900
$53,780	$77,300	$84,120.25	$64,100

4. Redo Programming Project 3 assuming that faculty members earning less than $50,000 receive a 3-percent raise, those earning more than $70,000 receive a 3.5-percent raise, and all others receive a 2.5-percent raise. For each faculty member, print the raise percentage as well as the amount.

5. Patients required to take many kinds of medication often have difficulty in remembering when to take their medicine. Given the following set of medications, write a function that prints an hourly table indicating what medication to take at any given hour. Use a counter variable `clock` to go through a 24-hour day. Print the table based on the following prescriptions:

Medication	Frequency
Iron pill	0800, 1200, 1800
Antibiotic	Every 4 hours starting at 0400
Aspirin	0800, 2100
Decongestant	1100, 2000

6. After studying gross annual revenues of Broadway shows over a 20-year period, you model the revenue as a function of time:

$$R(t) = 203.265 \times (1.071)^t$$

where R is in millions of dollars and t is the years since 1984. Create the following C++ functions to implement this model:

`revenue`—calculates and returns R for an input parameter of t.

`predict`—predicts the year in which revenues (in millions) will first equal or exceed the value of the input parameter. For example, `predict(200)` would return 1984.

Write a main function that calls `predict` to determine when revenues will likely exceed $1 trillion (that is, 1,000 million). Then display a table of estimated revenues (in millions of dollars) for all the years from 1984 through the year when revenues should exceed $1 trillion. Round revenue estimates to three decimal places.

7. The square root of a number N can be approximated by repeated calculation using the formula

$$NG = 0.5(LG + N/LG)$$

where NG stands for *next guess* and LG stands for *last guess*. Write a function that implements this computation. The first parameter will be a positive real number, the second will be an initial guess of the square root of that number, and the third will be the computed result.

The initial guess will be the starting value of *LG*. The function will compute a value for *NG* using the formula above. To control the computation, we can use a `while` loop. Each time through the loop, the difference between *NG* and *LG* is checked to see whether these two guesses are almost identical. If so, the function returns *NG* as the square root; otherwise, the next guess (*NG*) becomes the last guess (*LG*) and the process is repeated (that is, another value is computed for *NG*, the difference is checked, and so forth).

For this problem, the loop should be repeated until the magnitude of the difference between *LG* and *NG* is less than 0.005. Use an initial guess of 1.0 and test the function for the numbers 4.0, 120.5, 88.0, 36.01, and 10,000.0.

8. Develop a collection of functions to solve simple conduction problems using various forms of the formula

$$H = \frac{kA(T_2 - T_1)}{X}$$

where *H* is the rate of heat transfer in watts, *k* is the coefficient of thermal conductivity for the particular substance, *A* is the cross-sectional area in m² (square meters), T_2 and T_1 are the Kelvin temperatures on the two sides of the conductor, and *X* is the thickness of the conductor in meters.

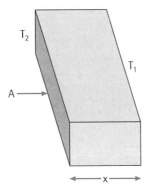

Define a function for each variable in the formula. For example, function `calcH` would compute the rate of heat transfer, `calcK` would figure the coefficient of thermal conductivity, `calcA` would find the cross-sectional area, and so on.

Develop a driver function that interacts with the user in the following way:

```
Respond to the prompts with the data known. For the
unknown quantity, enter -999
```

```
Rate of heat transfer (watts) : 755.0
Coefficient of thermal conductivity (W/m-K) : 0.8
Cross-sectional area of conductor (m^2) : 0.12
Temperature on one side (K) : 298
Temperature on other side (K) : -999
Thickness of conductor (m) : 0.003
```

$$H = \frac{kA(T_2 - T_1)}{X}$$

```
Temperature on the other side is 274 K.
H = 755.0 W                    T2 = 298 K
k = 0.800 W/m-K                T1 = 274 K
A = 0.120 m^2                  X = 0.0003 m
```

9. Write a program to model a simple calculator. Each data line should consist of the next operation to be performed from the list below and the right operand. Assume the left operand is the accumulator value (initial value of 0). You need a function scan_data with two output parameters that returns the operator and right operand scanned from a data line. You need a function do_next_op that performs the required operation. do_next_op has two input parameters (the operator and operand) and one input/output parameter (the accumulator). The valid operators are:

+   add

−   subtract

*   multiply

/   divide

^   power (raise left operand to power of right operand)

q   quit

Your calculator should display the accumulator value after each operation. A sample run follows.

```
+ 5.0
result so far is 5.0
^2
result so far is 25.0
/ 2.0
result so far is 12.5
q 0
final result is 12.5
```

10. Write a function that reads a problem involving two common fractions such as 2/4 + 5/6. After reading the common fractions problem, call a function to perform the indicated operation (call addFrac for +, call

multiplyFrac for *, and so on). Pass the numerator and denominator of both fractions to the function that performs the operation; the function should return the numerator and denominator of the result through its output parameters. Then display the result as a common fraction. (Hint: Use functions readFracProblem and getFrac; see Listings 6.3 and 6.4.)

11. Write a function to calculate the day number for a given day represented by three type int values (the function input). The day number should be between 1 and 365 (366 if the year is a leap year). Also, write a function that returns true if its first date (first three int arguments) comes after its second date (last three int arguments). Then write a recursive function that determines the number of days between two dates, each represented by three integers. Use the following algorithm:

If the first date comes after the second date

    Reverse the dates and calculate the days between them

Else if the year of both dates is the same

    The result is the day number of the second date minus

    the day number of the first date

Else

    The result is the day number of the second date +

    the number of days between the first date and the last

    day of the previous year

    The recursive function requires the second date to follow the first. If it doesn't, the task under the first condition should return the result of calling the function with the arguments reversed, so the second date will follow the first in this next call.

    If the dates are in the correct order and the year is the same (tested by the second condition), the result is just the difference in the day numbers for each date. Otherwise, the last task calculates the result by adding the day number of the second date to the number of days between the first date and the end of the year just before the year of the second date. For example, if the second date is January 5, 2003, the result is 5 + the number of days between the first date and December 31, 2002. The next call to the function will calculate the latter value either by executing the second task (if 2002 is the year of the first date) or by adding 365 (the number of days in 2002) to the difference between the first date and December 31, 2001, and so on.

Answers to Quick-Check Exercises

1. call; definition, prototype; prototype

2. value (or call-by-value)

3. reference (or call-by-reference), &, after

4. variable, expression

5. call-by-reference; call-by-value

6. void

7. stub

8. black-box testing

9. 16, 8
   8, 5
   10, 5
   8, 5

10. 16, 8
    16, 5
    10, 5
    16, 10

11. A function can return values by using a `return` statement or by assigning the values to be returned to reference parameters.

Robert Sebesta

Dr. Sebesta received his Ph.D. in Computer Science from Penn State University. He retired from the faculty of the University of Colorado at Colorado Springs in 2005, after teaching computer science for 35 years. Dr. Sebesta currently works on revisions of his books and teaches programming languages and Web programming part-time. He is the author of several books, including Concepts of Programming Languages *and* Programming the World Wide Web.

What is your educational background, and how did you decide to study computer science?
I have a B.S. in Applied Mathematics (University of Colorado at Boulder), an M.S. in Computer Science (Penn State), and a Ph.D. in Computer Science (Penn State). I decided to study computer science for two reasons: (1) I minored in computer science as an undergraduate and enjoyed programming, and (2) most of the jobs available for someone with a B.S. in applied math were in software development. I decided that if I was going to be a software developer, I needed more education in computer science.

What was your first job in the computer industry?
I worked half-time in a government research lab during my last two years of undergraduate school. I was a programmer for a small group of scientists who were doing research on wave propagation.

Which person in the field has inspired you most?
One early inspiration for me was the researcher for whom I worked as an undergraduate, Bob Lawrence. He was very interested in computer applications in his research. I learned much about scientific computing and in the process discovered that I really enjoyed doing that kind of work.

Do you have any advice about programming in C++?
Because of its widespread use in industry, all undergraduate students in computer science must learn it. However, by most reasonable measures, C++ is a large, complex language that includes more insecurities than some other languages, such as Java and C#. Because of its complexity and insecurities, C++ programs are more difficult to maintain than programs written in some other languages.

What advice do you have for students entering the computer science field?
First, computer science is not an easy discipline, so plan on spending large amounts of time studying and working on programming projects. Although the job market is certainly not as strong as it was in the 1990s, there are many jobs available in software development.

What is the most challenging part of teaching programming?
Because only a small percentage of people can easily become skilled programmers, the challenge for educators is to find ways to teach as many of the others as we can.

How has C++ evolved in the last few years?
Although new class libraries are always being created, the language itself has not changed much in the last few years. The changes that would be required to make the language less complex and more reliable are substantial and unlikely to happen.

What is your vision for the future of the C++ programming language?
I think C++ will remain a very popular language in industry, in part because there is a great deal of legacy software that is written in C++. However, the popularity of C++ has been eroded by the widespread use of Java and, more recently, C#.

chapter seven

Simple Data Types

Learning Objectives

- To learn how to define constants using the #define compiler directive
- To understand the differences between fixed-point and floating-point representations of numbers
- To learn about additional data types for representing very large integers and real numbers, and the range of numbers that can be represented by these different data types
- To learn how to manipulate character data using functions in library cctype
- To understand the encoding of character data using the ASCII character set
- To learn how to write and use bool functions in programming
- To understand how to use enumeration types and enumerators to define a data type and its associated values

SO FAR WE'VE used four *predefined data types* of C++: int, float, char, and bool. In this chapter, we look more closely at these data types and introduce some variants of them. We examine the forms in which these types of values are stored in memory, and we introduce some new operators that can be applied to these types. We also introduce the *enumeration type*. A characteristic shared by all of these data types is that only a single value can be stored in a variable of the type. Such types are often referred to as *simple* or *scalar data types*.

7.1   Constants Revisited

The #define Compiler Directive

We begin by reexamining the concept of constants in C++. Constant definitions have the form

```
const type identifier = constant;
```

where *constant* is a value of the same type as the identifier.

C++ provides another way to define important constants. The #define line is a compiler directive that can be used to associate an identifier with a particular sequence of characters called the *replacement-text*. The general form of the #define line is as follows:

```
#define identifier replacement-text
```

Once this line appears in a program, any occurrence of *identifier* (not enclosed in quotes and not part of another name) will be replaced by the associated *replacement-text* during compilation. The *identifier* has the same form as any C++ identifier. The *replacement-text* can be any sequence of characters. It's not a character string, so it's not enclosed in quotes.

EXAMPLE 7.1

We can use either the constant declaration

```
const float PI = 3.14159;
```

or the #define line

```
#define PI 3.14159
```

to associate the constant PI with the value 3.14159. In the first form, C++ allocates a memory cell named PI and stores 3.14159 in that cell. In the second form, the compiler replaces all textual references to the identifier PI by the constant 3.14159 during the compilation process, just as a word processor would perform the substitution. Using this form, PI is simply an identifier; it's not treated as a variable and has no storage associated with it.

The #define line is often used to name constants in the C language. Because C++ permits const declarations, we rarely use the #define line.

EXERCISES FOR SECTION 7.1

Self-Check

1. Which of the constants declared below are valid and which are invalid? Explain your answers briefly.

```
const int MAXINT = 32767;
const int MININT = -MAXINT;
const char FIRST_FEMALE = "Eve";
const int MAX_SIZE = 50;
const int MIN_SIZE = MAX_SIZE - 10;
const int ID = 4FD6;
const int KOFFMAN_AGE = 67;
const int FRIEDMAN_AGE = z66;
const float PRICE = $3,335.50;
const float PRICE = 3335.50;
const float PRICE = "3335.50";
```

2. Why would you declare an identifier as a constant rather than as a variable?

3. Explain the difference between the #define line and the constant declaration. Which is preferred in C++?

7.2 Internal Representations of Numeric Data Types

In this section, we look at the numeric data types and discuss the differences in their representations.

Fixed-Point and Floating-Point Data Types

The data types int and float are used to represent numeric information. We use integer variables as loop counters to represent data, such as exam scores, that do not have fractional parts. In most other instances, we use type float numeric data.

You may be wondering why it's necessary to have two numeric types. Can the data type float be used for all numbers? The answer is yes, but on many computers, operations involving integers are faster than those involving type float numbers and less storage space may be needed to store integers. Also, operations with integers are always precise, but there may be some loss of accuracy when dealing with type float numbers.

These differences result from the way type float numbers and integers are represented internally in a computer's memory. All data are represented in memory as strings of *binary digits*, or *bits* (0s and 1s). But the binary string stored for the integer 13 isn't the same as the binary string stored for the type `float` number 13.0. The actual internal representation depends on the computer, but the general forms are consistent in all computers. For example, the integer 13 would be represented as 1101 preceded by a sequence of 0 digits.

The internal representation of floating-point data is analogous to scientific notation. Recall that in scientific notation 3.57×10^3 refers to the same number as 3570. Similarly, 3.57×10^{-4} refers to 0.000357.

The storage area for a floating-point number is segmented into a *characteristic* and a *mantissa*. Usually, the mantissa is a binary fraction between 0.5 and 1.0 for positive numbers (and between −0.5 and −1.0 for negative numbers). The characteristic is normally a power of 2. The mantissa and characteristic are chosen to satisfy the formula

$$float\text{-}number = mantissa \times 2^{characteristic}$$

Because the size of a memory cell is finite, not all floating-point numbers (in the mathematical sense) can be represented precisely in the range of type `float` numbers provided on your computer system. We'll talk more about this later.

Besides the capability of storing fractions, the range of numbers that may be represented in type `float` form is considerably larger than for the integer form. For example, positive type `float` numbers on microcomputers might range between 10^{37} (a very small fraction) and 10^{37} (a rather large number), whereas positive type `int` values might range from 1 to +32767 (2^{15}). The actual ranges depend on the particular C++ compiler and the computer being used. Specifically, they depend on the number of bits that the compiler uses to store these different data types.

Integer Types

C++ provides three sizes of integers: `short int` (or `short`), `int`, and `long int` (or `long`). The actual lengths corresponding to the sizes are implementation-defined. C++ does, however, place some restrictions on the lengths of *short integers* (minimum of 16 bits) and *long integers* (minimum of 32 bits). It also requires that the following must be true:

- Short integers may be no longer than type `int` values.
- Type `int` values may be no longer than long integers.

The use of short integers can save space in programs with large volumes of integer data. However, as we've noted, the largest positive integer that may be stored in a short integer on most computers is $2^{15} \times 1$, or 32767. (Remember, one bit is used for the sign of the integer, leaving 15 bits to store the magnitude of the integer. See the Self-Check Exercises at the end of this section for more details.) This may not always be sufficient for storing and manipulating your data.

Floating–Point Types

C++ provides three sizes of floating-point types: `float`, `double`, and `long double`. As with integers, these are implementation-defined, but with the following restrictions: `double` isn't less precise than `float`, and `long double` isn't less precise than `double`. Some C++ compilers provide a `double` type with approximately twice the precision of `float` and a `long double` type with twice the precision of `double`.

Types of Numeric Literals

The data type of a numeric literal is determined in the following way. If the literal has a decimal point, then it's considered to be of type `float`. For example, −67.345 and 2.998E+5 (read as 2.998×10^5 or 299800.0) are floating-point literals. A literal written with a decimal scale factor is also considered to be a floating-point literal whether or not it has a decimal point. For example, the value 5E2 is considered type `float` (with a value of 500.0) because it has a scale factor.

Value Ranges for Integer and Floating–Point Types

C++ provides names for the ranges of integer and floating-point types. Some of these names, their interpretations, and the values they represent are shown in Table 7.1. These definitions are included along with many others in the standard C++ libraries named `climits` and `cfloat`. The values shown in this table are acceptable minimum (or maximum) values for these constant identifiers; the actual values are computer dependent.

Numerical Inaccuracies

The representation of floating-point data can cause numerical inaccuracies to occur in floating-point computations. Just as certain numbers cannot be represented exactly in the decimal number system (for example, the fraction 1/3 is 0.333333 . . .), some numbers cannot be represented exactly in floating-point form. The **representational error** will depend on the number of bits used in the mantissa: the more bits, the smaller the error.

representational error
An error that occurs when a finite number of bits is used to represent a real number.

Table 7.1   Special C++ Constants

Name	Value	Interpretation
		From `climits`
CHAR_BIT	8	Number of bits in a character type item
INT_MAX	+32767	Maximum value of int (16 bits)
INT_MIN	−32768	Minimum value of int (16 bits)
LONG_MAX	+2147483647L	Maximum value of long integer (32 bits)
LONG_MIN	−2147483648L	Minimum value of long integer (32 bits)
SHRT_MAX	+32767	Maximum value of short integer (16 bits)
SHRT_MIN	−32768	Minimum value of short integer (16 bits)
Name	Value	**From `cfloat`** Interpretation
FLT_DIG	6	Number of decimal digits of precision (32-bit float type)
FLT_MAX	1E+37	Maximum floating-point number
FLT_MIN	1E−37	Minimum floating-point number
FLT_EPSILON	1E−5	Minimum positive number x such that $1.0 + x$ does not equal 1.0
DBL_DIG	10	Decimal digits of precision for double
DBL_EPSILON	1E−9	Minimum positive number x such that $1.0 + x$ does not equal 1.0
LDBL_DIG	10	Decimal digits of precision for long double

The number 0.1 is an example of a number that has a representational error. The effect of a small error can become magnified through repeated computations. As a result, the loop shown next may fail to terminate on some computers because the effect of adding 0.1 to itself ten times isn't exactly 1.0.

```
for (float trial = 0.0;
        trial != 1.0;
        trial += 0.1) {
    ...
}
```

If the loop repetition test is changed to trial < 1.0, the loop might execute 10 times on one computer and 11 times on another. This is yet another reason why it's best to use integer variables whenever possible in loop repetition tests.

Other problems can occur when manipulating very large or very small real numbers. If you add a large number to a small number, the larger number may "cancel out" the smaller number—resulting in a **cancellation error.**

cancellation error
An error due to applying an arithmetic operator to two operands of very different magnitudes; the effect of the smaller number is lost.

If *x* is much larger than *y*, then *x* + *y* may have the same value as *x* (for example, 1000.0 + 0.0001234 is equal to 1000.0 on some computers).

If two very small numbers are multiplied and the result is too small to be represented accurately, it will be represented as zero. This phenomenon is called **arithmetic underflow.** Similarly, if two very large numbers are multiplied, the result may be too large to be represented. This phenomenon, called **arithmetic overflow,** is handled in different ways by C++ compilers. Arithmetic overflow can occur when processing very large integer values as well.

arithmetic underflow
An error in which a very small computational result is represented as zero.

arithmetic overflow
An error due to an attempt to represent a computational result that is too large.

Mixing Types: Promotions

In Chapter 2 (Section 2.6), we first introduced the notion of mixed-type expressions and assignments with type `int` and `float` data. In Chapters 3 and 6, we discussed the correspondence of formal and actual arguments. We recommended that you match the type of an actual argument in a function call with its corresponding formal parameter type.

C++ allows many uses of mixed types: in expressions, in assignment, and in argument passing. When data values of mixed type are used in expressions, the compiler examines the operands involved with each operation and *converts* (or *promotes*) mixed operands to make them the same. For example, short integers and characters would be promoted to type `int`, type `int` to type `float`, and type `float` to `double`. The result of the operation is the same type as the operands after promotion.

For example, in the expression

```
3 + x / 2
```

where x is type `float`, the constant 2 is promoted to `float` before the division is performed. Because the result of the division is type `float`, the constant 3 would be promoted to `float` before the addition is performed.

All such conversions are intended to be *value-preserving.* For the most part, an integral conversion (`char` to `int`, `short int` to `int`) won't alter the value of the data. This is also true when integers are converted to floating point, except that some loss of accuracy can occur because not all type `float` values can be precisely represented in the computer.

Type Conversions

Conversions similar to those just described for expressions are performed whenever mixed assignments are specified. Again the conversions are intended to preserve value. However, value preservation sometimes isn't possible when the type conversion is in the "other direction." In these cases, actual changes in value are likely to occur. For example, the assignment of a type `float` value to an integer variable will result in the *truncation* (chopping off) of the fractional part of the floating-point value (the assignment of the value 13.78 to the integer variable m stores the integer 13 in m). A few other examples are shown next.

```
i = 3.89;     // Truncates floating-point value 3.89.
              // Stores 3 in i (type int).
ch = 64.97;   // Truncates floating-point value 64.97.
              // Stores character with ASCII value 64
              //      ('@') in ch (type char).
printInt(27.7);   // Argument 27.7 is converted to 27.
                  // Function printInt has the prototype
                  // void printInt(int);
```

Type Casting

Besides relying on automatic conversion, you can specify an explicit type conversion operation using a **cast**. For example, if sum and n are type `int` and average is type `float`, we can use the statement

```
average = float(sum) / float(n);
```

to perform an accurate computation of the average value that retains the fractional part of the result. The casting operator `float` in the expression `float(sum)` converts the value of sum to a type `float` number before the division, so the division result is type `float`. Without casting, a type `int` result would be calculated. The actual values stored in sum and n are still type `int` and aren't changed by the casting operation.

Although we cast both operands in the expression above, we need to cast only one. The other would be converted automatically because of the way C++ evaluates mixed-type expressions.

Notice that the expression

```
average = float(sum / n);
```

wouldn't achieve the desired goal of retaining the fractional part of the average value. The cast takes place after the integer division, so a real number with a fractional part of zero would be assigned to variable average.

EXAMPLE 7.2

Sometimes we want to compute the value of a positive number rounded to two decimal places. The statement

```
x = float(int(x * 100.0 + 0.5)) / 100.0;
```

uses the casting operators int and float to accomplish this. For example, if x is 7.0562, the argument for the cast operator int would be 706.12 (705.62 + 0.5). The result of this cast operation would be the integer 706. The cast operator float converts 706 to a floating-point number. The result of dividing by 100.0 is assigned to variable x (value is 7.06).

EXERCISES FOR SECTION 7.2

Self-Check

1. What is the largest positive integer that may be stored (with sign) in a type int variable of size 2 bytes (16 bits)?

2. How does a cancellation error differ from a representational error?

3. In Example 7.2, what is the value of the assignment statement

   ```
   x = float(int(x * 100 + 0.5)) / 100.0;

   for x = 6.875? For x = - 6.875?
   ```

   Write an if statement that rounds to two decimal places for negative numbers as well as positive numbers.

4. Write the algorithm for a decision step that rounds any real number to n decimal places.

5. What is the value of the following expressions?

   a. float (int (3.45))

   b. int (5.65) + float (7.9)

   c. int (5.65) + 7.9

   d. int (5.65 + 7.9)

Programming

1. Write a C++ program to display the largest long integer and largest type double value that can be used on your computer system.

2. Write a function that has two formal input parameters, a real number x and an integer n. The function result should be x rounded to n decimal places. Use the if statement in Self-Check Exercise 4.

7.3   Character Data and Functions

C++ provides a character data type for storing and manipulating individual characters such as those that compose a person's name, address, and other personal data. We use the type specifier char to declare character variables. A type char literal consists of a single printable character (a letter, digit, punctuation mark, or the like) enclosed in single quotes. We can also use escape sequences (see Section 2.3) to represent character literals. We can associate a character value with a constant identifier or assign it to a character variable. We can compare character values using the equality and relational operators.

```
const char STAR = '*';
const char ENDLINE = '\n';
char nextLetter;
nextLetter = 'C';
if (nextLetter >= 'A')
```

To understand the result of an order comparison (using a relational operator), you must know something about the way your computer represents characters internally. Each character has its own unique numeric code; the binary form of this code is stored in a memory cell to represent a character value. C++ compares these binary numbers using the relational operators in the normal way.

The number of bits used to store a character value must be sufficient to store any member of the character set being used by your C++ language system. The ASCII (American Standard Code for Information Interchange) character set is most often used in C++ systems. In ASCII, one byte (8 bits) is used to represent characters. Only the rightmost 7 bits are used, so the numeric codes for all character values are in the range 0 to 127 (the value of $2^7 - 1$).

If you examine the ASCII code shown in Appendix A, you'll see that consecutive codes (decimal code values 48 through 57) represent the digit characters '0' through '9' respectively. The order relationship shown below holds for the digit characters:

'0'<'1'<'2'<'3'<'4'<'5'<'6'<'7'<'8'<'9'.

For the uppercase letters 'A', 'B', ... 'Z', the following order relationship holds:

'A'<'B'<'C'< . . . <'X'<'Y'<'Z'.

In the ASCII code, these characters are also represented using consecutive decimal values (decimal code values 65 through 90).

A similar situation is true for lowercase letters. Once again, the expected order relationship holds in the ASCII code:

```
'a'<'b'<'c'<. . .<'x'<'y'<'z'.
```

The lowercase letters have the consecutive decimal code values 97 through 122 in ASCII.

In ASCII, the printable characters have codes from 32 (the code for a blank or space) to 126 (the code for the symbol ~). The other codes represent nonprintable control characters (represented in a C++ program using escape sequences). Sending a control character to an output device causes the device to perform a special operation, such as returning the cursor to column one, advancing the cursor to the next line, or sounding a beep.

Because characters are represented by integer codes, C++ permits conversion of type char to type int and vice versa. For example, you could use the following to find out the code for a question mark:

```
cout << "Code for ? is " << int('?') << endl;
```

The next example uses the casting operator char to convert an integer to a character.

EXAMPLE 7.3

A *collating sequence* for characters is the ordering of characters according to their numeric codes. The program in Listing 7.1 displays part of the C++ collating sequence for the ASCII character set. It lists the characters with numeric codes 32 through 126, inclusive. The first character displayed is a blank (numeric code 32); the last one is the tilde (numeric code 126).

Some Useful Character Functions

Table 7.2 lists several useful character functions found in the C++ standard library cctype. The first two functions, tolower and toupper, change the case of a letter. They take a type char argument and return a type char result. If the argument for tolower is an uppercase letter, tolower returns its lowercase equivalent (that is, 'c' for an argument of 'C'). If the argument for tolower isn't an uppercase letter, tolower returns its argument unchanged. The remaining functions are used to test a character argument

Listing 7.1   ASCII collating sequence illustration

```cpp
// File: collate.cpp
// Displays part of the character collating sequence

#include <iostream>
using namespace std;

int main()
{
    const MIN = 32;     // smallest numeric code
    const MAX = 126;    // largest numeric code
    char nextChar;      // output - character form of next code

    // Display sequence of characters.
    for (int nextCode = MIN; nextCode <= MAX; nextCode++) {
        nextChar = char(nextCode);
        cout << nextChar;
        if (nextChar == 'Z')
            cout << endl;
    }

    return 0;
}
```

```
!"#$%&'()*+,-./0123456789;;<=>?@ABCDEFGHIJKLMNOPQRSTUVWXYZ
[/]^_'abcdefghijklmnopqrstuvwxyz{ } ~
```

to see if it's a particular kind of character (for example, is it a letter?). All the test functions take a type `char` argument, and all return a type `bool` result (either `true` or `false`).

EXAMPLE 7.4

Sometimes we want to convert a digit character to an equivalent number. For example, the digit character `'7'` should convert to the number 7. Function `digitToNumber` (Listing 7.2) performs this conversion. If its input argument isn't a digit character, function `digitToNumber` returns −1.

We use the `bool` function `isdigit` to determine whether parameter `ch` contains a digit character (a character in the set `{'0', '1', '2',... '9'}`).

Table 7.2 Some Character Functions from the Standard Library cctype

Function Prototype	Purpose
char tolower(char)	If c is uppercase, this function returns the corresponding lowercase letter; otherwise, returns c.
char toupper(char)	If c is lowercase, this function returns the corresponding uppercase letter; otherwise, it returns c.
bool isalnum(char)	Returns true if either isalpha(c) or isdigit(c) is nonzero; otherwise, returns false.
bool isalpha(char)	Returns true if either isupper(c) or islower(c) is true; otherwise, returns false.
bool iscntrl(char)	Returns true if c is a control character; otherwise, returns false.
bool isdigit(char)	Returns true if c is a digit character ('0', '1', '2',...,'9'); otherwise, returns false.
bool isgraph(char)	Returns true if c is a printable character (other than a space); otherwise, returns false.*
bool islower(char)	Returns true if c is a lowercase letter; otherwise, returns false.
bool isprint(char)	Returns true if c is a printable character (including the space); otherwise, returns false.
bool ispunct(char)	Returns true if c is a printable character other than a space, letter, or digit; otherwise, returns false.
bool isspace(char)	Returns true if c is a space, newline, formfeed, carriage return, tab, or vertical tab; otherwise, returns false.
bool isupper(char)	Returns true if c is an uppercase letter; otherwise, returns false.

*A printable character is any character in the ASCII table between the space (ASCII value 32) and the tilde (~, ASCII value 126).

Listing 7.2 Function digitToNumber

```
// Returns the number corresponding to its argument
//    if its argument is a digit character; otherwise
//    returns −1.
int digitToNumber(char ch)
{
    if (isdigit(ch))
        return (int(ch) − int('0'));
    else
        return −1;
}
```

We read the `if` statement in Listing 7.2 as follows:

If ch is a digit character, execute the statement
```
      return (int(ch) - int('0'));
```
else execute the statement
```
      return false;
```

The expression

```
int(ch) - int('0')
```

yields the difference between the code for the character stored in ch and the code for `'0'`. This difference is the number we're seeking. For example, if ch is `'7'`, its code is 55 and the code for `'0'` is 48.

Follow a similar process if you want to determine the relative position of a letter in the alphabet. For example, if letChar is a type char variable storing an uppercase letter, the expression

```
int(letChar) - int('A')
```

returns the position in the alphabet of letChar relative to A (at position 0).

EXERCISES FOR SECTION 7.3

Self-Check

1. Evaluate the following C++ expressions using the ASCII character set.

    a. `int('d') - int('a')`

    b. `char((int('M') - int('A')) + int('a'))`

    c. `int('7') - int('0')`

    d. `char(int('5') + 1)`

2. What is the purpose of the type cast operators int and char used in the previous exercise?

3. Briefly explain the result of each of the following function references. (First indicate the type of the result and then its actual value.)

    a. `isdigit('a');`

    b. `isdigit('7');`

    c. `isdigit(9);`

    d. `toupper('#');`

    e. `tolower('A');`

    f. `tolower('p');`

    g. `digitToNumber('0');`

4. In Listing 7.2, what is the effect of the if statement?

5. What values are returned by digitToNumber for the three data characters: x, $, 3?

Programming

1. Write your own version of function toupper (call it myToupper). (Hint: See Self-Check Exercise 1b.)

2. Write your own version of function islower (call it myIslower).

3. Write a C++ function called getDigitValue that reads data characters until it reads a digit character. Your function should return the numeric value of the first digit character read. Your function should use functions isdigit and digitToNumber (from Listing 7.2).

7.4 Type **bool** Data and Logical Expressions

Type bool data was introduced in Chapter 2, and we've used type bool expressions as conditions in if statements and for loop control. There are only two type bool literals—true and false. We now describe some additional features of logical expressions.

Complementing Logical Expressions

We use the logical operator ! (not) to form the complement or opposite of a condition. If a logical expression is true, then its complement is false and vice versa.

The ability to complement a condition is useful when you write if and while statements in C++. For example, certain expressions involving the use of the ! operator are more difficult to read and think about than an equivalent *complement expression* written without the ! operator. We can complement a simple condition just by changing the relational operator as shown below.

Operator	Operator in Complement
<	>=
<=	>
>	<=
>=	<
==	!=
!=	==

If a simple logical expression such as $!(x <= y)$ is used in a condition, its equivalent condition may be obtained by removing the ! operator and complementing the relational operator. This process would yield the simpler but equivalent condition $x > y$.

DeMorgan's theorem explains how to complement a compound logical expression:

1. Write the complement of each simple logical expression.

2. Change each && (and) to || (or) and each || to &&, respectively.

DeMorgan's Theorem

$!(expression_1$ && $expression_2)$ $!(expression_1$ || $expression_2)$

is the same as   is the same as

$!expression_1$ || $!expression_2$ $!expression_1$ && $!expression_2$

Another way to complement a logical expression is to precede the entire expression with the not (!) operator. Table 7.3 shows the complements of more complicated logical expressions as determined by applying DeMorgan's theorem. We see that flag and swap are type bool variables; next is type char; and x, y, m, and n are type int. In the complement of the expression on the first line, the relational operators are complemented (for example, >= is changed to <) and the operator && (and) is changed to || (or). The last two lines show two complements of the same expression. In the last line, the expression is complemented by simply inserting the logical operator ! (not) in front of the entire condition. Any logical expression can be complemented in this way.

Table 7.3 Complements of Logical Expressions

Expression	Complement
x >= 1 && x <= 5	x < 1 || x > 5
!flag || x <= y	flag && x > y
flag && !swap	!flag || swap
(n % m == 0) && flag	(n % m != 0) || !flag
next == 'A' || next == 'a'	next != 'A' && next != 'a'
next == 'A' || next == 'a'	!(next == 'A' || next == 'a')

Type **bool** Functions

Most of the functions listed in Table 7.2 are examples of type bool functions—they return either true or false values. We use these functions to
determine the status of type char variables. You can write similar functions,
give them meaningful names, and use them to write clear and concise
conditions with calls to these functions.

EXAMPLE 7.5

We can use bool functions to simplify loop repetition conditions. For example, a bill-paying
program should continue to pay monthly bills as long as the account balance is positive and
there are more bills to pay. The main processing loop might have the heading

```
while (balance > 0.0 && moreBills())
```

Loop exit occurs if the balance becomes zero or negative or if the user indicates there are
no more bills to pay.

Function moreBills should ask the user if there are more bills. Listing 7.3 shows
one possible implementation. The function returns true if the user enters Y or y after
the prompt Any more bills (Y/N):.

Inside the loop, we use the toupper function to set the character in answer to
uppercase. This step simplifies the loop repetition condition (see Self-Check Exercise 4).
The do-while loop executes until answer is either Y or N. The loop repetition condition is equivalent to

```
!(answer == 'Y' || answer == 'N')
```

After loop exit, the statement

```
return (answer == 'Y');
```

evaluates the condition in parentheses (type bool) and returns its value (true or
false). This is simpler than using an if statement to return either true or false (see
Programming Exercise 3).

Input and Output of Type **bool** Data

When you display type bool data, the value false displays as the integer 0
and true displays as the integer 1. Similarly, you must enter 0 (false) and
1 (true) to represent type bool data. These restrictions aren't likely to affect
you, since you usually won't want to read bool data and will only display
bool data during debugging. If you want to read or display false and true

Listing 7.3 Function moreBills

```cpp
// Returns true if the user has more bills to pay
bool moreBills()
{
    char answer;            // Stores user's answer

    do {
        cout << "Any more bills (Y/N): ";
        cin >> answer;
        answer = toupper(answer); // to uppercase
    } while (answer != 'Y' && answer != 'N');

    return (answer == 'Y');
}
```

as type `bool` data (instead of 0 or 1), insert the following lines of C++ code before the input or output statements.

```cpp
cin.setf(ios::boolalpha);    // to read true/false
cout.setf(ios::boolalpha);   // to display true/false
```

EXERCISES FOR SECTION 7.4

Self-Check

1. Write the complements of the conditions below. Assume the variables are all of type `int` except for `flag` (type `bool`). Use DeMorgan's theorem.

   a. `x <= y && x == 25`

   b. `x > y && x != 15 || z <= 7`

   c. `x != 15 || z == 7 && x <= y`

   d. `flag || !(x != 15)`

   e. `!flag && x > 8`

2. What does the following function do:

   ```cpp
   bool inRange(int item, int min, int max)
   {
       return (item >= min && item <= max)
   }
   ```

   What values can the function return?

3. The loop below uses function `readInt` from Exercise 2. Describe what the loop does and the value that n will have after loop exit. Also, explain the comment at the end of the loop and write the condition in a simpler way using the complement operator.

```
int n;
do {
        cout << "Enter a number in the range 1 to 10: ";
        cin >> n;
} while (inRange(n, 1, 10) == false); // == false is
                                      // not necessary
```

4. Trace the execution of function `moreBills` for the data characters q, y.

5. Rewrite the `if` statement below using a single assignment statement. Which is more efficient?

```
if (x > y)
    xBigger = true;
else
    xBigger = false;
```

Programming

1. Write a type `bool` function that has two integer input parameters m and n and returns `true` if the value of m is a divisor of n and `false` otherwise.

2. Write a loop that continues prompting and reading exam scores until the user enters a score that is in range (0 through 100). Use function `inRange` from Self-Check Exercise 2.

3. Rewrite function `moreBills` using a `while` statement.

4. Rewrite the loop in Self-Check Exercise 3, using a `while` statement.

7.5 Enumeration Types

Good solutions to many programming problems require new data types. For example, in a budget program you might distinguish among the following categories of expenses: entertainment, rent, utilities, food, clothing, automobile, insurance, and miscellaneous. C++ allows you to associate a numeric code with each category by creating an **enumeration type** that has its own list of meaningful values.

enumeration type
A user-defined data type with a list of values for that type.

For example, the enumerated type `expense` has eight possible values:

```
enum expense {entertainment, rent, utilities, food,
              clothing, automobile, insurance,
              miscellaneous};
```

Defining type expense as shown causes the identifier `entertainment` to be associated with the integer 0, `rent` to be associated with the integer 1, and so on. We can use our new type name `expense` in variable declarations just as we would use a standard type such as `int` or `double`. Here is a declaration of variable `expenseKind`:

```
expense expenseKind;
```

We can manipulate variable `expenseKind` and its eight possible values (called **enumerators**) just as we would any other integers. The `switch` statement that follows tests the value of `expenseKind` and displays an appropriate message.

enumerator
An identifier defined in an enumeration type.

```
switch (expenseKind)
{
case entertainment : cout <<
                            "Postpone until after your payday";
                            break;
case rent          : cout <<
                            "Pay before first of the month"; break;
 . . .
case miscellaneous : cout <<
                            "Do you really need that?";
}
```

The `switch` statement with enumerators is more readable than one with integer values. This is the primary motivation for using enumeration types. For example, without enumerators, we would write the first case as `case  0`, which has no special meaning.

EXAMPLE 7.6

The enumeration type **day** declared below has the values **sunday**, **monday**, and so on.

```
enum day {sunday, monday, tuesday, wednesday,
               thursday, friday, saturday}; // days of the week
```

The enumerator **sunday** has the value 0; **monday** has the value 1, and so on.

We can alter this default association by explicitly specifying a different association for some or all of the identifiers in an enumeration type, as shown in the next two examples.

EXAMPLE 7.7

The 12 enumerators for enumeration type `month` are associated with the constant integer values 1, 2, 3, ..., 12. Because the value 1 is specified for enumerator `jan`, enumerator `feb` has the value 2, enumerator `mar` has the value 3, and so on.

```
enum month {jan = 1, feb, mar, apr, may, jun, jul, aug,
               sep, oct, nov, dec};
```

Enumeration Type Declaration

Form: *enum enumeration-type {enumerator-list};*

Example: enum `classId` {`freshman, sophomore,`
                   `junior, senior};`

Interpretation: A new integral data type (an *enumeration-type*) is declared. The enumerators associated with this type are specified in the *enumerator-list*. The enumerators in the list may be identifiers. The enumerator values start at 0 and increase by one.

If an *enumerator* is defined using the form

         identifier = constant-expression

the enumerator is given the value of the *constant-expression*. The values of subsequent enumerators increase by increments of one until another enumerator is defined using this form. The values associated with enumerators in a particular enumeration type do not have to be unique. However, an enumerator, like any other identifier, cannot appear in more than one enumeration type declaration within its scope of definition.

Characters as Enumerator Values

Because characters also have integer values, you can use character constants to specify the value of an enumerator. In this case, the value of the enumerator is determined by the character's numeric code.

EXAMPLE 7.8

We can define an enumeration type to associate names with some of the common special characters.

```
enum specialChars
```

```
{backspace = '\b', bell = '\a', newline = '\n',
 return = '\r',      tab = '\t',  vtab = '\v'};
```

The value of the enumerator **backspace** is the ASCII code for the control character '\b'. We can use the enumerator **backspace** to represent the backspace character in our C++ code.

***

Comparisons Involving Enumeration Types

The order relationship among the enumerators of an enumeration type is fixed when the enumeration type is declared. For example, for types **day** and **expense**, the following order relationships are all true:

```
sunday < monday
wednesday != tuesday
wednesday == wednesday
wednesday >= tuesday
entertainment < rent
other >= automobile
utilities != food
```

Distinctions among Integral Types

When using enumeration types, it's important to remember that each declaration of an integral type is different from all the others (and therefore also different from the **int** type). These different types cannot be mixed in an expression. The expressions

```
entertainment + wednesday
```

and the order relation

```
entertainment < wednesday
```

would cause a syntax error because the values shown are associated with two different enumeration types.

Reading and Writing Enumeration Type Values

Enumeration types are defined by the programmer, so their values aren't known in advance, and the C++ input/output systems cannot read or write these values. But you can write your own functions for this purpose. The next example illustrates one approach to displaying the value of an enumeration variable in a readable form.

Notice that the switch statement shown in Listing 7.4 has enumerators as case labels. Make sure you do not attempt to use a character string (such as "green") as a case label. Enumerators are allowed as case labels; character strings aren't.

EXAMPLE 7.9

Function writeColor in Listing 7.4 displays a character string that represents a value of type color.

```
enum color {red, green, blue, yellow};
```

If the value of eyeColor (type color) is defined, the statement

```
writeColor(eyeColor);
```

displays the value of eyeColor as a string.

Listing 7.4   Function to display a value of type color

```
// Displays the value of thisColor
// Pre : thisColor is assigned a value.
// Post: The value of thisColor is displayed as a string
void writeColor
   (color thisColor)     // IN: color to display as a string
{
   // Display color value as a string.
   switch (thisColor)
   {
      case red:
         cout << "red ";
         break;
      case green:
         cout << "green ";
         break;
      case blue:
         cout << "blue ";
         break;
      case yellow:
         cout << "yellow ";
         break;
      default:
         cout << "*** ERROR: Invalid color value."
              << endl;
   }
}
```

EXAMPLE 7.10

Function `readColor` in Listing 7.5 "reads" an enumerator value. It does this by reading a character representing a color (R, G, B, Y) and then returning the enumerator corresponding to that color (red for R, and so on). If `eyeColor` is type `color`, you could use the statements

```
cout << "Reading eye color";
eyeColor = readColor();
```

to assign to `eyeColor` a color value based on a data character.

Listing 7.5   Function to read a value of type `color`

```
// Reads a color value
// Returns the color value corresponding to a data character.
color readColor()
{
    // Local data   . . .
    char colorChar;            // storage for data character

    // Continue reading until data character is valid.
    do
    {
        cout << "Enter first letter of color (R,G,B, or Y): ";
        cin >> colorChar;
        colorChar = toupper(colorChar);   // to uppercase

        // Return color value if valid character read.
        switch(colorChar)
        {
            case 'R' : return red;
            case 'G' : return green;
            case 'B' : return blue;
            case 'Y' : return yellow;
            default : cout << "Try again!" << endl;
        } // end switch
    } while (true);
}
```

The `switch` statement returns the enumerator corresponding to the first valid color character read. Instead of using a break statement, we return immediately to the calling function. The loop executes forever (its repetition condition is `true`), so executing one of the `return` statements is the only way to exit the loop.

PROGRAM STYLE   Using `returns` in a `switch` Statement

Usually we end each case in a `switch` statement with a `break` statement, and we end a function with a single `return` statement. In some situations, replacing every `break` with a `return` statement can lead to more readable code. If you want to return after executing every case in a `switch` statement, consider using `return` statements instead of a `break`.

Placement of Enumeration Type Declarations

When you use enumeration types, you'll normally need to provide functions similar to `readColor` and `writeColor`. Because these functions (and possibly other functions) need to reference the enumeration type `color` and its enumerators, you must declare the enumeration type before the function prototypes. This gives the enumeration type global scope and enables all functions to reference it and its enumerators. Listing 7.6 shows a small driver program that declares and uses enumeration type `color`.

Enumeration Types as Cast Operators

You can use enumeration types as cast operators. For the enumeration type `month` from Listing 7.7

```
enum month {jan = 1, feb, mar, apr, may, jun, jul, aug,
            sep, oct, nov, dec};
```

the cast operation `month(3)` returns the enumerator (`mar`) in the list above corresponding to 3. Function `readMonth` (Listing 7.7) uses this feature to return the type `month` enumerator corresponding to an integer read as data. First, it calls function `getIntRange` (Listing 5.9) to read an integer in the range 1 through 12. Next it casts this value to type `month` and returns the result.

Listing 7.6   Using enumeration type `color`

```
// File: color.cpp
// Tests the enumeration type color.

#include <iostream>
using namespace std;

enum color {red, green, blue, yellow};
```

(continued)

Listing 7.6   Using enumeration type `color` (continued)

```cpp
// Function prototypes
void writeColor(color);
color readColor();

int main()
{
    color eyeColor, hairColor;

    cout << "Reading eye color" << endl;
    eyeColor = readColor();
    cout << endl << "Reading hair color" << endl;
    hairColor = readColor();

    cout << endl << "Eye color is ";
    writeColor(eyeColor);
    cout << ", hair color is ";
    writeColor(hairColor);
    cout << endl;

    return 0;
}
// Insert functions readColor and writeColor here.
```

```
Reading eye color
Enter first letter of color (R,G,B, or Y): e
Try again!
Enter first letter of color (R,G,B, or Y): b
Reading hair color
Enter first letter of color (R,G,B, or Y): Y
Eye color is blue, hair color is yellow
```

Listing 7.7   Function to read a value of type month

```cpp
// Reads a month value as an integer
// Returns the corresponding month value
month readMonth()
{
    // Local data  ...
    int monthValue;          // storage for integer data
```

(continued)

Listing 7.7 Function to read a value of type month (continued)

```
        // Read a valid integer.
        cout << "Reading month"
        monthValue = getIntRange(1, 12);

        return (month(monthValue));
}
```

EXERCISES FOR SECTION 7.5

Self-Check

1. What are the integer values associated with the type `color` enumerators? With the type `day` enumerators? With the type `specialChars` enumerators?

2. Evaluate each of the following, assuming before each operation that today (type `day`) is wednesday.

   a. `int(monday)`   **b.** `int(today)`

   c. `today < tuesday`   **d.** `day(int(today) + 1)`

   e. `wednesday + monday`   **f.** `int(today) + 1`

   g. `today >= thursday`   **h.** `wednesday + thursday`

3. Indicate whether each sequence of type declarations below is valid or invalid. Explain what is wrong with each invalid sequence.

   a. `enum logical {true, false};`

   b. `enum letters {A, B, C};`
       `enum twoLetters {A, B};`

   c. `enum day {sun, mon, tue, wed, thu, fri, sat};`
       `enum weekDay {mon, tue, wed, thu, fri};`
       `enum weekEnd {sat, sun};`

   d. `enum trafficLight {red, yellow, green};`
       `int green;`

4. Trace the execution of function `readMonth` in Listing 7.7 for data values of 15 and 7. What value is returned by the function?

Programming

1. Write a `switch` statement with a selector expression of type `day` (see Example 7.6) that displays a message indicating the corresponding

day of the week followed by the message " is a weekday" or " is a weekend day". For example, if the selector expression value is Sunday, the message "Sunday is a weekend day" should be displayed.

2. Write function writeMonth for enumeration type month.

7.6   Iterative Approximations

Numerical analysis is the branch of mathematics and computer science that develops algorithms for solving computational problems. Problems from numerical analysis include finding solutions to sets of equations, performing operations on matrices, finding roots of equations, and performing mathematical integration. The next case study illustrates a method for iteratively approximating a root of an equation.

Many real-world problems can be solved by finding roots of equations. A value k is a **root** of an equation $f(x) = 0$ if $f(k)$ equals zero. If we graph the function $f(x)$, as shown in Figure 7.1, the roots of the equation are those points where the x-axis and the graph of the function intersect. The roots of the equation $f(x) = 0$ are also called the *zeros* of the function $f(x)$.

root (zero of a function)
A function argument value that causes the function result to be zero.

The *bisection method* is one way of approximating a root of the equation $f(x) = 0$. This method repeatedly generates approximate roots until a true root is discovered or until an approximation is found that differs from a true root by less than *epsilon*, where *epsilon* is a very small constant (for example, 0.0001). The approximation can be found if we can isolate the true root and the approximate root within the same interval whose length is less than *epsilon*. In our next case study, we develop a function to implement this method of iterative approximation.

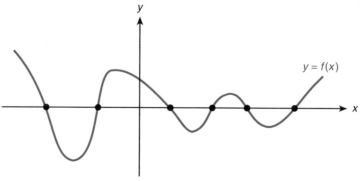

Figure 7.1   Six roots for the equation f(x) = 0

Function Parameters

Although we could develop a bisection function to find roots of one specified function, our bisection function would be far more useful if we could call it to find a root of any function, just by specifying the name of the function in the call. To do this, we must be able to include a function in the parameter list of another function. Declaring a function parameter is accomplished by simply including a prototype of the function in the parameter list. For example, if you want to write a function evaluate that evaluates another function at three different points and displays the results, write evaluate as shown in Listing 7.8. Then you can call evaluate either with library functions that take a type double argument and return a type double result or with your own function that meets these criteria. Table 7.4 shows two calls to evaluate along with the output generated.

Listing 7.8   Using a function parameter

```
// Displays value of f(x) at x = x1, x2, and x3
void evaluate(
    double f(double),      // IN: the function to evaluate
    double x1,             // IN: argument for first call
    double x2,             // IN: argument for second call
    double x3)             // IN: argument for third call
{

    cout << f(x1) << ", " << f(x2) << ", " << f(x3) << endl;

}
```

Table 7.4   Calls to Function evaluate and the Output Produced

Call to evaluate	Output Produced
evaluate(sqrt, 0.25, 25.0, 100.0);	f(0.25000) = 0.50000 f(25.00000) = 5.00000 f(100.00000) = 10.00000
evaluate(sin, 0.0, 3.14159, 0.5 * 3.14159);	f(0.00000) = 0.00000 f(3.14159) = 0.00000 f(1.57079) = 1.00000

case study   **Bisection Method for Finding Roots**

PROBLEM

Develop a function `bisect` that approximates a root of a function `f` on an interval that contains an odd number of roots.

ANALYSIS

A program that is to call function `bisect` should first tabulate function values to find an appropriate interval in which to search for a root. If a change of sign occurs on an interval, that interval must contain an odd number of roots. Figure 7.2 shows two such intervals. If there is no change of sign, the interval may contain no roots.

Let us assume that $[x_{left}, x_{right}]$ is an interval on which a change of sign does occur and in which there is exactly one root. Furthermore, assume that the function $f(x)$ is continuous on this interval. If we bisect this interval by computing its midpoint x_{mid}, using the formula

$$x_{mid} = \frac{x_{left} + x_{right}}{2.0}$$

there are three possible outcomes: the root is in the lower half of the interval, $[x_{left}, x_{mid}]$; the root is in the upper half of the interval, $[x_{mid}, x_{right}]$; or $f(x_{mid})$ is zero. Figure 7.3 shows these three possibilities graphically.

A fourth possibility is that the length of the interval is less than *epsilon*. In this case, any point in the interval is an acceptable root approximation.

DATA REQUIREMENTS
Function Inputs

`double xLeft`	*// left endpoint of interval*
`double xRight`	*// right endpoint of interval*
`double epsilon`	*// error tolerance*
`double f(double farg)`	*// function whose root is sought*

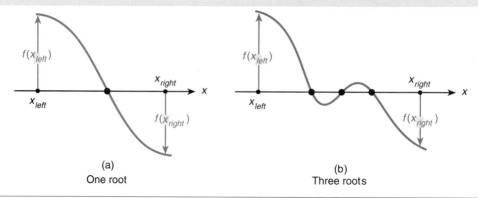

(a)
One root

(b)
Three roots

Figure 7.2   Change of sign implies an odd number of roots

Function Outputs

```
double root       // approximate root of f
bool error        // indicates whether error detected
                  // during root search
```

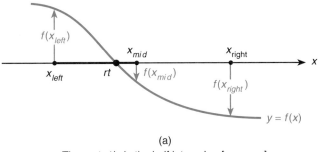

(a)

The root *rt* is in the half interval $[x_{left}, x_{mid}]$.

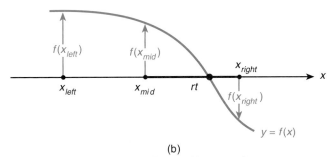

(b)

The root *rt* is in the half interval $[x_{mid}, x_{right}]$.

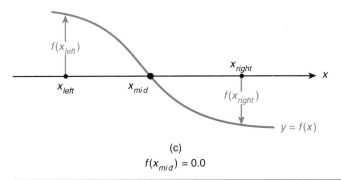

(c)

$f(x_{mid}) = 0.0$

Figure 7.3 Three possibilities that arise when the interval $[X_{left}, X_{right}]$ is bisected

DESIGN

The initial interval on which to search for a root is defined by the input parameters xLeft and xRight. Before searching this interval, we must verify that it contains an odd number of roots. If it does, we need to repeatedly bisect the interval, searching the half containing an odd number of roots until we find a true root or until the length of the interval to search is less than epsilon.

INITIAL ALGORITHM

1. Set error flag to true if the interval contains an even number of roots and return −999.0 if error flag is true.

2. Repeat as long as the interval is greater than tolerance and the root is not found

   3. Compute the function value at the midpoint
   4. if function value at xMid is zero
         Root is found – return xMid.
      else if the root is in the left half of the interval
         Reset xRight to xMid.
      else if the root is in the right half of the interval
         Reset xMid to xRight.

5. Return the midpoint of the final interval.

LOCAL VARIABLES FOR FUNCTION bisect

```
double xMid;            // midpoint of interval
double fLeft, fRight;   // function values at xLeft, xRight,
double fMid;            // and xMid
```

Refinement of Step 1

1.1 fLeft = f(xLeft);

1.2 fRight = f(xRight);

1.3 Set error to true if the signs of fRight and fLeft are the same; otherwise, set error to false.

1.4 if error is true, return −999.0

IMPLEMENTATION

Listing 7.9 shows an implementation of this algorithm. We have added display lines to make function bisect self-tracing.

TESTING

The program shown in Listing 7.9 looks for approximate roots of the function $f(x)$ on the interval [xLeft, xRight]. The left and right endpoints, xLeft

Listing 7.9 Find a function root using the bisection method

```cpp
// File: bisect.cpp
// Finds the root of a function using the bisection method
#include <iostream>
#include <cmath>

using namespace std;

// Function prototypes
double bisect (double, double, double, double f(double), bool&);
double f(double);

int main()
{

    double xLeft, xRight;      // end points of interval
    double epsilon;            // error tolerance
    double root;               // root found by bisect
    bool  error;               // error flag

    // Get endpoints and tolerance
    cout << "Enter interval endpoints: ";
    cin >> xLeft >> xRight;
    cout << "Enter tolerance: ";
    cin >> epsilon;

    // Use bisect function to look for root of function f
    root = bisect (xLeft, xRight, epsilon, f, error);

    // Display result
    if (!error)
       cout << "Root found at " << root
            << "\nValue of f(x) at root is: " << f(root);
    else
       cout << "There may be no root in [" << xLeft
            << ", " << xRight << "]" << endl;

    return 0;
}

// Implements bisection method to find a root of function f
// in interval [xLeft, xRight].
// PRE: xLeft, xRight, and epsilon are defined.
// POST: Returns midpoint of xLeft and xRight if the difference
//       between these values is <= epsilon. Returns true to
```

(continued)

Listing 7.9   Find a function root using the bisection method (continued)

```cpp
//  error if there is no root.
double bisect
    (double xLeft,                  // IN:  endpoints of interval
     double xRight,                 //       for possible root
     double epsilon,                // IN:  error tolerance
     double f(double),              // IN:  the function
     bool&  error)                  // OUT:  error flag
{
     double xMid;                   // midpoint of interval
     double fLeft, fRight;          // function values at xLeft, xRight,
     double fMid;                   //  and xMid

     // Compute function values at initial endpoints of interval
     fLeft = f(xLeft);
     fRight = f(xRight);

     // If no change of sign in the interval, there is no unique root
     error = (fLeft * fRight) > 0;   // test for same sign - set error
     if (error) return -999.0;       // no root - return to caller

     // Repeat while interval > error tolerance
     while (fabs (xLeft - xRight) > epsilon)
     {
          // Compute function value at midpoint
          xMid = (xLeft + xRight) / 2.0;
          fMid = f (xMid);

          // Test function value and reset interval if root not found
          if (fMid == 0.0)          // xMid is the root
             return xMid;           // Return the root
          else if (fLeft * fMid < 0.0)    // root in [xLeft, xMid]
             xRight = xMid;
          else                      // root in [xMid, xRight]
             xLeft = xMid;

          // Display next interval
          cout << "New interval is [" << xLeft
             << ", " << xRight << "]" << endl;
     }

     // Return midpoint of last interval
     return (xLeft + xRight) / 2.0;
}
```

(continued)

Listing 7.9 Find a function root using the bisection method (continued)

```
// Function whose root is being found.
// PRE: x is defined.
// POST: Returns f (x)
double f(double x)
{
    return 5 * pow (x, 3.0) - 2 * pow (x, 2.0) + 3;
}
```

```
Enter interval endpoints: -1.0 1.0
Enter tolerance: 0.00001
New interval is [-1, 0]
New interval is [-1, -0.5]
New interval is [-0.75, -0.5]
New interval is [-0.75, -0.625]
New interval is [-0.75, -0.6875]
New interval is [-0.75, -0.71875]
New interval is [-0.734375, -0.71875]
New interval is [-0.734375, -0.726562]
New interval is [-0.730469, -0.726562]
New interval is [-0.730469, -0.728516]
New interval is [-0.729492, -0.728516]
New interval is [-0.729004, -0.728516]
New interval is [-0.729004, -0.72876]
New interval is [-0.729004, -0.728882]
New interval is [-0.729004, -0.728943]
New interval is [-0.729004, -0.728973]
New interval is [-0.729004, -0.728989]
New interval is [-0.729004, -0.728996]
Root found at -0.729
Value of f(x) at root is: 1.45582e-05

Enter interval endpoints: 5.0 7.0
Enter tolerance: 0.0001
There may be no root in [5, 7]
```

Figure 7.4 Two sample runs of bisection program with trace

and xRight, and the tolerance, epsilon, are inputs from the user. The main function gets these three inputs, calls function bisect, and displays the results. Each call to bisect passes a function name as the fourth argument. Figure 7.4 shows the results of two runs of the program in Listing 7.9.

EXERCISES FOR SECTION 7.6

Self-Check

1. Find endpoints of an interval one unit long in which a root of $f(x)$ is found for function f from Listing 7.9.

2. It is unusual for a program to use equality comparison of two type double values as in

   ```
   if (fMid == 0.0)
   ```

   Find a function and an interval that would cause this test to evaluate to true.

Programming

1. Revise the program in Listing 7.9 so that if the user enters an interval longer than one unit, the program checks one-unit segments of the interval until a subinterval is found with different signs for the values of function f. The program should then call bisect with this subinterval and function f.

7.7 Using Type char Data to Control a Graphics Program (Optional)

The program in Listing 7.10 uses type char variable shapeCh to control the operation of a shape drawing program. The program draws a collection of shapes whose type (circle, square, or ellipse) and position is selected by the user (see Figure 7.5).

After the prompt to type in a character is displayed at the top of the window, the character typed by the user is read into shapeCh and converted to uppercase. The sentinel-controlled while loop repeats until the user types in q or Q. Within the main loop body, the statement

```
drawShape(shapeCh);
```

calls function drawShape to draw the shape specified by shapeCh.

Function drawShape first prompts the user to click the mouse to set the desired position of the shape. The first statement below

```
clearmouseclick(WM_LBUTTONDOWN);
while (!ismouseclick(WM_LBUTTONDOWN)) {
    delay(PAUSE);
}
```

clears any left mouse button clicks (WM_LBUTTONDOWN) that may have occurred in the past. Then the while loop continues executing (pausing the program) until the user clicks the left mouse button. The predefined graphics

Listing 7.10   Drawing different shapes at user selected positions

```
// File: randomShapes.cpp
// Generates shapes of random colors and sizes at positions selected by user

#include <graphics.h>
#include <cstdlib>

using namespace std;

// Function prototype
void drawShape(char);

int main()
{
    int width;                          // width of screen
    int height;                         // height of screen
    char shapeCh;                       // specifies kind of shape

    width = getmaxwidth();
    height = getmaxheight();
    initwindow(width, height, "Position Shapes");
    outtextxy(100, 10,
      "SELECT A SHAPE BY TYPING A CHARACTER IN BRACKETS BELOW -- C, S, E, OR Q");
    outtextxy(100, 30, "[C]IRCLE | [S]QUARE) | [E]LLIPSE | [Q]UIT");

    // Draw shapes until user selects QUIT
    shapeCh = toupper(getch());         // Get character from keyboard
    while (shapeCh != 'Q')
    {
        drawShape(shapeCh);             // Draw shape
        shapeCh = toupper(getch());     // Get next shape
    }

    closegraph();
    return 0;
}

// Draw the selected shape
// Pre: shapeCh is defined
// Post: Draws the shape selected at the position selected by mouse
void drawShape
    (char shapeCh)   // IN: shape to display or Q to quit
{
    const int PAUSE = 100;              // time to display frame
    int x, y;                           // shape center point
```

(continued)

Listing 7.10   Drawing different shapes at user selected positions (continued)

```
// Wait for mouse click
outtextxy(100, 50, "POSITION SHAPE BY CLICKING MOUSE");

clearmouseclick(WM_LBUTTONDOWN);
while (!ismouseclick(WM_LBUTTONDOWN))
{
    delay(PAUSE);
}

setcolor (BLACK);            // Overwrite mouse click prompt
outtextxy(100, 50, "POSITION SHAPE BY CLICKING MOUSE ");

// Set shape size and color randomly
getmouseclick(WM_LBUTTONDOWN, x, y);
int size = rand() % 100 + 20;        // 20 <= size <= 119
int color = rand() % 15 + 1;         // 1 <= color <= 15
setcolor(color);
setfillstyle(SOLID_FILL, color);

// Draw shape selected by user at mouse position (x, y)
switch (shapeCh)
{
    case 'C' : fillellipse(x, y, size, size);
               break;
    case 'S' : bar(x - size/2, y - size/2, x + size/2, y + size/2);
               break;
    case 'E' : fillellipse(x, y, size, size / 2);
               break;
    case 'Q' : outtextxy(100, 50, "CLOSING WINDOW");
               return;
    default  : outtextxy(100, 50, "NOT A VALID SHAPE");
               return;
}

}
```

constant `WM_LBUTTONDOWN` means that the function is responding to left mouse button events.

After the mouse click occurs, the call to function `outtextxy` "erases" the prompt to click the mouse by overwriting it in black. The statement

```
getmouseclick(WM_LBUTTONDOWN, x, y);
```

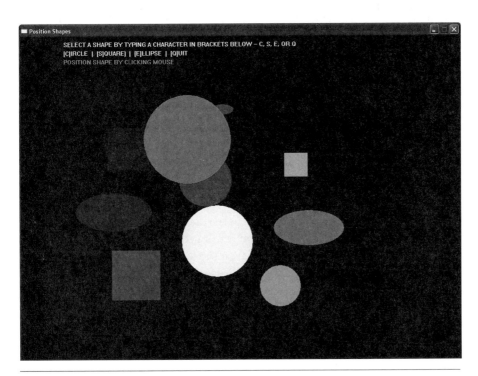

Figure 7.5   Drawing Random Shapes

stores in x and y (function output parameters) the coordinates of the mouse when it was clicked. The shape, size, and color are selected randomly (discussed later) and then the `switch` statement draws the shape selected by `shapeCh`. No shape is drawn if `shapeCh` is Q or an invalid character (not C, S, E, or Q).

Generating Random Numbers

Library `stdlib` provides a function `rand` that generates a pseudo-random integer. (They are called pseudo-random numbers because the sequence of numbers generated will eventually repeat, but they are certainly random enough for our purposes.) In the statements below, the first call to `rand` generates a random integer and the `%` operator yields a random value between 0 and 99. In the second statement, the random value generated is between 0 and 14. We add 1 to it because we don't want to give `color` the value 0 (`BLACK`) which is the default background color.

```
int size = rand() % 100 + 20;      // 20 <= size <= 119
int color = rand() % 15 + 1;       // 1 <= color <= 15
```

Seeding the Random Number Generator

The sequence of numbers that is generated depends on an integer value that **seeds** the random number generator, or provides it with a starting value for the computation of random numbers. If no starting value is provided by the programmer, a constant default value is used, so the sequence of numbers will be the same each time the program runs. To seed the random number generator with a different starting value each time, your program should execute the statement

```
srand(time(NULL));
```

before the first call to function `rand` where function `time` (defined in library `time.h`) returns an integer value representing the system clock. (The value `NULL` is discussed in Chapter 13.) Because the system clock is always changing, the random number generator will use a different starting value each time the program runs, thereby generating a different sequence of random numbers. In Listing 7.10, the call to `srand` should be placed before the `while` loop in the main function.

Table 7.5 New Functions for Graphics and Random Numbers

Function Prototype	Purpose
`clearmouseclick(int)`	Clears any pending events for the argument.
`getmouseclick(int, int&, int&)`	Returns the (x, y) position of the mouse through its second and third arguments when the event specified by its first argument occurs.
`ismouseclick(int)`	Returns true if the event specified by its first argument occurs; otherwise, returns false.
`int rand()`	Returns a random integer.
`srand(time(NULL))`	Seeds the random number generator with a value based on the system clock.

EXERCISES FOR SECTION 7.7

Self-Check Exercises

1. Explain why the call to function `srand` cannot appear in function `drawShape`.

2. Trace the execution of the `randomShapes` program if the user enters the character sequence `S, C, R, D, E, Q`?

3. Explain how the color used to draw the mouse click prompt is determined.

4. Describe how you might design a different interface that would enable the user to select a figure type by clicking a button (a small bar) that shows the name of the shape.

Programming

1. Explain what would need to be done to add another filled shape such as rectangle with a random width and length of a reasonable size.

2. Describe the modifications needed for a random selection of the shape to draw. Assume you have declared an enumeration type

```
enum shape {circle, square, ellipse);
```

3. Write method getShape that implements the interface designed in Self-Check Exercise 4.

4. Modify the program in Listing 7.10 so that each object is placed in a random position. The number of objects should also be a random value between 10 and 30.

7.8 Common Programming Errors

Be careful when writing complicated expressions, especially those involving the use of parentheses. Watch out for the following errors.

- *Omitting pairs of parentheses:* This error will often go undetected by the compiler because the resulting expression may be syntactically valid even though it's logically incorrect. For example, the statement

```
m = y2 - y1 / x2 - x1;
```

might be intended to compute the slope of a line through two points, $(x1, y1)$ and $(x2, y2)$, in the xy-plane. Yet because of the missing parentheses, the expression will actually compute m as

```
y2 - (y1 / x2) - x1
```

- *Unbalanced parentheses:* Omitting a single left or right parenthesis is also quite common in programming. This error will be detected by the compiler, causing a message such as "parse error before)".

    To help prevent such errors in the use of parentheses, review the C++ operator precedence rules summarized in Appendix D. Also, you can break a complicated expression into subexpressions that are separately assigned to temporary variables, and then manipulate these temporary variables. For example, instead of the single assignment statement

```
z = sqrt(x + y) / (1 + sqrt(x + y));
```

write the three assignment statements

```
temp1 = sqrt(x + y);
temp2 = 1 + temp1;
z = temp1 / temp2;
```

which have the same effect. Using three assignment statements is also more efficient because the square root operation is performed only once; it's performed twice in the single assignment statement above.

- *Mixing operators and operands of different types:* It's easy to make mistakes when writing expressions using mixed data types. To make matters worse, most errors of this nature aren't detected by the compiler. The expressions `'3' + '4'` and `grossPay != '3'` (grossPay of type `float`) are syntactically correct but will yield an unexpected and undesirable result at execution time.

  The best advice we can give for avoiding these problems is to not mix data types in the first place. Instead, use casting operators to specify explicitly all desired conversions.

- *Operator precedence errors:* Because of the operator precedence hierarchy in C++, very little use of parentheses is normally required when writing expressions involving relational and equality operators. The one major exception lies in the use of the not operator, `!`, which has a higher precedence than most of the other operators used so far. For example, if x is true and y is false, then `!x && y` is false, but `!(x && y)` is true.

  We list the precedence of operators in Appendix D. Notice that the unary operators have a higher precedence than the others (except for parentheses) and that they associate right to left, instead of left to right. Logical expressions such as

  ```
  -5.0 <= x && x <= 5.0
  ```

  may be written correctly without parentheses. You may find such expressions easier to read when parentheses are used:

  ```
  (-5.0 <= x) && (x <= 5.0)
  ```

- *Using enumeration types:* When declaring enumeration types, remember that the enumerators must be identifiers. Strings, characters, and numbers aren't allowed. Make sure that the same enumerator does not appear in more than one enumeration-type declaration in a given declaration scope. Remember that there are no standard functions available to read or write the values of an enumeration type.

  C++ treats enumeration and `char` data as integral data types (having integer values) and it's therefore possible to perform the standard arithmetic and relational operations on values of these data types. You must be careful, however; neither the compiler nor the run-time system will attempt to verify that the results of the arithmetic operations fall within the range of meaningful values for these types. Remember, each enumeration type you define is considered to be a different integral type, so you shouldn't mix enumerators from different types in the same expression.

You can't assign a type `int` value to an enumeration type without first applying the appropriate type casting operator. Use the statement

```
today = day(i);          // correct assignment
```

to assign the value of integer `i` to `today` (type `day`), not the statement

```
today = i;               // incorrect assignment
```

Chapter Review

1. Type `int` and `double` data have different internal representations. Type `int` values are represented as binary numbers with the leftmost bit containing the sign of the number. Type `double` data are represented by a binary exponent and mantissa.

2. Additional integer types are `short` and `long`. Type `short` typically represents a smaller range of integers than type `int`; type `long` represents a larger range.

3. Additional floating-point types are `double`, which typically represents a larger range than type `float`, and `long double`, which may represent an even larger range.

4. Arithmetic with floating-point data may not be precise, because not all real numbers can be represented exactly. Other types of numerical errors include cancellation error and arithmetic overflow and underflow.

5. Type `char` data are represented by storing a binary code value for each symbol. ASCII is a commonly used character code.

6. The character function library `cctype` contains several useful character functions for converting the case of a letter (`tolower` and `toupper`) and for testing the kind of data stored in a type `char` variable (`isdigit`, `isletter`, and so on).

7. DeMorgan's theorem describes how to complement a logical expression involving logical operators. For example, the expression `!((x < y) || (y > z))` is equivalent to `(x >= y) && (y <= z)`.

8. Data types in C++ can be declared using the reserved word `enum`. Defining an enumeration type requires listing the identifiers that are the values (enumerators) of the type. Each value is represented by an integer. Using enumeration types makes programs more readable because you can choose enumerators that are meaningful for a particular application.

9. A variable or expression can be cast to another type by writing the new type's name before the value to convert and enclosing the value in parentheses. Such a cast is a very high-precedence operation.

Summary of New C++ Constructs

Construct	Effect
Integer Variants	
`const long INT_BIG = 123456789L;`	A long integer constant
`const short INT_SMALL = 32;`	A short integer constant
Floating-Point Variants	Provides additional accuracy over `float`
`double x;`	
Enumeration Types	
`enum coins {penny=1, nickel=5,` `dime=10, quarter=25, halfDollar=50};`	A data type for representing United States coins and their values

Quick-Check Exercises

1. **a.** Evaluate the logical expression

   ```
   flag && ((m % n) == 0)
   ```

   when `flag` is `true`, m is 16, and n is 5.
   b. Is the outer pair of parentheses required?
   c. What about the inner pair?
   d. Write the complement of this expression in two ways.

2. Assuming m and k are integers (k = 13),

   a. What value is assigned to m by the statement

   ```
   m = 2.5 + k / 2;
   ```

   b. If m is type `float`, what is the value assigned to m?
   c. Rewrite the assignment statement in part (a) so that the addition and division become type `float` operations and the fractional part of the result is truncated before the assignment to m.
   d. If k is type `int`, is the division in `float(k / 2)` integer division or real division? Explain.

3. What is the value of each of the following?

   a. `char(int('a'))`
   b. `char(int('a') + 3)`
   c. `char(int('z') - 20)`
   d. `char(int('z') - 32)`
   e. `int('z') - 32`
   f. `ch - '0'` (where ch is any digit character)

4. If ch contains the character 'a', what is the value of the expression

```
isdigit(ch) || iscntrl(ch)
```

What kind of an expression is this?

5. Can an enumerator of the enumeration type day be assigned to a variable of another enumeration type? In other words, is the assignment

```
today = entertainment
```

valid if today is a variable of type day and entertainment is an enumerator of type expense?

6. Assume that two variables aren't of the same integral type (int, long int, char, enumeration, and so on).

a. Can they be mixed in the same arithmetic expression?
b. Can one be assigned to the other?

7. Under what circumstance can a type int variable or value be assigned to a variable of an enumeration type?

8. What is wrong with the following enumeration type declarations?

```
enum prime {2, 3, 5, 7, 11, 13};
enum vowels {'a', 'e', 'i', 'o', 'u'};
```

9. Write a function with the prototype

```
bool isUpperCase(char);
```

that returns true if its argument is an uppercase letter. Write a while loop that uses this function in a repetition condition. The loop should ignore any characters entered by the user that aren't uppercase letters. After loop exit, the input variable should store the first uppercase letter that is entered.

Review Questions

1. Explain why it's useful to have a data type int for integers instead of using data type float for all numbers.

2. List and explain three computational errors that may occur in type float expressions.

3. a. Write an enumeration type declaration for fiscal as the months from July through June.
   b. Write an enumeration type declaration for winter as December through February.

     c. Can you declare both enumerated types in the same function? Explain your answer.

4. Write a function for writing the value of a variable of type season as a string:

```
enum season {winter, spring, summer, fall};
```

5. Write a bool function isWeekend that returns true if the value of today (of type day; see Listing 7.6) is a weekend day. Otherwise the function should return false.

6. Write a switch statement that tests to see if the type day variable today is a working day (Monday through Friday). Display the message "Workday" or "Weekend". Also, write an if statement that does this. Remember you can compare enumerators of the same type using the relational operators.

7. Write an if statement that will write out true or false according to the following conditions: either flag is true or color is red, or both money is plenty and time is up.

8. Write a function that returns true if a worker's hours (the function input) are greater than 40. Otherwise, the function should return false.

9. What are the rules followed by C++ when type float variables are mixed with type double variables?

10. Write a C++ function that receives an integer argument between 0 and 9, inclusive, and returns an equivalent character value (for example, '0' for 0, '1' for 1).

Programming Projects

1. An integer *n* is divisible by 9 if the sum of its digits is divisible by 9. Develop a program to determine whether or not the following numbers are divisible by 9:

```
n = 154368
n = 621594
n = 123456
```

2. Redo the previous programming project by reading each digit of the number to be tested into the type char variable digit. Form the sum of the numeric values of the digits. (Hint: The numeric value of digit is int (digit) - int ('0').)

3. If a human heart beats on an average of once per second (60 beats per minute), how many times does the heart beat in a lifetime of 78 years? (Use 365.25 for the number of days in a year.) Rerun your program for a heart rate of 75 beats per minute. Implement the program first using beats per minute and years as integers and total beats and all constants as type `double`. Then try changing all type `double` data to type `float` and see what happens. Can you explain the difference (if any) in the execution output of the two versions?

4. A number is said to be *perfect* if the sum of its divisors (except for itself) is equal to itself. For example, 6 is a perfect number because the sum of its divisors (1 + 2 + 3) is 6. The number 8 is said to be *deficient* because the sum of its divisors (1 + 2 + 4) is only 7. The number 12 is said to be *abundant* because the sum of its divisors (1 + 2 + 3 + 4 + 6) is 16. Write a program that lists the factors of the numbers between 1 and 100 and classifies each number as perfect, deficient, or abundant.

5. Write a program for printing a bar graph summarizing the rainfall in Bedrock for one year. Include the average monthly rainfall and the maximum monthly rainfall during the year as part of the program output.

   Prompt the user for the amount of rainfall for a particular month and instruct the computer to send an appropriate output line to the printer. Assume that no one month will have more than 14 inches of rainfall. Your graph should resemble the following:

   Write functions corresponding to the prototypes shown below as part of your solution.

```
January    |* * * * * * * * * * * * * * * *
           |
February   |* * * * * * * * * * * *
           |
March      |
           |
December   |* * * * * * * * * * * * * * * * * * * * * * * * * * * * * * * *
           |-----1-----2-----3-----4-----5-----6-----7-----8-----9...
```

                        Inches of Rainfall

```
// Write the month value as a string
void writeMonth
   (int);        // IN – month to be written as a string

// Get rainfall for month; update totals
// User is prompted for inches of rainfall during a
month.
// Max inches and total inches are updated to contain
//    the maximum and total inches of rainfall input so far.
void getMonthlyTotal
```

```
(int,            // IN — current month
 float&,         // OUT — inches of rain for month
 float&,         // INOUT — max inches of rain
 float&);        // INOUT — total inches of rain
```

```
// Draw bar of length given by inches
// Draw a bar whose length is computed from inches with
//   label determined by the value of month.
void drawBar
    (int,        // IN: the month to be written as a string
     float);     // IN: the inches of rain for the month
// Draw scale and label at bottom of graph
void drawScaleLine();
```

6. The interest paid on a savings account is compounded daily. This means that if you start with *startbal* dollars in the bank, at the end of the first day you'll have a balance of

```
startbal * (1 + rate/365)
```

dollars, where *rate* is the annual interest rate (0.10 if the annual rate is 10 percent). At the end of the second day, you'll have

```
startbal * (1 + rate/365) * (1 + rate/365)
```

dollars, and at the end of *n* days you'll have

```
startbal * (1 + rate/365)n
```

dollars. Write a program that processes a set of data records, each of which contains values for `rate`, `startbal`, and `n` and computes the final account balance.

7. Experiments that are either too expensive or too dangerous to perform are often simulated on a computer when the computer is able to provide a good representation of the experiment. Find out how to call the random-number generator (usually a function returning a floating-point value in the range 0 to 1) for your C++ system. (Look up the functions `rand` and `srand` in the library `cstdlib`.) Write a program that uses the random-number generator to simulate the dropping of glass rods that break into three pieces. The purpose of the experiment is to estimate the probability that the lengths of the three pieces are such that they might form the sides of a triangle.

   For the purposes of this experiment, you may assume that the glass rod always breaks into three pieces. If you use the line segment 0 to 1 (on the real number line) as a mathematical model of the glass rod, a random-number generator (function) can be used to generate two numbers between 0 and 1 representing the coordinates of the breaks. The triangle inequality (the sum of the lengths of two sides of a triangle are always greater than the length of the third side) may be used to test the length of each piece against the lengths of the other two pieces.

To estimate the probability that the pieces of the rod form a triangle, you'll need to repeat the experiment many times and count the number of times a triangle can be formed from the pieces. The probability estimate is the number of successes divided by the total number of rods dropped. Your program should prompt the user for the number of rods to drop and allow the experiment to be repeated. Use a sentinel value of 21 to halt execution of the program.

8. Julian day numbers are used to provide a number for a day of the year so that calculations can be performed relatively easily to determine the difference between two dates. For example, if you wanted to determine the number of days between the day you were born and today, this would be a very tedious calculation. You would need to determine how many days followed the day you were born in that year, how many days were in each year between the year you were born and the current year, and how many days were in the current year up to today. This is complicated by the fact that leap years have 366 days (see Programming Project 11 in Chapter 6). The Julian day number for a day is the number of days that have elapsed between that day and a base date of January 1, 4713 B.C.E. Code the following algorithm for computing the Julian day number as a type long function where day is an integer from 1 to 31, month goes from 1 to 12, and year goes from -4713 (4713 B.C.E.) to whatever.

```
long julianDayNumber(int month, int day, int year)
{
    jyear = year;
    jmonth = month;
    if (year < 0)
        increment jyear by 1;          // no year 0
    if (month > 2)
        increment jmonth by 1;
    else
        increment jmonth by 13 and decrement jyear by 1

    long julian = floor(362.25 * jyear) +
                  floor(30.6001 * jmonth) +
                  day + 1720995.0;
      if the argument date is not before October 15, 1582
          int jCorrection = 0.01 * jyear;
          julian = julian + 2 - jCorrection +
                  0.25 * jCorrection;
      return julian;
}
```

Write and test a function to calculate the Julian day number for a given day. (The date October 9, 1995 is Julian day 2,450,000; the date October 15, 1582 is Julian day number 2,299,161.) Use this function to determine how many days you've been alive.

9. A baseball player's batting average is calculated as the number of hits divided by the official number of at-bats. In calculating official at-bats, walks, sacrifices, and occasions when hit by the pitch are not counted. Write a program that takes data containing player numbers and batting records. Trips to the plate are coded in the batting record as follows: H—hit, O—out, W—walk, S—sacrifice, P—hit by pitch. The program should output for each player the input data followed by the batting average.

```
Sample data:
12 HOOOWSHHOOHPWWHO
4  OSOHHHWWOHOHOOO
7  WPOHOOHWOHHOWOO
Corresponding output:
Player 12's record: HOOOWSHHOOHPWWHO
Player 12's batting average: 0.455

Player 4's record: OSOHHHWWOHOHOOO
Player 4's batting average: 0.417

Player 7's record: WPOHOOHWOHHOWOO
Player 7's batting average: 0.364
```

10. The rate of decay of a radioactive isotope is given in terms of its half-life H, the time lapse required for the isotope to decay to one-half of its original mass. The isotope cobalt-60 (^{60}Co) has a half-life of 5.272 years. Compute and print in table form the amount of this isotope that remains after each year for five years, given the initial presence of an amount in grams. The value of *amount* should be provided interactively. The amount of ^{60}Co remaining can be computed by using the following formula:

$$r = amount \times C^{(y/H)}$$

where *amount* is the initial amount in grams, C is expressed as $e^{-0.693}$ ($e = 2.71828$), y is the number of years elapsed, and H is the half-life of the isotope in years.

11. In this chapter, we studied the bisection method for finding a root of an equation. Another method for finding a root, Newton's method usually converges to a solution even faster than the bisection method, if it converges at all. Newton's method starts with an initial guess for a root, x_0,

and then generates successive approximate roots $x_1, x_2, \ldots, x_j, x_{j+1}, \ldots$, using the iterative formula

$$x_{j+1} = x_j - \frac{f(x_j)}{f'(x_j)}$$

where $f'(x_j)$ is the derivative of function f evaluated at $x = x_j$. The formula generates a new guess, x_{j+1}, from a previous one, x_j. Sometimes Newton's method will fail to converge to a root. In this case, the program should terminate after many trials, perhaps 100.

Figure 7.6 shows the geometric interpretation of Newton's method where x_0, x_1, and x_2 represent successive guesses for the root. At each point x_j, the derivative $f'(x_j)$ is the slope of the tangent to the curve, $f(x)$. The next guess for the root x_{j+1} is the point at which the tangent crosses the x axis.

From geometry, we get the equation

$$\frac{y_{j+1} - y_j}{x_{j+1} - x_j} = m$$

where m is the slope of the line between points (x_{j+1}, y_{j+1}) and (x_j, y_j). In Figure 7.6, we see that y_{j+1} is zero, y_j is $f(x_j)$, and m is $f'(x_j)$; therefore by substituting and rearranging terms, we get

$$-f(x_j) = f'(x_j) \times (x_{j+1} - x_j)$$

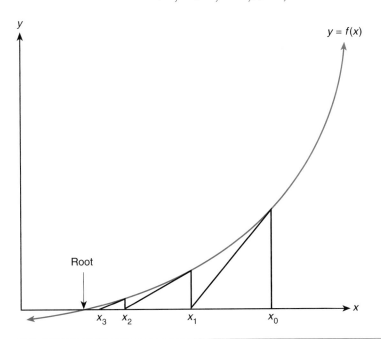

Figure 7.6   Geometric interpretation of Newton's method

leading to the formula shown at the beginning of this problem.

Write a program that uses Newton's method to approximate the nth root of a number to six decimal places. If $x^n = c$, then $x^n - c = 0$. Finding a root of the second equation will give you $\sqrt[n]{c}$. Test your program on $\sqrt{2}$, $\sqrt[3]{7}$, and $\sqrt[3]{-1}$. Your program could use $c/2$ as its initial guess.

12. You would like to find the area under the curve

$$y = f(x)$$

between the lines $x = a$ and $x = b$. One way to approximate this area is to use line segments as approximations of small pieces of the curve and then to sum the areas of trapezoids created by drawing perpendiculars from the line segment endpoints to the x-axis, as shown in Figure 7.7. We will assume that $f(x)$ is nonnegative over the interval $[a, b]$. The trapezoidal rule approximates this area T as

$$T = \frac{h}{2}\left(f(a) + f(b) + 2\sum_{i=1}^{n-1}f(x_i)\right)$$

for n subintervals of length h:

$$h = \frac{b - a}{n}$$

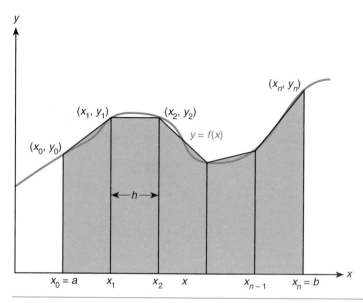

Figure 7.7   Approximating the area under a curve with trapezoids

Write a function `trap` with input parameters a, b, n, and f that implements the trapezoidal rule. Call `trap` with values for n of 2, 4, 8, 16, 32,
64, and 128 on functions

$$g(x) = x^2 \sin x \qquad\qquad (a = 0, b = 3.14159)$$

and

$$h(x) = \sqrt{4 - x^2} \qquad (a = -2, b = 2)$$

Function h defines a half-circle of radius 2. Compare your approximation to the actual area of this half-circle.

Note: If you have studied calculus, you will observe that the trapezoidal
rule is approximating

$$\int_a^b f(x)dx$$

13. Since communications channels are often noisy, numerous ways have
been devised to ensure reliable data transmission. One successful
method uses a checksum. A checksum for a message can be computed
by summing the integer codes of the characters in the message and
finding the remainder of this sum divided by 64. The integer code for a
space character is added to this result to obtain the checksum. Since this
value is within the range of the displayable characters, it is displayed as
a character as well. Write a program that accepts single-line messages
ending with a period and displays the checksum character for each
message. Your program should continue displaying checksums until
the user enters a line with only a period.

14. A finite state machine (FSM) consists of a set of states, a set of transitions, and a string of input data. In the FSM of Figure 7.8, the named
ovals represent states, and the arrows connecting the states represent
transitions. The FSM is designed to recognize a list of C++ identifiers
and nonnegative integers, assuming that the items are ended by one
or more blanks and that a period marks the end of all the data. The
following table traces how the diagrammed machine would process a
string composed of one blank, the digits 9 and 5, two blanks, the letter K, the digit 9, one blank, and a period. The machine begins in the
start state.

Write a program that uses an enumerated type to represent the
names of the states. Your program should process a correctly formatted
line of data, identifying each data item. Here is a sample of correct input
and output.

Input:

```
rate   R2D2   48   2 time   555666
```

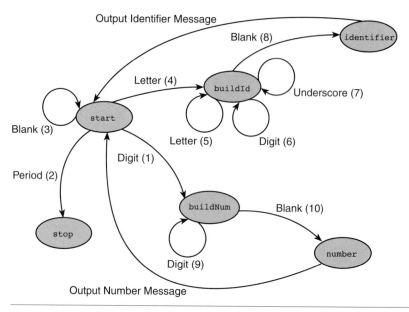

Figure 7.8 Finite state machine for numbers and identifiers

Output:

```
rate — Identifier
R2D2 - Identifier
48 - Number
2 - Number
time - Identifier
555666 - Number
```

Trace of Figure 7.8 FSM on data " 95 K9 ."

State	Next Character	Transition
start	' '	3
start	'9'	1
buildNum	'5'	9
buildNum	' '	10
number		Output number message
start	' '	3
start	'K'	4
buildId	'9'	6
buildId	' '	8
identifier		Output identifier message
start	'.'	2
stop		

Use the following code fragment in `main`, and design function `transition` to return the next state for all the numbered transitions of the FSM. If you include the header file `ctype.h`, you can use the library function `isdigit` which returns 1 if called with a digit character, 0 otherwise. Similarly, the function `isalpha` checks whether a character is a letter. When your program correctly models the behavior of the FSM shown, extend the FSM and your program to allow optional signs and fractional parts (that is, a decimal point followed by zero or more digits) in numbers.

```
currentState = start;
do {
    if (currentState == identifier) {
        cout << " - Identifier\n"
        currentState = start;
    } else if (currentState == number) {
        cout << " - Number\n";
        currentState = start;
    }
    cin >> transitionChar;
    if (transitionChar != ' ')
        cout << transitionChar;
    currentState = transition(currentState,
                              transitionChar);
} while (currentState != stop);
```

Graphics Projects

15. Modify the program in Listing 7.10 to call a function `getShape` to determine the shape to draw. The main function should display a small icon for each shape. Function `getShape` should return a `char` indicating which icon was clicked and then draw it at the position selected by the user.

16. Write a program that displays a collection of random shapes with white borders. Each time the user clicks in a shape, it should "disappear" from the screen. (Hint: Repaint it black.)

Answers to Quick-Check Exercises

1. **a.** `false`

   b. The outer pair isn't required.

   c. The inner pair isn't required.

   d. `!(flag && (m % n == 0)` or `!flag || (m % n != 0)`

2. **a.** m = 2.5 + 13 / 2; 8 is assigned to m (the integral part of 8.5).

   b. 8.5 is assigned to m.

   c. m = int(2.5 + float(k) / 2.0); 9 is assigned to m (the integral part of 2.5 + 6.5).

   d. In float(k / 2) the division of k by 2 is type int. It's performed first and then the result is cast to type float.

3. **a.** 'a'   **b.** 'd'   **c.** 'f'   **d.** 'R'   **e.** 82

   f. The result is the integer form of the character—for example, 7 if ch is '7'.

4. false || false is false; this is a logical expression involving calls to two type bool functions.

5. no

6. **a.** Yes, but carefully. Remember that these data are each considered to be different C++ types and are subject to the C++ conversion/promotion rules in Section 7.2.

   b. The same applies to assignment except that integer type values may not be assigned to variables of enumeration types.

7. This can happen only if the enumeration variable's type cast is applied to the type int variable or value before the assignment (for example, today = day(i);).

8. Type int and char values aren't allowed as enumerators in enumeration types.

chapter eight

Streams and Files

Learning Objectives

- To learn how to use external files for program input and output
- To learn how to read program data from input streams (type `ifstream`) and write program results to output streams (type `ofstream`)
- To become familiar with functions for manipulating streams in the C++ library `fstream`
- To learn when and how to use functions `get`, `getline`, and `ignore` to read character and string data
- To learn how to use manipulators in the C++ library `iomanip` to format output

THIS CHAPTER DISCUSSES streams and files in C++. It describes the input and output facilities provided by the C++ libraries that support stream input and output. The chapter will also present more about the standard input/output streams, `cin` and `cout`, how to use disk files for input/output, and how to format data items that are written to output streams.

8.1   The Standard Input/Output Streams

stream
A sequence of characters used for program input or output.

A **stream** is a sequence of characters used for program input or output. So far, we've used the *standard input stream* (named `cin`) and the *standard output stream* (named `cout`). Including the `iostream` header file enables a program to access these streams. When we first introduced streams in Chapter 2, we mentioned that `cin` and `cout` are objects of type `istream` and `ostream` respectively. The user-defined types `istream` and `ostream` are defined by classes in the `iostream` library, and `cin` and `cout` are declared as objects of these types. Normally, `cin` is connected to your keyboard, so when a program reads characters from `cin`, it reads characters typed at the keyboard. Similarly, `cout` is connected to your display, so writing characters to the standard output stream object `cout` displays these characters on your screen.

During input, the stream operators must convert sequences of characters into their appropriate internal representations before storing them in memory. For example, if the character sequence starting with `123.45` (digit character 1, digit character 2, and so on) is being read into a type `float` variable, the stream extraction operator `>>` must convert this sequence to the floating point form of the real number 123.45 for storage. If the same character sequence (`123.45`) is being read into a type `int` variable, only the first three characters will be extracted and converted into a fixed point number (binary equivalent of 123) for storage. The characters (`.45`) remain in the stream. Finally, if this sequence is being read into a type `char` variable, only the first character (`'1'`) is extracted and stored.

During output, the reverse process takes place. When writing a floating point number to an output stream, the insertion operator `<<` must first convert its internal representation to a sequence of characters and then write this character sequence to the output stream. A similar process takes place for the other data types in C++ (see Figure 8.1).

Any character, whether printable or not, may be read from or written to a stream. Thus nonprintable characters such as `'\a'` and `'\n'` may also be read from or written to streams. As their name suggests, these characters are not displayed. Rather, on many computers, they cause special actions to occur, such as sounding a beep (`'\a'`) or moving the cursor to the beginning of the next line (`'\n'`).

EXAMPLE 8.1

newline character
A character that partitions a stream into a sequence of lines.

The **newline character** (`'\n'`) partitions a stream into a sequence of lines. We call this a *logical partition*, because it reflects the way we often think and talk about a stream. Don't forget, however, that a stream is physically just a sequence of characters with the newline character interspersed. For example, the following represents a stream of two lines of data consisting of letters, blank characters, `'.'` (a period), and `'!'` (an exclamation point). The symbols `<nwln>` represent the newline character.

```
This is a stream!<nwln>It is displayed as two lines.<nwln>
```

The <nwln> character separates one line of data in the stream from the next. The letter I following the first <nwln> is the first character of the second line. If we were to display this stream, each <nwln> character would cause a *line feed* and a *carriage return*, ensuring that everything that follows it would appear at the beginning of a new line. The displayed stream would appear as follows:

```
This is a stream!
It is displayed as two lines.
```

A stream has no fixed size. As we write (insert) information to a stream, we're simply adding characters to the end of the stream (increasing its size). The C++ stream output library functions keep track of the size of the stream. As we read (extract) information from a stream, the C++ stream input library functions keep track of the last character read using an *input stream buffer pointer*. Each new attempt to get information from an input stream begins at the current position of this pointer.

When reading data from a stream using the extraction operator >>, any leading *white space* (blanks, tabs, and newline characters) is skipped until the

Output conversion (from internal representation to characters)

```
cout << "Enter " << setw(3) << n << " float values separated by a blank."
```

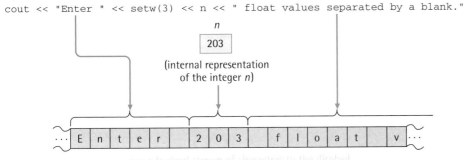

Input conversion

```
cin >> month >> day >> year;
```

Figure 8.1 Conversion of data during stream input/output

first non-white-space character is found. This is the case whether you're reading data into a type char, int, float, or bool variable or into a type string object. After the data characters are extracted, the input stream buffer pointer is advanced to the next character to be read.

EXAMPLE 8.2

For the input stream

```
        CIS 642   ...
    the line
    cin >> ch;              //ch is a type char variable
```

causes the five blanks (indicated by the symbol [blank]) at the start of the stream to be skipped. The character c is then extracted from the stream and stored in the variable ch (type char). The stream buffer pointer then is positioned at the character I.

When reading a numeric value, all characters that are part of the numeric value (a sign, digits, and so on) are processed until a character that's not legally part of a number in C++ is read. At this point, the number processed is returned to the program. If no digits are read before an illegal numeric character is encountered, the value returned is not defined.

EXAMPLE 8.3

If myAge and n are type int, for the input stream

```
    347an old man
```

the line

```
    cin >> myAge;      // myAge is a type int variable
```

reads the characters 347 and stops when the character a is encountered. The integer value 347 would be stored in myAge. The stream buffer pointer then points to the character a. If the next input statement is

```
    cin >> n;          // n is a type int variable
```

reading would stop as soon as the a is encountered, and the result stored in n would be undefined.

EXAMPLE 8.4

Consider the input stream consisting of exam score *records* (three initials and a score) for each of four students, where each record is entered as a single line, with the return key pressed after each score is typed:

```
flf 78<nwln>ebk 89<nwln>jas 95<nwln>pac 66<nwln>
```

Assuming that the variable `score` is type `int`, and `firstInit`, `midInit`, and `lastInit` are type `char`, the C++ instructions

```
for (int i = 0; i < numStudents; i++)
{
    cin >> firstInit >> midInit >> lastInit >> score;
    // Process the information just read.
    ...
}
```

may be used to read in this information. If `numStudents` is 4, this loop would extract (read) four data elements (three characters and an integer) at a time from the stream just shown until all four student records have been processed. In each `for` loop iteration, the next student's initials would be extracted and stored in the character variables, `firstInit`, `midInit`, and `lastInit`, and the integer that follows them would be read and stored in `score`.

The newline character in the stream has no special impact on the processing of the data just shown. Leading white space, including blanks and the newline character, is always skipped when reading a data element using `cin`. After the score for the first student has been read, the input stream buffer pointer is positioned at the `<nwln>` character that stopped the processing:

```
flf 78<nwln>ebk 89<nwln>jas 95<nwln>pac 66<nwln>
        ↑
```

When reading data for the second student, the white space (`<nwln>`) that precedes this student's first initial is skipped. If we replace each newline with a blank, the processing would be the same. In fact, if there were no white-space characters anywhere in the line, the processing of the line would not change (Listing 8.1). In this case, the letter **e** would terminate the reading of the first score, and **e** would then be read as the first initial of the second student.

Listing 8.1   An input stream without white space

```
flf78ebk89jas95pac66
```

Reading One Character at a Time

In many situations, we want to treat white space the same way as any other character. The following examples illustrate how this might be done using the stream input and output functions get and put, which are part of the C++ iostream library. Function get is used to read one character at a time; function put is used to display one character at a time.

EXAMPLE 8.5

The program in Listing 8.2 counts and displays the number of characters in each line of a stream entered at the keyboard. It also counts and displays the number of lines in the stream. The outer loop repeats as long as the condition !cin.eof() is true. Function eof (end-of-file) detects the end of a stream of characters. This function returns a value of false as long as there are more characters to be read in a stream. When the end of the stream is reached, it returns the value true. Consequently the outer loop repeats until the end of the stream is reached. You indicate the end of a stream by typing a special control character which is system dependent. On PCs, you enter this character by pressing and holding the control key and then pressing z (ctrl-z). On UNIX computers, the character ctrl-d is used.

The inner loop condition (next != nwln) is true as long as the newline character has not been read. Therefore, this inner loop processes all of the characters in the current data line, including the blanks. The put function displays each character in the line after it is read. When the newline character is read by the inner call to get, the inner while loop expression evaluates to false, and loop exit occurs. At this point, the newline is displayed (marking the end of the current line of output), the line count is incremented, and the number of characters in the line is displayed. This sequence of steps repeats as long as the outer loop condition is true.

Notice that the eof function does not return a value of true until after the get function reads the end-of-file character <eof> that marks the end of a stream. We use dot notation to indicate which stream (cin or cout) is involved in each stream operation (for example, cin.eof()).

We summarize the new functions together with other stream input/output functions in Table 8.1. The open, fail, and close functions are used only with external file streams, described in the next section.

Listing 8.2   Processing individual characters in a stream

```cpp
// File: countChars.cpp
// Counts number of characters in a line and lines in a stream

#include <iostream>
using namespace std;

#define ENDFILE "CTRL-Z"

int main()
{
   const char NWLN = '\n';   // newline character
   char next;                // next character in current line
   int charCount;            // number of characters in current line
   int lineCount;            // keeps track of number of lines in file

   lineCount = 0;
   cout << "Enter a line or press " << ENDFILE << ": ";
   cin.get(next);            // get first char of new line
   while (!cin.eof())
   {
      charCount = 0;         // initialize character count for new line
      while (next != NWLN)
      {
         cout.put(next);
         charCount++;        // Increment character count.
         cin.get(next);      // Get next character.
      }  // end inner while

      cout.put(NWLN); // Mark end of current display line.
      lineCount++;
      cout << "Number of characters in line " << lineCount
           << " is " << charCount << endl;
      cout << "Enter a line or press " << ENDFILE << ": ";
      cin.get(next);                  // Get next character.
   }  // end outer while

   cout << endl << endl << "Number of lines processed is "
        << lineCount << endl;
   return 0;
}
```

(continued)

Listing 8.2 Processing individual characters in a stream (continued)

```
Enter a line or press CTRL-Z: This is one.
This is one.
Number of characters is 12
Enter a line or press CTRL-Z: Hello!
Hello!
Number of characters is 6
Enter a line or press CTRL-Z: CTRL-Z
Number of lines processed is 2
```

Table 8.1 The File Manipulation Member Functions

Member Function	Purpose
fs.open(*fname*);	Opens stream *fs* for input or output. Connects the stream *fs* to the external file designated by *fname*.
fs.get(*ch*);	Extracts the next character from stream *fs* and places it in the character variable *ch*.
fs.put(*ch*);	Inserts (writes or displays) character *ch* into stream *fs*.
fs.close();	Disconnects stream *fs* from its associated external file.
fs.eof();	Tests for the end-of-file condition on stream *fs*. Returns true when the end-of-file is reached. This is detected when a program attempts to read the <eof> character marking the end of a file.
fs.fail();	Returns true if an operation on stream *fs* such as open failed to execute properly.

PROGRAM STYLE Using a Stream in a Condition

As an alternative to using the eof function to test for the end of a stream, C++ programmers can test the status of the stream by using the stream name directly in a condition. For example, to test whether an input operation on stream cin was successful, you can evaluate the condition (cin) just after the input operation. If the input operation in question was cin.get(next), you can use the condition (cin.get(next)). Because an input operation on stream cin returns a reference to stream cin, the status of stream cin is tested. The condition value is true if the input operation was successful; the condition value is false if the input operation was unsuccessful (for example, because the <eof> character was read).

Using this technique, we can write the outer loop control for Listing 8.2 as shown next.

```
cout << "Enter a line or press " << ENDFILE << ": ";
while (cin.get(next)) // get first char of new line
```

```
{
    // insert loop body including inner while loop.
    . . .
    cout << "Enter a line or press " << ENDFILE << ": ";
}   // end outer while
```

This loop repeats until the user enters the `<eof>` character instead of a data line. Notice that the input operation (`cin.get(next)`) appears only in the loop repetition condition. In Listing 8.2, we called function get twice: just before entering the loop and at the end of the loop body.

EXERCISES FOR SECTION 8.1

Self-Check

1. Explain what would happen in Listing 8.2 if the function calls `cin.get(next)` were replaced by `cin >> next;`.

2. Let x be type `float`, n type `int`, and c type `char`. Indicate the contents of each variable after each read operation is performed on the input stream below.

   1374 37 15.125 pqr*<nwln>233 $ <nwln>

   Assume the input stream buffer is reset to the first character before each file read operation.

   a. `cin >> n >> x; cin >> c >> n;`

   b. `cin >> n; cin.get(c);`

   c. `cin >> x >> n >> c; cin.get(c); cin >> n;`

   d. `cin >> c >> n >> x; cin >> c;`

   e. `cin >> c >> c >> c >> x >> n;`

3. Write one input statement that reads the input stream for Self-Check Exercise 2 and stores `15.125` in x, `233` in n, and `$` in c.

4. What would happen to the displayed output for Listing 8.2 if the line `cout.put(NWLN);` were omitted from the program?

5. Describe the behavior of the program in Listing 8.2 if the statement containing the innermost `cin.get` were omitted.

6. Describe the behavior of the program in Listing 8.2 if the input stream being processed were empty (contained no data at all).

7. Explain the problem that occurs when the statement

```
cin >> n >> ch1 >> ch2 >> m;
```

reads the following data line

```
3abc 452
```

Note: `ch1`, `ch2` are type `char`; `m`, `n` are type `int`.

Programming

1. Write a function that simulates what the extraction operator does when it reads an integer value. Your function should skip leading whitespace and read each digit character until it reaches a nondigit character. Your function should return the numeric value of the digit characters read. For example, if it reads the digit characters 3, 4, 5, your function should return the number 345. (Hint: Accumulate the numeric value by adding the numeric value of the current digit character (`int(dig) - int('0')`) to ten times the numeric value for the previous digit characters. If the previous sum is 34 and 5 is the next digit character, the next sum is 340 + 5 or 345.)

8.2   External Files

Interactive versus Batch Processing

So far this chapter focused on interactive input. Interactive programs read their input data from the `cin` stream associated with the keyboard, and they display their output to the `cout` stream associated with a display. This mode of operation is fine for small programs. However, as you begin to write larger programs, you'll see that there are many advantages to using external data files. External files are stored on a secondary storage device, normally a disk, and are semipermanent. They will remain on the disk until you delete or overwrite them.

You can create an external data file using a text editor in the same way that you create a program file. Once the data file is entered in computer memory, you can carefully check and edit each line and then save the final data file as a disk file. When you enter data interactively, you don't always have the opportunity to examine and edit the data. Also, the data are processed as they are entered—they are not saved permanently.

batch processing
Reading data from an external file instead of through interaction with the user.

After the data file is saved on disk, you can instruct your program to read from the data file rather than from the keyboard. This mode of execution is called **batch processing**. Because the program data are supplied before execution begins, prompting messages are not required for batch programs. Instead, batch programs should contain display statements that print back, or **echo-print**, those data values read by the program. This provides a

echo-print
The immediate display of a value read as data.

record of the values read and processed in a particular program run, which can be useful, especially for debugging and testing.

In addition to giving you the opportunity to check for errors in your data, using data files provides another advantage. A data file can be read many times. Therefore, during debugging you can rerun the program many times without needing to type in the test data each time.

You can also instruct your program to write its output to a disk file rather than display it on the screen. When output is written to the screen, it disappears when it scrolls off the screen and cannot be retrieved. However, if program output is written to a disk file, you have a permanent copy of it. You can get a **hard copy** of the file—a permanent copy on paper—by sending it to your printer, or you can read it using an editor or word processor.

Finally, you can use the output generated by one program as a data file for another program. For example, a payroll program may compute employee salaries and write each employee's name and salary to an output file. You could then run a second program (for example, a program that prints employee checks) that uses the output from the payroll program as its input data file.

hard copy
A permanent copy of program output on paper.

Directory Names for External Files

To access a file in a program, you must know the file's directory name. The directory name consists of the path to the file followed by the file name. For example, on a PC you'd use the directory name `C:\MyFiles\Payroll.txt` for a file named `Payroll.txt` stored in directory `MyFiles` on disk drive `C`. The details of providing directory names are system-dependent. If your program and external files are in the same disk directory, you can usually refer to the external file using just its file name.

File names must follow whatever conventions apply on a particular computer system. For example, UNIX computers don't permit blanks in file names. We use the *extension* `.txt` to designate data files.

Attaching Streams to External Files

We mentioned earlier that the input and output stream objects `cin` and `cout` are attached to the keyboard and display, respectively, by the C++ language system. However, to read from or write to an external data file, we must first attach or connect a stream object to that file.

In C++, we use the `open` statement (see Table 8.1) to connect a stream object to an external file. We show how to do this next.

EXAMPLE 8.6

For security reasons, it is a good idea to have a backup or duplicate copy of a file in case the original is lost. The program in Listing 8.3 creates a copy of a file by writing each character in the input file (file `inData.txt`) to the output file (file `outData.txt`).

Before we can read or write an external file in a program, we must first declare a stream object for each stream/file to be processed by our program. In Listing 8.3, the declarations

```
ifstream ins;
ofstream outs;
```

involve two new data types: `ifstream` (input file stream) and `ofstream` (output file stream). Both are defined in the C++ library `fstream`. Once the stream objects have been declared, we can open the files:

```
ins.open(inFile);
outs.open(outFile);
```

This function communicates with the operating system and attaches a stream (`ins`, for example) to the external file specified as the argument (`ins` is connected to `inFile`). We show the connections established by the `open` statements in Listing 8.3.

The use of the `#define` compiler directive enables us to associate the name of a stream used by the program (for example, `inFile`) with the actual directory name of an external file (such as `inData.txt`). This association enables us to easily reuse this program with different input and output files. All we would need to change are the two `#define` lines in the program, and the program would be ready to run with different files.

The `if` statement after the call to the `open` function tests whether the `open` operation was successful. If the last operation on stream object `ins` failed, function `fail` returns true. If the last operation succeeded, function `fail` returns false. You should always test whether an `open` operation is successful and terminate execution of the program if the value returned by `fail` is true. A return with the value `EXIT_FAILURE` (defined in library `cstdlib`) may be used to report unsuccessful termination to the operating system.

Listing 8.3   Copying a file

```cpp
// File: copyFile.cpp
// Copies file InData.txt to file OutData.txt

#include <cstdlib>      // for the definition of EXIT_FAILURE
#include <fstream>     // for external file streams
using namespace std;

// Associate stream objects with external file names
```

(continued)

Listing 8.3   Copying a file (continued)

```cpp
#define inFile "InData.txt"      // directory name for inFile
#define outFile "OutData.txt"    // directory name for outFile

// Functions used ...
// Copies one line of text
int copyLine(ifstream&, ofstream&);

int main()
{
    int lineCount;      // output: number of lines processed
    ifstream ins;       // ins is an input stream
    ofstream outs;      // outs is an output stream

    // Open input and output file, exit on any error.
    ins.open(inFile); // connects ins to file inFile
    if (ins.fail())
    {
        cerr << "*** ERROR: Cannot open " << inFile
            << " for input." << endl;
        return EXIT_FAILURE;    // failure return
    }
    outs.open(outFile); // connect outs to file outFile
    if (outs.fail())
    {
        cerr << "*** ERROR: Cannot open " << outFile
            << " for output." << endl;
        return EXIT_FAILURE;    // failure return
    }

    // Copy each character from inData to outData.
    lineCount = 0;
    while (!ins.eof())
    {
        if (copyLine(ins, outs) != 0)
            lineCount++;
    }

    // Display a message on the screen.
    cout << "Input file copied to output file." << endl;
    cout << lineCount << " lines copied." << endl;

    ins.close();        // close input file stream
    outs.close();       // close output file stream
```

(continued)

Listing 8.3   Copying a file (continued)

```
      return 0;            // successful return
}


// Copy one line of text from one file to another
// Pre:     ins is opened for input and outs for output.
// Post:    Next line of ins is written to outs.
//          The last character processed from ins is <nwln>;
//          the last character written to outs is <nwln>.
// Returns: The number of characters copied.
int copyLine
     (ifstream& ins,        // IN: ins stream
      ofstream& outs)       // OUT: outs stream
{
   // Local data . . .
   const char NWLN = '\n';              // newline character

   char nextCh;                         // inout: character buffer
   int charCount = 0;                   // number of characters copied

   // Copy all data characters from stream ins to
   //     stream outs.
   ins.get(nextCh);
   while ((nextCh != NWLN) && !ins.eof())
   {
      outs.put(nextCh);
      charCount++;
      ins.get(nextCh);
   }  // end while

   // If last character read was NWLN write it to outs.
   if (!ins.eof())
   {
      outs.put(NWLN);
      charCount++;

   }
   return charCount;
}  // end copyLine
```

```
Input file copied to output file.
37 lines copied.
```

Besides the standard iostreams `cin` and `cout`, there's another standard stream, `cerr`, the *standard error stream*, which is usually connected to your display. The `if` statement just discussed writes an error message to stream `cerr` when an error occurs in attempting to open the input file.

The program in Listing 8.3 uses the `get`, `put`, and `eof` functions with external files. It also uses the function `close` to disconnect each external file before the program terminates. This is a good programming practice.

Function `copyLine`

In the main function in Listing 8.3, the loop that does the actual copying follows the `open` instructions. This loop calls function `copyLine` to copy one line of information at a time from the input file to the output file. Function `copyLine` returns the count of characters in the line just read. The `main` function loop counts the number of lines copied. Loop repetition continues as long as the end of the input file has not been reached. After loop exit, the number of lines copied is displayed on the screen and both files are closed.

Function `copyLine` copies one line of the input file to the output file. The `while` loop header in `copyLine`

```
while ((nextCh != NWLN) && !ins.eof())
```

controls a loop that copies one character at a time as long as neither a new-line character nor the end of the input file has been encountered. When either of these events occurs, loop exit occurs. If the newline character caused loop exit (`!ins.eof()` is true), a newline character is written to the output file before `copyLine` returns to the main function.

Reading from or writing to a file stream modifies the file position pointer associated with the stream. For this reason, we must pass all file stream arguments by reference.

More on the Newline Character

Let's review how function `copyLine` processes newline characters. Consider the input file shown next:

```
This is a text file!<nwln>It has two lines.<nwln><eof>
```

When the first `<nwln>` is read during the execution of the `while` loop, the input and output files (and their respective stream buffer pointers) would appear as follows:

Input file

```
This is a text file!<nwln>It has two lines.<nwln><eof>
                          ↑
```

Output file

```
This is a text file!
                    ↑
```

If the lines

```
// If last character read was NWLN write it to outData.
if (!ins.eof())
{
    outs.put(NWLN);
    charCount++;
}
```

were omitted from copyLine, the <nwln> character just read from the input file would not be written to the output file. As this continued throughout the program, the output file OutData.txt would contain all the characters in InData.txt, except for the line separators:

```
This is a text file!It has two lines.
```

The call to function put following the while loop in function copyLine ensures that a newline character is written to the output file at the end of each complete line. Once the <nwln> has been copied to the output file, control is returned to the calling program. When copyLine is called the next time, the input and output files would appear as shown below:

Input file

```
This is a text file!<nwln>It has two lines.<nwln><eof>
                          ↑
```

Output file

```
This is a text file!<nwln>
                          ↑
```

The first call to function get (just prior to the while loop in copyLine) causes the next character (the I in It) to be read. This loop continues copying characters from input to output until the second newline is encountered. This newline then is copied to the output file, and control is returned to the calling function. What happens upon the next call to copyLine is left as an exercise at the end of this section (see Self-Check Exercise 1).

In Microsoft Visual C++, the newline character is actually a pair of characters representing the carriage return and line feed. Since we define NWLN as the line feed character '/n' and the line feed is the second character of the pair, this should not affect the examples in this chapter.

Using `getline` with a File Stream

Instead of writing our own function copyLine, we can use function getline to read each line of the file stream into a string object. We can replace the main function loop in Listing 8.3 with the one below.

```
string line;              // Next data line
lineCount = 0;
getline(ins, line);
while (line.length() != 0)
{
    lineCount++;
    outs << line << endl;
    getline(ins, line);
}
```

In this loop, each function call

```
getline(ins, line);
```

reads the next data line into string object line. If the number of characters read is nonzero, we increment lineCount, write the current line to stream outs, and repeat the process.

PROGRAM STYLE   Reading a File Name

In Listing 8.3, we use the #define compiler directive to specify the actual directory name of an external file:

```
#define inFile "InData.txt"
```

This instructs the compiler to replace inFile in the open statement with the string "InData.txt":

```
ins.open("InData.txt");
```

Sometimes program users need to enter interactively the name of a data file. You can enable this to happen by removing the compiler directive above and replacing the open statement with the statements:

```
string fileName

cout << "Enter the input file name: ";
cin >> fileName;
ins.open(fileName.c_str());
```

The file name that's typed in after the prompt will be read into string `fileName` and associated with stream `ins`. The function call `fileName.c_str()` converts the string in `fileName` to a C-style string, which has a different format than a C++ string. The `open` statement has a C-style string (see Section 9.9) as its argument.

EXERCISES FOR SECTION 8.2

Self-Check

1. Examine the file copy program shown in Listing 8.3 and provide a complete, step-by-step description of the processing of this file.

   ```
   This is a text file!<nwln>It has two lines.<nwln><eof>
   ```

2. What is the purpose of the `close` function, the `open` function, and the `eof` function?

3. What are some of the advantages to having external (permanent) storage files in which to store program input and output?

Programming

1. Rewrite the program shown in Listing 8.2 (counting the number of characters in a line and lines in a stream) to read from an external file named `MyData.txt` (rather than from the keyboard). Also, display the total number of characters in the file including the newline characters.

2. Rewrite the copy program shown in Listing 8.3 as a reusable function component with two arguments—specifically, the input and output file streams. The function should return an integer indicating the number of lines copied (0, if the input file is empty).

3. List the changes needed in Listing 8.3 to enable the user to type in the file name.

8.3   Using External Files for Communication between Programs

The following case study shows how one program can communicate with another using an intermediate disk file. If one program writes its output to a disk file rather than to the screen, a second program may use this output file as its own data file.

case study   **Preparing a Payroll File**

PROBLEM STATEMENT

You've been asked to write two programs for processing the company payroll. The first program reads a data file consisting of employee salary data. The data for each employee is stored in a single data record containing the employee's first and last names, hours worked, and hourly rate, as shown next for a file consisting of three data records:

```
Jim Baxter          35.5  7.25<nwln>
Adrian Cybriwsky    40.0  6.50<nwln>
Ayisha Mertens      20.0  8.00<nwln><eof>
```

The first program reads the input for each employee and computes the employee's gross salary as the product of the hours worked and the hourly pay rate. Next, it writes the employee's name and gross salary to an output file and accumulates the gross salary amount in the total company payroll. After processing all employees, it displays the total payroll. Processing the sample input file above would create the sample output file:

```
Jim Baxter          $257.38<nwln>
Adrian Cybriwsky    $260.00<nwln>
Ayisha Mertens      $160.00<nwln><eof>
```

The second program reads the file above as its data file and prints payroll checks based on its contents. For example, the first check issued should be a check for $257.38 made out to Jim Baxter.

PROBLEM ANALYSIS

We'll write the first program now and leave the second one as Programming Project 1 at the end of this chapter. As already explained, our program reads each employee record, computes the gross salary, and writes the employee's name and salary to the output file. Finally, the gross salary is added to the payroll total.

DATA REQUIREMENTS

Streams Used

```
ifstream eds      // employee data information
ofstream pds      // payroll data information
```

Problem Input (from stream eds)

for each employee:
```
string firstName
string lastName
float hoursWorked
float hourlyRate
```

Problem Output (to stream pds)

for each employee:
```
string firstName
string lastName
float salary
```

Problem Output (to stream cout)

```
float totalPayroll      // total company payroll
```

PROGRAM DESIGN

Function main prepares the streams and associated files for input and output. It then calls function processEmp to process the data for the company employees and determine the total company payroll amount. After the return from processEmp, the function main displays the final payroll total. We show the algorithm for function main next.

ALGORITHM FOR FUNCTION main

1. Prepare streams and associated files for processing.

2. Process all employees and compute payroll total.

3. Display the payroll total.

ANALYSIS AND DESIGN FOR processEmp

Function processEmp reads each employee's data record from the input file and writes a corresponding output record to the output file. The function interface and algorithm follow.

INTERFACE FOR processEmp

Input Arguments

```
ifstream eds      // input stream - employee data stream
ofstream pds      // output stream - payroll data stream
```

Output Arguments

(none)

Function Return Value

```
float totalPayroll            // total company payroll
```

ALGORITHM FOR `processEmp`

1. Initialize payroll total to 0.0.

2. While there are more employees

   2.1. Read employee's first and last names and salary data from `eds`.

   2.2. Compute employee's salary.

   2.3. Write employee's first and last names and salary to `pds`; add it to payroll total.

IMPLEMENTATION

We show the C++ code for function `main` in Listing 8.4. Only the three streams `cout`, `eds` (employee data stream), and `pds` (payroll data stream) and the total payroll variable need to be visible in this function. The individual employee data (first and last name, hours worked, hourly rate, and salary) will be used exclusively in `processEmp` and therefore are not declared until needed. Function `main` has no need to know this information.

Listing 8.5 shows function `processEmp`. We declare variables `firstName`, `hours`, `rate`, and `salary` as local variables in `processEmp` because they are referenced only in `processEmp`. Notice that the lines

```
eds >> firstName >> lastName >> hours >> rate;
```

and

```
pds << firstName << " " << lastName
    << " " << salary << endl;
```

are written in exactly the same form that we've been using since Chapter 2 for doing stream I/O with streams `cin` and `cout`. We simply changed the names of the streams to `eds` and `pds`.

Listing 8.4   Creating a payroll file (function `main`)

```cpp
// File: payrollFile.cpp
// Creates a company employee payroll file
//     computes total company payroll amount

#include <fstream>    // required for file streams
#include <cstdlib>    // for definition of EXIT_FAILURE
using namespace std;

// Associate streams with external file names
#define inFile "EmpFile.txt"   // employee file
#define outFile "Salary.txt"   // payroll file

// Functions used . . .
// PROCESS ALL EMPLOYEES AND COMPUTE TOTAL
float processEmp(ifstream&, ofstream&);

int main()
{
    ifstream eds;          //input: employee data stream
    ofstream pds;          //output: payroll data stream
    float totalPayroll;    // output: total payroll

    // Prepare files.
    eds.open(inFile);
    if (eds.fail ())
    {
        cerr << "*** ERROR: Cannot open " << inFile
             << " for input." << endl;
        return EXIT_FAILURE; // failure return
    }

    pds.open(outFile);
    if (pds.fail())
    {
        cerr << "***ERROR: Cannot open " << outFile
             << " for output." << endl;
        eds.close();
        return EXIT_FAILURE; // failure return
    }

    // Process all employees and compute total payroll.
    totalPayroll = processEmp(eds, pds);
```

(continued)

Listing 8.4   Creating a payroll file (function main) (continued)

```cpp
        // Display result.
        cout << "Total payroll is $" << totalPayroll << endl;

        // Close files.
        eds.close();
        pds.close();

        return 0;
}
// Insert processEmp here.
```

```
Total payroll is $677.38
```

TESTING

For the sample data file shown in the problem statement, function processEmp would create the output file also shown in the problem statement. After the return from processEmp, the main function would display the line

```
Total payroll is $677.38
```

Before you run this program, type in the data file using an editor and save it in the same directory as your program. Make sure you press the RETURN key after typing the last line.

Listing 8.5   Implementation of processEmp

```cpp
// File: payroll.cpp
// Process all employees and compute total payroll amount
// Pre:  eds and pds are prepared for input/output.
// Post: Employee names and salaries are written from eds to pds
//        and the sum of their salaries is returned.
// Returns: Total company payroll
float processEmp
    (ifstream& eds,       // IN: employee file stream
     ofstream& pds)       // IN: payroll file stream
{
    string firstName;     // input: employee first name
    string lastName;      // input: employee last name
    float hours;          // input: hours worked
```

(continued)

Listing 8.5   Implementation of `processEmp` (continued)

```
    float rate;          // input: hourly rate
    float salary;        // output: gross salary
    float payroll;       // return value - total company payroll

    payroll = 0.0;
    // Read first employee's data record.
    eds >> firstName >> lastName >> hours >> rate;
    while (!eds.eof())
    {
        salary = hours * rate;
        pds << firstName << " " << lastName
            << " " << salary << endl;
        payroll += salary;
        // Read next employee's data record.
        eds >> firstName >> lastName >> hours >> rate;
    } // end while

    return payroll;
} // end processEmp
```

EXERCISES FOR SECTION 8.3

Self–Check

1. In the payroll program:

    a. What would be the effect, if any, of leading blanks in an employee record (see Listing 8.5)?

    b. What would be the effect of blank lines (empty data records)?

2. Write a statement that reads the information in the record below from stream `eds` into string variables `first` and `last` and float variables hours and rate.

    ```
    Karina Haavik     30.0      7.75<nwln>
    ```

3. Show how you could use the `getline` function and the extraction operator to read the employee's data when that data is written on two lines.

    ```
    Karina Haavik<nwln>
    30.0     7.75<nwln>
    ```

4. Write an algorithm for a revised payroll program with two data files. In the first one, each record contains an employee name and hourly rate; in

the second one, each record contains an employee name and hours worked during the current pay period. The revised program should generate the same output file as the original. There should be a record for each employee in both data files and the records should be in the same order by employee name. Report an error if this is not the case.

5. Redo the previous question assuming the employee names are in no particular order. You will need to find the record in file 2 that corresponds to the one in file 1. It will be necessary to close file 2 and reopen it before processing the next record in file 1.

Programming

1. Write a program that reads from file `Salary.txt` produced by the payroll program and displays the total salary for all employees and their average salary.

2. Modify function `processEmp` to count the number of records processed and to return this value as well as the total payroll. Return both values through output parameters.

3. Write the program for Self-Check Exercise 4.

4. Write the program for Self-Check Exercise 5.

8.4 More on Reading String Data

Each employee in the employee data file has a first name and a last name. If we want to allow more flexibility (for example, a middle initial or middle name), we can use the `getline` function first introduced in Section 3.7 to read the entire name and store it in a string object. To do this correctly, we need to separate the employee name from the rest of the data in the employee record. We show a modified data file next that uses the pound character '#' to mark the end of each employee name:

```
Jim Andrew Baxter#      35.5    7.25<nwln>
Adrian Cybriwsky#       40.0    6.50<nwln>
Ayisha W. Mertens#      20.0    8.00<nwln><eof>
```

We can identify the pound character as a string delimiter symbol by passing it as the third argument in a call to function `getline`. The statement

```
getline(eds, name, '#');     // # is string delimiter
```

extracts from input stream `eds` a sequence of characters ending with # and stores all characters except the # in string object `name`.

Using *ignore* to Advance Past the Newline Character

Often we use the `getline` function to extract a sequence of characters up to and including a newline character. However, remember that `getline` does not skip leading white space, so if a newline character is encountered at the beginning of the characters to be extracted, `getline` will stop immediately and won't perform the expected task.

This can happen when both the extraction operator and the `getline` function are used to extract data from the same input stream. To illustrate, let's consider putting each employee's data on two lines instead of using # as a delimiter character after the name:

```
Jim Andrew Baxter<nwln>
35.5    7.25<nwln>
Adrian Cybriwsky<nwln>
40.0    6.50<nwln>
Ayisha W. Mertens<nwln>
20.0    8.00<nwln><eof>
```

We can use the next `while` loop to read and process all records of this file. For each employee, it reads the contents of the first line into string object `name` and the contents of the second line into variables `hours` and `rate`. Loop exit occurs when the end of the data file is reached.

```
payroll = 0.0;

// Get name of first employee.
getline(eds, name);
while (!eds.eof())
{
    // Get current employee salary data.
    eds >> hours >> rate;
    salary = hours * rate;
    pds << name << " " << salary << endl;
    payroll += salary;

    // Get name of next employee.
    getline(eds, name);
}   // end while
```

Given our six-line data sample, the first call to `getline` reads the first employee's name. Executing the first input statement in the loop

```
eds >> hours >> rate;
```

advances the input stream buffer pointer for stream eds to the <nwln> character at the end of the second line:

```
35.5    7.25<nwln>
            ↑
```

If we leave the input stream buffer pointer here, the next call to getline (to extract the second employee's name) would process just the <nwln> without reading any characters into string object name. The **null string**—an empty string containing zero characters—would be stored in name.

null string
An empty string containing zero characters.

At this point, the next character in the stream would be the first letter of an employee's name (the A in Adrian). The next input statement to execute

```
eds >> hours >> rate;
```

attempts to read a number into hours and into rate. Because the next character to read is the letter A, each read operation terminates immediately. The value of hours and rate are undefined, so an output record with an empty name and meaningless payroll data will be written to the output file.

One way to skip the newline character and avoid this problem is to use the fstream function ignore just before the call to getline in the while loop:

```
// Get name of next employee.
eds.ignore(100, '\n');    // skip through first '\n'
getline(eds, name);
```

This call to the ignore function skips up to 100 characters in the specified stream (eds) until the character argument '\n' is encountered. The character argument is also extracted and ignored. The ignore acts like an input operation except it does not store the characters extracted from the stream. Table 8.2 summarizes the functions getline and ignore.

Table 8.2 Functions getline and ignore

`getline(istream& ins, string& str)`	Reads all characters from input stream ins up to the first newline into string str. The newline character is extracted but not stored.
`getline(istream& ins, string& str, char delimiter)`	Reads all characters from input stream ins up to the first occurrence of delimiter into string str. The character is extracted but not stored.
`ins.ignore(int n, char delimiter)`	Extract (but do not store) up to n characters from stream ins through the first occurrence of the deliminator character. If the delimiter is one of the first n characters, it will be extracted but not stored.

EXERCISES FOR SECTION 8.4

Self-Check

1. Change `processEmp` (Listing 8.5) to write the name and salary for a given employee on separate lines. Explain the changes that have to be made.

2. Explain the differences between using the input operator `>>` and function `getline` to read string data.

3. Explain the effect of the statement

   ```
   eds.ignore(80, '*');
   ```

4. If we use `getline(eds, name, '#')` in `processEmp` (Listing 8.5) to read an employee's name:

   a. What would be the effect, if any, of trailing blanks and the `<nwln>` character at the end of an employee data record in the input stream?

   b. What would be the effect, if any, of leading blanks in an employee record in the input stream?

Programming

1. Write a function `skipNewline` that reads one character at a time in the designated stream up to and including the next newline (if any), and then leaves the stream pointer at the first character in the stream after the newline. Function `skipNewline` should require only one argument—the stream for which the skip operation is to be carried out.

2. Write a function `compress` that removes all white space (blanks and newline characters) from a file. Function `compress` should have two arguments, the input file and the output file.

8.5 Input/Output Manipulators

Section 5.3 described the input/output manipulator `setw`, which controls the width of an output field. Earlier, we introduced an additional manipulator, `endl`, which is used to insert the newline character into an output stream. In this section, we complete the discussion of i/o manipulators by introducing three other manipulators: `setprecision`, `fixed`, and `showpoint`. The manipulators are defined in libraries `iostream` and `iomanip`.

EXAMPLE 8.7

The next output statement uses three manipulators to control the appearance of **x** (type **float**).

```
cout << "The value of x is "
     << fixed
     << showpoint
     << setprecision(4) << x << endl;
```

The manipulator **fixed** causes real numbers to be displayed in decimal rather than scientific notation. The manipulator **showpoint** ensures that the decimal point will always appear (even for whole numbers) and that trailing zeros will be shown. The manipulator **setprecision(4)** sets the precision to four decimal places. These manipulators remain in effect (until changed) for future output statements.

Next we show how the earlier output statement would display some sample values of x. Notice that all the numbers have a decimal point followed by four digits.

```
The value of x is 3.4500
The value of x is 67.1234
The value of x is —1.0000
The value of x is 567890.5123
```

Table 8.3 shows some of the manipulators. To use **setw** and **setprecision**, you need to include library **iomanip**. To use the others, you

Table 8.3   Input/Output Manipulators

setw(int n)	Sets the width of the next output value only to the argument. After output, the width returns to the default of 0.
setprecision(int n)	Sets the precision to the argument. The default is 6.
boolalpha	Enables false and true to be extracted from an input stream or inserted into an output stream as values of type bool variables. The default is to use 0 for false and 1 for true.
noboolalpha	Resets bool input/output to the default values (0 and 1).
fixed	Causes all floating-point numbers to be displayed in decimal notation.
scientific	Causes all floating-point numbers to be displayed in scientific notation.
showpoint	Causes a decimal point to always be displayed.
noshowpoint	A decimal point may not be displayed for whole numbers.
left	Left-adjust output in field.
right	Right-adjust output in field (the default).
skipws	Skip white space on input (the default).
noskipws	Don't skip white space on input.

need to include library `iostream`. The last pair of manipulators, `skipws` and `noskipws`, affects input operations only.

The manipulator `left` changes justification from right-justification (the default) to left-justification. Often, it is preferable to display strings left-justified in a field. After displaying the string, the manipulator `right` should be used to reset justification to the default.

EXERCISES FOR SECTION 8.5

Self-Check

1. Show the effect of executing the output statement

   ```
   cout << scientific << showpoint << setprecision(2)
        << setw(10) << 235.423
        << setw(10) << 13.45 << endl;
   ```

2. How would the output for Self-Check Exercise 1 change if manipulator `scientific` were used instead of `fixed`?

3. Show the effect of executing the output statement

   ```
   cout << setw(10) << left << "Janis"
        << setw(10) << right << "Joplin" << endl;
   ```

   How many blanks would appear between the two strings?

4. Answer Self-Check Exercise 3 with the words `left` and `right` transposed.

Programming

1. Write a program fragment that displays the table below. Left-align each column heading with the columns of numbers that follow. Leave 10 spaces between the column headings.

   ```
   n          n x n
   1          1
   2          4
   3          9
   . . .
   12         144
   ```

2. Write a program fragment that displays the symbol for some common mathematical constants in one column, the constant name in the second column, the constant's value in scientific notation in the third column, and in normal decimal notation in the fourth column. The columns should be neatly aligned. The constant value should be displayed accurate to 5 decimal points. Some constants are pi (π), the gravitational constant (g), and Euler's number (e).

8.6 Common Programming Errors

When you first start using external files, there are many opportunities for error. The operating system must be able to connect an external file to its associated input stream. Your program must be able to correctly determine when all the data in a file have been read. We discuss some common errors next.

- *Connecting streams and external files:* To use an external file in your program, you first must declare a stream object and establish a connection between the file name as it is known to the operating system and the name of the stream object in your program. In C++, you establish this connection with function open. Once you establish this connection, use the stream name in all references to the file in your program. Normally, you won't receive a compiler or an execution-time diagnostic if a call to the open function fails to open a file successfully. For this reason, use function `fail` to verify that function open did its job. If the operating system was unable to find the file you were trying to connect to stream ins, the function call ins.`fail()` will return true.

- *Using input and output streams incorrectly:* Always be careful to prefix each call to a file processing function with the correct stream name. For example, using an output stream name with a file input operation such as get will cause a compiler error message such as "Get is not a member of ofstream". This message indicates that you've incorrectly tried to use the get function with an output file stream.

- *Reading past the end of a file:* An execution time error such as "attempt to read beyond end of file" will occur if a read operation is performed after all data in a file have been processed. The most likely cause for such an error is a loop that executes once too often.

- *Matching data in an input stream to input data stores:* Make sure that the order and type of the data stores (objects and variables) listed after the extraction >> operators are consistent with the order and type of the data in the specified stream. Usually you won't get a run-time error because of data inconsistencies. Instead, incorrect and sometimes undefined information will be stored. When debugging and testing a program, start by echo-printing the values stored in input variables to verify that your test data was read correctly. Remember that any character (not just white space) that's not a valid numeric character will terminate the reading of a numeric input value. The numeric value of the characters read to that point will be stored. If no characters were read, the value stored is undefined.

- *White space and input:* For all input involving the extraction operator, leading white space is ignored—even when reading a single character or character string. If your program requires that white space be treated as any other character, use function get to read a single character at a time.

Trailing white space also terminates the extraction of characters for strings and for numeric data. You can read a string that contains white space by using the member function `getline`. However, you must use some character (often the newline) to mark the end of the string to be extracted.

- *Proper handling of the newline character during input:* When reading character or string data mixed with numeric data, you must make sure that you handle the newline character properly. Often, you must use the `ignore` function to skip over a newline character at the end of a number before reading a string that ends with a newline.

- *Input/output settings:* Most format settings will remain set in a particular state until changed. However, the field width setting always reverts back to your system default value (usually `0`) if it is not set again prior to the input or output of the next data element. When this occurs, data elements may be inserted into an output stream with no separating blanks and will be hard to read.

Chapter Review

1. Function `get` is used to extract characters from an input stream and function `put` to insert characters into an output stream. Unlike the extraction operator `>>`, the `get` function does not skip white space.

2. The operating system keeps a directory of all external files associated with your computer. These files are known to the system by an external file name.

3. The C++ `iostream` library function `open` establishes a connection between the external file name and the name of the stream to be processed by your program.

4. Input streams should be declared as type `ifstream` objects and output streams as type `ofstream` objects.

5. The `eof` function can be used to test for the end of a stream and the `close` function to disconnect an external file from its associated stream.

6. The newline character breaks a stream into a sequence of lines. Be especially careful reading string data when the string delimiter is the newline character. In this case, leading newline characters won't be skipped but will terminate data entry. Use the `ignore` function to skip over a leading newline character. You can also pass a third argument to the `endline` function if you want to use a different character as a string delimiter.

7. The input/output manipulators in Table 8.3 are used to control the format or appearance of displayed output.

Summary of New C++ Constructs

Construct	Effect
Stream Declarations	Declares ins and outs as stream variables.
`ifstream ins;` `ofstream outs;`	
open, fail, and close operations on Data File Streams	
`ins.open(inData);`	Establishes the connection between the external file named inData and the stream ins.

`if (ins.fail())`
`{`
`   cerr << "Oops! " << endl;`
`   return EXIT_FAILURE;`
`}`
	Displays an error message and returns immediately if the open operation failed.

`ins.close();`	Closes or disconnects stream ins.
Input/Output with get, put, getline, and ignore	
`ins.get(ch);`	Gets the next character from the stream ins.
`ins >> i;`	The next integer is read from file ins as a string of characters, then converted to a binary number and stored in i.
`outs.put(ch);` `outs << i;`	Puts the character in ch to the stream outs, followed by a sequence of characters representing the value of i.
`ins.ignore(80, '\n');`	Extracts and skips up to 80 characters in input stream ins up to and including the first occurrence of the delimiter '\n'.
`getline(ins, name);`	Extracts the characters in input stream ins through the next newline and stores all characters except the newline in name.
`getline(ins, name, '#');`	Extracts the characters in input stream ins through the next character # and stores all characters except the # in name.
End-of-File Function	

`ins.get(ch);`
`while (!ins.eof())`
`{`
`   outs.put(ch);`
`   ins.get(ch);`
`}`
	Data characters are read from stream ins and written to stream outs until the end of the stream is reached.

Quick-Check Exercises

1. The statement

   _____ . _____ (_____);

   associates external file `data.txt` with stream `ins`.

2. Write a condition that's true when the operation described above for stream `ins` does not succeed.

3. The _____ character separates a stream into lines.

4. When would you use `getline` to read a string from a stream rather than the extraction operator `>>` ?

5. What function often needs to be called after `getline` and why?

6. Correct the C++ program segment shown below. Explain the changes you make.

   ```
   while (!ins.eof())
   {
       ins.get(ch);
       outs.put(ch);
   }
   ```

7. What does the symbol `endl` represent? What do we call this symbol in C++? Where is it defined?

8. Write a call to function `getline` that extracts up to 60 characters from stream `ins` or all characters through the first `*` character.

9. Write an output statement that displays the value of x right-justified in a field of width 10, in decimal notation with four decimal places of precision.

10. If x has the value `34.567`, show how x would be displayed by the statement:

    ```
    outs << fixed << setprecision(2) << x << "*"
        << scientific << x << endl;
    ```

11. What error could occur if you forget to close an output file?

Review Questions

1. List three advantages to using files for input and output as opposed to the standard input and output you've used so far in this course.

2. Explain how `get` and `cin` differ in reading data items from a stream.

3. **a.** Explain why there are usually three distinct names associated with a file.

   b. What conventions are followed for choosing each name?

   c. What does the name appearing in a program represent?

    d. Which name appears in the stream variable declaration?

    e. Which name is known to the operating system?

4. Let x and y be type `float`, m and n type `int`, ch1 and ch2 type `char`, and str type `string`. Show the final contents of each variable affected by the input operations below. Indicate any errors that might occur when the statements in each part execute. Assume that the input stream pointer is reset to the first input character before each part executes.

```
345.27 wxyz <nwln>
50 40<nwln>
```

    a. `ins >> x >> y >> ch1 >> ch2 >> str;`
       `ins >> x >> m >> n;`

    b. `ins >> m >> n >> x >> ch1 >> ch2 >> str;`

    c. `ins >> x >> y >> str;`
       `ins >> m >> ch1 >> n >> ch2 >> str;`

    d. `ins >> m >> n >> x >> str;`

5. Write a loop that reads up to ten integer values from a data file and displays them on the screen. If there are not ten integers in the file, the message `"That's all, folks"` should be displayed after the last number.

6. Write a function that copies several data lines typed at the keyboard to an external file. The copy process should be terminated when the user enters an empty line (indicated by two consecutive newlines).

7. Explain how the following manipulators format output data.

    a. The manipulator `right` when inserting a string of length 6 in a field of size 20

    b. The manipulator `noshowpoint` when inserting a floating-point value such as `65.0` into an output stream

    c. The manipulator `setprecision(5)` when inserting a floating-point value such as `25.635248` into an output stream

    d. The manipulator `setw` when inserting an integer value such as `250` into a field of width 8 in an output stream

    e. The manipulator `scientific` when inserting a floating-point value such as `25000143.6352` into an output stream

Programming Projects

1. Write a program system that prints payroll checks using the file produced by the payroll program described in Section 8.3. The format of the checks should be similar to the one shown in Figure 8.2.

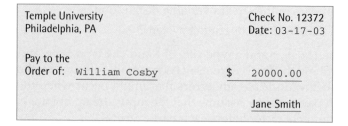

Figure 8.2   Format of check for Programming Project 1

2. Each year the state legislature rates the productivity of the faculty of each of the state-supported colleges and universities. The rating is based on reports submitted by the faculty members indicating the average number of hours worked per week during the school year. Each faculty member is rated, and the university receives an overall rating. The faculty productivity ratings are computed as follows:

a. Highly productive means over 55 hours per week reported.

b. Satisfactory means reported hours per week are between 35 and 55.

c. Overpaid means reported hours per week are less than 35.

   Read the following data from a data file:

Name	Hours
Herm	63
Flo	37
Jake	20
Maureen	55
Saul	72
Tony	40
Al	12

Your program should include functions corresponding to the function prototypes shown below as part of your solution.

```
// Displays table heading
void printHeader();

    // Displays productivity ranking given hours worked
void displayProductivity
   (float); // IN: hours worked per week

// Reads and displays one faculty name from a data stream file
void processName
   (ifstream&);   // IN: stream of names and hours worked
```

```
// Reads data lines from file facHours and displays body
//      of table. Returns number of faculty and sum of hours
//      worked.
// Uses: processName and displayProductivity.
void processData
   (ifstream&,    // IN: stream containing names and hours
    int&,          // INOUT: count of number of faculty
    float&);       // INOUT: sum of hours worked by faculty
```

3. Write a program system that reads several lines of information from a data file and prints each word of the file on a separate line of an output file followed by the number of letters in that word. Also print a count of words in the file on the screen when done. Assume that words are separated by one or more blanks. Reuse as many functions introduced in the text or in the C++ library as possible.

4. Compute the monthly payment and the total payment for a bank loan, given the following:

a. Amount of loan
b. Duration of loan in months
c. Interest rate for loan

Your program should read in one loan at a time, perform the required computation, and print the values of the monthly payment and the total payment.

Test your program with at least the following data (and more if you want).

Loan	Months	Rate
16000	300	6.50
24000	360	5.25
30000	300	5.0
42000	360	5.0
22000	300	4.5
100000	360	4.25

(Hints:

a. The formula for computing a monthly payment is

$$monthPay = \frac{ratem \times expm^{months} \times loan}{expm^{months} - 1.0}$$

where

ratem = rate / 1200.0,

expm = (1.0 + ratem).

b. The formula for computing the total payment is

```
total = monthlyPay * months.
```

Use type `double` data for all calculations.

5. Use your solution to Programming Project 4 as the basis for writing a program that will write a data file containing a table of the following form:

Loan Amount: $1000

Interest rate	Duration (years)	Monthly payment	Total payment

The output file produced by your program should contain payment information on a $1000 loan for interest rates from 4 percent to 7 percent with increments of 0.25 percent. The loan durations should be 20, 25, and 30 years.

6. Whatsamata U. offers a service to its faculty in computing grades at the end of each semester. A program will process three weighted test scores and will calculate a student's average and letter grade (A is 90 to 100, B is 80 to 89, and so on). It will read the student data from a file and write each student's ID, test score, average, and grade to an output file.

Write a program system to provide this valuable service. The data will consist of the three test weights followed by three test scores and a student ID number (four digits) for each student. Calculate the weighted average for each student and the corresponding grade. This information should be printed along with the initial three test scores. The weighted average for each student is equal to

```
weight1 x score1 + weight2 x score2 + weight3 x score3
```

For summary statistics, print the "highest weighted average," "lowest weighted average," "average of the weighted averages," and "total number of students processed." Sample data:

```
0.35   0.25   0.40        (test weights)
100    76    88   1014    (test scores and ID)
```

7. Write a program to read in a string of characters that represent a Roman numeral and then convert it to Arabic form (an integer). The character values for Roman numerals are as follows:

M	1000
D	500
C	100
L	50
X	10
V	5
I	1

Test your program with the following data: LXXXVII (87), CCXIX (219), MCCCLIV (1354), MMDCLXXIII (2673), MCDLXXVI (1476).

8. Because text files can grow very large, some computer systems supply a handy utility program that displays the head and tail of a file where the head is the first four lines and the tail is the last four lines. Write a program that asks the user to type in a file name and then displays the head of the file, a line of dots (three or four dots will do), and the tail of the file. If the file is eight lines long or less, just display the entire file.

9. Write a program to manage a dictionary. Your dictionary should be stored on a text file named `diction.txt` and consist of an alphabetized list of words, one per line. When a user enters a word, scan the dictionary looking for the word. If the word is in the dictionary, say so. If not, display the dictionary word immediately preceding and the word immediately following so the user can see words that are close in spelling. Then ask whether the user wants to add this new word to the dictionary. If the answer is yes, do so and go back to request the next word.

   To insert a word into a file in alphabetical order, simply copy the file to a new, temporary file named `diction.tmp` and move words one at a time from this temporary file back to the original file, inserting the new word when you reach its correct position alphabetically.

10. Write a program that reads two input files whose lines are ordered by a key data field. Your program should merge these two files, writing an output file that contains all lines from both files ordered by the same key field. As an example, if two input files contain student names and grades for a particular class ordered by name, merge the information as shown below.

File 1	File 2	Output file
Adams C	Barnes A	Adams C
Jones D	Johnson C	Barnes A
King B		Johnson C
		Jones D
		King B

You must read one line of a file at a time and either write it or the last line read from the other data file to the output file. A common merge algorithm is the following:

Read a line from each data file
While the end of both files has not been reached
    If the line from file 1 is smaller than the line from file 2
        Write the line from file 1 to the output file and read a new line from file 1.

Else

Write the line from file 2 to the output file and read a new
line from file 2.

Write the remaining lines (if any) from file 1 to the output file.
Write the remaining lines (if any) from file 2 to the output file.

11. Assume there are two input files for a payroll program. The first contains the employee's name (a string), id number (an integer), and
hourly rate (a real number). The second contains the employee's id
number and hours worked (a real number). The records in the first file
are ordered by name and the records in the second file are ordered by
id number. If a person did not work during the current time period,
there will be no record in the second file for that person. Write a file of
payroll records to an output file for all employees. Each record should
contain the employee name followed by # followed by the hours
worked, hourly rate, and pay amount. Use a space as a separator
between items in the output file. There should be a record in the
output file for every person including those who did not work in that
pay period.

12. Write a program that reads data about rainfall for several cities stored
in separate data files. Records in the first data file begin with the city
name followed by a pair of numbers for each of the 12 months of the
previous year. The first item in each pair is the number of days in
the month and the second is the number of days with rain. Records in
the second data file begin with the city name followed by the amount of
rain in inches for all 12 months of the previous year. Write an output file
with a collection of records for each city. The first record will contain
the city name. The second record will contain table headings ("month",
"days with rain", "average rainfall", "average per rainy day"). There
should be 12 additional lines of output, one for each month.

Example: (data shown for January and February)

data file 1:

Sarasota   31   15   28   10   . . .

data file 2:

Sarasota   5.0   35.0   . . .

Output file:

Sarasota	days with	average	average per
month	rain	rainfall	rainy day
January	15	0.16	0.33
February	10	1.25	3.50

. . .

13. InternetLite Corporation is an Internet service provider that charges customers a flat rate of $7.99 for up to 10 hours of connection time. Additional hours or partial hours are charged at $1.99 each. Write a function `charges` that computes the total charge for a customer based on the number of hours of connection time used in a month. The function should also calculate the average cost per hour of the time used (rounded to the nearest cent), so use two output parameters to send back these results. Write a second function `roundMoney` that takes a real number as an input argument and returns as the function value the number rounded to two decimal places. Write a main function that takes data from an input file `usage.txt` and produces an output file `charges.txt`. The data file format is as follows:

Line 1: current month and year as two integers

Other lines: customer number (a 5-digit number) and number of hours used

Here is a sample data file and the corresponding output file:

Data file `usage.txt`

```
10  2009
15362      4.2
42768      11.1
11111      9.9
```

Output file `charges.txt`

```
Charges for 10/2009
```

Customer	Hours used	Charge per hour	Average cost
15362	4.2	7.99	1.90
42768	11.1	11.97	1.08
11111	9.9	7.99	0.81

14. Write a `void` function that will merge the contents of two text files containing chemical elements sorted by atomic number and will produce a sorted file of binary records. The function's parameters will be three file pointers. Each text file line will contain an integer atomic number followed by the element name, chemical symbol, and atomic weight. Here are two sample lines:

```
11        Sodium      Na    22.99
20        Calcium     Ca    40.08
```

The function can assume that one file does not have two copies of the same element and that the binary output file should have this same property. (Hint: When one of the input files is exhausted, do not forget to copy the remaining elements of the other input file to the result file.)

15. Write a program that takes words from a text file and prints each one on a separate line of an output file followed by the number of letters (alphabetic characters) in the word. Any leading or trailing punctuation marks should be removed from the word before it is printed. When all the text has been processed, display on the screen a count of the words in the file. Assume that words are groups of nonwhitespace characters separated by one or more whitespace characters.

Answers to Quick-Check Exercises

1. `ins.open("data.txt");`

2. `(ins.fail())`

3. newline or `'\n'`

4. You'd use `getline` when the string may contain an embedded blank.

5. If the next item to be read is a string, you need to call function `ignore` to advance past the newline character.

6. ```
ins.get(. . .);
while (!ins.eof())
{
    outs.put(. . .);
    ins.get(. . .);
}
```

   The original version will attempt to insert a character into the stream `outs` even after the end of file has been encountered (and there are no more characters to be processed). There will be two copies of the last character read.

7. `endl` represents the newline character; it is a manipulator defined in library `iostream`.

8. `getline(ins, 60, '*');`

9. ```
cout << setw(10) << fixed << showpoint
        << right << setprecision(4) << x << endl;
```

10. `34.57*3.46e+01`

11. The information in the output buffer may not be appended to the end of the output file, so the output file may be incomplete.

Anita Borg

Dr. Anita Borg was a computer science pioneer who made it her goal to revolutionize both the world of technology and women's role in it. She was the founding director of the Institute for Women and Technology, an organization whose mission is to increase the impact of women on all aspects of technology and to increase the positive impact of technology on the lives of the world's women. She also created Systers, one of the oldest global electronic networks of women in computer science, and co-founded the Grace Hopper Celebration of Women in Computing, a prestigious conference for women in the computer science field. In 1999, President Clinton appointed her to the Commission of the Advancement of Women and Minorities in Science, Engineering, and Technology (CAWMSET), and in 2002 she received the Heinz Award for Technology, the Economy and Employment.

Anita Borg died in April 2003, as the fourth edition of this book was being prepared for publication. We were honored to have this inspirational computer scientist contribute an interview to this book's third edition in 1999, and that interview is included here.

Why did you decide to study computer science, and how did you become interested in the field?
I started as a math major in college, and I later taught myself COBOL from program instruction manuals. Then I went back to school and majored in computer science, and just got completely hooked. I loved the problem solving and the challenge. I loved figuring out how to make these contraptions do what I wanted them to do.

What was your first job in the industry, and what did it entail?
My very first job, in 1969, was writing some simple programs for an insurance company. Once I was out of graduate school, I worked for a startup, where I was the lead designer of a fault-tolerant version of the UNIX operating system.

What kind of projects are you doing for the Institute for Women and Technology?
One project is a partnership with MIT, Purdue, Texas A&M, and Santa Clara University, where interdisciplinary groups of students and faculty develop technology projects based on ideas that come out of workshops with nontechnical women in the local community, brainstorming about ways in which technology could have

a positive impact on their families and communities. One of the ideas is a family scheduler that helps coordinate all members of the family.

What is a typical day like for you?
Running an organization is a very busy thing. I spend my time between writing and communicating with people, either on the phone or via e-mail. I probably give two talks a week. This fall I've been traveling. I give speeches, hold meetings, and find out what women in other countries are doing. For instance, the Third World Organization for Women in Science brought 300 female scientists and engineers from 60 developing countries together to discuss science and technology for sustainable human development. I gave the keynote speech on information technology.

What do you do as a member of CAWMSET?
We've conducted hearings and collected information and next we will put together a report that will be recommendations to the nation, both to the president and Congress, to the states and to industry about how to improve representation of women and minorities in science.

What advice do you have for students entering the computer science field?
I think that it is very, very important to get involved in projects that are connected to real needs and to experience what that's like. So, if there's some way to work on something that is not just an abstract problem, where there are real customers and real users, where you can see the reality of this stuff, it's just incredibly valuable.

I envision a transformation from a technology-driven world in which we wind up with solutions in search of problems to one in which we really look at the problems that are out there and let those drive the technology. This definitely is not happening. The technology culture is one in which we train students to talk to and listen to other brilliant technologists. We train them to believe that by talking to other brilliant technologists, they will come up with ideas for projects and research to work on. Most students don't understand that ordinary people have tremendously brilliant ideas for things that they could work on that would then really push the boundaries of technology.

Besides technical skills, what kind of skills do you think are most important to have for students wanting to go into computer science?
Technical skills are clearly core. However, I think that students should strive for a very broad background, educationally. I think students should study some art, some political science, some sociology, and really try to get as broad a background as they can as undergraduates, because all of that helps them to think. Building an ability to think well in a variety of different disciplines, on a variety of different topics, is really important.

Students should also have a lot of understanding of cultural differences internationally. They should make an effort to get international experience if possible. We are building tools that are at the cutting edge of connecting the entire world; we can't build this stuff in a vacuum.

chapter nine

Data Structures: Arrays and Structs

Learning Objectives

- To learn how to declare and use arrays for storing collections of values of the same type
- To understand how to use a subscript to reference the individual values in an array
- To learn how to process the elements of an array in sequential order using loops
- To learn a method for searching an array
- To learn a method for sorting an array
- To become familiar with Big-O notation for estimating an algorithm's efficiency
- To learn how to declare and use structs to store collections of values of different types
- To understand how to use dot notation to reference the individual values in a struct
- To learn how to use multidimensional arrays for storing tables of data
- To understand how to use arrays whose elements are structs
- To learn how to use character arrays and C-style strings

SIMPLE DATA TYPES, whether built in (`int`, `float`, `bool`, `char`) or user defined (for example, enumeration type `day`), use a single variable to store a value. To solve many programming problems, it's more efficient to group data items together in main memory than to allocate a different variable to hold each item. For example, it's easier to write a program that processes exam scores for a class of 100 students if you can store all the scores in one area of memory and can access them as a group. C++ allows a programmer to group such related data items together into a single composite structured variable. Without such a structured variable, we'd have to allocate 100 different variables to hold each individual score.

In this chapter, we look at two structured data types: the array and the struct. For an array, all items in the collection are the same data type, and we use a subscript to distinguish between them just as we use x_i to reference the ith item in a list. The struct, on the other hand, is an aggregate item that has components of different types. We also study arrays of arrays (multidimensional arrays) and arrays of structs.

9.1   The Array Data Type

array
A collection of data items stored under the same name.

array element
Each individual element in an array.

An **array** is a collection of data items associated with a particular name—for example, all the exam scores for a class of students could be associated with the name scores. We can reference each individual item—called an **array element**—in the array. We designate individual elements by using the array name and the element's position, starting with 0 for the first array element. The first element in the array named scores is referred to as scores[0], the second element as scores[1], and the tenth element as scores[9]. In general, the kth element in the array is referred to as scores[k-1].

C++ stores an array in consecutive storage locations in main memory, one item per memory cell. We can perform some operations, such as passing the array as an argument to a function, on the whole array. We can also access individual array elements and process them like other simple variables.

Array Declaration

Arrays in C++ are specified using *array declarations* that specify the type, name, and size of the array:

```
float x[8];
```

C++ associates eight memory cells with the name x. Each element of array x may contain a single floating-point value. Therefore, a total of eight floating-point values may be stored and referenced using the array name x.

EXAMPLE 9.1

Assume **x** is the array shown in Figure 9.1. Table 9.1 shows some statements that manipulate the elements of this array. Figure 9.2 shows the array after the statements in Table 9.1 execute. Note that only **x[2]** and **x[3]** are changed.

x[0]	x[1]	x[2]	x[3]	x[4]	x[5]	x[6]	x[7]
16.0	12.0	6.0	8.0	2.5	12.0	14.0	-54.5
First	Second	Third		...			Eighth

Figure 9.1   Array x

Table 9.1   Statements that Manipulate Elements of Array x in Figure 9.1

Statement	Explanation
cout << x[0];	Displays the value of x[0], or 16.0.
x[3] = 25.0;	Stores the value 25.0 in x[3].
sum = x[0] + x[1];	Stores the sum of x[0] and x[1], or 28.0, in the variable sum.
sum += x[2];	Adds x[2] to sum. The new sum is 34.0.
x[3] += 1.0;	Adds 1.0 to x[3]. The new x[3] is 26.0.
x[2] = x[0] + x[1];	Stores the sum of x[0] and x[1] in x[2]. The new x[2] is 28.0.

x[0]	x[1]	x[2]	x[3]	x[4]	x[5]	x[6]	x[7]
16.0	12.0	28.0	26.0	2.5	12.0	14.0	-54.5
First	Second	Third		...			Eighth

Figure 9.2   Array x after execution of statements in Table 9.1

EXAMPLE 9.2

The declarations for the plant operations program shown below allocate storage for four arrays, onVacation, vacationDays, dayOff, and plantHours.

```
const int NUM_EMP = 10;      // number of employees
bool onVacation[NUM_EMP];
int vacationDays[NUM_EMP];
enum day {sunday, monday, tuesday, wednesday, thursday,
          friday, saturday};
day dayOff[NUM_EMP];
float plantHours[7];
```

The arrays onVacation and vacationDays (Figure 9.3) have 10 elements, each with subscripts 0 through 9 (value of NUM_EMP − 1). Each element of array onVacation can store a type bool value. The contents of this array indicate which employees are on vacation (onVacation[i] is true if employee i is on vacation). If employees 0, 2, 4, 6, and 8 are on vacation, the array will have the values shown in Figure 9.3. Array vacationDays shows the number of vacation days each employee has remaining.

	onVacation		vacationDays		dayOff
[0]	true	[0]	10	[0]	monday
[1]	false	[1]	12	[1]	wednesday
[2]	true	[2]	3	[2]	tuesday
[3]	false	[3]	8	[3]	friday
[4]	true	[4]	15	[4]	friday
[5]	false	[5]	5	[5]	monday
[6]	true	[6]	6	[6]	thursday
[7]	false	[7]	9	[7]	wednesday
[8]	true	[8]	10	[8]	tuesday
[9]	false	[9]	15	[9]	thursday

Figure 9.3   Arrays `onVacation`, `vacationDays`, and `dayOff`

The array `dayOff` (Figure 9.3) also has 10 elements. Each element stores an enumerator from the enumeration type day, and the value of `dayOff[i]` indicates the weekday employee i has off. Because the data stored in `onVacation[i]`, `vacationDays[i]`, and `dayOff[i]` relate to the ith employee, the three arrays are called **parallel arrays.**

parallel arrays
Two or more arrays with the same number of elements used to store related information about a collection of objects.

The array `plantHours` (Figure 9.4) has seven elements with subscripts 0 through 6. We can use the subscripts 0 through 6 or the enumeration type day to reference these elements. The array element `plantHours[sunday]` (or `plantHours[0]`) indicates how many hours the plant was operating during Sunday of the past week. The array shown in Figure 9.4 indicates that the plant was closed on the weekend, operating single shifts on Monday and Thursday, double shifts on Tuesday and Friday, and a triple shift on Wednesday.

plantHours[sunday]	0.0
plantHours[monday]	8.0
plantHours[tuesday]	16.0
plantHours[wednesday]	24.0
plantHours[thursday]	8.0
plantHours[friday]	16.0
plantHours[saturday]	0.0

Figure 9.4   Array `plantHours`

Array Initialization

The next example shows how to specify the initial contents of an array as part of its declaration.

EXAMPLE 9.3

The statements below declare and initialize three arrays (see Figure 9.5). The list of initial values for each array is enclosed in braces and follows the assignment operator =. The first array element (subscript 0) stores the first value in each list, the second array element (subscript 1) stores the second value, and so on.

```
const int SIZE = 7;
int scores[SIZE] = {100, 73, 88, 84, 40, 97};
char grades[] = {'A', 'C', 'B', 'B', 'F', 'A'};
char myName[SIZE] = {'F', 'R', 'A', 'N', 'K'};
```

The length of the list of initial values can't exceed the size of the array. If the list contains fewer elements than the array size allows, then the value of any element not initialized is system dependent (indicated by ? in Figure 9.5). If the size of the array is not specified, indicated by an empty pair of brackets [ ], the compiler sets the array size to match the number of elements in the initial value list.

Array scores (size 7)

100	73	88	84	40	97	?
[0]	[1]	[2]	[3]	[4]	[5]	[6]

Array grades (size 6)

'A'	'C'	'B'	'B'	'F'	'A'
[0]	[1]	[2]	[3]	[4]	[5]

Array myName (size 7)

'F'	'R'	'A'	'N'	'K'	?	?
[0]	[1]	[2]	[3]	[4]	[5]	[6]

Figure 9.5   Initialization of three arrays

EXAMPLE 9.4

The array declaration

```
string kidNames[] = {"Richard", "Debbie", "Robin",
                     "Shelley", "Dara"};
```

allocates storage for an array of five strings called **kidNames**, storing the string literals shown in the initialization list in this array. The statement

```
cout << kidNames[0] << '/' << kidNames[4] << endl;
```

displays the output line

```
Richard/Dara
```

Array Declaration

Form: *element-type array-name[size]*;
          element-type array-name[size] = {initialization-list};

Example: `char myName[5];`
            `float salaries[NUM_EMP];`
            `char vowels[] = {'A', 'E', 'I', 'O', 'U'};`

Interpretation: The identifier *array-name* describes a collection of array elements, each of which may be used to store data values of type *element-type*. The *size*, enclosed in brackets, [ ], specifies the number of elements contained in the array. The *size* value must be a constant expression consisting of constant values and constant identifiers. This value must be an integer and must be greater than or equal to 1. There is one array element for each value between 0 and the value *size* −1.

In the initialized array declaration, the *size* in brackets is optional. In this case, the number of values in the *initialization-list* determines the array size. The *initialization-list* consists of constant expressions of type *element-type* separated by commas. Element 0 of the array being initialized is set to the first constant, element 1 to the second, and so on.

Array Subscripts

array subscript
A value or expression enclosed in brackets after the array name, specifying which element to access.

subscripted variable
A variable followed by a subscript in brackets, designating a particular array element.

To process the data stored in an array, we must be able to access its individual elements. We use the array name (a variable) and the **array subscript** to do this. The array subscript is enclosed in brackets after the array name and selects a particular array element for processing. For example, if x is the array with eight elements shown earlier in Figure 9.2 and repeated below, then the **subscripted variable** x[0] (read as "x sub 0") references the first element of the array x, x[1] the second element, and x[7] the eighth element. The number enclosed in brackets is the array subscript.

x[0]	x[1]	x[2]	x[3]	x[4]	x[5]	x[6]	x[7]
16.0	12.0	28.0	26.0	2.5	12.0	14.0	-54.5
First element	Second element	Third element		. . .			Eighth element

Understanding the difference between an array subscript value and an array element value is key. The subscripted variable x[i] references a particular element of array x. If i has the value 0, the subscript value is 0, and x[0] is referenced. The value of x[i] in this case is 16.0. If i has the value 2, the subscript value is 2, and the value of x[i] is 28.0.

A subscript can be an expression of any integral type (int, long, short, char, or an enumeration type). However, to create a valid reference, the value of this subscript must be between 0 and one less than the array size. If i has the value 8, the subscript value is 8, and we can't predict the value of x[i] because the subscript value is out of the allowable range.

EXAMPLE 9.5

Table 9.2 shows some simple statements involving the array x shown above and in Figure 9.2. In these statements, i is assumed to be type int with value 5. Make sure you understand each statement. The two attempts to display element x[10], which is not in the array, may result in a run-time error, but they're more likely to display incorrect results.

The last cout line in Table 9.2 uses int(x[4]) as a subscript expression. Because this evaluates to 2, the value of x[2] (*not* x[4]) is displayed. If the value of int(x[4]) were outside the range 0 through 7, its use as a subscript expression would reference a memory cell outside the array.

Two different subscripts are used in each of the three assignment statements at the bottom of the table. The first assignment statement copies the value of x[6] to x[5] (subscripts i+1 and i); the second assignment statement copies the value of x[5] to x[4] (subscripts i−1 and i). The last assignment statement causes a syntax error because there is an expression to the left of the assignment operator.

Array Subscript

Form: *name[subscript]*

Example: x[3*i-2]

Interpretation: The *subscript* must be an integral expression. Each time a subscripted variable is encountered in a program, the *subscript* is evaluated and its value determines which element of array *name* is referenced. The *subscript* value should be between the range 0 and one less than the array size (inclusive). If the *subscript* value is outside this range, a memory cell outside the array will be referenced.

Table 9.2   Some Simple Statements Referencing Array x in Figure 9.2

Statement	Effect
`cout << 3 << ' ' << x[3];`	Displays 3 and 26.0 (value of x[3]).
`cout << i << ' ' << x[i];`	Displays 5 and 12.0 (value of x[5]).
`cout << x[i] + 1;`	Displays 13.0 (value of 12.0 + 1).
`cout << x[i] + i;`	Displays 17.0 (value of 12.0 + 5).
`cout << x[i+1];`	Displays 14.0 (value of x[6]).
`cout << x[i+i];`	Value in x[10] is undefined.
`cout << x[2*i];`	Value in x[10] is undefined.
`cout << x[2*i−3];`	Displays −54.5 (value of x[7]).
`cout << x[(int(x[4])];`	Displays 28.0 (value of x[2]).
`x[i] = x[i+1];`	Assigns 14.0 (value of x[6]) to x[5].
`x[i−1] = x[i];`	Assigns 14.0 (new value of x[5]) to x[4].
`x[i] − 1 = x[i−1];`	Illegal assignment statement. Left side of an assignment operator must be a variable.

EXERCISES FOR SECTION 9.1

Self-Check

1. What is the difference between the expressions x3 and x[3]?

2. For the following declarations, how many memory cells are reserved for data and what type of data can be stored there?
   a. `float prices[15];`
   b. `char grades[20];`
   c. `bool flags[10];`
   d. `int coins[5];`
   e. `string monthNames [12];`

3. Write array declarations for each of the following:
   a. Array names with element type string, size 100
   b. Array checks with element type float, size 20
   c. Array madeBonus with element type bool, size 7
   d. Array daysInMonth with element type int, size 12

4. Which of the following array declarations are legal? Defend your answer and describe the result of each legal declaration. For questions (a) and (e), use enumeration type day as defined in Example 9.2.
   a. `float payroll[friday];`
   b. `int workers[3] = {6, 8, 8, 0};`

c. `char vowels[] = {'a', 'e', 'i', 'o', 'u'};`

d. `int freq[12] = {0, 0, 3, 7, 10, 16, 28, 31};`

e. `day firstDay[] = {monday, friday, wednesday, saturday, friday};`

f. `string names [] = {"Harry", "Sally", "Don", "Sue"};`

Programming

1. Provide array type declarations for representing the following:

   a. A group of rooms (living room, dining room, kitchen, and so on) that have a given area

   b. A group of rooms as in part (a), but the array elements should indicate whether the room is carpeted

   c. Elementary school grade levels (0 through 6, where 0 means kindergarten) with a given number of students per grade

   d. A selection of colors (strings) representing the eye color of five people

   e. Answer (d) above assuming each array element stores an enumerator from the enumeration type below.

   `typedef color = {blue, green, hazel, brown, black};`

   f. An array `daysInMonth` with 31 (number of days in January) in element 0, 28 (number of days in February) in element 1, and so on.

9.2 Sequential Access to Array Elements

Many programs process all the elements of an array in sequential order, starting with the first element (subscript 0). To enter data into an array, print its contents, or perform other sequential processing tasks, use a for loop whose loop-control variable (i) is also the array subscript (x[i]). Increasing the value of the loop-control variable by 1 causes the next array element to be processed.

EXAMPLE 9.6

The array cube declared below stores the cubes of the first 10 integers (for example, `cube[1]` is `1`, `cube[9]` is `729`).

```
int cube[10];   // array of cubes
```

The for statement

```
for (int i = 0; i < 10; i++)
    cube[i] = i * i * i;
```

initializes this array as shown in Figure 9.6.

[0]	[1]	[2]	[3]	[4]	[5]	[6]	[7]	[8]	[9]
0	1	8	27	64	125	216	343	512	729

Figure 9.6   Array cube

EXAMPLE 9.7

In Listing 9.1, the statements

```
const int MAX_ITEMS = 8;
float x[MAX_ITEMS];  // array of data
```

allocate storage for an array **x** with subscripts 0 through 7. The program uses three **for** loops to process the array. The loop-control variable **i**, with **i** in the range (0 <= i <= 7), is also the array subscript in each loop. The first **for** loop,

```
for (int i = 0; i < MAX_ITEMS; i++)
    cin >> x[i];
```

reads one data value into each array element (the first item is stored in **x[0]**, the second item in **x[1]**, and so on). The **cin** line executes for each value of **i** from 0 to 7; each repetition causes a new data value to be read and stored in **x[i]**. The subscript **i** determines the array element to receive the next data value. The data shown in the first line of the sample execution of Listing 9.1 cause the array to be initialized as shown in Figure 9.1.

Listing 9.1   Displaying a table of differences

```
// File: showDiff.cpp
// Computes the average value of an array of data and displays
//     the difference between each value and the average
#include <iostream>
#include <iomanip>
using namespace std;

int main()
{
    const int MAX_ITEMS = 8;
    float x[MAX_ITEMS];              // array of data
    float average;                   // average value of data
    float sum;                       // sum of the data

    // Enter the data.
    cout << "Enter " << MAX_ITEMS << " numbers:";
    for (int i = 0; i < MAX_ITEMS; i++)
        cin >> x[i];
```

(continued)

Listing 9.1   Displaying a table of differences (continued)

```
// Compute the average value.
sum = 0.0;                              // initialize sum
for (int i = 0; i < MAX_ITEMS; i++)
    sum += x[i];                        // add next element to sum
average = sum / MAX_ITEMS;              // get average value

cout << "The average value is " << average << endl << endl;

// Display the difference between each item and the average.
cout << "Table of differences between x[i] and the average."
     << endl;
cout << setw(4) << "next" << setw(8) << "x[next]"
     << setw(14) << "difference" << endl;
for (int i = 0; i < MAX_ITEMS; i++)
    cout << setw(4) << i << setw(8) << x[i]
         << setw(14) << (x[i] - average) << endl;

return 0;
}
```

```
Enter 8 numbers: 16 12 6 8 2.5 12 14 -54.5
The average value is 2

Table of differences between x[i] and the average.
   i        x[i]      difference
   0         16           14
   1         12           10
   2          6            4
   3          8            6
   4         2.5          0.5
   5         12           10
   6         14           12
   7        -54.5        -56.5
```

The second **for** loop accumulates the sum of all eight elements of array **x** in the variable **sum**. Each time the **for** loop body repeats, the statement

```
sum += x[i];            // add next element to sum
```

adds the next element of array **x** to **sum**. Table 9.3 traces the first three loop iterations. The last **for** loop displays a table showing each array element, **x[i]**, and the difference between that element and the average value, **x[i] − average.**

Table 9.3   Trace of Second `for` Loop in Listing 9.1 (three iterations)

Statement Part	i	x[i]	sum	Effect
`sum = 0.0;`			0.0	Sets sum to zero
`for (i = 0; i < MAX_ITEMS; i++)`	0	16.0		Sets i to zero
`sum += x[i];`			16.0	Add x[0] to sum
increment and test i	1	12.0		1 < 8 is true
`sum += x[i];`			28.0	Add x[1] to sum
increment and test i	2	6.0		2 < 8 is true
`sum += x[i];`			34.0	Add x[2] to sum

Strings and Arrays of Characters

A `string` object uses an array whose elements are type `char` to store a character string. That's why the position of the first character of a string object is 0, not 1. If `name` is type `string`, we can use either `name[i]` or `name.at(i)` to access the `i`th character in string `name`.

EXAMPLE 9.8

The program in Listing 9.2 forms a *cryptogram*, or coded message, by replacing each letter in a message (a data string) with its code symbol. For example, in the simple next-letter-substitution code, we want to replace all **a**s with **b**, all **b**s with **c**, and so on. In Listing 9.2, the string constant **ALPHABET** contains all 26 lowercase letters and the string **CODE** contains the corresponding code symbols that appear under each letter.

The for loop heading

```
for (int i = 0; i < message.length(); i++)
```

processes each character in string message from the first to the last (subscript `message.length()` − 1). The statement

```
message[i] = CODE.at(pos);
```

replaces the letter in **message[i]** with its corresponding code symbol. This statement executes only if the value of **pos** is between **0** and **25**, or when function **find** is able to locate the lowercase form of **message[i]** in string **ALPHABET**. See Table 3.3 to review the string functions.

Listing 9.2   Cryptogram generator

```cpp
// File: cryptogram.cpp
// Displays a cryptogram.

#include <string>
#include <iostream>
#include <cctype>
using namespace std;

int main()
{
    const string ALPHABET = "abcdefghijklmnopqrstuvwxyz";
    const string CODE =     "bcdefghijklmnopqrstuvwxyza";
    string message;         // message to encode
    char ch;                // next message character
    int pos;                // its position

    cout << "Enter a string to encode: ";
    getline(cin, message);

    // Encode message.
    for (int i = 0; i < message.length(); i++)
    {
        ch = tolower(message.at(i));    // ch to lowercase
        pos = ALPHABET.find(ch);        // find position of ch
        if ((pos >= 0) && (pos < 26))
            message[i] = CODE.at(pos);
    }

    cout << "The cryptogram is        : " << message << endl;

    return 0;
}
```

```
Enter a string to encode: This is a string.
The cryptogram is        : uijt jt b tusjoh.
```

EXERCISES FOR SECTION 9.2

Self-Check

1. **a.** If an array has 10 elements, what is displayed by the fragment
    below?

```
for (int i = 9; i >= 0; i--)
    cout << i << " " << x[i] * x[i] << ",";
cout << endl;
```

b. What is displayed by the fragment below?

```
i = 0;
while (i < 10)
{
    cout << x[i] << " ";
    i += 2;
}
cout << endl;
```

2. The sequence of statements below changes the initial contents of array x displayed by the program in Listing 9.1. Describe what each statement does to the array and show the final contents of array x after all statements execute.

```
i = 2;
x[i] = x[i] + 10.0;
x[i-1] = x[2*i-1];
x[i+1] = x[2*i] + x[2*i+1];
for (int i = 4; i < 7; i++)
    x[i] = x[i+1];
for (int i = 2; i >= 0; i--)
    x[i+1] = x[i];
```

3. Trace the execution of the for loop in Listing 9.1 when the string read into message is "4 Hearts."

Programming

1. Write program statements that will do the following to array x, shown in Listing 9.1:

   a. Display all elements with odd subscripts on one line.

   b. Calculate the sum of the elements with odd subscripts only.

2. Write a loop that displays the characters in string message in reverse order.

3. Write a program to store in string reverse the characters in string message in reverse order and to display "Is a palindrome" if message and reverse contain the same string.

9.3 Array Arguments

The C++ operators (for example, <, ==, >, +, −) can be used to manipulate only one array element at a time. Consequently, an array name in an expression will generally be followed by its subscript. The next example shows the use of array elements as function arguments.

Array Elements as Arguments

EXAMPLE 9.9

You can use function **exchange** (see Listing 9.3) to switch the contents of its two floating-point arguments. The formal parameters **a1** and **a2** are used for both input and output and are therefore passed by reference.

This function may be used to exchange the contents of any two floating-point variables. The statement

```
exchange(x, y);
```

switches the original contents of the floating-point variables **x** and **y**.

This function may also be used to exchange the contents of any pair of elements of a floating-point array. For example, the function call

```
exchange(s[3], s[5]);
```

switches the contents of array elements **s[3]** and **s[5]** (see Figure 9.7). C++ treats the call to **exchange** in the same way as the earlier call involving **x** and **y**. In both cases, the contents of two floating-point memory locations (**s[3]** and **s[5]**) are exchanged.

Besides passing individual array elements to functions, we can write functions that have arrays as arguments. Such functions can manipulate some, or all, of the elements corresponding to an actual array argument.

Listing 9.3 Function to exchange the contents of two floating-point memory locations

```
void exchange
    (float& a1, float& a2)            // INOUT
{
    // Local data    . . .
    float temp;
    temp = a1;
    a1 = a2;
    a2 = temp;
}
```

s[0]	s[1]	s[2]	s[3]	s[4]	s[5]	s[6]	s[7]
16.0	12.0	28.0	26.0	2.5	12.0	14.0	-54.5

s[0]	s[1]	s[2]	s[3]	s[4]	s[5]	s[6]	s[7]
16.0	12.0	28.0	12.0	2.5	26.0	14.0	-54.5

Figure 9.7   Array **s** before (top) and after (bottom) exchange of **s[3]** and **s[5]**;

Passing an Array Argument

We can pass an entire array to a function by writing its name with no subscript in the argument list of a function call. What is actually stored in the function's corresponding formal parameter is the address of the initial array element. In the function body, we can use subscripts with the formal parameter to reference the array's elements. However, the function manipulates the actual array, not its own personal copy, so an assignment to one of the array elements by a statement in the function changes the contents of the actual array.

The next two examples illustrate the use of arrays as function arguments. We assume the calling function declares three floating-point arrays, x, y, and z, each of size 5:

```
const int MAX_SIZE = 5;          // size of arrays
float x[MAX_SIZE];
float y[MAX_SIZE],
float z[MAX_SIZE];
```

EXAMPLE 9.10

Function **sameArray** in Listing 9.4 determines whether two arrays, represented by formal array parameters a and b, are identical. We consider two arrays to be identical if the first element of one is the same as the first element of the other, the second element of one is the same as the second element of the other, and so on.

We can determine that the arrays are not identical by finding a single pair of unequal elements. Before each iteration, the second part of the **while** loop condition

```
while ((i < size-1) && (a[i] == b[i]))
```

compares the ith elements of the actual arrays corresponding to formal array parameters a and b. Loop exit occurs when a pair of unequal elements is found or just before the last pair is tested.

Listing 9.4 Function `sameArray`

```cpp
// File: sameArray.cpp
// Compares two float arrays for equality by comparing
//    corresponding elements

// Pre:  a[i] and b[i] (0 <= i <= size-1) are assigned
//       values.
// Post: Returns true if a[i] == b[i] for all i in range
//       0 through size - 1; otherwise, returns false.

bool sameArray
    (float a[],                 // IN: float arrays to be compared
     float b[],
     const int size)            // IN: size of the arrays
{
    // Local data  ...
    int i;              // loop control variable and array subscript
    i = 0;
    while ((i < size-1) && (a[i] == b[i]))
        i++;

    return (a[i] == b[i]);      // define result
}
```

After loop exit, the statement

```cpp
return (a[i] == b[i]);              // define result
```

defines the function result (true or false). If loop exit occurs because the pair of elements with subscript i is not equal, the function result is false. If loop exit occurs because the last pair of elements is reached (i equal to size-1), the function result will be true if these elements are equal and false if they're not.

As an example of how you might use function **sameArray**, the **if** statement

```cpp
if (sameArray(x, y, MAX_SIZE))
    cout << "The arrays x and y are identical. " << endl;
else
    cout << "The arrays x and y are different. " << endl;
```

displays a message indicating whether the actual argument arrays **x** and **y** are identical.

Notice that we write the actual array **x** without brackets in the function call. Also, we declare formal array parameter **a** as **float a[ ]** in the parameter list for function **sameArray**. We discuss the reasons for this after the next example.

EXAMPLE 9.11

The assignment statement

```
z = x + y;      // invalid array operation
```

is invalid because the operator + can't be used with array arguments. However, we can use function **addArray** (see Listing 9.5) to add together, element by element, the contents of any two floating-point arrays of the same size. The function stores the sum of each pair of elements with subscript i in element i of a third floating-point array. The function call

```
addArray(MAX_SIZE, x, y, z);
```

causes the addition of corresponding elements in arrays **x** and **y** with the result stored in the corresponding element of array **z**.

Figure 9.8 shows the argument correspondence for arrays established by the function call

```
addArray(MAX_SIZE, x, y, z);
```

Because C++ always passes arrays by reference, arrays **a**, **b**, and **c** in the function **addArray** data area are represented by the addresses of the actual arrays **x**, **y**, and **z** used in the call. Thus the values of the elements of **x** and **y** used in the addition are taken directly from the arrays **x** and **y** in the calling function, and the function results are stored directly in array **z** in the calling function. After execution of the function, $z[0]$ will contain the sum of $x[0]$ and $y[0]$, or 3.8; $z[1]$ will contain 6.7; and so on. Arrays **x** and **y** will be unchanged. In fact, the use of the reserved word **const** in front of the formal parameters **a** and **b** ensures that the contents of the corresponding actual arguments (**x** and **y**) can't be changed by the function. We use **const** in the declaration of formal parameter **size** for the same reason.

Notice that the formal parameter list in Listing 9.5 doesn't indicate how many elements are in the array parameters. Because C++ doesn't allocate space in memory for a copy of the actual array, the compiler doesn't need to know the size of an array parameter. In fact, since we don't provide the size, we have the flexibility to pass to function **addArray** three arrays of any size. In each call to **addArray**, the first argument tells the function how many elements to process. In the function prototype, we use **float[ ]** to represent each formal array parameter:

```
void addArray(int, const float[], const float[], float[]);
```

Listing 9.5   Function `addArray`

```
// File: addArray.cpp
// Stores the sum of a[i] and b[i] in c[i]

// Sums pairs of array elements with subscripts ranging from 0
//       to size-1
// Pre:  a[i] and b[i] are defined (0 <= i <= size-1)
// Post: c[i] = a[i] + b[i] (0 <= i <= size-1)

void addArray
  (int size,               // IN: the size of the arrays
   const float a[],        // IN: the first array
   const float b[],        // IN: the second array
   float c[])              // OUT: result array
{
   // Add corresponding elements of a and b and store in c.
   for (int i = 0; i < size; i++)
       c[i] = a[i] + b[i];
}
```

Figure 9.8   Argument correspondence for `addArray(MAX_SIZE, x, y, z);`

We summarize important points about arrays as function arguments next.

> ### Arrays as Function Arguments
>
> - In C++, arrays are passed by reference. Therefore, a formal array parameter in a function (**c** in Listing 9.5) represents the address of the first element of the actual array argument (**z** in Figure 9.8). All references to the formal array parameter are therefore references to the corresponding actual array argument in the calling function.
> - In a function definition or a function prototype, we use empty brackets [ ] to inform the compiler that a formal parameter represents an array. We don't need to specify the size of this array because the compiler doesn't allocate storage for a copy of the actual array in the called function data area.
> - The reserved word **const** indicates a formal array parameter that can't be changed by a function. If a function attempts to modify the contents of such an array, the compiler will generate an error message.
> - In the function call, write the name of an actual argument array without using brackets after the array name.

EXERCISES FOR SECTION 9.3

Self-Check

1. In function `sameArray`, what will be the value of `i` when the statement

   ```
   return (a[i] == b[i]);
   ```

   executes if array `a` is equal to array `b`? If the third elements don't match?

2. Write the `return` statement for `sameArray` using an `if` statement.

3. Rewrite the `exchange` and `sameArray` functions to work with integer operands rather than floating-point operands.

4. Describe how to modify function `addArray` to obtain a new function, `subtractArray`, that performs an element-by-element subtraction of two integer arrays of the same size.

5. Explain why the size of an array must be passed as an argument to a function that processes an array.

Programming

1. Write a function that assigns a value of `true` to element `i` of the output array if element `i` of one input array has the same value as element `i` of the other input array; otherwise, assign a value of `false`.

2. Write a function `scalarMultArray` that multiplies an entire floating-point array `x` (consisting of n elements) by a single floating-point scalar `c`. Array `x` should be used for input/output.

9.4 Reading Part of an Array

Often a programmer doesn't know in advance exactly how many elements will be stored in an array. As an example, let's say you're writing a program to process exam scores. There may be 150 students in one section, 200 in the next, and so on. Because you must declare the array size before program execution begins, you must allocate enough storage space so that the program can process the largest expected array without error.

When you read the array data into memory, you should begin filling the array starting with the first element (at subscript 0) and be sure to keep track of how many data items are actually stored in the array. The part of the array that contains data is called the **filled subarray.** The *length* of the filled subarray is the number of data items that are actually stored in the array.

filled subarray
The portion of a partially filled array that contains data.

EXAMPLE 9.12

Function readScores in Listing 9.6 reads and stores in its array argument **scores** up to **MAX_SIZE** exam scores, where **MAX_SIZE** is an input argument that represents the size of the actual array corresponding to **scores**. The output argument **sectionSize** represents the length of the filled subarray and is initialized to zero. Within the loop, the statements

```
scores[sectionSize] = tempScore;    // save score just read
sectionSize++;
```

store the score just read (value of **tempScore**) in the next array element and increment **sectionSize**. After loop exit, the value of **sectionSize** is the length of the filled subarray **array**. The **if** statement displays a warning message when the array is filled (when **sectionSize** equals **MAX_SIZE**).

Listing 9.6   Function readScores

```
// File: readScores.cpp
// Reads an array of exam scores for a lecture section
//    of up to MAX_SIZE students.

// Pre: None
// Post: The data values are stored in array scores.
//       The number of values read is stored in sectionSize.
//       (0 <= sectionSize < MAX_SIZE).
```

(continued)

Listing 9.6   Function `readScores` (continued)

```cpp
void readScores
   (int scores[],          // OUT: array to contain all scores read
    const int MAX_SIZE,    // IN: max size of array scores
    int& sectionSize)      // OUT: number of elements read
{
   // Local data  . . .
   const int SENTINEL = -1;         // sentinel value
   int tempScore;                   // temporary storage for each score

   // Read each array element until done.
   cout << "Enter next score after the prompt or enter "
        << SENTINEL << " to stop." << endl;
   sectionSize = 0;                 // initial class size

   cout << "Score: ";
   cin >> tempScore;
   while ((tempScore != SENTINEL) && (sectionSize < MAX_SIZE))
   {
      scores[sectionSize] = tempScore;      // save score just read
      sectionSize++;
      cout << "Score: ";
      cin >> tempScore;
   } // end while

   // Sentinel was read or array is filled.
   if (tempScore != SENTINEL)
   {
      cout << "Array is filled!" << endl;
      cout << tempScore << " not stored" << endl;
   }
}
```

Often when processing array data, we prefer to read the data from a file rather than type it in each time. Function `readScoresFile` (Listing 9.7) performs this operation assuming `ifstream` parameter `ins` is associated with a data file. We based this function on `readScores`. The major difference is the addition of parameter `ins` and the use of the `eof` function to detect the end of the data file instead of using a sentinel value. Also, we removed the prompts. If you prefer to use a sentinel value, the only change to function `readScores` in Listing 9.6 would be to add parameter `ins`, replace `cin` by `ins`, and delete all prompts.

Listing 9.7   Function `readScoresFile`

```cpp
// File: readScoresFile.cpp
// Reads an array of exam scores for a lecture section
//    of up to MAX_SIZE students from a file.

// Pre: None
// Post: The data values are read from a file and stored
//       in array scores.
//       The number of values read is stored in sectionSize.
//       (0 <= sectionSize < MAX_SIZE).
void readScoresFile
   (ifstream& ins,        // IN: input stream of scores
    int scores[],         // OUT: array to contain all scores read
    const int MAX_SIZE,   // IN: max size of array scores
    int& sectionSize)     // OUT: number of elements read
{
    // Local data . . .
    int tempScore;               // temporary storage for each score

    // Read each array element until done.
    sectionSize = 0;             // initial class size
    ins >> tempScore;
    while (!ins.eof() && (sectionSize < MAX_SIZE))
    {
        scores[sectionSize] = tempScore;   // save score just read
        sectionSize++;
        ins >> tempScore;
    } // end while

    // End of file reached or array is filled.
    if (!ins.eof())
    {
        cout << "Array is filled!" << endl;
        cout << tempScore << " not stored" << endl;
    }
}
```

EXERCISES FOR SECTION 9.4

Self-Check

1. Describe the changes necessary to use function `readScores` for reading floating-point data.

2. In function readScores, what prevents the user from entering more than MAX_SIZE scores?

3. Explain how you would modify function readScoresFile if the number of scores to read was included in the data file. Where should this number be placed?

Programming

1. Rewrite readScoresFile so that it stops reading when either a sentinel value is read, the end of the file is reached, or the array is filled.

9.5 Searching and Sorting Arrays

This section discusses two common problems in processing arrays: searching an array to determine the location of a particular value and sorting an array to rearrange the elements in an ordered fashion. As an example of an array search, we might want to search the array scores to determine which student, if any, got a particular score. An example of an array sort would be rearranging the array elements so that they're in increasing order by score. This would be helpful if we wanted to display the list in order by score or if we needed to locate several different scores in the array.

Finding the Smallest Value in an Array

We begin by solving a different kind of search problem: finding the smallest value in a subarray.

1. Assume that the first element is the smallest so far and save its subscript as "the subscript of the smallest element found so far."

2. For each array element after the first one

    2.1. If the current element < the smallest so far

        2.1.1. Save the subscript of the current element as "the subscript of the smallest element found so far."

Function findIndexOfMin in Listing 9.8 implements this algorithm for any subarray of floating-point elements. During each iteration of the loop, minIndex is the subscript of the smallest element so far and x[minIndex] is its value. The function returns the last value assigned to minIndex, which is the subscript of the smallest value in the subarray. Arguments startIndex and endIndex define the boundaries of the subarray, x[startIndex] through x[endIndex], whose smallest value is being found. Passing these subscripts as arguments results in a more general function. To find the minimum element in the entire array, pass 0 to startIndex and the array size − 1 to endIndex.

Listing 9.8   Function `findIndexOfMin`

```
// File: arrayOperations.cpp
// Finds the subscript of the smallest value in a subarray.

// Returns the subscript of the smallest value in the subarray
// consisting of elements x[startindex] through x[endindex]
// Returns -1 if the subarray bounds are invalid.
// Pre: The subarray is defined and 0 <= startIndex <= endIndex.
// Post: x[minIndex] is the smallest value in the array.

int findIndexOfMin
    (const float x[],       // IN: array of elements
     int startIndex,        // IN: subscript of first element
     int endIndex)          // IN: subscript of last element
{
    // Local data . . .
    int minIndex;               // index of the smallest element found
    int i;                      // index of the current element

    // Validate subarray bounds
    if ((startIndex < 0) || (startIndex > endIndex))
    {
        cerr << "Error in subarray bounds" << endl;
        return -1;                          // return error indicator
    }

    // Assume the first element of subarray is smallest and check
    //    the rest.
    // minIndex will contain subscript of smallest examined so far.
    minIndex = startIndex;
    for (i = startIndex + 1; i <= endIndex; i++)
        if (x[i] < x[minIndex])
            minIndex = i;

    // Assertion: All elements are examined and minIndex is
    //    the index of the smallest element.
    return minIndex;                        // return result
} // end findIndexOfMin
```

Note that function `findIndexOfMin` returns the subscript (or index) of the smallest value, not the smallest value itself. Assuming `smallSub` is type `int`, and `yLength` is the number of array elements containing data, the following statements display the smallest value in array y.

```
smallSub = findIndexOfMin(y, 0, yLength - 1);
if (smallSub != -1)
    cout << "Value of smallest element in array y is "
        << y[smallSub] << endl;
else
    cerr << "Error - invalid array range" << endl;
```

PROGRAM STYLE   Assertions as Comments

Normally we use a comment to document the purpose of the statements that follow it. In Listing 9.8, we introduced a different kind of comment called an **assertion**—a statement about the program that must be true at this point in the program. Instead of summarizing the intent of the statements that follow it, an assertion helps clarify the rationale for those statements. Programmers sometimes use assertions to help them prove that a program is correct. We'll use them to describe the expected status or state of the program.

assertion

A comment that makes a statement about the program that must be true.

Array Search

We can search an array for a particular element by comparing each array element, starting with the first (subscript 0), to the target, the value we're seeking. If a match occurs, we have found the target in the array and can return its subscript as a search result. If we test all array elements without finding a match, we return −1 to indicate that the target was not found. We choose −1 because no array element has a negative subscript.

INTERFACE FOR A SEARCH FUNCTION

Input Arguments

```
int items[]      // array to search
int size         // number of items to be examined
int target       // item to find
```

Output Arguments

(none)

Returns

Subscript of the first element of the array containing the target (return −1 if no element contains the target)

We use the linear search algorithm below and implemented in Listing 9.9 to search the input array for the target value.

1. For each array element

    1.1. If the current element contains the target

    1.2. Return the subscript of the current element.

2. Return −1.

Listing 9.9   The function `linSearch`

```cpp
// File: arrayOperations.cpp
// Searches an integer array for a given element (the target)

// Array elements ranging from 0 to size −1 are searched for
//     an element equal to target.
// Pre:  The target and array are defined.
// Post: Returns the subscript of target if found;
//          otherwise, returns −1.

int linSearch
    (const int items[],        // IN: the array being searched
     int target,               // IN: the target being sought
     int size)                 // IN: the size of the array
{
    for (int next = 0; next < size; next++)
        if (items[next] == target)
            return next;            // found, return subscript

    // Assertion: All elements were tested without success.
    return −1;
}   // end linSearch
```

Sorting an Array in Ascending Order

Many programs execute more efficiently if the data they process are sorted before processing begins. For example, a check-processing program executes more quickly if all checks are in order by checking account number. Other programs produce more readable output if the information is sorted before it's displayed. For example, your university might want your instructor's grade report sorted by student ID number. In this section, we describe one simple sorting algorithm.

EXAMPLE 9.13

The *selection sort* is a fairly intuitive sorting algorithm. To perform a selection sort of an array of *n* elements (subscripts 0 through $n - 1$), we locate the smallest element in the array and then switch the smallest element with the element at subscript 0, thereby placing the smallest element at location 0. We then locate the smallest element remaining in the subarray with subscripts 1 through $n - 1$ and switch it with the element at subscript 1, thereby placing the second smallest element at location 1. We continue this process until all elements have been placed in their correct locations.

DATA REQUIREMENTS FOR A SORT FUNCTION

Input Arguments

```
float items[]    // array to sort
int n            // number of items to sort
```

Output Arguments

```
int items[]      // original array sorted in ascending order
```

Local Variables

```
int i            // subscript of first element in each subarray
int minSub       // subscript of each smallest item located by
                 // findIndexOfMin
```

ALGORITHM

1. Starting with the first item in the array (subscript 0) and ending with the next-to-last item:

    1.1. Set i equal to the subscript of the first item in the subarray to be processed in the next steps.

    1.2. Find the subscript (`minSub`) of the smallest item in the subarray with subscripts ranging from i through n−1;

    1.3. Exchange the smallest item found in step 1.2 with item i (exchange `items[minSub]` with `items[i]`).

Figure 9.9 traces the operation of the selection sort algorithm on an array with four elements. The first array shown is the original array. Then we show each step as the next smallest element is moved to its correct position. The shaded portion of each array represents the subarray that is sorted. We stop when the next to last element is placed in its correct position, so n−1 exchanges will be required to sort an array with n elements.

We can use function `findIndexOfMin` (see again Listing 9.8) to perform step 1.2. Function `selSort` in Listing 9.10 implements the selection sort algorithm. Local variable `minSub` holds the index of the smallest value found so far in the current subarray. At the end of each pass, we call function `exchange` (see again Listing 9.3) to exchange the elements with subscripts `minSub` and `i`. After execution of function `selSort`, the array element values will be in increasing order.

The selection sort illustrates the importance of component reuse in problem solving and program engineering. We always strive to break down a complicated problem into simpler subproblems so that we can solve many of these subproblems using existing and tested components. Occasionally, we may need to make some minor modification to these components to adapt them to the current problem. But this is preferable to designing, implementing, and testing a new function from scratch.

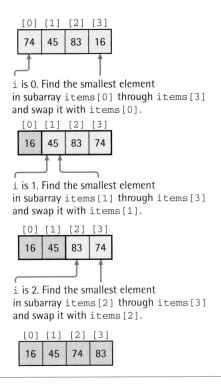

i is 0. Find the smallest element
in subarray items[0] through items[3]
and swap it with items[0].

i is 1. Find the smallest element
in subarray items[1] through items[3]
and swap it with items[1].

i is 2. Find the smallest element
in subarray items[2] through items[3]
and swap it with items[2].

Figure 9.9   Trace of selection sort

Listing 9.10   Function selSort

```
// File: arrayOperations.cpp

// Sorts an array (ascending order) using selection sort algorithm
//     Uses exchange and findIndexOfMin
// Sorts the data in array items (items[0] through items[n–1]).
// Pre:  items is defined and n <= declared size of actual argument
//       array.
// Post: The values in items[0] through items[n–1] are in
//       increasing order.
void selSort(float items[], int n)
{
    // Local data . . .
    int minSub;  // subscript of each smallest item located by
                 // findIndexOfMin

    for (int i = 0; i < n–1; i++)
    {
```

(continued)

Listing 9.10   Function `selSort` (continued)

```
    // Find index of smallest element in unsorted section of
    //    items.
    minSub = findIndexOfMin(items, i, n-1);

    // Exchange items at position minSub and i
    exchange(items[minSub], items[i]);
  }
}
```

EXERCISES FOR SECTION 9.5

Self-Check

1. For the linear search function in Listing 9.9, what happens if

   a. the last element of the array matches the target?

   b. several elements of the array match the target? The subscript of which one will be returned?

2. Trace the execution of the selection sort on the following list:

   55   34   56   76   5   10   25   34

   Show the array after each exchange occurs. How many comparisons are required? How many exchanges?

3. How could you modify the selection sort algorithm to arrange the data items in the array in descending order (smallest first)?

4. Modify the exchange function (Listing 9.3) to work for integer data.

5. In selection sort, there is no need to exchange the value in element i with the smallest value found if the smallest value is the same as the one at position i. How would you modify the algorithm to avoid this unnecessary exchange? How would this change affect the number of comparisons? How would it affect the number of exchanges?

6. Discuss how you could modify function `linSearch` to write a function `linSearchOrder` that performs a more efficient search of an array that has been sorted.

Programming

1. Write a function to count the number of items in an integer array having a value greater than 0.

2. Another method of performing the selection sort is to place the largest value in position n−1, the next largest in n−2, and so on. Write this version.

3. Write function `linSearchLast` that finds the last occurrence of a target value in an array.

4. Rewrite function `selectSort` by writing step 1.2 of the algorithm (Find index of smallest item . . .) as a loop with loop control variable `j` instead of calling function `findIndexOfMin`.

5. Write function `linSearchOrder` described in Self-Check Exercise 6.

9.6   Analyzing Algorithms: Big-O Notation

Often we want to estimate the efficiency of an algorithm. In this section, we provide a brief introduction to the topic of algorithm analysis, focusing on the searching and sorting algorithms just introduced.

There are many algorithms for searching and sorting arrays. Because arrays can be very large, these operations can become time-consuming, so we need to know the relative efficiency of various algorithms for performing the same task. Because it's difficult to get a precise measure of the efficiency of an algorithm or program, we normally try to approximate the effect on an algorithm of a change in the number of items, n, that the algorithm processes. This way, we can see how an algorithm's execution time increases with n, so we can compare two algorithms by examining their growth rates.

Usually, growth rates are described in terms of the largest contributing factor as the value of n gets large (for example, as it grows to 1,000 or more). If we determine that the expression

$$2n^2 + n - 5$$

expresses the relationship between the processing time of an algorithm and n, we say that the algorithm is an $O(n^2)$ algorithm, where O is an abbreviation for "the order of magnitude." This notation is known as big-O notation. The reason that this is an $O(n^2)$ algorithm rather than an $O(2n^2)$ algorithm or an $O(2n^2 + n - 5)$ algorithm is that the dominant factor in the relationship is the n^2 term. For large values of n, the largest exponent term has by far the greatest impact on our measurements. For this reason, we tend to ignore the "smaller" terms and constants.

Analysis of a Search Algorithm

To search an array of n elements using the linear search function, we have to examine all n elements if the target is not present in the array. If the target is in the array, then we have to search only until we find it. However, the target could be anywhere in the array—it's equally as likely to be at the beginning of the array as at the end. So, on average, we have to examine $n/2$ array elements to locate a target value in an array. This means that linear search is an O(n) process; that is, the growth rate is linear with respect to the number of items being searched.

Analysis of a Sort Algorithm

To determine the efficiency of a sorting algorithm, we normally focus on the number of array element comparisons and exchanges that it requires. Performing a selection sort on an array of n elements requires $n - 1$ comparisons during the first pass, $n - 2$ during the second pass, and so on. Therefore, the total number of comparisons is represented by the series

$$1 + 2 + 3 + \ldots + (n - 2) + (n - 1)$$

The value of this series is

$$\frac{n \times (n - 1)}{2} = n^2/2 - n/2$$

At the end of each pass through the unsorted subarray, we exchange the smallest value with the array element at position `i`. Therefore, the number of exchanges is n and the growth rate for exchanges is O(n).

Because the dominant term in the expression for the number of comparisons shown earlier is $n^2/2$, the selection sort is considered an O(n^2) process and the growth rate is said to be quadratic (proportional to the square of the number of elements). What difference does it make whether an algorithm is an O(n) or O(n^2) process? Table 9.4 shows the evaluation of n and n^2 for different values of n. A doubling of n causes n^2 to increase by a factor of 4. Because n^2 increases much more rapidly than n, the performance of an O(n) algorithm is not as adversely affected by an increase in array size as is an O(n^2) algorithm. For large values of n (say, 100 or more), the difference in the performances of an O(n) and an O(n^2) algorithm is significant (see the last three lines of Table 9.4).

Other factors besides the number of comparisons and exchanges affect an algorithm's performance. For example, one algorithm may take more time preparing for each exchange or comparison than another. Also, one algorithm might exchange subscripts, whereas another might exchange the array elements themselves. The second process can be more time consuming. Another measure of efficiency is the amount of memory required by an algorithm. Further discussion of these issues is beyond the scope of this book.

Table 9.4 Table of Values of n and n^2

n	n^2
2	4
4	16
8	64
16	256
32	1024
64	4096
128	16384
256	65536
512	262144

EXERCISES FOR SECTION 9.6

Self–Check

1. Determine how many times the cout line is executed in each of the following fragments. Indicate whether the algorithm is $O(n)$ or $O(n^2)$.

   a. ```
for (i = 0; i < n; i++)
    for (j = 0; j < n; j++)
        cout << i << ' ' << j;
```

   b. ```
for (i = 0; i < n; i++)
    for (j = 1; j <= 2; j++)
        cout << i << ' ' << j;
```

   c. ```
for (i = 0; i < n; i++)
    for (j = n; j > 0; j-)
        cout << i << ' ' << j;
```

   d. ```
for (i = 0, i < n; i++)
    for (j = 0; j < i; j++)
        cout << i << " " << j << endl;
```

2. What does it mean for a term to dominate an equation? To get a feel for the answer, calculate the value of n, $n^2 + n - 5$, $n^2 - n + 5$, and $2n^2$ for values of $n = 1, 10, 100, 1000,$ and 10000. You may want to write a small program to do this. Notice that each value of n is 10 times the previous value.

Programming

1. Write a program to compute and print the values of y1 and y2 (below) for *n*, from 10 to 1000 inclusive, in increments of 25. Does the result surprise you?

$$y1 = 100n + 10$$
$$y2 = 5n^2 + 2$$

9.7   Multidimensional Arrays

The array data structure allows a programmer to organize information in arrangements that are more complex than the linear or one-dimensional arrays discussed so far. We can declare and use arrays with several dimensions of different sizes.

Multidimensional Array Declaration

Syntax: *element-type aname*[*size*$_1$][*size*$_2$] ... [*size*$_n$] **;**

Example: `float table[NROWS][NCOLS];`

Interpretation: The array declaration allocates storage space for an array *aname* consisting of *size*$_1$ × *size*$_2$ × ... × *size*$_n$ memory cells. Each memory cell can store one data item whose data type is specified by *element-type*. The individual array elements are referenced by the subscripted variables *aname*`[0][0]` **. . .** `[0]` through *aname*[*size*$_1$ −1][*size*$_2$ −1] ... [*size*$_n$ −1]. An integer constant expression is used to specify each *size*$_i$.

Declaring Two–Dimensional Arrays

two-dimensional array
An array used to store information that is normally represented as a two-dimensional table.

Two-dimensional arrays, the most common multidimensional arrays, store information that we normally represent in table form. Let's first look at some examples of two-dimensional arrays—game boards, seating plans, and matrixes.

EXAMPLE 9.14

The array declaration

```
char ticTacToe[3][3];
```

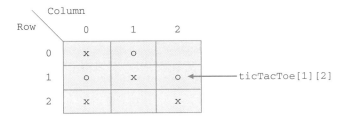

Figure 9.10   A tic-tac-toe board stored as array ticTacToe

allocates storage for a two-dimensional array (`ticTacToe`) with three rows and three columns. This array has nine elements, each of which must be referenced by specifying a row subscript (0, 1, or 2) and a column subscript (0, 1, or 2). Each array element contains a character value. For the array shown in Figure 9.10, the character 0 is stored in the subscripted variable

```
ticTacToe[1][2]
```

EXAMPLE 9.15

Your instructor wants to store the seating plan (Figure 9.11) for a classroom on a computer. The declarations

```
const int NUM_ROWS = 11;
const int SEATS_IN_ROW = 9;
string seatPlan[NUM_ROWS][SEATS_IN_ROW];
```

allocate storage for a two-dimensional array of strings called `seatPlan`. Array `seatPlan` could be used to store the first names of the students seated in a classroom with 11 rows and 9 seats in each row. The statement

Figure 9.11   A classroom seating plan

```
seatPlan[0][8] = "Gerry";
```

stores the string "Gerry" in the last seat of the first row.

Initializing Two-Dimensional Arrays

EXAMPLE 9.16

The statements

```
const int NUM_ROWS = 2;
const int NUM_COLS = 3;
float matrix[NUM_ROWS][NUM_COLS] = {{5.0, 4.5, 3.0},
                                    {-16.0, -5.9, 0.0}};
```

allocate storage for the array matrix with two rows and three columns. In the initialization list enclosed in braces, each inner pair of braces contains the initial values for a row of the array matrix, starting with row 0, as shown below.

	col 0	col 1	col 2
row 0	5.0	4.5	3.0
row 1	-16.0	-5.9	0.0 ← matrix[1][2]

Nested Loops for Processing Two-Dimensional Arrays

You must use nested loops to access the elements of a two-dimensional array in row order or column order. If you want to access the array elements in row order (the normal situation), use the row subscript as the loop control variable for the outer loop and the column subscript as the loop control variable for the inner loop.

EXAMPLE 9.17

The nested **for** statements that follow display the seating plan array from Figure 9.11 in tabular form. The top row of the table lists the names of the students sitting in the last row of the classroom; the bottom row of the table lists the names of the students sitting in the first row of the classroom (closest to the teacher).

```
for (int row = NUM_ROWS - 1; row >= 0; row--)
{
    for (int seat = 0; seat < SEATS_IN_ROW; seat++)
        cout << setw(10) << seatPlan[row][seat];
    cout << endl;
}
```

Two-Dimensional Arrays as Function Arguments

You can pass two-dimensional arrays as function arguments. In the function call, simply list the actual array name, just as you would for one-dimensional arrays. In the formal argument list, you must list the column dimension, but the row dimension is optional. For example, you could use the function prototype

```
float sumMatrix
    (float table[][NUM_COLS],     // IN: array to be summed
        int rows)                 // IN: number of rows
                                  //        (rows > 0)
```

for function sumMatrix (see Listing 9.11), which calculates the sum of all the elements in an array of floating-point values with NUM_COLS (a constant) columns. The second function argument represents the number of rows to be included in the sum. You can use the statement

```
total = sumMatrix(matrix, NUM_COLS);
```

to assign to total the sum of the element values in the array matrix from Example 9.16.

You may be wondering why you only need to specify the column dimension (NUM_COLS) in the declaration of the formal array parameter table. Because the array elements are stored in row order, starting with row 0, C++ must know the number of elements in each row (value of NUM_COLS) in order to access a particular array element. For example, if NUM_COLS is 3, the first row is stored in array positions 0, 1, and 2, the

Listing 9.11   Function `sumMatrix`

```
// File: sumMatrix.cpp
// Calculates the sum of the elements in the first rows
//    of an array of floating point values
//    with NUM_COLS (a constant) columns.
// Pre: The type int constant NUM_COLS is defined (NUM_COLS > 0)
//       and the array element values are defined and rows > 0.
// Post: sum is the sum of all array element values.
// Returns: Sum of all values stored in the array.
float sumMatrix
   (float table[][NUM_COLS],    // IN: array to be summed
    int rows)                   // IN: number of rows in array
                                //       (rows > 0)

{
    float sum = 0.0;            // sum of all element values
                               // - initially 0.0
    // Add each array element value to sum.
    for (int r = 0; r < rows; r++)
      for (int c = 0; c < NUM_COLS; c++)
         sum += table[r][c];

    return sum;
}
```

second row is stored in array positions 3, 4, and 5, and so on. C++ uses the formula

```
NUM_COLS * r + c
```

to compute the array position for array element `table[r][c]`. For example, array element `table[1][0]`, the first element in the second row, is stored at array position 3 * 1 + 0 (array position 3).

Arrays with Several Dimensions

C++ doesn't limit the number of dimensions an array may have, although arrays with more than three dimensions are rare. The array `sales` declared here

```
const int PEOPLE = 10;
const int YEARS = 5;
float sales[PEOPLE][YEARS][12];
```

is a three-dimensional array with 600 (value of $10 \times 5 \times 12$) elements that may be used to store the monthly sales figures for the last five years for the 10 sales representatives in a company. Thus `sales[0][2][11]` represents the dollar amount of sales for the first salesperson (person subscript is 0) during December (month subscript is 11) of the third year (year subscript is 2). As you can see, three-dimensional and higher arrays consume memory space very quickly.

EXAMPLE 9.18

The following fragment finds and displays the total dollar amount of sales for each of the 10 sales representatives.

```
// Find and display the total dollar amount of sales by
//     person
for (int person = 0; person < PEOPLE; person++)
{
    totalSales = 0.0;
    // Find the total sales for the current person.
    for (int year = 0; year < YEARS; year++)
        for (int month = 0; month < 12; month++)
            totalSales += sales[person][year][month];

    cout << "Total sales amount for salesperson "
        << person << " is " << totalSales << endl;
}
```

Because we're displaying the total sales amount for each person, we use the salesperson subscript (`person`) as the loop control variable in the outermost loop. We set the value of `totalSales` to zero before executing the inner pair of nested loops. This pair accumulates the total sales amount for the current salesperson. The statement beginning with `cout` displays the accumulated total for each individual.

EXERCISES FOR SECTION 9.7

Self-Check

1. Assuming the following declarations

```
const int MAX_ROW = 9;
const int MAX_COL = 5;
float matrix[MAX_ROW][MAX_COL];
```

answer these questions:

a. How many elements are in the array `matrix`?

b. Write a statement to display the element in row 3, column 4.

c. How would you reference the element in the last column of the last row?

d. How would you reference the element in the exact middle of the array?

2. Write the declarations for a multidimensional array used to store the number of students enrolled in each section of the introductory programming course. Four different professors teach the course and each one teaches three sections. Answer this question if the course is taught at three campuses and there are five sections at each campus.

3. Explain why it isn't necessary to specify the first dimension (number of salespeople) when you declare a formal parameter that is an array with the same form as the one in Example 9.18. Describe the storage order for elements of this array in memory. Give a formula that will compute the position of array element `sales[i][j][k]`.

Programming

1. For the array `matrix` declared in Self-Check Exercise 1, do the following:

a. Write a loop that computes the sum of the elements in row 4.

b. Write a loop that computes the sum of the elements in column 3.

c. Write nested loops that compute the sum of all the array elements.

d. Write nested loops that display the array elements in the following order: display column 3 as the first output line, column 2 as the second output line, column 1 as the third output line, and column 0 as the fourth output line.

2. For the array `sales` in Example 9.18, do the following:

a. Write a program fragment that displays the total sales amount in a table whose rows are years and whose columns are months.

b. Write a program fragment that displays the total sales amount for each year and the total for all years.

9.8   The Struct Data Type

struct
A data structure that can be used to store a collection of related data items with different types.

Arrays are useful data structures for storing a collection of data elements of the same type. But many programming problems require us to store collections of related data that have different types. We can use a **struct** to accomplish this. For example, we can use a struct to store a variety of information about a person, such as name, marital status, age, and date of birth. The individual component of a struct is called a **member.** In this section, we show how to declare and process structs.

member
An individual component
of a struct.

Declaring a Struct Type and Struct Variables

EXAMPLE 9.19

The manager of a software firm has asked you to keep organized, accessible information about her staff. As part of her plan, she would like certain information about each employee. An example might look like this:

ID: 1234
Name: Noel Goddard
Gender: Female
Number of dependents: 0
Hourly rate: 12.00
Total wages: 480.00

This information can be stored in a struct with six data elements. The struct type declaration describes the format of each struct including the name and type of each data element, or *struct member.* To store the preceding information, you can use the struct type `employee` shown next with two integer fields, a `string` field, a character field (for `gender`), and two `float` fields:

```
struct employee
{
    int id;
    string name;
    char gender;
    int numDepend;
    float rate;
    float totWages;
};
```

The above sequence of C++ statements (ending with a semicolon) defines a new struct data type named `employee` consisting of six members. There is no memory associated with this type. However, once it has been defined, you can declare *structure variables* of this type. The declaration

```
employee organist, janitor;
```

allocates storage space for two variables, `organist` and `janitor`, in the form defined by the structured type `employee`. Thus the memory allocated for these variables consists

id	1234
name	Noel Goddard
gender	F
numDepend	0
rate	12.00
totWages	480.00

Figure 9.12   The struct variable `organist`

of storage space for six distinct values. The variable `organist` shown in Figure 9.12 stores the values presented earlier in the example.

As with other identifiers in C++ programs, use member names that describe the information to be stored and select a data type that's appropriate for that kind of information. For example, struct type `employee` uses a string field for storage of an employee's name.

`struct` Type Declaration

Form: `struct` *struct-type*
          `{`
               type$_1$ id-list$_1$;
               type$_2$ id-list$_2$;

               .
               .
               .

               type$_n$ id-list$_n$;
          `};`

Example: `struct complex`
          `{`
                  `float realPart, imaginaryPart;`
          `};`

Interpretation: The identifier *struct-type* is the name of the struct being declared. Each *id-list$_i$* is a list of one or more member names of the same type separated by commas, and each *id-list$_i$* is separated from the next *id-list* of a possibly different type by a semicolon. The data type of each member in *id-list$_i$* is specified by *type$_i$.*

You must declare a struct type before you can declare any variables of that type. We recommend that you declare a struct type before the function prototypes in a program system. This placement makes the struct type global, which means that all functions in the program system can use it. Make sure you follow the closing brace with a semicolon.

Accessing Members of a Struct

We can access a struct member using the **member access operator,** a period placed between a struct variable name and a member name for that struct type. If `s` is a struct variable and `m` is a member of that struct, then `s.m` accesses member `m` of the `struct s`.

member access operator
The period placed between a struct variable name and a member name for that struct type.

EXAMPLE 9.20

The statements below store data in the struct variable `organist`. Refer back to Figure 9.12 to view the contents of `organist` after these statements execute.

```
organist.id = 1234;
organist.name = "Noel Goddard";
organist.gender = 'F';
organist.numDepend = 0;
organist.rate = 12.00;
organist.totWages = 480.0;
```

Once data are stored in a struct, they can be manipulated in the same way as other data in memory. For example, the assignment statement

```
organist.totWages += (organist.rate * 40.0);
```

computes the organist's new total wages by adding this week's wages to her previous total wages. The computed result is saved in the struct member `organist.totWages`.

The statements

```
cout << "The organist is ";
switch (organist.gender)
{
    case 'F': case 'f':
        cout << "Ms. ";
        break;
    case 'M': case 'm':
        cout << "Mr. ";
        break;
    default:
        cout << organist.gender
             << " is bad character for gender!" << endl;
}
cout << organist.name << endl;
```

display the organist's name after an appropriate title (`"Ms."` or `"Mr."`); the output line follows:

```
The organist is Ms. Noel Goddard
```

EXERCISES FOR SECTION 9.8

Self-Check

1. For variable `organist` in Example 9.20 describe the effect of each valid statement below or indicate that it is not valid.
   ```
   organist.rate *= 2;
   cout << organist;
   organist.totWages = organist.rate * 40.0;
   if (organist.gender == 'F')
       cout << "Female";
   ```

2. Explain what is wrong with the statement below, which is supposed to set an employee's gender.
   ```
   employee.gender = 'M';
   ```

Programming

1. A catalog listing for a textbook consists of the author's name as well as the title, edition, publisher, and year of publication. Declare a struct `catalogEntry` and a variable `cPlusBook` and write assignment statements that store the relevant data for a C++ textbook in `cPlusBook`.

2. A company represents each part in an inventory by its part number, a descriptive name, the quantity on hand, and the price. Define a struct `part`.

9.9 Structs as Operands and Arguments

Programmers often need to write functions that process entire structs. In this section we discuss passing structs as function arguments and other operations on entire structs.

Struct Copy or Assignment

We can copy all of the members of one struct variable to another struct variable of the same type. If `organist` and `janitor` are both struct variables of type `employee`, the statement

```
organist = janitor;   // Copy janitor to organist
```

copies each member of `janitor` into the corresponding member of `organist`.

Passing a Struct as an Argument

A struct can be passed as an argument to a function, provided the actual argument is the same type as its corresponding formal parameter. The use of structs

as arguments can shorten argument lists considerably, because one argument
(a struct variable) can be passed instead of several related arguments.

EXAMPLE 9.21

You have been asked to organize a grading program, which keeps track of a student's
name, three exam scores, the average exam score, and letter grade based on the average.
Previously you would have stored these data in separate variables, but now you can
group them together as a struct.

```
struct examStats
{
    string stuName;
    int scores[3];
    float average;
    char grade;
};

int main ()
{
    examStats aStudent;
```

Struct variable **aStudent** (type **examStats**) contains all the data regarding the
student's exam performance. Notice that member **scores** is an array of integers. We
use the notation **aStudent.scores[0]** to access the first element of this array.
Figure 9.13 shows a sketch of variable **aStudent**.

Function **printStats** (Listing 9.12) displays the value stored in each member of
its struct argument (type **examStats**). For the sample data shown, the statement

```
printStats(aStudent);
```

would display the following output:

```
Exam scores for Judy: 55 90 87
Average score: 77.3333
Letter grade : C
```

stuName	Judy
scores	55 90 87
average	77.3333
grade	C

Figure 9.13   Variable **aStudent**

Listing 9.12   Function `printStats`

```
// File: printStats.cpp
// Prints the exam statistics

// Pre:  The members of the struct variable stuExams are
//       assigned values.
// Post: Each member of stuExams is displayed.

void printStats
   (examStats stuExams)      // IN:
                             // the struct to be displayed
{
    cout << "Exam scores for " << stuExams.stuName << ": "
    cout << stuExams.scores[0] << ' ' << stuExams.scores[1]
         << ' ' << stuExams.scores[2] << endl;
    cout << "Average score: " << stuExams.average << endl;
    cout << "Letter grade : " << stuExams.grade << endl;
}
```

In `printStats`, the struct argument was declared as a value argument, so storage is allocated for a copy of its actual argument in the function data area. You can pass a struct as a reference argument, as illustrated in the next section.

Reading a Struct

Function `readEmployee` in Listing 9.13 reads data into the first five members of a struct variable of type `employee` represented by the reference parameter `oneEmployee`. The address of the actual struct argument is stored in the function data area, so `oneEmployee.id` references member `id` of the actual struct argument. The function call

```
readEmployee(organist);
```

causes the data read to be stored in struct variable `organist`.

Listing 9.13   Function `readEmployee`

```
// File: readEmp.cpp
// Reads one employee record into oneEmployee

#include <string>
#include <iostream>
```

(continued)

Listing 9.13 Function `readEmployee` (continued)

```
// Pre: None
// Post: Data are read into struct oneEmployee

void readEmployee
  (employee& oneEmployee)   // OUT: The destination for the data read
{
    cout << "Enter a name terminated with the symbol # : ";
    getline(cin, oneEmployee.name, '#');
    cout << "Enter an id number: ";
    cin >> oneEmployee.id;
    cout << "Enter gender (F or M): ";
    cin >> oneEmployee.gender;
    cout << "Enter number of dependents: ";
    cin >> oneEmployee.numDepend;
    cout << "Enter hourly rate: ";
    cin >> oneEmployee.rate;
}
```

A Struct as a Function Result

A function can return a struct result. Function `readEmp` does this. See programming Exercise 1.

```
employee readEmp()
{
    employee oneEmployee;   // function result
    // Read data into one Employee

    . . .
    return  oneEmployee;
}
```

Efficiency of Reference Arguments

For efficiency reasons, programmers sometimes prefer not to pass structs as value arguments because C++ must make a local copy of a struct passed as a value argument in the called function's data area. But they can still get the protection afforded by value arguments by using the word const in a formal parameter declaration. For example, the function header

```
void printStats
  (const examStats& stuExams) // IN:
                              // the struct to be displayed
```

declares `stuExams` as a reference argument that can't be changed by the execution of function `printStats`. Instead of making a local copy of the actual struct argument during a call to `printStats`, C++ passes the actual argument's address to function `printStats`. This enables `printStats` to access the data stored in its actual argument, but C++ doesn't allow `printStats` to modify the data in its actual argument.

EXERCISES FOR SECTION 9.9

Self-Check

1. For variables `aStudent` and `bStudent` (type `examStats` in Example 9.21), describe the meaning of each of the valid references below and the value(s) referenced. Which are invalid?

   a. `aStudent.stuName`

   b. `aStudent.stuName[0]`

   c. `examStats.stuName`

   d. `aStudent.scores[3]`

   e. `aStudent.scores[2]`

   f. `examStats.scores[0]`

   g. `aStudent = bStudent;`

   h. `aStudent.scores[0] = bStudent.grade;`

2. Write statements that calculate the average score for `aStudent` and assign a letter grade based on a straight scale (90–100 an A, 80–89 a B, and so on).

3. You can return a struct as a function result. This means it would be possible to write a function `readEmp` with prototype

   ```
   employee readEmp();
   ```

   to read in an employee's data. Write a statement to call `readEmp` to read in an organist's data.

Programming

1. Write function `readEmp` described in Self-Check Exercise 3.

2. Write a function that reads in the data for a struct of type `date`:

   ```
   struct date
   {
       string month;
       int day;
       int year;
   };
   ```

   The function should return the values read through a single argument of type `date`.

3. Consider the struct employee given in Example 9.14. Write a function `printEmployee` to print all the members of a structure variable of type employee and show how you would call it.

4. Write a function that updates a selected score for a student (type `examStats` in Example 9.21). The function parameters should be the struct to be changed, the score index, and the new score. The function should verify that the index is in range. It should return the old score. If the index is not in range, it should return −999

9.10 Arrays of Structs

In Example 9.21 we showed a struct with an array component. You can also create arrays whose elements are structs.

EXAMPLE 9.22

The declaration

```
employee company[10];
```

allocates storage for an array with 10 elements of struct type **employee** (see Figure 9.14). We use the subscripted variable **company[0]** to access the first element (a struct) of this array. We use the notation **company[9].name** to access the name component (a string) of the last employee.

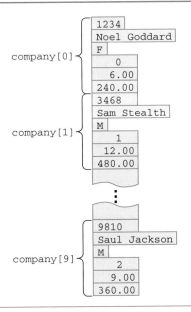

Figure 9.14   Sketch of array **company**

EXAMPLE 9.23

Array **company** provides storage for 10 elements of type **employee**, and function **readEmployee** (see again Listing 9.13) reads data into a single type **employee** variable. Function **readCompany** (Listing 9.14) reads data into all 10 elements of array **company**. The statement

```
readEmployee(company[i]);
```

reads employee data into the array element with subscript i. Because i goes from 0 through 9, all 10 elements receive data.

Listing 9.14   Function **readCompany**

```cpp
// File: readCompany.cpp
// Reads 10 employee records into array company

// Pre: None
// Post: Data are read into array company
void readCompany
   (employee company[])   // OUT: array being read
{
   // Read 10 employees.
   for (int i = 0; i < 10; i++)
   {
      cout << "Enter data for employee " << i+1 << ":" << endl;
      readEmployee(company[i]);
   }
}
```

EXAMPLE 9.24

C++ provides a great deal of flexibility in the use of arrays and structs. The struct type **gradeBook** declared next has three components. The last component is an array of 100 structs of type **examStats** (see again Example 9.21) containing exam data for each student. Figure 9.15 shows a sketch of variable **mySection** (type **gradeBook**).

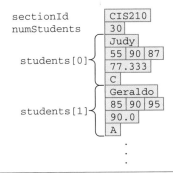

Figure 9.15   Sketch of variable `mySection`

```
struct gradeBook
{
    string sectionId;
    int numStudents;            // Count of students in section
    examStats students[100];    // Storage for 100 students
};

gradeBook mySection;
```

You use `mySection.sectionId` to access the section ID number, and use `mySection.numStudents` to access the count of students. You use `mySection.students[0]` to access the data for the first student (struct type `examStats`). You use `mySection.students[0].stuName` to access the first student's name and `mySection.students[0].scores[0]` to access her first exam score. You use `mySection.students[numstudents-1]` to access the data for the last student in the section.

EXERCISES FOR SECTION 9.10

Self-Check

1. For array `company`, describe the meaning of each of the valid references below. Which are invalid?

   a. `company[1].gender`

   b. `id.company[0]`

   c. `company[9]`

   d. `company[10]`

   e. `company[1].employee`

   f. `company[1].employee.gender`

   g. `company[9].name`

   h. `company[2].company[1]`

2. For variable `mySection` (Figure 9.15), write the correct way to reference each data item described below.

    a. First student's name   **e.** First student's score on the first exam

    b. Section ID   **f.** Number of students in the section

    c. All data for the last student   **g.** Last student's average

    d. First student's letter grade   **h.** Last student's score on the last exam

3. For variable `company` (Figure 9.14), show how you'd reference each of the data items below.

    a. Noel Goddard   **c.** Sam Stealth

    b. 3468   **d.** 1234

Programming

1. Write a function that displays the data in variable `mySection`. Use function `printStats` (Listing 9.12) to display each student's data.

2. Write a function that decreases each employee's total wages in array `company` (Figure 9.14) by a specified percentage (a function argument) for a tax deduction. Assume that data field `totWages` contains the employee's salary amount.

3. Write a function that computes and returns the average score for a particular student. The function should have a `section` parameter and an `int` parameter—the student's index.

4. Write a function that changes an exam score for a particular student in a section (a parameter). Your function should call the function described in Programming exercise 4 of Section 9.9.

9.11   Strings as Arrays of Characters (Optional)

Before C++ had a string class as part of its standard library, a string in C++ (or C) was stored in an array of characters. These strings are often called *C-Style strings*. For historical reasons, we show how to process strings stored as arrays of characters in this section.

Declaring and Initializing an Array of Characters

The declaration

```
char name[] = "Jackson";
```

or

```
char name[8] = "Jackson";
```

[0]	[1]	[2]	[3]	[4]	[5]	[6]	[7]
'J'	'a'	'c'	'k'	's'	'o'	'n'	'\0'

Figure 9.16 Array name

allocates storage for an array of eight characters and stores each character of the string literal `"Jackson"` in an element of that array (see Figure 9.16). Recall that you don't need to declare the size of an array when you provide initial values for its elements. The last character stored is `'\0'`, the **null character**, that C++ uses to denote the end of a string in a character array. C++ actually stores each string literal that occurs in a program as an array of characters terminated by the null character.

Reading and Writing Character Arrays

You can display the string stored in `name` as an entity by using the extraction operator

```
cout << name << endl;
```

Or you can use the following loop to display each individual character in the array.

```
// Display each character up to '\0'
int i = 0;
while (name[i] != '\0') {
   cout << name[i];
   i++;
}
```

In either case, all characters up to, but not including, the null character are displayed.

The declaration

```
char flower[10];
```

allocates storage for a string of at most nine characters because the last character stored should always be the null character. You can read a string into array `flower` by using the insertion operator

```
cin >> flower;
```

Or you can read each individual character from a data line using a sentinel-controlled loop as shown in the following fragment. The loop reads each individual character and stores it in the next array element, starting with the one at position 0. Loop repetition stops when either the newline character is read or nine data characters are stored in the array. The statement following the loop is critical; however, it's easy to forget. Its purpose is to store the null character after the last data character stored in the array. The test j < 9 ensures that at most 9 data characters will be stored and there will be space in the array for the null character.

```cpp
int j = 0;
char ch;

cin.get(ch);                // read first character
while (ch != '\n' && j < 9) {
   flower[j] = ch;          // store data character
                            // in next array element
   j++;
   cin.get(ch);            // read next character
}
flower[j] = '\0';          // terminate string with
                            // null character
```

You can't assign a string literal to a character array that has already been declared. We discuss how to store a string literal in an array next.

Some Useful Functions for Character Arrays

The standard library cstring has several useful functions for manipulating strings stored in character arrays (called *C-style strings*). You can use function strlen to return the length of a C-style string. The null character is not counted, so the function call

```cpp
strlen(name)
```

returns 7 for the array shown in Figure 9.16.

You can't assign a string to a character array after storage has been allocated to the array. However, you can use the string copy function, strcpy, to change the contents of a character array. The statement

```cpp
strcpy(flower, "Rose");
```

stores the five characters 'R', 'o', 's', 'e', '\0' in the character array flower (size 10). Take care not to overflow the storage area allocated to a character array. The assignment statement

```cpp
strcpy(flower, "Chrysanthemum");  // string is too long
```

will overwrite data in memory cells that follow the ones allocated to array flower. This could lead to execution errors because C++ doesn't prevent string overflow from happening.

In Section 8.3, we mentioned that the standard string library has a method `c_str` that converts a C++ string to an array of characters (C-style string). We used that function to enable the user to provide the external file name (needed for function `open`) as a data item. The argument of `open` must be a C-style string. If `fileName` stores a standard C++ string and `aStream` is a stream, the statement below associates stream `aStream` with the file whose name is stored in `fileName`.

```
aStream.open(fileName.c_str());
```

Another useful string function, `atoi`, is found in the standard library `cstdlib`. You can use `atoi` to convert a numeric string consisting of only digit characters to a type int value. If the `string` variable `yearStr` stores a numeric string (for example, "2009"), the fragment below stores the corresponding integer value (2009) in year (type int). The argument of `atoi` is the C-style string corresponding to `yearStr`.

```
year = atoi(yearStr.c_str());
```

EXERCISES FOR SECTION 9.11

Self-Check

1. Correct the errors in each of the statements below.

```
char dayName[] = "Sunday";
cout << "length is " << dayName.length();
char monthName[5];
monthName = "February";
string fName = "data.txt";
aStream.open(fName);
string year = "2004";
year++;
char initial[3];
initial[0] = 'E';  initial[1] = 'B';  initial[2] = 'K';
```

Programming

1. Write a function `readCharArray` that reads the data to be stored in its character array argument from a data line. The second function argument should be the declared size of the array. The function should store the null character after the last character read into the array. If too many characters are provided, ignore any extra characters at the end of the line.

2. Write a function `concat` that returns through its third character array argument, the concatenation of its first two arguments. The fourth argument

should be the declared size of the output array. If the declared size is too small to store the entire result, store only the characters that will fit without causing overflow.

9.12   Graphics Programs with Arrays (Optional)

In this section, we use arrays in graphics programs to draw a polygon and also to draw a grid or a two-dimensional table. We begin by drawing a polygon.

Drawing a Polygon

Rectangles and squares have four sides, but there are times when you want to draw a triangle (three sides) or a closed figure that has more than four sides. The `graphics.h` library has two functions that do this: `drawpoly` and `fillpoly`. Both functions require an array argument that stores the points to be displayed. The coordinates of each point are stored in consecutive elements of the array. For `drawpoly`, the polygon must be closed; that is, the first point should be repeated as the last point.

EXAMPLE 9.25

In Figure 3.14, a house was drawn as a rectangle on top of a square. We can draw the outline of a house as a polygon using the following statements.

```
//                    (x, y)
int poly[12] = { 100, 200,      // top-left corner
                 300, 100,      // roof peak
                 500, 200,      // top-right corner
                 500, 400,      // bottom-right corner
                 100, 400,      // bottom-left corner
                 100, 200       // top-left corner
               };
drawpoly(6, poly);
```

The first argument for **drawpoly** is the number of points to draw. The array size is 12 because there are two elements for each point. For example, `poly[0]`, `poly[1]` are the x, y coordinates for the first point.

The program in Listing 9.15 draws a painted house by calling **fillpoly** instead of **drawpoly**. Each time the user presses a key, the fill pattern and color changes. Figure 9.17 shows one example.

Listing 9.15   Drawing and filling a polygon

```cpp
// File: drawPolygon.cpp
// Draws a house shape and fills it with random patterns
#include <graphics.h>
#include <cstdlib>
#include <ctime>

int main()
{
    //                    (x, y)
    int poly[12] = { 100, 200,     // top-left corner
                     300, 100,     // roof peak
                     500, 200,     // top-right corner
                     500, 400,     // bottom-right corner
                     100, 400,     // bottom-left corner
                     100, 200      // top-left corner
                   };

    char message [] =
            "Press a key to repaint house - press Q to quit";
    initwindow(640, 500, "House");
    outtextxy(100, 450, message);

    srand(time(NULL));
    char ch = '*';
    while (toupper(ch) != 'Q') {
        int color = rand() % 16;
        int fill = rand() % 12;
        setfillstyle(fill, color);
        fillpoly(6, poly);
        ch = getch();
    }

    closegraph();           // close the window
}
```

PROGRAM STYLE   Using an Array of Characters to Store a Prompt

Method outtextxy in the graphics library expects a C-style string as its
third argument. That is the reason for the warning message: deprecated
conversion from string constant to char* when you use a literal
string as the third argument. You can avoid this warning if you store the
literal string in an array of characters and then pass the name of this array as
an argument to outtextxy.

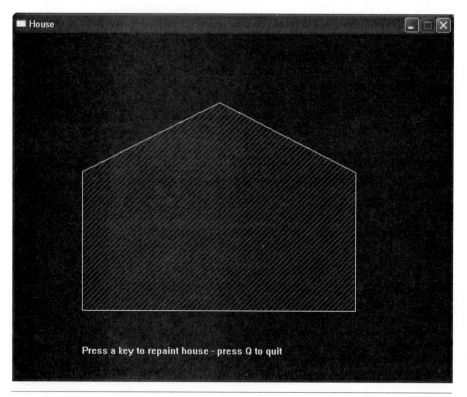

Figure 9.17   A painted house

```
char message[] =
      "Press a key to repaint house – press Q to quit");
outtextxy (100, 450, message);
```

Drawing a Grid

In game programs, we often need to draw a two-dimensional grid pattern to show the current state of the game and record the position of a new move. Listing 9.16 is a program that draws the grid shown in Figure 9.18. The program constants can be changed to allow different size grids and cells. In the main function, the two-dimensional array `gridArray` stores the color values to be displayed in each cell, starting with row 0 which happens to have all black cells (color value is 0). This array is passed to function `drawGrid`.

The body of function `drawGrid` contains a pair of nested loops to access each element of `gridArray`. For element `gridArray [r] [c]`, the statements

```
rectangle(c*CELL_SIZE, r*CELL_SIZE,     // top-left corner
          c*CELL_SIZE + CELL_SIZE,      // bottom-right
          r*CELL_SIZE + CELL_SIZE) ;    //      corner
```

Listing 9.16   Program to draw a two-dimensional grid

```cpp
// File: drawGrid.cpp
// Draws a grid and displays the row, column of a selected cell
#include <graphics.h>
#include <iostream>

using namespace std;

const int NUM_ROWS = 5;
const int NUM_COLS = 6;
const int CELL_SIZE = 50;   // dimensions of a square cell

                            // function prototypes
void drawGrid(int[][NUM_COLS]);
void reportResult(int&, int&, int&);
void recolor(int, int, int, int);

int main()
{
   int gridArray[NUM_ROWS][NUM_COLS] = { {0, 0, 0, 0, 0, 0},
                                         {2, 4, 2, 4, 2, 4},
                                         {1, 2, 3, 4, 5, 6},
                                         {2, 3, 4, 15, 6, 7},
                                         {5, 5, 5, 5, 5, 5}
                                       };

   int width = CELL_SIZE * NUM_COLS;
   int height = CELL_SIZE * NUM_ROWS + 100;
   int row, column;            // row and column of cell clicked
   int color;                  // color of cell clicked

   initwindow(width, height, "Grid - Press a key to close");

   drawGrid(gridArray);

   char message[100] = "Select a cell by clicking it";
   outtextxy(100, height - 50, message);
   reportResult(row, column, color);
   cout  << "You clicked the cell in row " << (row + 1)
         << ", column " << (column + 1) << endl;

   recolor(row, column, color, HATCH_FILL);

   getch();
   closegraph();
}
```

(continued)

Listing 9.16   Program to draw a two-dimensional grid (continued)

```
// Draw the grid corresponding to the color values in gridArray
// Pre:    Array gridArray is defined
// Post:   A two-dimensional grid is drawn with the same number
//         rows and columns as gridArray. The cell at row r,
//         column c has the color value of gridArray[r][c].
void drawGrid(int gridArray[][NUM_COLS])
{
   int color;                    // color of cell

   // Draw a grid cell for each array element
   for (int r = 0; r < NUM_ROWS; r++) {
      for (int c = 0; c < NUM_COLS; c++) {
            setcolor(WHITE);                          // border color
            // Draw cell border
            rectangle(c*CELL_SIZE, r*CELL_SIZE,    // top-left corner
                     c*CELL_SIZE + CELL_SIZE,      // bottom-right
                     r*CELL_SIZE + CELL_SIZE);     // corner
            // Fill the cell
            color = gridArray[r][c] % 16;
            setfillstyle(SOLID_FILL, color);
            floodfill(c*CELL_SIZE + 1, r*CELL_SIZE + 1, WHITE);
      }
   }
}

// Report the results of a mouse click by the user.
// Pre:    The grid is displayed
// Post:   The row, column, and color of the cell selected
//         are returned through row and column.
void reportResult(int& row, int& column, int& color)
{
   int x, y;          // (x, y) position of mouse click

   clearmouseclick(WM_LBUTTONDOWN);
   while (!ismouseclick(WM_LBUTTONDOWN)) {
      delay(100);
   }
   getmouseclick(WM_LBUTTONDOWN, x, y);

   // Convert x (y) pixel position to row (column)
   row = y / CELL_SIZE;
   column = x / CELL_SIZE;
```

(continued)

Listing 9.16   Program to draw a two-dimensional grid (continued)

```
    color = getpixel(x, y);   // get pixel color
}

// Recolors a selected grid cell with a new color and pattern.
// Pre:     The cell row and column and new color
//          and pattern are are defined.
// Post:    The selected cell is refilled.
void recolor(int row, int column,
             int newColor, int pattern)
{
    setfillstyle(pattern, newColor);
    floodfill(column*CELL_SIZE + 1, row*CELL_SIZE + 1, WHITE);
}
```

draws a rectangle associated with row r, column c of the array. The x-coordinates of the pixels in the rectangle's sides depend on the value of c—the larger c is, the further to the right the rectangle is positioned. Adding CELL_SIZE to the x-coordinate of the left side gives the

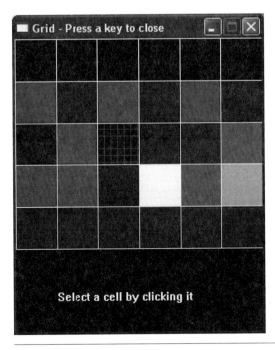

Figure 9.18   Two-dimensional grid

x-coordinate of the rectangle's right side. The y-coordinate values for the rectangle depend on the value of r and are calculated in a similar manner. The statements

```
color = gridArray [r][c] % 16;
setfillstyle (SOLID_FILL, color) ;
floodfill (c*CELL_SIZE + 1, r*CELL_SIZE + 1, WHITE) ;
```

fill the rectangle just drawn with the color value stored in grid [r][c].

After the grid is drawn, the main function prompts the user to select a cell by clicking in it. Method reportResult calls getmouseclick to store in (x, y) the coordinates of the pixel clicked. The statements

```
row = y / CELL_SIZE;
column = x / CELL_SIZE;
```

convert the pixel coordinates to a row and column value which are returned to the main function. The graphics function getpixel returns an integer representing the color value of the cell that was selected.

```
color = getpixel (x, y) ;   // return of pixel at (x, y)
```

The values of color, row, and column are outputs of reportResult.

After the return from reportResult, the main function adds 1 to row and column before displaying the cell's grid position because non-programmers tend to think of the first row of a grid as row 1 and not row 0, Next, the main function calls function recolor to change the fill pattern, but not the color, of the cell that was clicked. Figure 9.18 shows the grid after the user clicks the cell in row 3, column 3.

Table 9.5 shows the new graphics functions.

Table 9.5 Functions in graphics Library

Function	Purpose
drawpoly (int size, int poly[])	Draws a closed polygon with size vertices. poly [0], poly[1] are (x, y) for the first point, poly[2], poly[3] are (x, y) for the second point, and so on. The last pair of array elements, poly[size−2] and poly [size−1], should be the same as poly[0] and poly[1].
fillpoly (int size, int poly[])	Fills the specified polygon with color and fill style as specified in the previous call to setfillstyle.
int getpixel (int x, int y)	Returns the color value at pixel (x, y).

Self–Check

1. Sketch the polygon corresponding to the following array.

   {100, 200, 300, 400, 200, 500, 50, 300, 250, 400, 100, 200}

2. What changes would be needed to draw a grid with 10 rows and 20 columns whose cells are twice as high as they are wide?

Programming

1. Draw a polygon that is a six-sided star.

2. Draw a polygon that resembles the shape of a horse.

3. Write and test the program for Self-Check Exercise 2.

4. Modify function `drawGrid` to display a tic-tac-toc board. Use the color value RED to represent moves for player X, GREEN for player O, and the background color for unfilled cells. The moves for player X are in the middle of the first row, in the first and third cells in the second row, and in the third cell in the third row. Player O should be in the first cell in the first row, the middle cell in the second row and in the first cell in the third row.

5. In Listing 9.16, the main function specifies the array element values for `gridArray` when it is declared. Change the declaration so that the array values are not specified. Write and call a function `loadGrid` that loads the array by reading its element values from a data stream.

9.13 Common Programming Errors

Most errors in using arrays are due to subscript range errors. Be especially careful when writing loops that process arrays. Make sure that the subscript values at the loop boundaries are within range.

- *(Arrays) Out-of-range subscript references:* Array subscript references that are out-of-range (less than zero, or greater than or equal to the array size) won't be detected by the compiler or the run-time system. Instead, they will cause access to memory locations outside the range of the array, causing unpredictable program behavior.

  Such errors are very difficult to identify; they may not become readily apparent until a statement in your program executes that appears unrelated to the point where the problem occurred. It's the programmer's responsibility to prevent these errors from happening.

- *(Arrays) Unsubscripted array references:* Arrays may be used as function arguments. However, unsubscripted array references in expressions are invalid and will generate an error message. For example, if x is an integer array and y is an integer, the expression

```
y = y + x;
```

will generate an error message.

- *(Arrays) Subscripted references to nonarray variables:* Subscripted references to nonarray variables, such as the reference b[10] in

```
a = a + b[10];
```

where a and b are both simple variables, causes an error message to be generated indicating an "Invalid operation."

- *(Arrays) Mixing types in passing arrays to functions:* When array arguments are passed to functions, differences between actual argument and formal parameter types will produce error messages. For example, passing an integer array actual argument when a character array is expected will cause the compiler to generate a message such as

```
"Type mismatch in parameter y in call to findMatch."
```

- *(Structs) References to a struct member with no prefix:* Always use the member access operator (a period) when referencing a member of a variable of some structured type. If you don't use the period, the compiler assumes that you're referencing a variable that isn't part of a structured variable.

- *(Structs) Reference to a struct member with incorrect prefix:* If v is a structured variable with a member named comp and x is a structured variable with no member of that name, then the reference x.comp will generate an "Undefined symbol 'comp'" message. If you use a struct type name (for example, coord) instead of a struct variable name before the dot, then a message such as "Improper use of typedef 'coord'" might be generated. This tells you that the a user-defined type name (coord, in this case) has been used illegally.

- *(Structs) Missing semicolon following a struct declaration:* If the semicolon required at the end of a struct declaration is missing, a variety of error messages might be generated, depending on what follows the declaration. Frequently, another declaration will follow the faulty one. If so, the second declaration is considered part of the struct, and the compiler will generate a diagnostic such as "Too many types in declaration."

- *(For multideminesional arrays) Subscript errors:* When you use multidimensional arrays, make sure the subscript for each dimension is always in range and that the subscripts are in the correct order. If you use nested for loops to process the array elements, check carefully that the loop control variables used as array subscripts are in the correct order and that they are in range at the loop boundaries. The order of the loop control variables determines the sequence in which the array elements are processed.

- *(For multidimensional arrays) Improper use of brackets:* Don't write all the subscripts inside one pair of brackets. For example, use x[i][j], not x[i, j].

Chapter Review

1. A data structure is a grouping of related data items in memory.

2. An array is a data structure used to store a collection of data items of the same type.

3. To reference an array element, a subscript is placed in brackets immediately after the array name.

4. The initial element of array x is referenced as x[0]. If x has *n* elements, the final element is referenced as x[n-1].

5. A for loop whose counter variable runs from 0 to one less than an array's size enables us to reference all the elements of an array in sequence by using the loop counter as the array subscript.

6. For an array declared as a local variable, space is allocated in the function data area for all the array elements.

7. For an array declared as a function parameter, space is allocated in the function data area for only the address of the initial element of the actual array argument.

8. A struct is a data structure used for storing a collection of related data items of different types.

9. The individual members of a struct are accessed by placing the name of the member after the name of the struct, separating the two by the member access operator (a period).

10. The time required to perform a linear search of an array is proportional to the size of the array, so the growth rate for linear search is $O(n)$.

11. The time required to perform a selection sort on an array is proportional to the size of the array squared, so the growth rate for linear search is $O(n^2)$.

12. You can model a variety of problem data using combinations of C++ arrays and structs.

13. You can model tables and board games with two-dimensional arrays. You can use an array with three dimensions to represent a company's sales volume broken down by salesperson, year, and quarter.

Summary of New C++ Constructs

Construct	Effect
Array Declaration	
`int cube[10];` `int count[10];`	cube and count are arrays with 10 type int elements.
Array References	
`for (i = 0; i < 10; i++)` `    cube[i] = i * i * i;`	Saves i cubed in the ith element of array cube.
`if (cube[5] > 100)` `    cout << cube[0] << cube[1];`	Compares cube[5] to 100. Displays the first two cubes if cube[s] is larger.
struct Declaration	

`struct part`
`{`
`   int id;`
`   int quantity;`
`   float price;`
`};`
	A struct part is declared with data fields that can store two ints and a float value.

`part nuts, bolts;`	nuts and bolts are struct variables of type part.
struct References	
`totalCost = nuts.quantity *` `           nuts.price`	Multiplies two members of nuts.
`cout << bolts.id;`	Displays the id field of bolts.
`bolts = nuts;`	Copies struct nuts to bolts.
Two-Dimensional Array	
`int matrix[10] [5];`	matrix is a two-dimensional array with 10 rows and 5 columns.

`sum = 0;`
`for (int i = 0; i < 10; i++)`
`   for (int j = 0; j < 5; j++)`
`     sum += matrix[i][j];`
	Stores the sum of all elements of array matrix in sum.

Array of Structs	
`part store[50];`	Allocates storage for an array store whose 50 elements are structs of type part.
`store[49] = nuts;`	Stores nuts in last element of array store.

Quick-Check Exercises

1. What structured data types were discussed in this chapter? What is a structured data type?

2. Which fundamental types can't be array subscript types? Array element types?

3. Can values of different types be stored in the same array?

4. When an array is initialized, you don't need to declare the size of the array. (True/False)

5. An array is always passed by reference. (True/False)

6. When can the assignment operator be used with array elements? With entire arrays? Answer the same questions for the equality operator.

7. The elements of an array can be accessed in _____ order; however, use a _____ statement to access the elements of an array in sequential order.

8. What is the primary difference between an array and a struct? Which would you use to store the catalog description of a course? Which would you use to store the names of the students in the course?

9. When can you use the assignment operator with struct operands? When can you use the equality operator?

10. For aStudent declared as follows, provide a statement that displays the name of a student in the form *last name, first name.*

```
struct student
{
    string first;
    string last;
    int age;
    int score;
    char grade;
}; // end student

student aStudent;
```

11. How many members are there in struct student?

12. Write a function that displays a variable of type student.

13. Explain the reason you might use const student& stu in a parameter list instead of student stu.

14. What control structure can be used to sequentially access all the elements in a multidimensional array?

15. List the storage sequence for elements of the two-dimensional array matrix with 3 rows and 2 columns.

16. Write a program segment to display the sum of the values in each column of a 5×3 array table with type float elements. How many column sums will be displayed? How many elements are included in each sum?

17. Write a type declaration for a data structure that stores a baseball player's name, salary, position (pitcher, catcher, infielder, outfielder, utility),

batting average, fielding percentage, number of hits, runs, runs batted in, and errors.

18. Write the type declaration for a data structure that stores the information in the previous exercise for a team of 25 players.

19. For the data structure described in Quick-Check Exercise 18, write a program segment that displays the data for the first five players.

Review Questions

1. Identify the error in the following code segment. When will the error be detected?

```cpp
int main()
{
    int x[8];
    for (int i = 0; i <= 8; i++)
        x[i] = i;
    return 0;
}
```

2. Declare an array of floating-point elements called week that can be referenced by using any day of the week as a subscript. Assume sunday is the first subscript.

3. Does C++ give you a compile-time error or a run-time error if you have a subscript out of the valid range?

4. Write a C++ program segment to print out the index of the smallest and the largest character in an array letters of 20 characters.

5. The arguments for a function are two arrays of type float and an integer that represents the length of the arrays. The function copies the first array in the argument list to the other array using a loop structure. Write the function.

6. How many exchanges are required to sort the following list of integers, using the selection sort? How many comparisons are required?

    20 30 40 25 60 80 15

7. Declare a struct called subscriber that contains the member's name, streetAddress, monthlyBill (how much the subscriber owes), and which paper the subscriber receives (morning, evening, or both).

8. Write a C++ program to read and then display the contents of the variable competition declared as follows:

```
struct olympicTrial
{
        string event;
        string entrant;
        string country;
        int place;
};

olympicTrial trackMeet;
```

9. Identify and correct the errors in the following program:

```
int main()
{
    struct summerHelp
    {
        string name;
        int empID;
        string startDate;
        float payRate
        int hoursWorked;
    }

    summerHelp operator;

    summerHelp.name = "James Borden";
    summerHelp.startDate = "June 1, 2004";
    summerHelp.hoursWorked = 29.3;
    cout << operator << endl;
    return 0;
}
```

10. Declare the proper data structure to store the following student data:

    studentName, GPA, major, and address (consisting of streetAddress, city, state, zipCode). Use whatever data types are most appropriate for each member.

11. Declare a data structure that can be used to store the number of times the 26 letters of the English alphabet occur in five different documents.

12. Write a function that determines the total number of times a selected letter (the argument) occurs in all five documents.

13. Write the declarations for the array cpuArray that will hold 20 records of type cpu. The struct cpu has the following fields: idNumber (a string), make (a string), location (a string), and ports (integer).

    Use the following declarations for questions 14 through 16:

    const int NUM_EMPLOYEES = 20;

```
struct employee
{
        int id;
        float rate;
        float hours;
};    // end employee
employee allEmployees[NUM_EMPLOYEES];
```

14. Write the function `totalGross` that will return the total gross pay given the data stored in the array `allEmployees`.

15. Write a program fragment that displays the ID number of each employee who works between 10.0 and 20.0 hours per week.

16. Write a program fragment that displays the ID number of the employee who works the most hours.

17. Write the declarations for an array of structs that can be used to store all the top 40 hits for one week of the year. Assume that the data stored for each hit is the title, artist, production company, cost, and month of issue (an enumerator).

18. Answer the previous question for a data structure that stores the same data for each of the 52 weeks of a year.

Programming Projects

1. Write a program to read *n* data items into two arrays, x and y, of size 20. Store the products of corresponding pairs of elements of x and y in a third array, z, also of size 20. Print a three-column table that displays the arrays x, y, and z. Then compute and print the square root of the sum of the items in z. Make up your own data, with *n* less than 20.

2. Write a program for the following problem. You're given a file that contains a collection of IDs and scores (type int) for an exam in your computer course. You're to compute the average of these scores and assign grades to each student according to the following rule:

   If a student's score is within 10 points (above or below) of the average, assign a grade of satisfactory. If a student's score is more than 10 points above average, assign a grade of outstanding. If a student's score is more than 10 points below average, assign a grade of unsatisfactory.

   The output from your program should consist of a labeled three-column list that shows each ID, score, and corresponding grade. As part of the solution, your program should include functions that correspond to the function prototypes that follow.

```
// reads exam scores into array scores
void readStuData
    (ifstream &rss,       // IN: data file
     int scores[],        // OUT: the scores
     int id[],            // OUT: the IDs
     int &count,          // OUT: Number of students read
     bool &tooMany);      // OUT: A flag to indicate that more
                          // than MAX_SIZE scores items are in
                          // input file.


// computes average of count student scores
float mean(int scores[], int count);


// Displays a table showing each student's ID, score and
   grade
// on a separate line
// Uses: printGrade
void printTable(int score[], int ID[], int count);


// Prints student grade after comparing oneScore to average
void printGrade(int oneScore, float average);
```

3. Redo Programming Project 2 using a struct to store each student's data and an array of structs to store the whole class. The struct should have a data member for id, score, and grade.

4. The bubble sort is another technique for sorting an array. A bubble sort compares adjacent array elements and exchanges their values if they're out of order. In this way, the smaller values "bubble" to the top of the array (toward element 0), while the larger values sink to the bottom of the array. After the first pass of a bubble sort, the last array element is in the correct position; after the second pass, the last two elements are correct, and so on. Thus, after each pass, the unsorted portion of the array contains one less element. Write and test a function that implements this sorting method.

5. The results of a survey of the households in your township are available for public scrutiny. Each record contains data for one household, including a four-digit integer identification number, the annual income for the household, and the number of household members. Write a program to read the survey results into three arrays and perform the following analyses.

   a. Count the number of households included in the survey and print a three-column table displaying the data. (Assume that no more than 25 households were surveyed.)

b. Calculate the average household income, and list the identification number and income of each household that exceeds the average.

c. Determine the percentage of households that have incomes below the poverty level. Compute the poverty level income using the formula

$$p = \$7000.00 + \$850.00 \times (m - 2)$$

where m is the number of members of each household. This formula shows that the poverty level depends on the number of family members, m, and that the poverty-level income increases as m gets larger. Test your program on the following data.

Identification Number	Annual Income	Household Members
1041	12,180	4
1062	13,240	3
1327	19,800	2
1483	35,000	7
1900	17,000	2
2112	28,500	6
2345	15,623	2
3210	3,200	6
3600	6,500	5
3601	11,970	2
4724	8,900	3
6217	10,000	2
9280	6,200	1

6. Assume that your computer has the very limited capability of being able to read and write only single-integer digits and to add two integers consisting of one decimal digit each. Write a program that can read two integers up to 20 digits each, add these integers together, and display the result. Test your program using pairs of numbers of varying lengths. (Hint: Store the two numbers in two int arrays of size 20, one digit per array element. If the number is less than 20 digits in length, enter enough leading zeros (to the left of the number) to make the number 20 digits long.) You'll need a loop to add the digits in corresponding array elements. Don't forget to handle the carry digit if there is one!

7. A number expressed in scientific notation is represented by its mantissa (a fraction) and its exponent. Write a function that reads a character string that represents a number in C++ scientific notation and stores the number in a struct with two members. Write a function that prints the contents of this struct as a real value. Also write functions that compute the sum, product, difference, and quotient of two numbers in scientific notation stored in two struct arguments. (Hint: The string −0.1234E20 represents a number in scientific notation. The fraction −0.1234 is the mantissa, and the number 20 is the exponent.)

8. A prime number is any number that's divisible only by one and itself. Write a program to compute all the prime numbers less than 1000. One way to generate prime numbers is to create an array of `bool` values that are true for all prime numbers, but are false otherwise. Initially set all the array entries to true. Then, for every number from 2 to 1000, set the array locations indexed by multiples of the number (but not the number itself) to false. When done, output all numbers whose array location is true. These will be the prime numbers.

9. Write a program that generates the Morse code for a sentence that ends in a period and contains no other characters except letters and blanks. After reading the Morse code into an array of strings, your program should read each word of the sentence and display its Morse equivalent on a separate line. The Morse code is as follows:

A .- B -... C -.-. D -.. E . F ..-. G --. H .... I .. J .--- K -.- L .-.. M --
N -. O --- P .--. Q --.- R .-. S ... T - U ..- V ...- W .-- X -..- Y -.--
Z --..

Your program should include `functions` corresponding to the prototypes shown next.

```
// Stores Morse codes read from codeFile in array code.
void readCode(ifstream& codeFile, string codeArray[]);

// Writes Morse equivalent for a letter.
void writeCode (string codeArray[], char letter);
```

10. Write an interactive program that plays the game of Hangman. Read the word to be guessed into `word`. The player must guess the letters belonging to `word`. The program should terminate when either all letters have been guessed correctly (player wins) or a specified number of incorrect guesses have been made (computer wins). (Hint: Use `solution` to keep track of the solution so far. Initialize `solution` to a string of symbols `'*'`. Each time a letter in `word` is guessed, replace the corresponding `'*'` in `solution` with that letter.)

11. Write a function that will merge the contents of two sorted (ascending order) arrays of type `double` values, storing the result in an array output parameter (still in ascending order). The function shouldn't assume that both its input parameter arrays are the same length but can assume

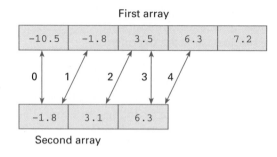

that one array doesn't contain two copies of the same value. The result array should also contain no duplicate values.

(Hint: When one of the input arrays has been exhausted, don't forget to copy the remaining data in the other array into the result array.) Test your function with cases in which (1) the first array is exhausted first, (2) the second array is exhausted first, and (3) the two arrays are exhausted at the same time (that is, they end with the same value). Remember that the arrays input to this function *must already be sorted.*

12. The *binary search* algorithm that follows may be used to search an array when the elements are sorted. This algorithm is analogous to the following approach for finding a name in a telephone book.

    a. Open the book in the middle, and look at the middle name on the page.

    b. If the middle name isn't the one you're looking for, decide whether it comes before or after the name you want.

    Take the appropriate half of the section of the book you were looking in and repeat these steps until you land on the name.

    ALGORITHM FOR BINARY SEARCH

    1. Let `bottom` be the subscript of the initial array element.

    2. Let `top` be the subscript of the last array element.

    3. Let `found` be false.

    4. Repeat as long as `bottom` isn't greater than `top` and the target has not been found.

        5. Let `middle` be the subscript of the element halfway between `bottom` and `top`.

        6. If the element at `middle` is the target

        7. Set `found` to `true` and `index` to `middle`.

            Else if the element at `middle` is larger than the target

8. Let top be middle $-$ 1.

     Else

9. Let bottom be middle + 1.

Write and test a function `binarySearch` that implements this algorithm for an array of integers. When there is a large number of array elements, which function do you think is faster: `binarySearch` or the linear search function of Listing 9.9?

13. The insertion sort algorithm is a more efficient means of sorting an array. This algorithm is analogous to the procedure that card players follow when picking up cards and inserting them in their hand to form a run in a particular suit. A player makes room for a new card by shifting over the ones that follow it and then inserting it where it belongs in the hand. In sorting an array, all values are available when you begin, but you can assume that the array is not sorted and start by inserting the value currently in the second array element by comparing it to the first element. This gives you a sorted subarray consisting of the first two elements. Next, you insert the value currently in the third array element where it belongs compared to the first two, which gives you a sorted subarray of three elements, and so on. You're finished after you insert the value in the last element. Follow the algorithm below to insert the next value in an array.

ALGORITHM FOR INSERTING THE NEXT VALUE

1. Save the value to be inserted in `newValue`.

2. Using a loop, compare `newValue` to the elements already inserted in the array starting with the last one inserted. If an element is larger than `newValue`, shift it to the next array element. Exit the loop when a value that is not larger than `newValue` is reached.

3. Insert `newValue` at the initial position of the last element that was shifted.

14. An algorithm that is an improvement over the insertion sort is called the Shell sort. It works by performing a series of insertion sorts over subarrays of the array being sorted. For example, if an array has 15 elements, the Shell sort may first do an insertion sort on the subarrays with elements 0, 7, 14 which are the elements starting with the first, that are separated by a gap of seven. Continuing with this process, it would then sort elements 1 and 8, also with a gap of 7. Then elements 2 and 9, and so on until it sorts the last subarray whose elements have a gap of 7 which is the subarray with elements 6 and 13. Next, it cuts the gap in half (new gap is 3) and repeats the process: doing an insertion sort on the subarray with elements 0, 3, 6, 9, 12, and then the subarray with elements 1, 4, 7, 10, 13, and finally the subarray with elements 2, 5, 8, 11, and 12. The next time the gap is cut in half it becomes 1, which causes Shell sort to do an

insertion sort on the entire array. This is always the final sort. The theory is that since the earlier sorts have put the array in some semblance of order, the later sorts for which n (the array size) is large will be much more efficient. It can be shown experimentally that Shell sort is close to $O(n \times \log n)$ whereas the regular insertion sort is $O(n \times n)$.

Write and test the Shell sort algorithm. Use an initial gap size of half the number of elements in the array to be sorted. If the gap size becomes 2, change it to 1 so that the entire array is sorted.

15. Write the declarations for an array of structs that can be used to store all the top 10 hits for every week of the year. Assume that the data stored for each hit is the title, artist, production company, cost, and month of issue (an integer). Write the following functions:

   1. Load the array with data from a data file. For testing purposes, use just five weeks.

   2. Display the top hit for every week of the year.

   3. Display the number of weeks each #1 hit has been #1.

   4. For a particular recording, determine how many weeks it has been #1, #2, and so on.

   5. For a particular hit, determine how many weeks it has been on the top 10 list.

   6. For a particular artist, determine how many weeks that artist has had n recordings on the top 10 list, where n is a function parameter.

16. The voting district in which you live is partitioned into five precincts. Write a program that reads the election results from each of these precincts and tabulates the total vote in your district for all of the candidates running for election. The program should begin by asking the user to enter the number of candidates, nmbrCandidates, running for office. It should then read the election returns for each precinct for each candidate, compute the total vote for each candidate, and display the input and the results in the form shown in the table.

   For each candidate, the program should also compute and display the percentage of the total vote. If there is one candidate whose percentage is better than 50 percent, display a message declaring that candidate to be the winner of the election. If there is no such candidate, display out a message indicating the names of the top two vote-getters and indicate that a run-off election will be required. The voting data should be stored in an indexed collection of structured elements, each of which contains the name of a candidate, the number of votes in each precinct for that candidate, and the total vote. The relevant information about each candidate should be modeled by a class containing the definitions of the necessary attributes and functions required for one candidate.

   Test your program for the data shown below and also when candidate C receives only 108 votes in precinct 4.

Precinct	Candidate A	Candidate B	Candidate C	Candidate D	Total Vote
1	192	148	1206	137	1683
2	147	190	1312	121	1770
3	186	112	1121	138	1557
4	114	121	1408	139	1782
5	267	113	1382	129	1891
Totals	906	684	6429	664	7683

17. Modify the previous programming project to make it an interactive, menu-driven program. Menu options should include the following:
    - initializing the vote table (prompt the user for the number of candidates, their names, and the number of votes in each precinct)
    - displaying the candidates' names and votes received (raw count and percentage of votes cast)
    - displaying the winner's name (or names of the top two vote-getters in the case of a run-off)
    - exiting the program.

Answers to Quick–Check Exercises

1. Arrays and structs. A structured data type is a named grouping of related values.

2. Floating-point types can't be used for array subscript types; all types can be element types.

3. no

4. true

5. true

6. Both the assignment and equality operators may be used with array elements. Neither the assignment operator nor the equality operator may be used with entire arrays.

7. random, `for` or `while`

8. The values stored in an array must all be the same type; the values stored in a struct don't have to be the same type. You would use a struct for the catalog item and use an array for the list of names.

9. The assignment operator may be used between structs of the same type. The equality operator may not be used to compare structs.

10. `cout << aStudent.last << ", " << aStudent.first << endl;`

11. five

12.
```
void writeStudent
    (student oneStu)              // IN: The data to display
{
    cout << "Student is " << oneStu.first << " "
         << oneStu.last << endl;
    cout << "Age is " << oneStu.age << endl;
    cout << "Score is " << oneStu.score << endl;
    cout << "Grade is " << oneStu.grade << endl;
}
```

13. The formal parameter const student stu& is a reference parameter whereas student stu is a value parameter. In the former, the data for the actual argument struct is referenced by the function but the data can't be changed. The latter creates a local copy of the actual argument, which requires extra storage and time. This extra time can be a factor for structs that store a lot of data.

14. nested for loops

15.
```
matrix[0][0], matrix[0][1], matrix[1][0], matrix[1][1],
matrix[2][0], matrix[2][1]
```

16.
```
for (int c = 0; c < 3; c++)
{
    columnSum = 0.0;
    for (int r = 0; r < 5; r++)
        columnSum += table[r][c];
    cout << "Sum for column " << c << " is "
         << columnSum << "." << endl;
}    // end for c
```
three column sums; five elements added per column

17. The data elements are of different types:
```
enum position {pitcher, catcher, infielder, outfielder,
               utility};
struct player
{
    string name;
    float salary;
    position place;
    float battingAve, fieldPct;
    int hits, runs, rbis, errors;
}; // end player
```

18.
```
player team[25];
```

19.
```
for (int i = 0; i < 5; i++)
    cout << team[i].name << " "
         << team[i].salary << endl;
```

Index